AVIATION CENTURY

THE
GOLDEN
AGE

THE
GOLDEN
AGE

RON DICK AND DAN PATTERSON

The BOSTON
MILLS PRESS

A BOSTON MILLS PRESS BOOK

© Ron Dick and Dan Patterson, 2004

First printing 2004

National Library of Canada Cataloguing in Publication

Dick, Ron, 1931-
Aviation century the golden age / Ron Dick and Dan Patterson.

Includes bibliographical references and index.
ISBN 1-55046-409-4

1. Aeronautics--History. I. Patterson, Dan, 1953- II. Title.

TL670.3.D53 2004   629.13'009   C2004-900963-X

Publisher Cataloging-in-Publication Data   (U.S.)

Dick, Ron, 1931-

Aviation century the golden age / Ron Dick ; and Dan Patterson. _ 1st ed.

[288] p. : ill. , photos. (chiefly col.) ; cm. (Aviation Century)

Includes bibliographical references and index.

Summary: From the adventures in flight between the world wars, to military aviation, aerial travelers and adventurers, record setters, entertainers, air shows and
aviation museums.

ISBN 1-55046-409-4

1. Airplanes _ History. 2. Aircraft industry – History. 3. Aeronautics—History.
I. Patterson, Dan, 1953- II. Title. III. Series.

629.13'009   22   TL670.3.D52Av   2004

Published in 2004 by BOSTON MILLS PRESS
132 Main Street,
Erin, Ontario N0B 1T0
Tel 519-833-2407
Fax 519-833-2195
books@bostonmillspress.com
www.bostonmillspress.com

IN CANADA:
Distributed by Firefly Books Ltd.
66 Leek Crescent
Richmond Hill, Ontario L4B 1H1

IN THE UNITED STATES:
Distributed by Firefly Books (U.S.) Inc.
P.O. Box 1338, Ellicott Station
Buffalo, New York 14205

Aviation Century series editor: Kathleen Fraser
Design: PageWave Graphics Inc.

The publisher acknowledges the financial support of the Government of Canada through
the Book Publishing Industry Development Program (BPIDP) for its publishing efforts.

HALF-TITLE PAGE *Roscoe Turner's Air Racer.*
PAGE 2 *A De Havilland Tiger Moth flies from Duxford into the evening sky.*
TITLE PAGE *A Sikorsky S-39, participant in the National Air Tour 2003, piloted by
Dick and Pat Jackson of Rochester, New Hampshire, and Bill Thaden of Kittery
Point, Maine.*
PAGE 6 *Famous Unlimited air racer* Miss America *casts an early-morning
silhouette.*

FRONT JACKET

MAIN IMAGE *The red Italian air racer — the Macchi-Castoldi MC.72 — was built to
win the Schneider Trophy, but did not compete due to development problems. This
aircraft holds the standing world speed record of 440 mph set in 1934.*
BOTTOM ROW
FAR LEFT Miss America *runs up her Rolls-Royce Merlin engine.*
CENTER LEFT *A replica Boeing P-26 from the United States Air Force Museum,
Dayton, Ohio.*
CENTER RIGHT *Waco Taperwing in flight.*
FAR RIGHT *Amelia Earhart's red Lockheed Vega, which she flew solo across the
Atlantic in 1932.*
BACK JACKET *The reliable Wright-Whirlwind engine and one of the most famous
airplanes of the aviation century, Lindbergh's* Spirit of St. Louis, *on display at the
National Air & Space Museum in Washington, D.C.*

Dedicated to aviators,
past, present
and of the future.

Contents

ACKNOWLEDGMENTS

THE PREPARATION OF ANY historical work is not usually an enterprise that can be undertaken successfully without help. This has proved to be especially true of the *Aviation Century* series. In expressing their appreciation for all the help and encouragement they were given in preparing this second volume, *Aviation Century The Golden Age*, Ron Dick and Dan Patterson must acknowledge once more many of those who contributed so much to the previous book, *Aviation Century The Early Years*. The repetition of their names and organizations here serves to emphasize the gratitude felt for their unstinting support during the five years of the project. Once again, however, the authors would like to apologize in advance to anyone who is not properly recognized. Although every effort has been made to ensure that sincere thanks are offered to everyone who made a contribution, the coverage may prove, in the end, to be as imperfect as the authors themselves. If an omission has been made, Ron and Dan would be glad to hear about it so that the oversight can be corrected later in the series.

In tackling the subjects chosen for the chapters of *Aviation Century The Golden Age*, it was necessary to enter the world of the military between the 20th century's World Wars, and to research perhaps the most colorful and adventurous era of human flight. The directors and staffs of the aviation museums and archives of North America and Europe were immensely helpful in gathering the material for the chapters in this book. The authors are particularly grateful to the directors and staffs of the Smithsonian's National Air & Space Museum, Washington, D.C.; the Museum of Flight, Seattle, Washington; the Virginia Aviation Museum, Richmond, Virginia; the USAF History Office; the United States Air Force Museum, Dayton, Ohio; the Museum of Naval Aviation, Pensacola, Florida; the U.S. Marine Corps Museum, Quantico, Virginia; the Canada Aviation Museum, Ottawa; the Canadian Warplane Heritage Museum, Hamilton, Ontario; the Royal Aeronautical Society, London; the Imperial War Museum, Duxford, U.K.; the Royal Air Force Museum, Hendon, and Cosford, U.K.; the Fleet Air Arm Museum, Yeovilton, U.K.; the Science Museum, London; the Shuttleworth Trust; the Musée de l'Air et de l'Espace, Le Bourget, France; the Museo Storico Aeronautica Militare, Vigna di Valle, Italy; the Museo Caproni, Trento, Italy; the Flygvapenmuseum, Linkoping, Sweden; the Muzeum Lotnictwa Polskiego, Krakow, Poland; and the Royal Australian Air Force Museum, Point Cook, Victoria, Australia.

David Brown of KJP, London, (now Calumet Photo) offered generous support and advice in the provision of photographic equipment while the authors were working in the United Kingdom. All the original color photography was completed by Dan Patterson. Archive photographs in this volume came from the collections of Wright State University;

the Smithsonian National Air & Space Museum; the Museum of Flight, Seattle; the USAF Museum; the National Museum of Naval Aviation, Pensacola; the Imperial War Museum; the Royal Air Force Museum, Hendon; the Royal Aeronautical Society; the Museo Caproni, Trento; and from the private collections of the Caproni family and the authors.

The authors wish to acknowledge the help of several people and their organizations in Dayton, Ohio: Blair Conrad and the Dayton Air Show; Ron Kaplan at the National Aviation Hall of Fame; and Ty Greenlees of the *Dayton Daily News*. In London, the staff of *Aeroplane Monthly* went out of their way to offer their expert advice and free use of the magazine's archives. Particular thanks go to Michael Oakey, Tony Harmsworth, Tanya Caffrey, Nick Stroud and Lydia Matharu.

A number of distinguished artists generously agreed to contribute their work to this series. *Aviation Century The Golden Age* includes paintings or drawings by Roy Grinnell, Gerald Coulson, Jim Dietz, Robert Taylor, Nicolas Trudgian, Michael Turner, Paul Rendel and Philip Castle. The authors are again most grateful to Pat Barnard, formerly of the Military Gallery, Bath, U.K., for all his help and encouragement. The present owners of the Military Gallery, Colin Hudson and Rick Taylor, have continued to offer support and have been kind enough to grant permission for the reproduction of works by many of the artists.

Particular thanks for their individual contributions go to Dr. Richard Hallion, Trish Graboske, Torn Allison, Scott Wiley, Dennis Parks, Katherine Williams, Bob Rasmussen, Hill Goodspeed, Irene Grinnell, David McFarland, Floyd McGowin, Donald Nijboer, Michael Fopp, Henry Hall, Phil Jarrett, Graham Mottram, Ted Inman, Colette Byatt, Clive and Linda Denny, Paddy Worth, Contessa Maria Fede Armani Caproni, Lieutenant General Antonino Lenzo, Dr. Orazio Giuffrida, Colonel Marco Scarlatti, Lieutenant Egidi and Air Marshal Alan Reed.

One essential fact underscores all of the efforts made by the authors and the various organizations and people involved in the production of this book. None of it would have been possible without the wholehearted support and limitless patience of the author's wives, Paul and Cheryl. For five years they have at one time or another indulged our fantasies, boosted our confidence, discouraged stagnation, calmed rising blood pressures, tolerated eccentric behavior, borne inconvenience, smiled in adversity, and dried our tears. Once again, we are grateful to them beyond measure. They have most thoroughly earned our love and thanks.

RON DICK AND DAN PATTERSON

FOREWORD
Alex Henshaw

FOR PEOPLE OF MY GENERATION, the technological development in aerodynamics has exceeded even the wildest dreams of our youth. That this extraordinary evolution has taken place within a lifespan is hard to believe. After I landed my ninetieth-birthday celebration flight, after over seventy years of solo flying, I was asked what I considered the best period in aviation during the past century. Without hesitation I said it had to be that disturbed period between the wars called the Golden Age of flying.

My introduction to this new world of aviation was at Brooklands in 1923. There was a small airfield there from which slow, lumbering aeroplanes rose from time to time giving joyrides. I was so fascinated that my father bought a ticket for both of us. I think the aircraft was a D.H.9, and the pilot, Captain Barnard. Although I was exhilarated and, in a way, bewildered, I cannot say that I enjoyed the flight. It was noisy, cold and uncomfortable, and I could not see a great deal as the biting wind made my eyes run. Whether this brief experience had any influence on my subsequent involvement in aviation, I am not at all sure. Like most boys at that age, I was seeking adventure, excitement, challenge — something demanding skill, daring and a test of personal courage while offering the rewards of worthwhile achievement. In later years, my entry into the realm of international air-racing and recordbreaking precipitated a level of emotion, tension and trauma unknown to but a few. Success in these endeavors opened doors and revealed opportunities undreamed of in my formative years.

In spite of post-WWI austerity, some aircraft firms survived and laid the foundations for unprecedented growth in the demand for light aircraft at a price the man in the street could afford. The de Havilland Company led the way, and I think the machine that did most to popularize air travel for the private aviator was the D.H. Puss Moth. It operated with the simplicity and comfort of a car, and intrepid pilots used it across ocean, jungle and desert to establish records that would have been inconceivable before. Closely following the example of de Havilland in the design and production of light aircraft in the United Kingdom were such firms as Avro, Percival, Airspeed and Miles. Asked today what I found most attractive about the Golden Age, I answer that it was the freedom of the sky to all who had the ability and wherewithal to take advantage of this modern magic carpet.

Two aspects of flying particularly absorbed my interest and concentration — handling tricky racing aircraft and navigating over wide expanses where a visual fix is impossible for hours on end. I came to rely on the chronometer, compass and slide rule as if my life depended on it — which it often did. Among contemporaries, I rated Frank Chichester and P.G. Taylor the two leading exponents of the art, and the pilots of Comet G-ACSS in the 1934 England-to-Australia air race displayed airmanship of the highest caliber. When I acquired Percival Mew Gull G-AEXF in 1937, I had two pipe dreams in mind. One was to record the fastest speed in the King's Cup Race, and I achieved that in 1938. The second was to attack my old friend Clouston's astonishing performance from England to the Cape and back. It is gratifying to be told now that the 1939 Mew Gull flight to and from the Cape is rated as one of the three most outstanding international record flights, and that as a solo flight it is judged in a class of its own. Furthermore, G-AEXF is acknowledged to be the only machine of any category ever to hold long-distance world records unbroken for over sixty-four years.

I was privileged to be able to fly and be involved in aviation throughout its most exhilarating period. It was a time of unparalleled challenge and excitement, thoroughly deserving its title of flight's Golden Age.

ALEX HENSHAW
NEWMARKET, ENGLAND
SEPTEMBER 2003

FOREWORD
Tom Poberezny

WHEN AN AIRPLANE FLIES overhead, our first reaction is to look up and marvel at the sight. A hundred years later, the miracle of flight continues to captivate people of all ages. This is why people visit airports to do nothing more than watch airplanes take off and land.

On December 17, 1903, Wilbur and Orville Wright solved the equation that made the magic possible, and they forever changed the world. Over the century of its existence, aerial transportation has changed where we live and how we live. It's become such an everyday part of life that many take it for granted.

Some people may not look up when an airliner whispers across the high sky, but at an air show or in an aviation museum, everyone's eyes are on the aircraft. In these places live the emotion and excitement of silk scarves and open cockpits and the opportunity to see, smell and touch the past that made aviation's present possible.

I have been fortunate to be extensively involved with both air shows and museums. Like many performers, I entered the air-show world through competition aerobatics, after competing in national and world events.

Competitive flying requires tenacity, dedication and training to balance safety with risk and put an airplane though its paces, expanding its envelope of performance to the very edge. Because judges decide who wins and who does not, aerobatic competition is also about matching wits and skills with the other pilots, all of whom vie for the officials' objective and subjective approval.

Freedom and creativity make the difference between competition and air-show flying. The same skill and dedication is demanded of the air-show pilots who trace their twisting, turning ballet across a three-dimensional stage in smoke, entertaining millions of people every year.

Air shows demonstrate a pilot's skill and the beauty, brute strength, noise and excitement of aviation in real time. Aviation museums elicit the same "ohs" and "ahs" in the minds of the people soaking up every detail of the artifact that has captured their attention.

Preserving our aviation heritage by telling what it is people have accomplished by designing, building and flying these airplanes is important because it inspires as well as educates and entertains. As head of the EAA AirVenture Museum in Oshkosh, Wisconsin, I have worked hard not only to preserve our aviation heritage and legacy, but also to exhibit significant examples in their natural environment — the sky — so people can touch, hear and smell aviation's history for themselves.

In many ways this book is an aviation museum and air show with covers. In words and pictures it chronicles the development of flight from our first flight, and it sets aerobatic pilots — and all others who fly — free to fly in the sky of our mind's eye.

As we celebrate one hundred years of powered flight, I am proud of aviation's contributions to the world. And I'm proud of contributions of air shows and aviation museums, because they inspire people to look up, to look at airplanes, and remind us of the beauty and inspiration of flight.

TOM POBEREZNY
PRESIDENT, EXPERIMENTAL AIRCRAFT ASSOCIATION
OSHKOSH, WISCONSIN, NOVEMBER 2003

PHOTOGRAPHER'S PREFACE
Dan Patterson

WHEN RON AND I began the process of assembling the *Aviation Century* project, we made up a list of all the locations and museums in the world we'd like to visit to make new images and research this rich history of aviation. The list grew to three pages that covered about a dozen countries on both sides of the Atlantic Ocean. Now, at the end of the process, that list is pretty dog-eared and covered with red checkmarks and crossed-out references, as well as many newer entries penciled into the margins. Remarkably, that list has been mostly accomplished. We set out not only to go to the great national museums where the icons of aviation are often kept, but also to seek out and find the hidden treasures of aviation history in small and often unsung collections. As we found out, these wonderful places are not on the usual beaten path, which made the discovery all the more enjoyable.

The National Air & Space Museum in Washington, D.C., was certainly prominent on our initial wish list, and Lindbergh's Ryan monoplane one of the items listed. We both felt that while I could photograph it from the balcony like everyone else, actually getting access to the plane was a pipe dream at best. Well, it turns out, dreams do come true.

The opportunity to make new photographs of Charles Lindbergh's *Spirit of St. Louis* was a once-in-a-lifetime event. This small airplane is perhaps *the* most recognized icon from all of aviation history. It has been in the collection of the National Air & Space Museum since Lindbergh gave it to the museum, and suspended above the museum floor for nearly all of its public display, unavailable for a close photographic study for a long time.

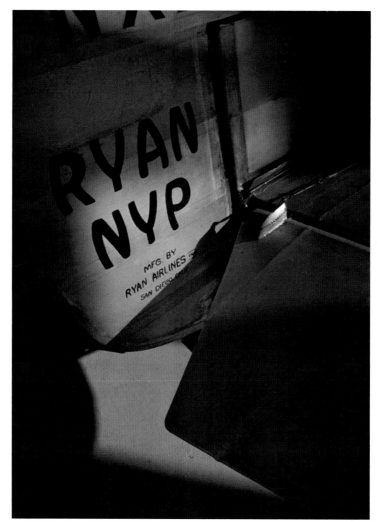

The rudder of Lindbergh's Spirit of St. Louis.

In late October of 2000 the leaky roof at the museum was undergoing repairs and the *Spirit* was to be moved. I had been in touch with Trish Graboske, publications director at the museum, about the move for several months, and about a week before the move she called and invited me to come to Washington. I would have three to four hours access to the *Spirit* on the 30th of October. I rearranged my schedule for the following week and on the 29th drove to Washington. I kept telling myself all along the 500-mile drive that this was just another job. . . that light was light, focus was focus and film was film. Don't be intimidated by the subject.

I arrived at the museum the afternoon of the 30th. I went through the same ritual that accompanies every photo shoot. Unload the carload of lights, lightstands, cables, tripod, and cameras, somewhere between 200 and 250 pounds of equipment. Sure that I had not left anything behind, I set off through the museum with this unwieldy cartload of "stuff."

The small silver airplane was in the open gallery at the west end of the museum. The museum's staff photographer was completing his work around the *Spirit* and putting away his lights. My first impression was how small this airplane was, and how fragile it seemed. I asked Trish again how much time I was allowed and if I would be sharing this time with other photographers. I was astounded to find that I was the only independent photographer invited to have this unique and now exclusive opportunity. I said again to myself, remember, this is just another job — and went to work.

As the afternoon wore on and I set up my lights and cameras, the warm and golden October sun was streaming through the huge glass wall and bathing this small silver painted piece of history in the kind of light that photographers just love. The small Ryan-built monoplane was covered in graffiti, signatures, initials, dates and locations where Lindbergh landed his airplane. Some of them were from Paris, but also from Belgium and from his later goodwill tour of South America. I found names penciled inside the ailerons and the door frames. The airplane has been preserved by the museum and not restored, so the character of this one-of-a-kind piece of human history is saved.

I was also allowed to be inside the airplane. Here was the place where Lindbergh faced the realization of his attempt, alone in this tiny space, sitting in the wicker pilot's seat for almost 34 hours, sometimes just above the waves and at other times several thousand feet above the North Atlantic. I found his handwritten pencil notes on the plywood instrument panel, still there since 1927.

Three days later as I drove the 500 miles back home, the realization of what I had been able to do started to sink in. This had not been "just another job." This was a chance to really look into the past through the window that the *Aviation Century* project has opened for me.

Dan Patterson
Dayton, Ohio
November 2003

INTRODUCTION
Air Vice-Marshal Ron Dick

THIS SECOND VOLUME of the *Aviation Century* series reveals the explosive development of aviation in the 1920s and 1930s. From 1918 onward, it became possible for the pure appeal of flying to the human spirit to be given wider expression. Flying ushered in the promise of three-dimensional freedom and challenged the adventurous to go ever faster, higher and further. Aircraft opened up new fields of exploration and brought the modern world closer to those living in remote areas. In some cases, the intrusion of the aircraft was far from welcome, since it came to enforce discipline among the unruly, or to change an ancient way of life forever. From the outset, the imagination of the general public was caught by the drama and romance of all this, and aviators' exploits often brought an element of excitement to the world's headlines.

For military aviators, the end of WWI proved to be a two-edged sword. Any post-WWI euphoria over the part played in the Allied victory by the air services was short-lived. Defense budgets were eviscerated and little money was available to continue the development of military aviation, particularly in the face of open hostility from the established services. For more than a decade, front-line squadrons everywhere continued to fly aircraft that strongly resembled those of 1918. Air power theories were expounded, and frequently accepted, but were unsupported by empirical evidence and were often proved unsound by the events of later years. In the 1930s, people were forced to confront the unthinkable — the prospect of a second world conflict only two decades after the "war to end all wars." Military aviation belatedly attracted funds, and dress rehearsals in Spain and China pointed the way to the future of war in the air. Open-cockpit biplanes were replaced by fast, heavily armed, metal monoplanes with enclosed cabins, and the threat of air assault on civilian populations was seen to be terrifyingly real.

> "There was no time to aim carefully. It was turn, attack, aim at the red circle, press the buttons, pull out, gain some height, turn back, get the next one in front of one's guns."
>
> GÜNTHER "FRANZL" LÜTZOW, IN AN ACCOUNT OF
> AIR COMBAT DURING THE SPANISH CIVIL WAR, 1937

There were many barriers for aviation to overcome in the years immediately following WWI. Most people still thought of flying as a great adventure, something normal folks did not do. Aircraft were fearsome creations and those who flew them, military or civilian, were superhuman daredevils. The barnstormers, a host of newly trained ex-military pilots flying surplus military aircraft, encouraged this view. It helped them to earn a precarious living by thrilling the public with outrageous airborne stunts. The shows they gave grew in time into spectacular flying circuses, in the process introducing flying machines to a wider audience. Safety regulations eventually tamed the barnstormers, but air shows nevertheless became an established part of the world's aeronautical calendar, bringing together public entertainment and commercial activity.

One notable aspect of flight has always been its promise of increased speed. From the earliest days, racing aircraft against one another was a popular sport. Some races, such as the Bendix Trophy in the U.S. or the England–Australia air race of 1934, were flown over long distances, but other races were flown over closed circuits at low level, with crowds cheering below. Whatever its form, air racing provided a competitive spur that helped to encourage aeronautical development, both civil and military, between the wars.

For many fliers, demonstrating their prowess in front of an air show crowd was not nearly enough. Aircraft offered them the chance to reach other parts of the world quickly, and to penetrate unknown regions by jumping over previously impenetrable barriers. The 1920s and 1930s were the Golden Age of flight, when trail-blazing men and women accepted astonishing challenges, often in fragile machines of limited capability. Despite the hazards and the price paid in lost lives, oceans and continents were crossed, and the polar regions conquered. Global point-to-point records were set up by pilots of limited experience in light aircraft, using basic navigation aids and flying into regions where few people had seen a flying machine and facilities were scarce. The competition to be first or fastest was fierce, and many aviators died trying to achieve aeronautical immortality. Those who achieved their goal and lived to tell the tale gained international celebrity and became as well known as film stars and leading politicians. Their globe-circling efforts made the world a smaller place, bringing every human society within reach of every other.

As the 20th century progressed, the fabric of the aviation story grew ever richer, woven together with tales of brave or foolhardy fliers and patterned with designs of increasingly capable aircraft. A clear need emerged not only to record aviators' deeds but also to care for aeronautical artifacts — aircraft, flying clothing, maps, charts, propellers, navigation equipment, engines, photographs and so on.

The people and machines associated with human flight became the inspiration for thousands of books and limitless images, and museums were created to preserve the paperwork and hardware of aviation. Enthusiasts did their bit by restoring old aircraft to flying condition, making it possible for younger generations to experience the sights and sounds of an earlier aviation age.

This volume of *Aviation Century* tells a tale of romance and adventure, of daring and bravado. Aviators shrink the world and prepare for war on a global scale. The stories of their achievements become the stuff of legend, and their machines are revered as artifacts of a Golden Age.

Ron Dick
Fredericksburg, Virginia
January 2004

CHAPTER 1

Military Aviation Between the Wars

*"If they ask me, what shall I say
To the folks back home, back England way?
Don't you worry, there's naught to tell
'Cept work and fly and bomb like hell.
With hills above and hills below
And rocks to pile where the hills don't go.
Nice soft sitting for those who crash
But 'War' you call it? Don't talk trash!
War's a rumor, war's a yarn.
This is the Peace of Waziristan."*

R.H. PEEL, FROM A POEM ABOUT
COLONIAL POLICING BY THE RAF ON THE
NORTHWEST FRONTIER OF INDIA IN THE 1920S.

WHEN THE GUNS FELL silent on the Western Front at the eleventh hour on the eleventh day of the eleventh month of 1918, and the killing stopped at last in the fields and skies of France, many of those who had survived found it hard to believe that the war really was finally over. The sudden release from the strain and tension of the interminable life and death struggle was almost too much to bear. At first, there were spontaneous demonstrations of joy and thanksgiving, both among the members of the armed forces and those who waited to welcome them home.

The reaction of Eddie Rickenbacker's 94th Squadron to the news was fairly typical; like many units based behind the front line, they started celebrating the night before:

> We all went a little mad. Shouting and screaming like crazy men, we ran to get whatever firearms we had, including flare pistols, and began blasting up into the sky. It was already bright up there. As far as we could see the sky was filled with exploding shells and rockets, star shells, parachute flares, streams of Very lights and searchlights tracing crazy patterns.
>
> [To add even more light, the 94th started a fire with barrels of gasoline.]
>
> Up roared a bonfire that could be seen for miles. We danced around that blazing pyre screaming, shouting and beating one another on the back. One pilot kept shouting over and over and over, "I've lived through the war, I've lived through the war!"

*OPPOSITE PAGE
The USAF Museum's collection of artifacts that belonged to outspoken air power advocate General Billy Mitchell includes his medals and the uniform jacket he is believed to have worn at his court martial in 1925. Also shown here are his spectacles, binoculars, and the pennant flown from his aircraft during the 1921 battleship trials.*

Designed during 1917 by Captain Georges LePere, a French aeronautical engineer, the LUSAC 11 was an attempt to get an American fighter into combat. (LUSAC stood for LePere U.S. Army Combat.) Designed to be a combination fighter and reconnaissance aircraft, it carried a pilot and an observer/gunner. Three prototypes were completed in April 1918, but WWI ended before flight testing was complete. The LUSAC 11 shown is on display at the USAF Museum, Dayton, Ohio.

The elation of the fighting men on Armistice Day was reflected in the rejoicing of people in towns and villages all over the world. Even in the defeated nations there was a sense of relief. Once the parties were over, however, and the initial surge of euphoria was spent, some postwar realities seized the public mind. The appalling price paid by the combatants began to be understood as the casualty figures were totaled and the depletion of national resources measured. Realization of the true scale of the disaster reinforced people's revulsion for warfare and induced a reaction against all things military. Surely, it was thought, mankind could not be so insane as to inflict such horrors on the world again. The international conflagration begun in 1914 must certainly have been "the war to end all wars."

Given the abhorrence generally felt for war and its machines, it is hardly surprising that peace brought with it a confusion of attitudes toward air forces. Reflecting the sentiment of the time, Winston Churchill, who had been and would be again one of air power's most vocal advo-cates, railed against "the aeroplane…this cursed hellish invention." The romantic association of aerial combat with ancient ideals of medieval chivalry, so recently and eagerly embraced, soon faded behind the threat of what might lie in the future, with civilian populations exposed to the prospect of mass destruction from the air. Uplifting images inspired by tales of airborne heroics were incompatible with terrifying concepts of total war waged indiscriminately by aerial armadas. Air power was a means by which the military, political, industrial and technological muscles of a nation's strength might be flexed together as never before, and the thought that it could reach out to touch every member of a population was particularly disturbing. It was a powerful argument in support of the view that war on such a scale must now be considered unthinkable. With peace so dearly bought, and nations so utterly exhausted by the struggle, was it sensible to maintain large armed forces? Retrenchment was the order of the day and military expenditures were among the first to feel the keenness of the budget cutter's knife.

The Pruning of the Air Power Tree

Among the armed forces of the victorious Allies, none shrank more drastically during the immediate postwar period than Britain's Royal Air Force. In November 1918, the RAF had 188 front-line squadrons and over 290,000 officers and men. With nearly 23,000 aircraft of all types on hand, it was the largest air force in the world. Little more than a year later, there were only twelve operational squadrons and the manpower figure was down to less than 32,000. By October 1924, after some punishing political battles, the front-line strength had been restored to a more respectable forty-three squadrons, but most of those were heavily occupied with duties overseas. Until late 1922, responsibility for Britain's home air defense rested with a single squadron of Sopwith Snipes.

The Italians ended the war with nearly 1,800 military aircraft, mostly of local manufacture, but that number dwindled rapidly in 1919, and, despite Douhet's advocacy for air power, military aviation in Italy was largely neglected until after Mussolini's rise to national leadership in 1922. The French behaved more circumspectly. Even after demobilization, the Aviation Militaire retained 180 front-line squadrons, deployed not only in France, but also in North Africa, and in French colonial territories in the Middle and Far East. The situation of the defeated Central Powers was quite different, limited as they were by the terms of the Versailles Treaty, signed in June 1919. The Austro-Hungarian Empire was dissolved, and aircraft of the newly independent Austrian Republic saw some action in the Carinthian War early in 1919, but by the end of that year, Germany, Austria and Hungary were obliged to disestablish their military air arms. A Control Commission was appointed to ensure that all of their aircraft and associated equipments were either destroyed or surrendered to the Allies.

American airmen felt that their potential had been unfulfilled. Entering the war late and poorly prepared, they had fought hard with what they had and won some notable victories, but they had not darkened the skies with fleets of American warplanes and they had not reached a point where the promise of their military aircraft had been fully redeemed.

Disappointment led to recrimination and a series of hearings and investigations from which criticisms spread widely. U.S. government departments, industry and the military were all blamed for lack of organization, indecision and poor judgment. The U.S. war machine had only just shifted into high gear, but now it went into reverse. An air arm that had grown from 1,200 men to nearly 200,000 in little more than eighteen months experienced the pains of contraction as it was cut to fewer than 10,000 by mid-1920. Reflecting the postwar mood of the country, the attitude of Congress toward military spending was unsympathetic and budgets were parsimonious. The $460 million of fiscal year 1919 fell to no more than $25 million in 1920. Politicians

Major General Benjamin D. Foulois was the Army's first pilot and a founding father of air power. He became Chief of the U.S. Army Air Corps on December 20, 1931. He was a flier's flier and liked flying his personal Douglas O-38F to inspect bases. He is seen here in 1914 as Captain Foulois, standing in front of a Burgess-Wright biplane.

intended for attacking cities. Furthermore, General Pershing delivered himself of the opinion that "an air force acting independently can of its own account neither win a war at the present time nor, so far as we can tell, at any time in the future." In what was seen by many air officers as a crushing defeat for their cause, Congress authorized the Air Service only as a combatant arm of the army limited to some 1,500 officers and 16,000 enlisted men, which was an indication of how much preaching the apostles of air power still had to do. In a front line of twenty-seven squadrons there were just four pursuit and four bombardment squadrons, only one of which was designated "heavy." The remaining nineteen squadrons were all tasked with observation, as were thirty-two balloon companies. The emphasis reflected the views still held by most senior army officers that aircraft were intended primarily for close support of troops on the battlefield.

In Russia, the Imperial Russian Flying Corps disintegrated with the coming of revolution in November 1917, some elements of the force siding with the revolutionaries and others opposing them. The Workers' and Peasants' Red Air Fleet (RKKVF) was established in May 1918, making do with what was left from the mayhem and operating a motley collection of types, including among the best of them SPAD VIIs, Nieuport 17s, and Sopwith 1½ Strutters. The Volga Military Flotilla also possessed several Grigorovich M.9 flying boats. Beginning with a force of some 300 aircraft in

found it difficult to imagine that any nation could pose a credible threat to the United States and they were quick to note that wartime expansion had provided the Air Service with thousands of aircraft and mountains of spares. It was the view of Congress that there was little need to spend money on more. American military airmen looked forward gloomily to many years in which their flying would be dominated by Curtiss Jennies and U.S.-built DH-4s.

The prospects for a change in the status of the U.S. Air Service were no more encouraging. In 1919, bills were presented in both the Senate and the House proposing the creation of an independent U.S. Air Force. The bills died, and Secretary of War Baker warned that the Air Service had better not get any ideas about building up a bomber force the front line, the Red Air Fleet was then involved in bitter and confused fighting for more than two years, primarily in the fragmented civil wars against "White" antirevolutionary forces. At various times the fighting spread over an immense area from the Black Sea to within the Arctic Circle, and from the Baltic to Siberia. The opposing "Whites" were given military assistance by a number of foreign countries. RAF squadrons flying Camels and D.H.9s served briefly in campaigns on the Volga and in the far north, around Archangel. By late 1921, the White forces had been separately defeated and the foreign intruders had been discreetly withdrawn.

In the war against Poland during 1920, the Red Air Fleet found itself opposed by a small Polish Air Force that, although haphazardly equipped with some sixty types of aircraft acquired from Germany, France, Britain and Italy, was well trained and resolute. Recalling the Lafayette Escadrille experience, it included the American volunteers of the "Kosciuszko Squadron." At one stage, with the Red Army at the gates of Warsaw, the Polish Air Force played a large part in saving the day, slowing the Russian spearheads by incessant pounding from the air until the Polish Army could launch a crushing counterattack. It was a crit-

ical action, since a Polish collapse would have given the Russians access to a Germany in chaos, when Communism had every prospect of taking root. In the words of the British Ambassador in Berlin, if the Poles had "failed to arrest the triumphant march of the Soviet Army at the Battle of Warsaw…the very existence of western civilization would have been imperilled." The Polish Air Force and the "Kosciuszkos" had every right to be proud of themselves when Lenin sued for peace and signed the Treaty of Riga in March 1921. In common with so many other elements of the Soviet state in the aftermath of war and revolution, the Red Air Fleet was reduced to a shambles, with most of its aircraft unserviceable or obsolete. Like air forces everywhere, it was badly in need of reorganization and reequipment.

However hard the military airmen of any country might argue the case for maintaining the capability of their forces, the funds available for defense expenditure in the post-WWI world were limited. National treasuries were sorely depleted and public opinion was not at all in favor of spending much money on armaments of any kind. In any event, the rapid demobilization of the massive forces existing at the end of the war led to huge surpluses of equipment, and it was felt that these should be used up before acquiring more. (British production in the summer of 1914 averaged ten aircraft per month. Four years later it was about 2,500 per month.) Orders involving thousands of aircraft were canceled, and aircraft industries that had mushroomed to meet wartime demands found themselves virtually overnight competing to exist on repair work or the supply of spares. Most aircraft manufacturers and their subcontractors diversified or went out of business. Productive capacity shrank to a mere fraction of its wartime volume and aircraft development stagnated.

In a remarkable recapitulation of the Escadrille Lafayette experience, American pilots formed the Kosciuszko Squadron and fought for Poland against the Bolsheviks in the 1919–1920 Soviet-Polish war. Cedric Fauntleroy (commander), Merian Cooper (founder and deputy commander), and Arthur Kelly were among the seventeen Americans who volunteered. They flew bombing and strafing missions against hordes of Russian troops, using whatever aircraft were available. These were mostly an assortment of Allied and German machines from WWI, including Austrian-built Albatros D.III fighters.

In WWI and between the wars, a number of French aircraft appeared as parasols, in which the single wing was placed above and clear of the fuselage. Morane Saulnier in particular favored the parasol, and produced several for the French military. An example of the parasol design is the Morane-Saulnier MS 181 F-AJXN owned by the Experimental Aircraft Association at Oshkosh, Wisconsin. A single-seat light aircraft, it is powered by a 60-horsepower Salmson radial engine and is capable of a modest 80 mph.

Independent Air Power Challenged

To ease the discomfort of the postwar economic climate, the British government in 1919 adopted the "Ten Year Rule," which assumed for planning purposes that Britain would not be involved in a major war for another ten years. This arbitrary assumption, used as justification for restricting defense spending to a minimum, was renewed each year until 1932. Rational discussion of defense issues was difficult in the circumstances. The Royal Air Force, having become the world's first independent air force in response to an urgent wartime need first to defend against and then to conduct strategic air operations, found that its continued survival was by no means assured. The older services did not relish having to feed another mouth from the meager defense budget cake, and they set out to strangle the infant air force soon after its birth. Repeated attacks were launched not only by the Army and Navy, but also by a number of prominent politicians, including, in 1922, Prime Minister Bonar Law, who announced it as his firm intention to get rid of the RAF. Sir Hugh Trenchard, the Chief of Air Staff, steadfastly maintaining that "the air is one and indivisible," rested his argument for the survival of his service on two solid pillars. First, while accepting the need to support operations by the other services, he insisted that an air force should be primarily a strategic arm, intended to strike at the heart of an enemy nation directly, something armies and navies were incapable of doing. Second, he suggested that the onerous duty of policing the trouble spots of the British Empire and its mandated territories could be most economically accomplished by relatively small numbers of aircraft, reducing the need to maintain large and expensive army garrisons overseas.

Looking Down on the Locals

Between the wars, the idea that control over large territories could be exerted successfully from the air was one that generated much debate. Effective control from the air alone was not often achieved, but there were many instances of aircraft being used by nations to influence events in their spheres of interest where air opposition was either absent or negligible. French airmen operated frequently against warring tribesmen in Morocco and Algeria, and they were also active in Syria, flying aircraft such as the Breguet 14 of WWI, the Potez 25, and the Breguet 19. In the Moroccan Rif War of 1921–26, Muhammad bin Abd al-Karim led a rebellion first against the Spanish colonial power and later against the forces of both France and Spain. The two European powers used aircraft extensively, and the French were successful in developing combined operations, with aircraft supporting troops equipped with tanks and armored cars. Twice aircraft were integrated into more complex plans, and cleared the way for amphibious assaults. The imaginative employment of aircraft in the fighting against al-Karim did much to ensure the campaign's success and demonstrated

considerable insight into the nature of "small wars," a problem that would prove increasingly troublesome as the century progressed.

The United States sent aircraft at various times to intervene in Santo Domingo, Haiti and, during the Sandino War, in Nicaragua. When Nicaraguan guerrillas surrounded the small U.S. garrison at Ocotal in July 1927, five DH-4s of the U.S. Marine Corps broke the siege by dive-bombing and machine-gunning the attackers. As the squadron commander reported: "We ended up by diving in from 1,000 feet and pulling out at about 300. Since the enemy had not been subjected to any form of bombing attack…they had no fear of us. They exposed themselves in such a manner that we were able to inflict damage which was out of proportion to what they might have suffered had they taken cover."

It was the first time that aircraft had rescued a beleaguered garrison from envelopment by superior forces. Later in the campaign, the aging DH-4s were replaced by Curtiss OC-2s and Vought O2Us, but the Marines went on dive-bombing, convinced that the precision of such a method of attack was especially effective in small-scale engagements.

Morane Saulnier loomed large at the 1933 Paris air show, with parasol designs prominently displayed. The MS 225 fighter in the foreground was adopted by the Armée de l'Air. With landing-gear fairings and a low-drag cowling for its 600-horsepower Gnome-Rhône Jupiter engine, its top speed approached 200 mph. The MS 225 was highly maneuverable and was flown by Michel D'Etroyat when he took second place in the 1934 World Aerobatic Championships.

At the same time, it was argued that dive-bombing would be the best way to attack surface ships. It was a suggestion that later led to the U.S. Navy's acquisition of specialized dive-bombers, and so eventually to the destruction of Japan's hopes of Pacific dominance.

Both in North Africa and Central America, air operations were generally carried out in support of action by ground forces. Elsewhere, it was the RAF more than any other service that, through necessity, used aircraft more independently, placing less reliance on the presence of troops. In Iraq especially, every effort was made to take the air control idea and develop it into a workable system, using open-cockpit biplanes that either dated from WWI or were hardly any different.

The RAF gave a startling demonstration of air control's possibilities as early as 1920. A rebel Dervish leader known as the "Mad Mullah" had been raiding and looting in Somaliland for twenty years, defying efforts made by thousands of troops to put an end to his depredations. The cost, in both financial and human terms, had been intolerably high. In January 1920, one squadron of D.H.9s was sent to begin a bombing campaign against the Mullah's strongholds, forcing him to seek sanctuary elsewhere. Pursued by RAF bombs and a small force from the Camel Corps, he fled the country and died bereft of power the following year. Once aircraft were introduced, twenty years of conflict were brought to an end in just three weeks. The delighted

British Colonial Secretary said it was "the cheapest war in history," and it proved to be the precursor of more ambitious operations in the 1920s and 1930s, mainly in the Middle East and on the frontiers of India. They in turn foreshadowed events in Iraq, Bosnia and Afghanistan over half a century later.

In the aftermath of WWI, Britain acquired League of Nations mandates for ensuring the "security and orderly development of Iraq, Palestine and Trans-Jordan." At the Cairo conference in 1920, Winston Churchill argued that the RAF should be given responsibility for both internal and external security in the Middle East, where border raiding and intertribal warfare were a way of life. In the former Mesopotamia, now Iraq, thirty-three battalions of infantry, six of cavalry, and sixteen artillery batteries were replaced by eight RAF squadrons (four squadrons of D.H.9As, one each of Bristol Fighters and Sopwith Snipes, and two of Vickers Vernon troop transports) supported by one infantry brigade and four squadrons of RAF armored cars. It was a challenge of daunting proportions. The Suez Canal and Middle East oil had combined to make the stability of the region vital to the

PRESENTED BY HIS HIGHNESS
THE NIZAM OF HYDERABAD
HYDERABAD Nº 12ᴬ

The Airco D.H.9A at the RAF Museum is one of seven No. 110 Squadron aircraft shot down during a daylight raid on Germany in October 1918. It is restored as Hyderabad No. 12A (to avoid No. 13!), one of the aircraft presented to No. 110 Squadron, RAF, by the Nizam of Hyderabad. No. 110 Squadron was the first to fly the D.H.9A (known as the "Nine-Ack") in action.

In the late 1930s, Geoffrey Morley-Mower was based on the northwest frontier of India, close to Afghanistan, and found himself "flying biplanes of ancient vintage over the most exotic frontier in the world, keeping order among tribes that had not changed since the invasion of India by Mahmud of Ghazni in the Middle Ages." Wing Commander Geoffrey F. Morley-Mower, DFC, AFC, RAF, is now a professor of English literature at James Madison University in Harrisonburg, Virginia. He has written two books about his RAF service: Flying Blind and Messerschmitt Roulette. BELOW Hawker Audax biplanes patrolling the frontier between India and Afghanistan.

Aircraft of No. 5 Squadron, RAF, dropping leaflets over the city of Lahore, India, after the outbreak of war in Europe. The message (in English and Urdu) read: "This leaflet might have been a Nazi bomb! Defend the Punjab by helping to buy warplanes. Give what you can afford today."

economy of the Western world. The few frail biplanes on which this responsibility rested seemed too insubstantial a force to bear the weight of such an important task.

The method of control was to warn recalcitrant tribesmen initially by dropping messages on their villages. If they were defiant, a further warning advised them to clear the area by a certain time or suffer the consequences. If it was doubted that the villagers could read, the written messages could be backed up by voice through loudspeakers mounted on aircraft. If the warnings were ignored and action proved necessary, the village would be bombed while its inhabitants sat on a nearby hillside and riflemen took shots at the bombers. The aim, as set out in the RAF War Manual, was "to interrupt the normal life of the enemy people to such an extent that a continuance of hostilities becomes intolerable." The manual said nothing about

> *"Would not the sight of a single enemy airplane be enough to induce a formidable panic? Normal life would be unable to continue under the constant threat of death and imminent destruction."*
>
> GIULIO DOUHET, *IL DOMINIO DELL'ARIA*, 1921

whether the aircrew might find life tolerable or not. Flying from the crushing heat of the plains, often above 120 degrees Fahrenheit, to bone-numbing cold at altitude could be a severe test for men and machines. Finding suitable clothing for the open-cockpit conditions was impossible, while wood and fabric structures suffered from the assault of extreme temperatures, sand, and remote and stony landing strips.

Controversial though it was, the system was quite effective, given that the aircraft involved were small in number and obsolete, and that they were operated on a financial shoestring from rudimentary bases. For the first time, it became possible to enforce the law and promote harmony in remote areas without occupying the country and killing large numbers of the population. Previously, peacemaking had involved sending troops to compel submission, and that had been a bloody business on

Frontier Patrol, *by Michael Turner. A Bristol fighter of 28 Squadron, RAF, on patrol over the northwest frontier of India in the 1920s.*

both sides. Even air control was not without its casualties. Tribesmen were killed when they ignored warnings, and their rifles shot down a few aircraft. However, the numbers were minimal compared to those of the army's operations, and the effects were longer lasting. Military expeditions into tribal areas were deeply resented. When troops withdrew, they usually did so under harassing fire, and then the tribes went back to their old ways. Aircraft, patrolling over the remotest villages, were not so intrusive, but their presence was a constant reminder that law-breaking would bring swift retribution from on high.

Sometimes circumstances justified sending troops in to pacify a situation, but aircraft could be useful then, too. In 1923, a Kurdish force descended on Kirkuk in northern Iraq. They assumed that the RAF would not bomb the city, and they believed it could not be reached by the army since heavy rains had made the roads impassable. However, troop carrier squadrons picked up the 14th Sikh Regiment from a railhead 75 miles to the south and flew them to Kirkuk. The raiders were surprised in the act of looting the bazaar, and the sudden appearance of disciplined troops sent them running for the hills. Shortly afterward, a local sheikh, noted for his anti-British activities, called on the District Officer. He wished, he said, to be regarded in future as pro-

British. "With my own eyes," he explained, "I saw hundreds of soldiers march into town, having flown through the air directly from London, where it is well known that there is an inexhaustible supply. Allah is great, but who can prevail against that?"

The RAF made good use of its transport aircraft, pioneering air mobility as a means of increasing the army's reach and capabilities. RAF transports scattered leaflets, deployed troops, served as air ambulances, delivered supplies, surveyed air routes, and conducted emergency evacuations. In the winter of 1928–29, when civil war broke out in Afghanistan, over 500 civilians of some twenty nationalities, together with the Afghan king, were airlifted to safety from Kabul to India. It was a demonstration of air mobility that the British Secretary of State for Aviation was quick to use as an illustration that military aircraft were not always destructive. The evacuation showed, he said, "that the aeroplane can be made an instrument of real help and benefit to humanity." True enough, but there was no denying that the flying machine, like its creator, would always have a darker side to its character.

Marshal of the Royal Air Force Sir Hugh "Boom" Trenchard, "Father of the Royal Air Force." He was a staunch advocate of independent air power and the bomber force's "knock-out blow."

AIR POWER PROPHETS AND CRUSADERS
The Service Comes First

Sir Hugh "Boom" Trenchard (his deep, penetrating voice earned him the nickname) had not always been in favor of independent air power. As commander of the RFC in France, he had argued against the Smuts proposals for the formation of the Royal Air Force on the grounds that the new service, faced with other priorities, would not be inclined to give the British Army as much close support as it needed. By the time he was established as the RAF's Chief of Air Staff, however, he had spent some months in command of the Independent Air Force, created for the purpose of long-range bombardment of Germany. The role appealed to his offensive spirit, and he came to believe that the destruction of a nation's industrial base and the will of its people to wage war could serve the troops on the ground as effectively as did close air support.

In a statement to the Supreme War Council at Versailles in the autumn of 1918, Trenchard set out the aims for an expanded Allied bombing offensive, saying:

"There are two factors — moral effect and materiel effect — the object being to obtain the maximum of each. The best means to this end is to attack the industrial centres where you:

a) Do military and vital damage by striking at the centres of supply of war material.

b) Achieve the maximum of effect on the most sensitive part of the whole German population — namely, the working class."

Here was a clear indication that civilians were considered to be legitimate targets on the grounds that they were part of the war machine. Trenchard was a single-minded man of great determination, and once converted to the idea of strategic air power, he became its ardent campaigner, but not only because he believed in its war-winning potential. It also formed one of the two pillars on which the survival of his service depended.

Public opinion in Britain was generally in favor of Trenchard's point of view. Fear of another continental commitment and its ground war horrors fostered the belief that it was infinitely preferable to build an air force that could leap over intervening armies and navies to destroy the fabric of an enemy nation. Trenchard himself maintained that this was the only way to approach a future war. He despised efforts to strengthen air defenses, an attitude he had held since his earliest days in France. In 1916, he wrote: "The aeroplane is not a defence against the aeroplane. But the opinion of those most competent to judge is that the aeroplane, as a weapon of attack, cannot be too highly estimated."

The records of a committee meeting held in 1923 reveal his contempt for defensive strategies: "[Sir Hugh Trenchard said that] fighter defence must be kept to the smallest possible number. It was, in the opinion of the Chief of Air Staff, in a sense only a concession to the weakness of the civilians, who would demand protection and cause the Cabinet to do likewise. These demands, he insisted, must be resisted as far as possible."

Trenchard preached that "attack is the best form of defence." He promoted the idea that the best way to defend Britain from air attack was to equip the RAF with a bomber force of crushing strength, which could, among other things, overpower and destroy the enemy air force on its bases. His was the doctrine of the "knock-out blow." Such forceful and inflexible views were instrumental in protecting the RAF, but they later had the paradoxical effect of generating serious problems for the service they sustained.

When Brigadier General William "Billy" Mitchell returned from France in 1918 he was thought by many (including himself) to be the ideal choice for appointment as Chief of the U.S. Army Air Service. The officers of the General Staff were not sure that they were ready for such a turbulent spirit in the post, however, and he was made Deputy Chief. He became "the hero of the Army's flyers," never ceasing to promote his ideas on the primacy of air power.

ing one in 1928 that said: "You have given us something worth doing. The RAF is 30,000 strong, too huge for you to have personal contact with many of us, but there is not a single barrack-room where your trumpet does not sound; and these thousands of your champions find no opponents. We grouse and grumble at everything and everybody, except you."

Martyr for the Cause
In the U.S. Air Service, Brigadier General Billy Mitchell had been profoundly influenced by Trenchard's views that aircraft were primarily offensive weapons that should be operated under unified command. These ideas took root in Mitchell's fertile mind and grew into the concepts with which he so forcefully sought to shape American air power. Many Air Service officers hoped that Billy Mitchell would be appointed Chief of Air Service when he returned from France. However, Mitchell's fiery reputation preceded him and the first peacetime Chief appointed was, from the U.S. Army's point of view, a sensibly conservative choice. Major General Charles Menoher was an infantry officer and not a pilot. Mitchell had to be content with being number two.

If they had hoped to keep Billy Mitchell quiet by making him a subordinate, the General

Whatever emotions Trenchard stirred in the breasts of his adversaries in the government and the older services, he was much loved by the men of the RAF. Inarticulate, obstinate and even unapproachable though he could be, his airmen believed he could do no wrong. The unpredictable Colonel T.E. Lawrence (Lawrence of Arabia), seeking to escape his unwanted celebrity, joined the RAF as Aircraftman 2nd Class Shaw. He wrote many letters to Trenchard, includ-

Staff were disappointed. He became "the gadfly of the General Staff and the hero of the Army's flyers." Central to Mitchell's vision of an independent air force was his conviction that air power could become a decisive strategic instrument. The total war concept inherent in his ideas was unpopular in both military and civilian circles. By suggesting that future wars could be decided by airmen before soldiers got involved, Mitchell was attacking arguments being made by the Army to bolster its budget for ground forces. The sailors were apoplectic over his belief that navies were made largely redundant by air power, and his insistence that modern war could no longer exclude women and children horrified almost everyone. "The entire nation," he said, "is, or should be, considered a combatant force." In the face of mounting opposition, Mitchell was persistent. He spoke in public, testified before Congressional committees, and wrote a book spelling out his air power gospel (*Our Air Force, the Keystone of National Defense,* William Mitchell, 1921.) At the same time, Mitchell pursued the day-to-day business of the Air Service with relentless energy. Papers were written on countless proposals — long-range bombers, aircraft that were amphibious or on skis, all-metal bombers, troop-carrying aircraft, armor-piercing bombs, large-caliber cannon, aerial torpedoes, civil defense, the encouragement of private flying — and so on, without pause.

Army officers often found Mitchell's zeal hard to live with, but their naval counterparts saw him as their mortal foe. One of the U.S. Navy's principal roles was to guard against any hostile approach to the American coasts. At the heart of this defense were the Navy's battleships, which

> *"[Hawaii] is where the blow will be struck, on a fine, quiet Sunday morning."*
>
> GENERAL BILLY MITCHELL, PREDICTING WAR WITH JAPAN, 1924

sailors considered almost invulnerable. Mitchell disparaged what he called an outdated notion, declaring that the day of the dreadnoughts was over, that aircraft could sink any ship afloat, and that the United States would be safer if the Air Service were to defend its coasts.

The Chief of Naval Operations was scathing about air power theories, saying: "I cannot conceive of any use that the fleet will ever have for aircraft." Faced with Mitchell's assault, he added: "Aviation is just a lot of noise." The Secretary of the Navy was even more intemperate. He said that he would be prepared to stand bareheaded on the deck of any capital ship under attack from the air.

After several newspapers had picked up Mitchell's theme and argued that battleships were indeed relics of the past, his campaign bore fruit. A number of ex-German warships and some old U.S. ships were made available for trial by air attack. The tests began against an ex-German destroyer in mid-July 1921. First, a wave of S.E.5s dropped 25-pound antipersonnel bombs and simulated strafing the ship from 200 feet. Sixteen Martin bombers followed, dropping two 300-pound bombs each from 1,500 feet. After the first pass by the Martins, the destroyer sank. On July 18,

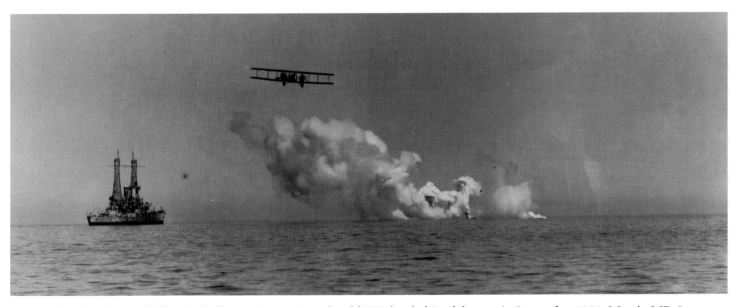

During the first phase of Billy Mitchell's exercises against the old U.S. battleship Alabama, *in September 1921, Martin MB-2 bombers laid smokescreens. Later aircraft dropped increasingly heavy bombs, finally sinking the ship with a 2,000-pound weapon dropped close alongside.*

the cruiser *Frankfurt* got similar treatment, being sunk by Martins carrying 600-pound bombs. A more serious challenge came on July 20 in the shape of the 27,000-ton battleship *Ostfriesland*. With a four-layered hull and water-tight compartments end to end, the ex-German warship was said to be unsinkable. The Martins struck on July 21, this time delivering the coup de grace with 2,000-pound bombs. In just 21 minutes, the unsinkable *Ostfriesland* was sunk.

By July 29, Mitchell was leading his bombers in mock raids on New York City, Philadelphia, Wilmington, Baltimore and Annapolis. In his report on the naval tests, Mitchell's conclusions were uncompromising. The bombers had demonstrated that any ship could be sunk by bombs and that American cities were vulnerable to assault from the air. The only proper defense could be provided by aircraft, and these should be operated by an independent air force. "Aviation," he insisted, "can only be developed to its fullest extent under its own direction and control. An efficient solution of our defensive needs will not exist until a Department of National Defense is organized."

A joint Army/Navy Board acknowledged the dangers of the air threat, and said it was imperative "as a matter of national defense to provide for the maximum possible development of aviation in both the Army and the Navy." However, the Board concluded that battleships "were still the backbone of the fleet and bulwark of the nation's sea defense." The certainty of that assertion seemed dubious after later bombing attacks on the battleship *Alabama* in September 1921, and on two more, the *Indiana* and the *Virginia*, in 1923. All three were sent to the bottom by Mitchell's bombers. It was rightly claimed that the trials were artificial in that the ships were stationary and not firing back, and the bombers were at relatively low level. Nevertheless, doubts were cast on the invulnerability of battleships to air attack, and, on the far side of the world, Japanese naval officers took note.

In 1924, Mitchell resumed his outspoken campaign with more speeches, articles and Congressional testimony. On October 24, 1924, after a tour of the Far East, Mitchell submitted a report to the War Department in which he said that war with Japan was almost inevitable. In a prediction of startling accuracy, he suggested that the Japanese would strike first at Pearl Harbor: "That is where the blow will be struck," he said, "on a fine, quiet Sunday morning." As he grew more strident, he gained something of a public following but his efforts were counterproductive in places where it mattered. He not only angered the Secretaries of War and the Navy and senior officers, he antagonized President Coolidge. When his tour of duty as Assistant Chief of Air Service expired in April 1925, Mitchell was not reappointed. He reverted to his permanent rank of colonel and was exiled to Texas. From there, his frustration burst the bounds of reason. On September 5, 1925, after Navy losses of an aircraft and the airship *Shenandoah*, Mitchell issued a statement to the press that indicted "the incompetency, criminal negligence and almost treasonable administration of our national defense by the Navy and War Departments." The court martial that Mitchell appeared to be seeking was duly ordered by the President and was held in Washington during the closing months of 1925.

Mitchell and his supporters (including such future leaders as Arnold, Spaatz, Olds and Eaker) knew that the verdict of the court was a foregone conclusion, but they made the best of it by treating the trial as a public hearing of the case for air power. As expected, Mitchell was found guilty of "conduct of a nature to bring discredit upon the military service," and sentenced to be suspended from the service for five years without pay. On February 1, 1926, he resigned from the Air Service to continue the fight as a civilian. By the following year he was trumpeting: "The airplane is the future arbiter of the world's destiny."

The onset of the Depression led the public to pay less attention to defense matters, and to Mitchell. He died almost a forgotten man in 1936. Ten years later, when many of his predictions had proved all too accurate, the farsightedness and courage, if not the diplomacy, of his stand were belatedly recognized when President Truman authorized the posthumous award of a special Medal of Honor to Billy Mitchell, air power visionary extraordinary.

> "A modern state is such a complex and interdependent fabric that it offers a target highly sensitive to a sudden and overwhelming blow from the air."
>
> B.H. LIDDELL-HART

Theory Above All

Perhaps the most intellectual of air power's advocates was Italy's Giulio Douhet. He had refined his ideas on aerial warfare during WWI, and in 1921 he published *Command of the Air*, a book that has gained the status of a classic for students of military doctrine, although it is probable that his work was little read outside Italy until it was translated into English in 1932. Sir John Slessor, an architect of Britain's air power in WWII, was among those who claimed never to have seen it. Be that as it may, Douhet's book articulates the interwar theory of strategic air power in its purist form, pulling together ideas drawn from a number of sources — traditional maritime strategies, his own limited experience, his observation of the bombing campaigns conducted by both sides in WWI, and perhaps even from such flights of the imagination as H.G. Wells' *War in the Air*. For Douhet, strategic bombing was the only sensible air power mission; all other roles were irrelevant.

Like Trenchard and Mitchell, Douhet believed that aircraft were the ultimate offensive weapons, against which there was no effective defense. He wrote: "Because of its independence of surface limitations and its superior speed the aeroplane is the offensive weapon par excellence." In his view of future war, armies and navies would be relegated to defensive roles, while the air force first seized command of the air and then launched a massive air assault on the enemy's cities, communications and industries to force a swift decision. Wars would be total, pitting national populations against one another and placing everyone in the firing line. Victory would go to the peoples who destroyed the material resources and overcame the moral resistance of their opponents. Like

Italy's Giulio Douhet. In 1921 he published Command of the Air, *a book setting out the theories of strategic air power. He believed that strategic bombing was the supreme air-power role, and all other uses of military aviation were secondary, if not wasteful or even wholly irrelevant.*

Trenchard, Douhet claimed that civilian morale would be vulnerable to air attack. He went so far as to say: "Would not the sight of a single enemy plane be enough to induce a formidable panic? Normal life would be unable to continue under the constant threat of death and imminent destruction." Convinced of the bomber's supremacy and quite sure of his own judgment, he argued that a major part of the national effort should go toward building a large bomber force that would be kept ready in peace to deliver the decisive blows once hostilities began.

Douhet's theories were developed from the point of view of an Italian and were not, when written, intended to be read universally. At least in part, his arguments were meant to support the case not only for a bomber force but also for an independent Italian Air Force. If many of his predictions were later shown to be questionable, the general trend of development he saw for aerial warfare proved reasonably close to the truth. Given the facts and experience available to him, it is perhaps understandable that he paid little attention to the possible effectiveness of fighters, promoted the impractical all-purpose "battle-plane," and thought civilian morale would be brittle under bombardment. These flaws were exposed in WWII, but they did not nullify Douhet's basic thesis on the significance of air power. The boldness of his line of thought, with its promise of swift, decisive action, was appealing, especially in the aftermath of a long and bloody ground war. Among those who felt its appeal was Benito Mussolini ("Il Duce"), who came to power in 1922 and appointed Douhet as Commissioner of Aviation in his Fascist government.

BRISTOL BULLDOG

The Bristol Bulldog was the RAF's standard front-line fighter of the 1930s. Ten of the thirteen home-defense squadrons were equipped with Bulldogs. It was a delightful aircraft to fly and much loved by its pilots, but its long period (for the time) of service reflected the lack of urgency in Britain's defense policies for most of the interwar years. The Bulldog joined its first RAF unit, No. 3 Squadron, in 1928, and was not finally phased out of the front line until 1937. By that time, it was clearly obsolete, still bearing a strong resemblance to its forbears of WWI — an open-cockpit biplane with fixed undercarriage and two rifle-caliber machine guns firing through the propeller. Its maximum speed was 174 mph. Having been the first, No. 3 Squadron was the last to fly the Bulldog, and within months was operating the Hurricane, an eight-gun monoplane nearly twice as fast. Even though it outlived its usefulness, the Bulldog is remembered as a classic of the period in the tradition of wind in the face and silk scarf fluttering in the breeze. In spite of the RAF's emphasis on bombers, it was the public image of the service in the early 1930s and air-show crowds thrilled to its smoke-trail aerobatics at the Hendon air shows.

In 1964, the aircraft seen here was in flying condition but crashed and was destroyed during an aerobatic display at the Farnborough Air Show. The aviation world thought the wreckage was beyond recovery. In five years of painstaking work, however, the RAF Museum rebuilt this aviation classic and restored it to its present immaculate condition. It was photographed by Dan Patterson at Hendon in the year 2000.

In the Hart light bomber, designed by Sydney Camm, Hawker Aircraft produced one of the most adaptable aircraft of the interwar years. Besides being built in a number of variants, it was the root design for a family of aircraft tasked with widely different roles — the Fury, Demon, Audax, Osprey, Nimrod, Hardy, Hind and Hector. They were the cream of the military biplane era, fast and maneuverable with beautifully harmonized controls. The Hart first reached No. 33 Squadron in January 1930, and some were operated by the RAF in India until 1941. This example can be seen in the RAF Museum at Hendon.

THE BIPLANE AIR FORCES

If the leading air power prophets differed in method and temperament, their theories were built on common foundations. They believed in the destructive power of long-range bombers, the impotence of defenses against them, and the fragility of industrial societies under aerial bombardment. Viewing air warfare through the lens of the 1920s, they exaggerated the first, underrated the second and badly overestimated the third. It was a case of theory running well ahead of capability. However, although strategic bombing theories were supported by little solid evidence, they offered conclusions that sounded all too probable, especially to those who had experienced a foretaste of what the aerial Armageddon might be like. Even so, although the claims of the prophets gave rise to some public apprehension, there were too few funds and too much conservative military inertia to permit any serious development of strategic air power capability. Indeed, as the years went by, it became apparent that the only powers maintaining an interest in strategic bombing were the United Kingdom and the United States, and even there, progress was less than impressive.

Generally speaking, the European continental powers were prisoners of their history, and so were primarily concerned with maintaining armies for the defense of long land frontiers. A few continental airmen appreciated the potential of strategic air power, but their military bureaucracies were drawn by traditional fears to support the needs of surface forces as a first priority. Even those European nations that followed Britain's lead and created independent air forces (Italy, 1923; Sweden, 1926; Germany, 1933; France, 1934) developed aircraft and doctrines that were designed for just that purpose. Given such attitudes and the meager budgets available, it is hardly surprising that the rewards of developing such complex machines as multi-engine, long-range bombers were thought to be insufficient to justify the immense investment of time and effort required. As a result, the aircraft in front-line service with air forces everywhere in the late 1920s were not so very different either in appearance or performance from those flown at the end of WWI.

From Douhet to Balbo

Italian aviation was neglected as badly as any during the four years after WWI, but the arrival of Mussolini's Fascist government brought about a change. To begin with, "Il Duce" appointed himself as both Prime Minister and Minister of Aviation. Within months, the Regia Aeronautica was formed by merging the air arms of the Italian army and navy, and steps were taken to modernize the force. Mussolini's imperial ambitions included the rehabilitation of Italian air power, and in 1926 that task was entrusted to General Italo Balbo. Douhet having retired,

Balbo concentrated more on the practical matters of building up the air force's strength and esprit de corps, and improving its prestige, than on developing new doctrine. By the early 1930s, he had built the Regia Aeronautica into a major air force with a first-line strength of over 1,200 aircraft, and its airmen had caught the headlines of the world's newspapers many times for their record-breaking achievements and crowd-pleasing displays. (See Chapter 2, The Continuing Challenge.)

The principal Italian fighter was the Fiat C.R.20, a delightfully agile little aircraft much loved by its pilots. However, it was still an open-cockpit biplane with fixed undercarriage, a top speed of less than 170 mph, and two Vickers machine guns firing through the propeller arc. René Fonck or Eddie Rickenbacker would have found it reasonably familiar. The backbone of the bomber force during this

Between July 1 and August 12, 1933, Marshal Italo Balbo commanded a formation of twenty-four specially equipped twin-hulled Savoia-Marchetti S.55X flying boats that were flown across Europe and the Atlantic to the United States. They visited the Chicago World's Fair and then returned to Rome. It was a dramatic display of airmanship and public relations. From then on, the term "Balbo" was commonly used to describe any large formation of aircraft.

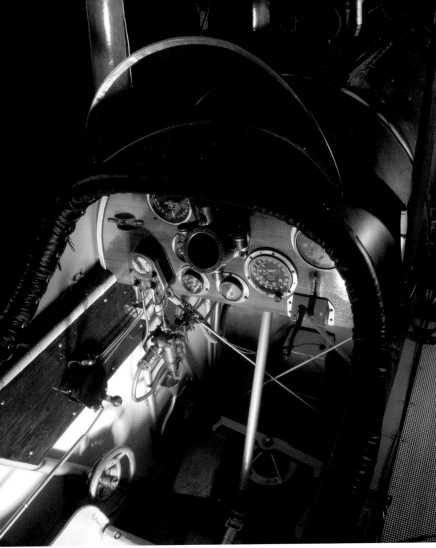

The layout of the post-WWI DH-4's cockpit retains the essential simplicity typical of wartime aircraft. Most people are right-handed, so that is the hand that grasps the stick and is entrusted with the important business of maneuvering the aircraft. The throttle and elevator trim wheel are on the left. When it was photographed in 1995, this DH-4 was on display at the USAF Museum, painted in the colors of Major General Mason Patrick, Chief of the U.S. Army Air Service from 1921 to 1926.

period was the Caproni Ca.73, a medium-sized twin-engined inverted sesquiplane built on lines that would have done credit to a flying boat. (A sesquiplane is a biplane with wings of unequal span, the upper normally being longer than the lower.) It, too, had open crew positions and was flat out at 107 mph. In an attempt to resurrect Douhet's ideas, Caproni did build the prototype of a similarly shaped but much larger six-engined bomber in 1929. The Ca.90 was for a while the largest landplane in the world, with a lower wing spanning 152 feet and an all-up weight of 66,000 pounds. It could carry nearly 18,000 pounds of bombs and had a range of 800 miles, but it still reflected its WWI lineage. The air force hierarchy was not impressed and turned away finally from the path marked by Douhet.

Failures in France

For some years after WWI, the French, concerned with colonial problems and determined to ensure compliance with the Treaty of Versailles, retained the world's largest and best-equipped air force, with new types replacing many of those in service at the end of the war. Notable was a partiality for parasol fighters such as the Wibault 72, a 150-mph machine, a few of which were still in service as late as 1936. That protracted lifespan is an indication of the difficulties faced by French airmen. Although they fought hard for air force independence, and finally achieved their goal in 1934, the French Air Force (Armée de l'Air) lived under the constraints of an interservice committee dominated by the army. In addition, French defense policy at one time or another suffered from the effects of political instability, penurious budgets, a touching faith in the ability of the League of Nations to enforce international disarmament, and the mistaken belief that any future threat from Germany could best be met by an army dug into strong fortifications. Although the Armée de l'Air remained one of the world's largest air forces, its equipment progressed only slowly, and its organization reflected its responsibility to support the army. Aircraft development often seemed to be in search of Douhet's "battle-plane," producing a series of slow, angular creatures

In the early 1920s, modified de Havilland DH-4s (DH-4Bs) carried the U.S. air mail. In their first year, DH-4Bs carried more than 775 million letters and became known as the workhorse of the air mail service. This DH-4B ("Old 249") is part of the atrium exhibit, Moving the Mail, at the National Postal Museum in Washington, D.C.

The Vickers Valentia was the RAF's principal transport aircraft in the Middle East and India in the 1930s. Two pilots sat in an open cockpit, and twenty-two troops could be accommodated in the cabin. Powered by two 600-horsepower Bristol Pegasus engines, it had a maximum airspeed of 120 mph and a range of 750 miles. Here three Valentias of No. 216 Squadron cruise over Cairo's Citadel.

such as the Amiot 143, an ugly monster intended to meet a specification for a "Multi-seater BCR" (Bombardment, Chasse, Reconnaissance) machine. Just as ungainly and impractical, and no less obsolescent as soon as they appeared, were the LeO 20 and the Potez 540. At a time when Hitler was rising to power and new technologies were accelerating aeronautical progress, the Armée de l'Air was hampered by poor equipment and mired in the army's defensive strategy. In little more than one decade, France had slipped from the position of being the world's leading military air power to one of struggling to catch up.

Trenchard's Air Force

Across the Channel, the RAF labored along on its meager share of an emaciated defense budget, surviving behind the shield of Trenchard's policies. By the time of his retirement in 1929, the RAF was unmistakably Trenchard's air force — secure in its independence, with professional staffs and well-established training facilities, but heavily biased toward its bomber arm. Overseas, in its colonial operations, the RAF performed well in its policing role, making the best of biplanes that were unsophisticated and often long overdue for retirement. At home, it was decided in 1923 that the RAF should have a front line capable of protecting Britain against the strongest air force within striking distance. This was operated by the French, who at that time had some 1,500

aircraft. A goal of fifty-two squadrons (thirty-seven bomber and fifteen fighter) was set for 1928, a date deferred each year until 1936 under the ten-year rule. However, although the RAF remained under strength, reequipment began and an extraordinary variety of new types appeared from the late 1920s onward. By the early 1930s, the principal RAF fighters were the Bristol Bulldog and the Armstrong-Whitworth Siskin, while the bombers ranged from the smaller Fairey IIIF and Fox, Hawker Hart and Horsley, to the larger Boulton-Paul Sidestrand, Handley Page Hinaidi, and Vickers Virginia. Varied and new they may have been, but all of them were biplanes and most of them closely resembled the aircraft of 1918.

If the RAF made progress anywhere in the 1920s it was in the public mind. Trenchard discouraged the glamorizing of individuals, but he knew the power of good publicity and approved of eye-catching events, such as record-breaking and trail-blazing flights, and the annual RAF Pageant at Hendon, designed to show off the service with spectacular displays on the ground and in the air. (See Chapters 2 and 3 for further details of record-breaking and air shows.) As the 1930s began, the RAF in the U.K. was a highly professional service, capable of demonstrating its spirit and its expertise in feats that drew the admiration of the public. Unfortunately, the RAF was also poorly equipped to conduct major operations of the kind envisaged by Trenchard, and it

The Martin MB-2, designed specifically as a night bomber, first flew in 1920. MB-2s were redesignated NBS-1 in a new Army designation scheme. These aircraft took part in the famous trials of July 21, 1921, in which the ex-German battlecruiser Ostfreisland *was sunk by aerial bombardment. Eight Army bombing squadrons used the NBS-1: the 11th, 20th, 49th and 96th Squadrons with the 2nd Bomb Group based at Langley Field in Virginia; the 23rd and 72nd Squadrons with the 5th Composite Group in Hawaii; and the 28th Squadron with the 4th Composite Group in the Philippines. The Martin bombers remained in service until replaced by Keystones in 1928–29. The MB-2 shown is a replica built specially for the USAF Museum, Dayton, with meticulous attention to detail.*

The Martin MB-1, introduced in 1918, was smaller and faster than its successor, but could carry only 1,000 pounds of bombs, a third of the MB-2's load. It also had a more complex four-wheeled main landing gear and engines mounted between the wings.

still had opponents in high places. In 1932, the Secretary of the Cabinet and of the Committee for Imperial Defence wrote: "It would be worth a lot to get rid of submarines and aircraft — which I have advocated for a long time."

American Adventures

American airmen faced similar difficulties as their service grew, but in the pioneering days after WWI, these did not often include restrictions. Local commanders were given latitude to wave the Air Service's flag as they saw fit. Lengthy absences of aircraft and crew from the home base were not seen as a problem, and fact-finding adventures were deemed at least as important as routine training. In the first transcontinental flight by the Air Service, Major Albert Smith

An F6C-3 Hawk of VF-1B (Fighting Squadron 1 of Battle Force).

led five Curtiss Jennies out of Rockwell Field, San Diego, on December 4, 1918. He reached Jacksonville on December 18 and returned to Rockwell on February 15, 1919, via Washington and New York. In the process, two aircraft crashed, two more were wrecked in severe weather, and several major overhauls were carried out. Forced landings were common, and pilots got used to landing in any relatively flat area and accepting the hazards. One pilot sent a message that he was delayed "due to cow eating wing." In his later report, he stated that the patches on his aircraft were proof that "some unprincipled bovine with a low sense of humor and a depraved appetite had eaten large chunks out of the lower wing panels and stabilizer." In September 1919, the Army took action to control its wayward

airmen. From that date, authorization for special flights had to be obtained from Air Service Headquarters in Washington.

Even controlled exercises had their excitements. The most important exercise for the Air Service under the new rules in 1919 was Mitchell's "transcontinental reliability and endurance test." It was meant to be a field maneuver "calculated to yield a far greater profit to the Air Service and the cause of aeronautics in general than any field maneuver ever did before." Navigation, meteorology, landing fields and other operational matters would be tested. An underlying reason for Mitchell's proposal was to gather facts on the problems of operating an air force that had suffered savage cuts and was flying obsolete aircraft over country with inadequate facilities. Any local commander could enter an aircraft and pilot, and Mitchell's "test" took on the character of a race, the prospect of which excited public interest.

The chosen route lay between New York and San Francisco, and could be flown either way, but all aircraft had to pass through twenty-nine control stations on the 2,700-mile flight. No night flying was allowed. Fifty-two DH-4s dominated the lineup, and they were joined by one D.H.9, seven S.E.5s, five Fokkers, three LUSAC 11s, two Martin bombers, one Ansaldo S.V.A.5, one Thomas-Morse MB-3, one SPAD, and one Bristol Fighter. Several of these failed to reach the starting line for one reason or another, including two fatal accidents.

> *"Why don't we just buy one airplane and let the pilots take turns flying it?"*
>
> CALVIN COOLIDGE, COMMENTING ON A WAR DEPARTMENT REQUEST FOR MORE AIRCRAFT.

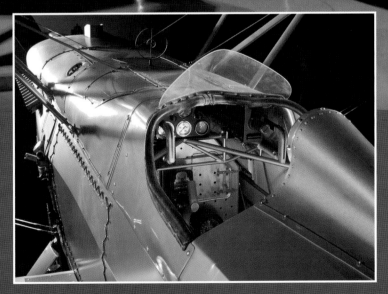

CURTISS HAWK

The F6C Hawk on display at the National Museum of Naval Aviation, Pensacola, Florida. The first of the series of Curtiss biplane fighters to carry the name Hawk was the P1 (F6C-1) of 1925. Throughout the 1920s, Curtiss produced biplanes in a bewildering range of designations for the U.S. Army, Navy and Marine Corps. Variations on the Curtiss theme were also flown as racing machines in the Pulitzer and Schneider Trophies, with considerable success. Much of the credit for the superior performance of these aircraft can be attributed to their Curtiss engines, particularly the 400-horsepower D-12, the world's first wet-sleeve monobloc aero-engine, and its developments. VF-5S, the Red Rippers at Hampton Roads, received F6Cs in 1927. (In 1948, The Red Rippers became VF-11.) The Red Rippers performed formation aerobatics with their Hawks at air shows in the late 1920s and are the unofficial forerunners of the Navy's Blue Angels flight demonstration team. In 1926, Hawks also played a major role in the development of dive-bombing tactics when they made a mock attack on elements of the Pacific Fleet. Even though the ships were warned of the exercise, complete surprise was achieved and it was concluded that there could have been no defense against the attack.

BOEING'S ALL-PURPOSE FIGHTER

USN F4B

Boeing Airplane Company was the principal supplier of fighter aircraft to the Navy during the period 1925–1933. During these years the company's products were at the center of some of the Navy's design and operational successes. The prototype F4B fighter made its first flight in 1928. Given the success of its predecessors, the F4B series incorporated no radical new designs. It featured straight wings rather than tapered ones, and its fuselage was a unique composite of welded steel tubing and bolted square dural tubing. There were later refinements within the series, including the addition of a ring cowling and incorporation of a semi-monocoque metal fuselage. The F4B-4 differed from earlier aircraft in the series in its enlarged tail and pilot headrest.

The first of ninety-two production F4B-4 aircraft joined the fleet in 1932. Five Navy and Marine Corps fighter squadrons were equipped with the type, which remained in front-line service until 1938.

LEFT AND TOP RIGHT This aircraft is on display at the National Museum of Naval Aviation, Pensacola. It began life as a P-12F, an Army version of the F4B, and was acquired by the museum in 1993. Century Aviation of Wenatchee, Washington, painstakingly restored the aircraft and converted it to the specifications of an F4B-4. It is painted in the markings of VF-6B, the "Felix the Cat" Squadron, which flew the F4B-4 from the deck of *Saratoga* (CV-3) during the period 1932–1936.

BOTTOM RIGHT A formation of three F4B-3s from VF-4M, U.S. Marine Corps, flying on June 21, 1933.

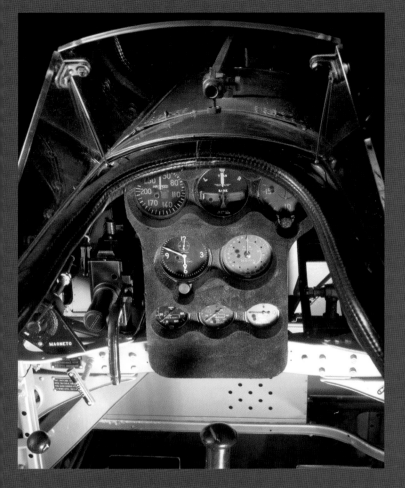

ARMY AIR CORPS P-12

LEFT The business end of a P-12E, Boeing's ubiquitous military biplane and the U.S. Army Air Corps' most successful fighter of the early 1930s. Powered by a 500-horsepower Pratt & Whitney R-1340-17 radial, the P-12E had a maximum speed of 189 mph and a service ceiling of 26,300 feet. Introduced in 1929, some P-12Es were still in service in 1941.

ABOVE LEFT Although some thought was given to the needs of the combat pilot in the design of the instrument panel, in the P-12E, he was still required to sit in an open cockpit shielded by a very small windscreen. At 20,000 feet, that would have been a challenge.

ABOVE RIGHT The P-12E was an early example of an aircraft with an all-metal stressed-skin fuselage, although its wings were still wooden and covered with fabric. The P-12E displayed by the USAF Museum is finished in the colors of the 6th Pursuit Squadron, based in Hawaii in the 1930s.

RIGHT Changing the engine of a P-12 in the field was simply a matter of putting a block and tackle in the right place.

LOENING AMPHIBIAN

RIGHT The Loening OA-1A merged fuselage and hull as a single
structure to gain the qualities of a small flying boat, but added
retractable wheels to become an amphibian. The need to keep the
propeller clear of the hull meant that the almost inevitable Liberty
engine had to be inverted. The OA-1A was by no means swift, but had
a range of 750 miles cruising at 90 mph.

ABOVE Loening OA-1A *San Francisco* was one of five amphibians sent
on the 22,000-mile Pan American Goodwill Tour of 1926–27. The
pilots were Captain Ira Eaker (seen here) and Lieutenant Muir "Sandy"
Fairchild. Both officers went on to become generals in WWII. Eaker
commanded first the USAAF's Eighth Air Force and then the Allied Air
Forces, Mediterranean.

Lieutenant Belvin Maynard's DH-4 was the first to arrive at San Francisco, and an S.E.5 flown by Major Carl "Tooey" Spatz led the west-to-east group into New York. (Spatz was the original spelling of his name, with the "a" pronounced "ah." He had it legally changed in 1938 to Spaatz in an effort to ensure correct pronunciation.) Twenty-six of the New York starters reached the west coast, and there were seven finishers from San Francisco. Seventeen of these thirty-three set off in a hastily authorized extension of the race into a round-trip; six of them made it back to New York and two to San Francisco. The double crossing was completed by five DH-4s, two S.E.5s and one Fokker. It had been a grueling ordeal for both men and machines. They had contended with rain, snow, ice and fog, and endured long periods of severe cold. They got lost, which was hardly surprising, given the weather,

the guidance of basic compasses, and the Post Office or Rand McNally state maps. Mechanical problems included engine failures, broken landing gear, splintered propellers, frozen water pumps, blown tires, leaking radiators, and damaged wings. The overall winner, Lieutenant Maynard, survived a forced landing after breaking a crankshaft. With his mechanic, he succeeded overnight in changing his Liberty engine for one retrieved from a crashed Martin bomber.

There were fifty-four accidents during the exercise, and these added seven deaths and two serious injuries to the fatal accidents suffered before the start. (One death in particular drew attention to some dangerous unofficial practices developed to overcome the DH-4's shortcomings. The main wheels were set well back and the aircraft had a tendency to nose over on soft ground. Some rear-seat airmen

RIGHT *A formation of nine Liberty-powered Keystone bombers flying from Kelly Field, Texas, in 1930.*
BELOW *The most abysmal failure in the attempt to produce a bomber with strategic reach was the Barling bomber (XNBL-1) of 1923. The monstrous Barling was thought by one observer to "be more likely to antagonize the air than to pass through it." A triplane with a wingspan of 120 feet, the Barling had two tailplanes and four fins and weighed more than 42,000 pounds. Powered by six Liberty engines, it could go no faster than 95 mph and was incapable of climbing over the modest heights of the Appalachians.*

ABOVE *A supercharged Liberty engine powered the open-cockpit LUSAC-11 when, on February 27, 1920, Major Rudolph "Shorty" Schroeder set a solo altitude record of 33,114 feet. When Schroeder landed at McCook Field after the record-breaking flight, his eyelids were frozen open.*

had taken to sliding back over the fuselage during landing to reach the tail and hold it down. Two did this in the course of the transcontinental exercise, and one was killed when thrown off.) The price had been high, but Mitchell, like Trenchard, believed that the more the Air Service could be kept in the public eye, the better, as the case for building a powerful air force was put together. Accidents were not good, but even they helped by drawing attention to the challenges of military flying, and to the hazards of flying obsolete aircraft. (With few funds for new equipment, the Air Service accident rate was appallingly high. Between July 1920 and June 1921, there were 330 major accidents resulting in the deaths of 69 aircrew from a strength of 900.)

Mitchell's efforts to develop aircraft with strategic reach were disappointing. The XNBL-1 Barling bomber was an impressive monster that seemed to tackle the problem by being bigger and having more of most things than its con-

temporaries. To one observer, it looked "more likely to antagonize the air than to pass through it." A triplane of 120-foot wingspan, the Barling had two tailplanes and four fins, and it weighed more than 42,000 pounds. Powered by six of the eternal Libertys, it first staggered into the air on August 22, 1923, from Wright Field. It later showed that it could lift its bomb-load off the ground, but was then incapable of carrying it more than 170 miles and could not drag its mass of struts and wires along at more than 95 mph. The last straw came when the Barling proved incapable of crossing the Appalachians to reach the east coast. It was hardly the creature of Billy Mitchell's air power dreams.

Other U.S. bombers followed more conventional lines, but none of them came close to matching Billy Mitchell's vision. The Martin MB-2 of 1920 was joined by the first of the Keystone bombers in 1923. Apart from a dozen Curtiss Condors ordered in 1927, Keystones monopolized Army

For ten years from 1923, Keystone bombers in various forms captured over 90 percent of the U.S. Army's bomber procurement. As Hitler rose to power in Germany, the U.S. Army's "strategic" bombers still had open cockpits, a maximum speed of 120 mph, and a range of less than 1,000 miles. Defensive armament was three .303 machine guns and the bomb-load was 2,500 pounds.

bomber procurement during the 1920s. Neither the Keystone nor the Condor differed in any really significant way from the WWI style of the MB-2. All three were open-cockpit, twin-engined biplanes capable of carrying bomb-loads of 2,500 pounds or so over ranges up to 800 miles. Engines improved and service ceilings rose to the 17,500 feet of the Condor, but maximum speeds remained stubbornly low at no more than 130 mph. Inadequate as strategic bombers, the Keystones and Condors at least kept the bombing force and its expertise alive while aeronautical technology struggled to catch up with strategic theory.

By the end of the 1920s, the state of the fighter art had advanced, but not by much. Boeing and Curtiss had cornered the market and produced some agile and attractive single-seaters, but they still resembled the biplanes of 1918. The Curtiss Hawk series, begun with the P-1 in 1925, led to the P-6E in 1929, an elegant design affectionately remembered as a worthy symbol of the Golden Age of flight. Besides being photogenic, the P-6E had a top speed of 197 mph and could reach 25,000 feet. It was, however, still an open-cockpit biplane armed with just two rifle-caliber machine guns firing through the propeller arc. As the decade drew to a close, Boeing provided a fighter with a 500-horsepower Pratt & Whitney radial engine. It was the P-12, and it proved reliable and popular, with over 350 delivered to the U.S. Army

Air Corps, but it represented an alternative to the Curtiss fighter rather than any noticeable improvement. The performance of the P-12 was similar to that of the P-6 and it was the last of the biplane fighters flown by the Army. Rapidly overtaken by technological advances in the 1930s, the last of the P-12s nevertheless managed to hang on until 1941 before being retired.

For all their obvious links with a bygone era of air warfare, the Army's biplane fighters did project a glamorous image of military flying for the American public to admire. Gaudily decorated in bright color schemes and unit insignia, they were a glorious sight at air shows. Pilots in leather helmets and silk scarves completed the picture and called forth memories of Rickenbacker and Luke. The aircraft were creatures of the past, but one thing about the Curtiss Hawks did point the way to the future. Their cowlings hid the 450-horsepower Curtiss D-12 engine or its 600-horsepower successor, the V-1570 Conqueror. The D-12 was a true technical watershed, a V-shaped aluminum monobloc that would have an influence on aviation until the advent of jet propulsion. Refinements raised the overall power and the power-to-weight and power-to-frontal-area ratios, but the essential elements of the engine remained unchanged. Rolls-Royce engineers studied a D-12 before they began the series of V-12s that culminated in the

Merlin, the engine that powered such famous WWII fighters as the Hurricane, Spitfire and Mustang.

A D-12 derivative was also fitted to an aircraft designed for ground attack. The Curtiss A-3 was a two-seater born out of the experience of attacking troops at low level in 1918 and the thought (perhaps even hope) that the DH-4s could not last forever. It first appeared in 1926 bearing a distinct family resemblance to the Curtiss Hawks. Armored and fitted with bomb-racks, it carried four forward-firing machine guns plus another two for the observer. Noticeably heavier than the Hawks, it was not very quick at 140 mph and would probably have been

hazardous to the health of its crews if operated in any major conflict. Even the A-3, however, was an improvement on the ground-attack aircraft designed by the Engineering Division at McCook Field. Built by Boeing, the GA-1 was a large, armored triplane with two Liberty engines driving pusher propellers. Its three crew members controlled eight machine guns and could drop a variety of bombs. There was even provision for a 37 mm cannon. It did fly, but not very well, and the Army changed its mind about a contract. The ubiquitous DH-4, loaded down with extra guns, filled in until the A-3 came along.

The remaining aircraft on the Army's strength during the 1920s included a plethora of observation, cargo and training machines. Notable among the observation aircraft was a series of biplanes from

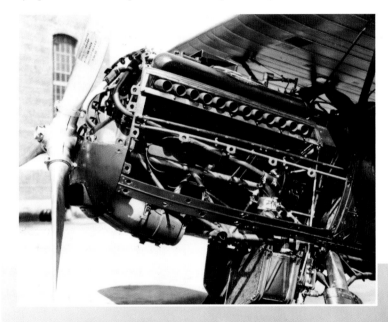

LEFT *The twelve-cylinder 600-horsepower Curtiss Conqueror powered the P-6E. Excellent though it was, the Conqueror could not haul the P-6E through the 200-mph barrier in level flight.*
BELOW *The Curtiss P-6E Hawk was one of the most attractive biplane fighters ever built and was much loved by its pilots. In 1932, the 17th Pursuit Squadron from Selfridge Field, Michigan, showed off its formation skills and its snowy owl emblem.*

Douglas that began with the O-2 in 1925 and continued until the O-38 of the early 1930s, developing from an open-cockpit, Liberty-engined two-seater resembling a DH-4 into a more sophisticated machine with a cockpit canopy and a Pratt & Whitney radial. Performance improvements were minimal, however, and none of them was capable of more than 150 mph. Even slower but more intriguing was the Loening OA-1. An amphibian built for the Army, it was a single-engined biplane dominated by a huge central float that contained retractable landing gear and was the foundation for a slab-sided fuselage. To raise the propeller clear of the protuberant float, the Liberty engine was inverted. Forty-five of these eccentricities were ordered by the Army between 1924 and 1928, primarily for use in the Hawaiian Islands and the Philippines, but deployed wherever lakes and rivers were liable to outnumber airfields.

The military cargo aircraft of the 1920s were mostly modified civilian airliners. Prominent among them were two designs by the Dutchman, Anthony Fokker. The T-2 high-wing monoplane of 1921 looked far too large for its power plant. Spanning 81 feet and nearly 50 feet long, its boxy frame was hauled along by a single Liberty engine. In 1927, this was joined by the Fokker C-2, built by Atlantic Aircraft Corporation in the United States, which was more reasonably provided with three Wright Whirlwind radials. Other trimotors in the stable were the Fords, C-3 and C-4. In the extraordinary category was another amphibian, the twin-engined Sikorsky C-6, a sesquiplane in which ten passengers were carried in a large hull tenuously suspended beneath twin booms trailing behind an impossibly high wing.

Outstanding aircraft may have been few and far between in the 1920s, but that did not stop the U.S. Army's aircrews from waving the air power flag and recording some outstanding performances in the air in the process. Faster, further, higher, longer — American airmen were prominent among those who pushed back the frontiers of flight. (See Chapter 2.) In 1926, the Air Service gained status by becoming the Air Corps, and by 1932 was equipped with sixteen pursuit, twelve bombardment, and four attack squadrons alongside thirteen observation squadrons. Examining the results of their efforts dispassionately, the Army's airmen saw that the Air Corps was better than it had been, but it was a long way from the air force they had hoped to create.

Red Resurrection

At the eastern end of Europe, the revolutionary Soviet regime appreciated the importance of airborne strength, and took steps to ensure that the Soviet Union would be self-sufficient. Flying schools and clubs, research institutes and academies were established, and efforts were made to improve public awareness of aviation. Until 1928 and the start of the first Soviet Five Year Plan, however, more than half the aircraft in use were foreign, and even thereafter reliance was placed on foreign engines. To accelerate the buildup of an aviation industry and an air force, the Soviet Union in 1922 began clandestine negotiations with its former German enemies. In exchange for the establishment of a Junkers aircraft factory at Fili, near Moscow, and for places at the German Army Staff College, the Soviets offered the Germans flying training facilities. It subsequently proved more economic for the Soviets to buy equipment directly from foreign suppliers, but during the time when the Junkers engineers were working at Fili, the Soviets gained considerably from the process of technology transfer.

The Red Air Fleet grew in strength in the 1920s, but there was little support for it becoming an independent service. The Russian experience with aircraft in WWI suggested that military aviation should be closely tied to the Red Army, and its doctrine developed to give close support and tactical bombing operations pride of place. Even though the Soviets had been impressed with Sikorsky's four-engined bombers and continued to build gigantic aircraft, their efforts seemed to have more to do with national pride than with any real desire to acquire a strategic capability.

Two designers were notable for producing the first Soviet types to be built in large numbers for the Red Air Fleet. By the end of Stalin's first Five Year Plan in 1933, designs by N.N. Polikarpov and A.N. Tupolev were strongly represented in operational squadrons. Tupolev's TB-1, a large twin-engined bomber of which some 200 were built, boasted several claims to fame. It flew from Moscow to New York in 1929, landed on drifting ice in the Arctic to rescue men from a trapped icebreaker, and was the parent aircraft in the 1931 trials in which two Tupolev I-4 fighters were carried aloft on its wings and then launched at 10,000 feet. Encouraged by the TB-1's success, the Tupolev factory went on to produce other huge aircraft in later years. Polikarpov's aircraft were at the other end of the scale. His I-5 fighter became operational in 1931. It had exceptional handling qualities and was the forerunner of a long line of highly maneuverable radial-engined fighters flown by the Red Air Fleet. It was while flying an I-5 that V.A. Stepanchonok became the first pilot ever to enter an inverted spin and recover to describe the maneuver. In some ways a more remarkable Polikarpov aircraft was the U-2 (later Po-2), an unimposing little trainer that first flew in 1927 and was still giving multirole service in WWII and Korea.

The Secrets of von Seeckt

Although the Luftstreitkräfte had been dismantled following WWI, and Article 198 of the Versailles Treaty stated that "The armed forces of Germany must not include any military or naval air forces," the Germans had not been idle in air power matters during the 1920s. General Hans von Seeckt was appointed Chief of Germany's small standing army in 1920. He later said that he saw it as his mission "to neutralize the poison in the disarmament clauses of the Treaty." His experience in WWI convinced him that success in future conflicts would come from the use of heavily armed and highly mobile ground forces closely supported by aircraft. This led him to the idea of the blitzkrieg and to the conclusion that he should find ways to avoid the restrictions of Versailles and begin building the forces to match his concept. As a first step, he selected 180 veteran pilots and put them in key positions in the Defense Ministry and other headquarters from which they could keep commanders informed of developments in aviation. Some even staffed aviation sections that, for the benefit of the Allied Control Commission, were hidden behind other names. Even at this early stage, von Seeckt looked forward confidently to a day when the German Air Force would be resurrected, led by his chosen few and created as an independent organization. (Von Seeckt's selection included officers such as Wever, Felmy, Sperrle, Kesselring and Stumpff, all of whom rose to the highest levels of the Luftwaffe.)

An essential element of von Seeckt's plan was the provision of military flying training for at least some German airmen. This was achieved through a secret agreement with the Soviet Union. Given their recent conflict and their

The Tupolev ANT-6 (military designation TB-3) was the world's first four-engine all-metal monoplane bomber, built with the Soviet love of the gargantuan in mind. It first flew on December 22, 1930, and 818 aircraft in several versions were built. TB-3s were involved in the conflicts of the USSR with Japan, Finland and Germany. In 1935, TB-3s acted as aircraft carriers in the extraordinary Zveno trials. In one of these, a TB-3 took off with two I-5 fighters above the wing and two I-16s below. In flight, an I-Z fighter hooked onto an under-fuselage trapeze. Six aircraft of four types were therefore flying as one. All five fighters were released to independent flight simultaneously.

respective positions in the political spectrum, neither nation had any reason to feel drawn to the other, but expediency provided mutual attraction. The Soviets wanted to construct an aircraft industry but lacked the expertise, and they needed some middle-rank officers to attend a professional staff college. The Germans were looking for a place where they could train military aircrews, an activity expressly forbidden by the Versailles Treaty. A marriage of convenience was arranged, and the Germans established themselves at Lipetsk, about 220 miles from Moscow. By 1926, the remote site had become a large airfield, complete with hangars, repair shops and living accommodation. Although disguised as a Soviet base, it was a fully operational German flying training school and flight test center.

The drafters of the Versailles Treaty meant to be implacable in their determination to destroy German air power, but they did not appreciate the significance of civil and private aviation. By the time the Paris Air Agreement of 1926 removed restrictions on civil aircraft manufacturing in Germany, the aircraft industry was well established and the German people had a claim to being the most air-minded in the world. The Deutcher Luftsportverband, an aviation society with 50,000 members, was officially encouraged by the Defense Ministry, which also supported gliding clubs and training organizations for aircraft technicians. Ostensibly, these things were done for the benefit of civil aviation, but the underlying intention was to create the nucleus around which a new air force could grow. Adolf Galland, the future fighter leader, became a glider pilot while still a schoolboy, and later went to Lufthansa for a flying course which, he said, involved aerobatics and "real fighter pilot training, including formation flying...only the guns were missing."

Hugo Junkers led the way for the aircraft industry. His first postwar aircraft was the F.13, a small all-metal passenger monoplane that served well into the 1930s and pioneered many of the European air routes. Other manufacturers followed, and by the early 1930s, Heinkel, Dornier, Messerschmitt, Arado and Focke-Wulf were all in production, most of them having ensured they kept abreast of advances in aviation technology by operating through subsidiaries abroad. At the same time, airlines sprang up haphazardly all over Germany. Recognizing the advantage of controlling that activity, von Seeckt saw to it that the man

LEFT *Future Luftwaffe pilots examining the cockpit of an Olympic glider in 1936. Ernst Udet, Germany's highest-scoring surviving First World War ace and one of the world's leading acrobatic pilots, persuaded the German Air Ministry to buy two Curtiss Hawks for the still-secret Luftwaffe to use in dive-bombing trials. The first German Hawk II was delivered in 1934 with civil registration D-3165. This became D-IRIS when the German system was changed.* BELOW LEFT AND RIGHT *The second was D-IRIK, the fuselage of which is now in the Aviation Museum, Krakow, Poland. It still bears the markings used by Ernst Udet during his aerobatic demonstrations at the Berlin Olympics in 1936.*

The first German bomber revealed to the world as the offensive weapon of the newborn Luftwaffe was the Dornier 23, which joined front-line squadrons in 1935. Despite the propaganda that accompanied its appearance, it was not an impressive machine. Slow, clumsy and defended by only three rifle-caliber machine guns, it was soon relegated to a supporting role in the bombing and gunnery schools.

chosen to head the Civil Aviation Department of the Ministry of Transport was his nominee, Ernst Brandenburg. From then on, civil aviation was under clandestine military control.

In 1926, the new state airline, Deutsche Luft Hansa, absorbed most of the private operators. Luft Hansa included among its directors Erhard Milch, another man who understood where German aviation was heading and kept in touch with with von Seeckt. Under Luft Hansa's cover, new airfields were built, more pilots trained, and better navigation aids introduced. Luft Hansa soon became the best-equipped airline in Europe, flying greater distances with more passengers than any other. (The one-word spelling, "Lufthansa," was adopted in 1934.) When the Allied Control Commission was abolished in 1927, it was not long before the German aircraft industry was producing aircraft with characteristics that were militarily useful. The building blocks were in place. All that was lacking for German air power's rebirth to begin was political will.

The Risen Luftwaffe

Before being named Chancellor of Germany in 1933, Adolf Hitler said: "In the air we shall of course be supreme. It is a manly weapon, a Germanic art of battle. I shall build the largest air fleet in the world." It was not quite as simple as that. Notwithstanding all the clandestine preparation, the Nazis came to power needing to overcome enormous difficulties in their bid to create an air force. There were too few

OPPOSITE AND ABOVE *The Bücker Bü133 Jungmeister is a classic aerobatic aircraft. It first appeared in the mid-1930s and soon became the preferred aircraft for aerobatic champions. In the 1960s, the first American to own a Jungmeister, Mike Murphy, said of it, "You don't fly it — you wear it. Now, thirty years later, it's still the nicest airplane to do aerobatics in. It never resists you. It's smiling all the time."*

trained officers, Luft Hansa's equipment and experience did not translate directly into military capability, and the aircraft industry was small and fragmented, apparently lacking the wherewithal for rapid, large-scale expansion. However, the problems of the Luftwaffe's birth were eased by the appointment of Hermann Göring as its leader. As Hitler's closest associate, Göring had sufficient political power to ensure that the new service would be independent of the army and would enjoy privileged status in the allocation of funds. It was fortunate, too, since Göring's political preoccupations took so much of his attention, that his principal subordinate was the able and energetic Milch, who added to his Luft Hansa chairmanship the post of State Secretary at the new Air Ministry. In January 1934, Milch introduced a production program that aimed to manufacture 4,021 military aircraft by the end of September 1935. Since the average monthly output of the German aircraft industry in 1933 had been thirty-one machines, this was an ambitious plan. Substantial expansion of existing aircraft factories was enabled by government loans, and other industrial concerns were encouraged to use their facilities for manufacturing aircraft. By the second half of 1935, the average monthly production figure had risen to 303, an increase of almost 1,000 percent in less than two years. Much of this was in the form of trainers, such as the Focke-Wulf Fw 44 and the Arado Ar.66; but there were also considerable numbers of Junkers 52/3m transports, and combat aircraft, such as Heinkel He 51 and Arado Ar.65 fighters, Heinkel He 45 and He 46 reconnaissance aircraft, and Dornier Do 11 and Do 23 bombers.

As the production capacity of the German aircraft industry rose, so its design teams grew in their ability to use new materials and techniques. By 1935, Milch was able to phase out biplanes and produce a new generation of monoplanes of notably improved performance. The Dornier Do 17, Junkers Ju 86 and Ju 87, Heinkel He 111 and Messerschmitt Bf 109 and Bf 110 were evaluated at the Luftwaffe's Rechlin test center and given the go-ahead. The twin-engined bombers in this group (Do 17, Ju 86, He 111)

TOP *The Handley Page Heyford, last of the fabric-covered "cloth bombers," was an anachronism in the late 1930s. The RAF bomber force was supposed to be able to strike a devastating blow against an enemy nation, but that would hardly have been possible with an aircraft that was flat out at 140 mph, defended by three Lewis guns, had no navigational aids worthy of the name, and had a range of less than 1,000 miles when carrying 1,600 pounds of bombs.*

BOTTOM *On July 6, 1935, King George V performed the first Royal Review of the Royal Air Force at Mildenhall. At this stage the RAF was still a biplane air force: Hawker Furies, Bristol Bulldogs, Hawker Harts and Audaxes, and Handley Page Heyfords were the most numerous types.*

were originally conceived in response to a Lufthansa requirement for fast airliners, but the link established between civil and military aviation ensured that each of them was designed with conversion to the bomber role in mind. During this early stage of the Luftwaffe's buildup, Milch showed himself to be a brilliant administrator, well able to handle the organizational and technical challenges of his job. Unfortunately for him (and for the Luftwaffe), his increasing influence, plus the fact that he enjoyed Hitler's respect and had been given the rank of general, earned him Göring's enmity. In a systematic campaign, Göring steadily eroded Milch's power, and began calling on less able people. One of these was Ernst Udet, the leading surviving German ace from WWI, to whom Göring entrusted the technical and production aspects of the Luftwaffe's buildup. Udet was a poor administrator, incapable of planning for the long term, and the origins of many of the problems subsequently suffered by the Luftwaffe can be traced to his bad management. Like his political masters, he was interested only in front-line numbers, and saw to it that most manufacturing capacity was devoted to the final product. Adequate inventories of spares were never provided. Even his personal preferences had their influence. For example, his love of dive-bombers led to his insistence that the admirable Junkers Ju 88 should be given a dive-bombing capability. The necessary design changes added to its weight, reduced its maximum speed, and delayed its introduction to service by at least a year.

In March 1935, the existence of the Luftwaffe was officially proclaimed, with Göring named as its Commander-in-Chief. General Walther Wever was made Chief of Staff of the new service, which had at its inception over 1,800 aircraft of all types and some 20,000 men. Wever was a man of remarkable intellectual powers. Unlike many of his contemporaries, he had a good grasp of Germany's national strategy, and believed in the need to build a well-balanced air force, with a strong strategic element. He encouraged the development of four-engined long-range bombers, such as the Junkers Ju 89 and the Dornier Do 19. Both programs were canceled after Wever was killed in an aircraft accident in 1936. If he had lived, they might have survived, although Germany probably

---

"Trumpets of Jericho"

NAME FOR SIRENS MOUNTED ON THE LANDING GEAR OF THE JUNKERS JU 87 DIVE-BOMBER

---

did not then have the resources to build both an air force principally designed to support the army and a strategic bombing force. In any case, deprived of Wever's advocacy, most Luftwaffe officers came to believe that their twin-engined bombers, five of which could be built for the cost of two with four engines, would be more than capable of dealing such strategic blows as were necessary against their likely continental enemies. One other four-engined bomber program was initiated in 1937, the Heinkel He 177, but it was not built in quantity and was bedeviled by engine problems. After 1936, the acquisition of a genuine strategic capability was not seriously considered by the Luftwaffe.

In the mid-1930s, the idea of the Luftwaffe was more impressive than the reality. Although there were problems inherent in its expansion, these were hidden from outside observers, and it was generally viewed as a military instrument to be feared. The Luftwaffe's sudden appearance on the world stage, seemingly fully fledged, and the brashness with which Nazi leaders spoke of its growing power unnerved other nations and helped to induce political paralysis in their governments. In March 1936, Hitler marched German troops into the demilitarized zone of the Rhineland. This aggressive move was accompanied by a demonstration of the Luftwaffe's strength, with impressive formations of aircraft covering the occupation throughout. The feat was actually managed by just two fighter squadrons that flew their He 51s backward and forward, landing at various airfields during the day and changing their markings at each stop to give the impression of greater numbers. According to Albert Speer, the Nazi Armaments Minister, Hitler remembered the occupation of the Rhineland as one of his most daring accomplishments. With more than a touch of exaggeration to embellish the scale of his bluff, he recalled Germany's military weakness at the time: "We had no army worth mentioning…. If the French had taken any action we would have been easily defeated…. and what air force we had then was ridiculous. A few Ju 52s from Lufthansa, and not even enough bombs for them." Exhilarated by the ease with which his neighbors had been intimidated into immobility, Hitler was encouraged to use the air weapon, or the thought of it, as one of the political tools that won him his bloodless victories in the 1930s.

FOR FEAR OF A GREAT WAR
French Follies

In France, the immediate reaction to the emergence of the Luftwaffe was one of indifference. The French were confident in the strength of their frontier defenses, the supposedly impregnable Maginot Line. As late as 1937, some of their senior officers were saying that they could defeat any possible German incursion by air with guns alone. Given the "veritable forest of guns" planted in the Maginot Line, it was believed that an enemy "would require an unrealizable supremacy of machines to get over the antiaircraft defenses." Such ill-founded opinions made it extremely difficult for those who maintained that French air power badly needed reestablishing.

Although the emphasis in France remained on the needs of the army, some measures were taken to improve the situation in the air, including the nationalization of the aircraft industry. This was supposed to increase aircraft production by some 40 percent in 1937, but instead there was a sharp reduction. Only 370 military aircraft were manufactured that year, and most of them were obsolescent. The fighters delivered included SPAD 510 biplanes, Loire 46 gull-wings, and

RIGHT *The prototype Dewoitine D.500 (R-008) first flew on June 18, 1932. Powered by a 690-horsepower Hispano-Suiza, it was armed with four machine guns and could reach 220 mph. D.500s began equipping French* escadrilles de chasse *in 1935. There were 102 built.*

Dewoitine D.500 series monoplanes. All had fixed undercarriages and open cockpits, even though their advertised service ceilings were above 30,000 feet. The bombers, such as the Farman F.222 and Bloch 210, were no more impressive, and adherence to the unrealistic BCR idea was perpetuated in the Bloch 131, which proved to be inadequate for any of its roles.

Albion Alarmed

As early as November 1932, British Prime Minister Stanley Baldwin reacted to stories of German militance in a famous warning, given to the House of Commons during a disarmament debate: "I think it is well for the man in the street to realize that there is no power on earth that can protect him from being bombed. Whatever people may tell him, *the bomber will always get through.* The only defence is offence, which means that you have to kill more women and children more quickly than the enemy if you want to save yourselves." (Italics added.)

Given the relative performance figures for fighters and bombers at the time, and the lack of both early warning and fighter control systems, Baldwin's doomsday pronouncement was uncomfortably close to the truth. Indeed, it has remained

LEFT Castles in the Air, No. 5, *by Philip Castle (from a series published in* Aeroplane Monthly*). The artist has contrasted the angularity of French aircraft between the wars with the smoother outlines of a Delahaye car and Brigitte Bardot. Counterclockwise, the aircraft are a Farman F221, Farman F-4-X (transport), Farman F221-10, Amiot 143, Aérienne Bordelaise AB21, Amiot 143, Breguet 460, and Potez 540.*

Top *The first production Hawker Hurricane (L1547) served for many months as a company test aircraft at Brooklands. Transferred to the RAF during the Battle of Britain, it was lost on October 10, 1940, while flying with No. 312 (Czech) Squadron.*
Bottom *The Supermarine Spitfire prototype (K5054) first flew on March 5, 1936, piloted by "Mutt" Summers. The Air Ministry in London were so impressed with the new fighter that on June 3, 1936, before the test program was completed, a contract was issued for 310 Spitfires.*

so even as technology has advanced. The subsequent history of air power shows that the only factor to have been even temporarily effective in preventing bombers from getting through to a target has been bad weather. If an attacking force has been determined, it has almost invariably bombed its target, even in the face of severe losses. The best that defenses have ever been able to hope for has been that they might minimize the damage and deter future attacks.

At the time that Baldwin made his "bomber" speech, the RAF had struggled up to a strength of forty-two squadrons, but in keeping with the Trenchard doctrine, only thirteen were equipped with fighters. The stark clarity of the strategic theory that influenced the RAF's operational policies contrasted sharply with the equipment provided to carry it out. Little serious thought, effort or money had been directed toward the practical realization of the strategic idea. There was also the political problem of having a doctrine that said that it was acceptable to attack cities and kill civilians. Whatever Baldwin said, people were so

horrified by the idea that the RAF felt it had to change its tune. Targets were now said to be factories, railway junctions and so on. Almost imperceptibly, it came about that a force conceived for attacking cities in daylight found itself being asked to find precise targets by night, even though the tools for the job were sadly lacking. Politically driven to use a rapier, the planners did not seem to notice that they were instead stuck with Trenchard's bludgeon, and a pretty small bludgeon at that. The engine of destruction still used by most heavy bomber squadrons and so responsible for delivering the RAF's "knock-out blow" was the Vickers Virginia. A huge, fabric-covered, open-cockpit biplane, the Virginia represented only a marginal improvement over the earliest heavy bombers, yet it was not finally withdrawn from service until 1937. The Handley Page Heyford, the last of the "cloth bombers," hung on even longer. Given their slow speed, limited range, small bomb-load, inadequate defensive armament, and lack of navigational aids, it is hard to imagine how such aircraft could have brought about the moral collapse of a major industrial nation, even in the minds of political and military leaders mesmerized by the strategic air power concepts of the time.

ART DECO FIGHTER

The P-26 was the first U.S. Army Air Corps fighter with Boeing's all-metal low cantilever wing. Important though such technological advances were, the P-26 was destined to be no more than an interim aircraft. Pretty to look at and delightful to fly, the P-26 earned the nickname "Peashooter" and was soon overtaken by other monoplane designs on both sides of the Atlantic. The USAF Museum's P-26A is finished in the bright colors of the squadron commander, 19th Pursuit Squadron, Wheeler Field, Hawaii.

OPPOSITE TOP The instrument layout had developed a little further than those of the biplane age, but the pilot still had to brave the elements in an open cockpit.

OPPOSITE BOTTOM Fitted with a Pratt & Whitney 600-horsepower R-1320-37 radial, a P-26A could manage a maximum speed of 234 mph and (with an open cockpit) reach an altitude of 27,000 feet. Its performance was not helped by the drag of the large radial engine, bracing wires and fixed undercarriage.

In October 1933, Hitler withdrew Germany from the World Disarmament Conference, and Winston Churchill among others rang alarm bells about the German Chancellor's intentions. Churchill's warnings that Germany was intent on creating the world's strongest air force helped to force the British government to the reluctant conclusion that the RAF needed building up. Prime Minister Baldwin announced that, in terms of air power, Britain must not be inferior to any nation within striking distance of its shores. A series of expansion schemes followed, and these were accompanied by considerable technical advances. In addition, the RAF's leadership began to pay more attention to the need to defend British air space. One indication of impending change came in 1934, when new fighter specifications were issued to the Hawker and Supermarine companies. The monoplane designs subsequently submitted by designers Sydney Camm and Reginald Mitchell were both powered by the Rolls-Royce PV-12 engine (soon to be named Merlin) and carried eight machine guns. Biplane fighters such as the Hawker Fury and the Gloster Gladiator continued in squadron service for several more years, much loved by their pilots, but their days were numbered. The leap forward in performance granted by the Hurricane and the Spitfire came just in time to enable the RAF to match the Luftwaffe in combat.

New bomber designs took wing in the late 1930s as the Fairey Battle and Bristol Blenheim light bombers, the Handley Page Hampden and Armstrong-Whitworth Whitley mediums and, the best of them, the Vickers Wellington. Most were to prove woefully inadequate when put to the test in war, but they were an unavoidable interim stage in the RAF's rush of expansion. Even as they entered service, work was underway on their successors — the more capable four-engined heavy bombers designed to meet a specification issued in 1936 for aircraft with genuine strategic reach and power.

Together with the reequipment programs, other schemes were initiated. In 1936, the RAF in the United Kingdom was split into functional commands — Bomber,

Fighter, Coastal, Training — and plans were laid that led to new airfields and ample reserves of men and machines. The shadow factory scheme was devised to involve the motor industry in the production of aircraft and components, and scientists were hard at work seeking a system that would allow aircraft to be detected at long range. The RAF still had a long way to go, but apprehensions about German rearmament had finally forced the British into one of their traditionally belated efforts to get organized.

Ups and Downs in America

Strategic air power theory had been fiercely debated in the United States during the 1920s but its progress was hampered there as elsewhere by the state of the art in bomber design. The early 1930s saw the introduction of techniques that were little short of revolutionary, promising dramatic advances in aircraft performance, and American designers were quick to make the most of them. A foretaste of things to come was given by the Boeing B-9 in 1931, but even this remarkable aircraft was overshadowed by the appearance only a few months later of the Martin B-10. The B-10 embodied so many new techniques and devices that it stands out as one of the most significant single advances in the history of military aircraft. Here for the first time was a cantilever monoplane of all-metal stressed-skin construction that had wing flaps, retractable landing gear, enclosed cockpits, a glazed gun turret, variable-pitch propellers, low-drag engine cowlings, and an internal bomb-bay with power-driven doors. Even the underpowered prototype could outrun the fighters then in service. The B-10's bomb-load of a little over one ton could have been bigger, and its combat range was only 700 miles, but it was seen as the harbinger of an American air power spring and it was soon adopted as the Air Corps' front-line bomber.

Such bright spots aside, the Depression of the early 1930s had its effect on the Air Corps. Annual maneuvers were abandoned, flying hours

sharply reduced, and live weapons training stopped. Accident rates went up and pay was cut. Worse was to come. In 1934, President Roosevelt canceled the air mail contracts held by commercial airlines because of irregularities. While new contracts were being drawn up, the U.S. Air Corps was asked to carry the mail. The rushed preparations brought dire predictions from a number of observers, including Eddie Rickenbacker, then a vice-president of American Airways. He warned that the airlines had aircraft specifically designed for the job, and that their pilots were experienced and well trained. In his opinion: "Either they are going to pile up ships all the way across the continent, or they are not going to be able to fly the mail on schedule."

Rickenbacker was to be proved right on both counts. The weather that winter was the worst for many years, and Air Corps pilots faced it in open cockpits equipped with poor instrumentation and inadequate navigation aids. The results were almost inevitable. By the time the Air Corps was relieved of responsibility for the mail in May 1934, little more than three months after it assumed the burden, there had been sixty-six crashes in which twelve men had died on mail routes and another six in training or ferrying flights. Fifteen others were in hospital recovering from injuries. Rickenbacker called it "Legalized murder!"

U.S. Army aircrew pose in front of their recently acquired Martin B-10s, sure that they have the most advanced bomber in the world in 1934.

The uproar caused by the air mail fiasco focused the attention of everyone, including President Roosevelt, on the state of the Air Corps. The recriminations led to positive results. The findings of an investigative board suggested major improvements in equipment and recommended that aircrew should carry out more training in night and bad weather flying and radio navigation, and that they should average a minimum of three hundred hours flying a year. However, while many findings were helpful to the Air Corps, the overall attitude of the committee reflected a lack of conviction among its members about the importance of air power. The report remarked on "the limitations of the airplane," and said that "The idea that aviation, acting alone, can control the sea lanes, or defend the coast, or produce decisive results…are all visionary, as is the idea that a very large and independent air force is necessary to defend our country." A lone voice on the committee recorded a dissenting view. Jimmy Doolittle, then with Shell, said that most of the members of the Board knew "as much about the future of aviation as they do about the sign writing of the Aztecs." His more formal statement said: "I believe that the future security of our nation is dependent upon an adequate air force," and reaffirmed his view that such an air force would be more effective if developed as a separate arm of the military.

Such disagreements never diverted American airmen from their goal of acquiring a strategic bomber force. In 1934, the War Department agreed to an Air Corps project to develop an aircraft much larger and of longer range than the B-10, on the grounds that an aircraft was needed that could reinforce either coast of the U.S. or its overseas possessions without refueling. The project, undertaken by Boeing, grew into a monster aircraft, the XB-15. Its sheer size — 149-foot wingspan and 70,000 pounds gross weight — made it an experiment in every sense of the word. Boeing engineers had new problems to solve at each stage of construction, and they took three and a half years to finish the job. Then they found that their design had outrun engine technology. The XB-15 was underpowered, and only one was ever built. Nevertheless, the lessons learned with the XB-15 were helpful in paving the way for two other Boeing bombers destined to leave their mark on aviation history in WWII.

Shortly after the contract for the XB-15 was awarded, Boeing was swept into a competition to build another bomber. The specification said that the aircraft should be multiengine and be able to carry at least a ton of bombs over a range of 1,020 miles at 200 mph. It was noted that the range and speed figures were minima and that it was desirable for the new bomber to have a range of 2,500 miles and a top speed of 250 mph. One further point added spice to the challenge. It was August 1934 and the Air Corps required bidders to provide aircraft for a flying competition at Wright Field in August 1935.

Three companies had aircraft at Wright Field on the appointed day. Martin came with the B-12, which was little more than an updated B-10. Douglas offered the DB-1, a twin-engined bomber developed from the DC-2 airliner. Boeing, however, stole the show with a completely new

The Boeing Model 299, forerunner of the B-17, soon after its rollout in July 1935. Note that it carries a civil registration number on the fin, since this was a company aircraft and did not belong to the U.S. Army.

Destined to be taken into service only as an interim measure, the Martin B-10 was nevertheless one of the most significant advances in the history of military aircraft. It combined all-metal stressed-skin construction, cantilever monoplane wings, flaps and retractable landing gear. The two cockpits and rotating gun turret were fully glazed. The two Wright Cyclone radials were smoothly cowled and had variable-pitch propellers. During trials in 1932, the B-10 could not be caught by the U.S. Army Air Corps fighters of the time and was immediately ordered into production. This is the last existing B-10 in the world and is on display at the USAF Museum.

The Seversky P-35 was the first single-seat, all-metal fighter with an enclosed cockpit and retractable landing gear in the U.S. Army Air Corps.
BELOW The prototype was first flown in 1935. A step beyond the P-26 though it was, the P-35 lacked armor and self-sealing tanks. Introduced to the front line in 1937, the P-35 was obsolete by the time of Pearl Harbor. However, the ancestry of a more famous and significant combat aircraft, the P-47 Thunderbolt, is revealed in the P-35's chubby lines. The only surviving example of the Seversky P-35 is on display at the USAF Museum. It has a fully restored cockpit and carries the insignia of the 19th Pursuit Squadron, Selfridge Field, Michigan.

four-engined aircraft. The Model 299 flew in nonstop from Seattle, having averaged 232 mph on the way. Two months later, after exhaustive tests, the 299 was clearly the front-runner in the competition. Then, on October 30, 1935, just after takeoff for its final test flight, the 299 reared up, stalled and crashed. The controls locks had been left engaged and the pilot could not lower the rising nose when the 299 left the ground. Boeing's hopes went up in smoke, and the DB-1, now the B-18, was declared the winner by default. Douglas received an immediate production contract for 133 aircraft.

The Air Corps, however, had seen enough of the 299 to know what they wanted. The accident, after all, had not been the fault of the aircraft. Approval was given for the acquisition of thirteen 299s for flying evaluation, plus one more for static tests. This first series was designated Y1B-17, but the press had already coined the name by which the public would recognize the aircraft. A Seattle reporter had been so amazed at the sight of a bomber with five gun positions that he was inspired to call it "a Flying Fortress." Bitter experience in combat would later reveal that the name, at least in the early B-17s, was an exaggeration of the truth, but it had a good sound and it stuck. It did not sound so good to the U.S. Army's General Staff, however. They were not convinced that B-17s were needed. The Deputy Chief of Staff harped on the theme that "our national policy contemplates defense, not aggression." This policy, adhered to since 1919, stood as a barrier to the building of effective U.S. armed forces at a time when Hitler had repudiated the Versailles Treaty and declared

general conscription for German youth, and when Japan was waging total war in China. When German troops rolled into the Rhineland, the U.S. Army's General Staff could still say that, in their preference for the B-17, the Air Corps had been led astray by "a quest for the ultimate in aircraft performance at the expense of practical military need." The B-18 was the Army's bomber of choice. Utterly sure of their case, the airmen took every opportunity of showing off the B-17 to the American public. They began appearing at conventions and expositions, and flew over a number of cities in formation, after which their speeds between cities were

The unusual nose on the Douglas B-18A was the result of a design that placed the bomb aimer's position above and in front of the front gunner. Its sharklike appearance belied the bomber's modest capabilities. Slow and poorly defended, the B-18 Bolo was obsolete almost as soon as it reached squadrons in 1937. This was the U.S. Army Air Corps' front-line bomber when Hitler's forces crossed the Polish border in 1939. The example preserved in the USAF Museum is marked as an aircraft of the 38th Reconnaissance Squadron in 1939.

Douglas B-18 Bolos in formation over Miami on Army Day in 1940.

always released for publication. In January 1938, Colonel Robert Olds broke the U.S. transcontinental record by flying from Langley, Virginia, to March Field, California in 12 hours, 50 minutes, and then flew back again in 10 hours, 46 minutes. Still more impressive were two extensive goodwill tours of South America, completed without serious incident in a blaze of favorable publicity. Even so, a 1938 memorandum from the Secretary of War said there was no requirement for four-engined bombardment aircraft.

Complicating the issue was the antagonism of the U.S. Navy, outraged because in May 1938 the Air Corps used the Italian transatlantic liner *Rex* to represent an enemy

fleet. In breach of the 1931 interservice agreement concerning air operations more than 100 miles from the coast, three B-17s set off from Mitchel Field, New York, to intercept a single ship some 700 miles out in the ocean. The weather was bad, with low cloud and rain, but the B-17s found the *Rex* as planned. The next day the achievement was on the front pages of newspapers all across the United States. *The New York Times* declared that the B-17's performance was "one from which valuable lessons about the aerial defense of the United States will be drawn." Insisting modestly that the flight had been routine for B-17 crews, the airmen were unprepared for the U.S. Navy's protest

The Douglas XB-19 was completed in May 1941 and was the largest American aircraft built until the Convair B-36 appeared in 1946. The XB-19 had a wingspan of 212 feet and a maximum gross weight of 162,000 pounds. It proved to be too demanding a concept for the technology of its time and only one was built.

about Army aircraft usurping blue water prerogatives. An embarrassed Army Chief of Staff sent down a verbal order restricting Air Corps activities to within 100 miles of the U.S. shoreline. The order was never formally issued, and therefore never properly rescinded, and its effects bedeviled Army aviation for many months.

The Navy's objections were real enough, but is was equally true that many other people, including Army officers, could see no justification for developing heavy bombers. In their opinion, Army aviation should be devoted to direct support of the land battle, and four-engined aircraft were not required for that. Twin-engined medium and light bombers were more than adequate. More to the point, two or even three of the smaller aircraft could be bought for the price of one heavy bomber. That argument held considerable appeal for politicians. In 1938, until the Munich crisis, the future for the B-17 did not look bright.

Aeronautical progress in the 1930s pushed the bomber into controversy not only because it raised questions about its role but also because it threatened to eliminate the performance gap between bombardment and pursuit aviation. By 1933, it was thought that bombers had enough speed and firepower to operate without support, and there were doubts that pursuit aircraft could intercept and engage at such high speeds. Seeking an answer to the pursuit problem, the Air Corps considered a number of solutions, including large multi-seat fighter aircraft

In December 1941, when the Japanese attacked Pearl Harbor, the U.S. Army Air Corps in the Philippines was equipped with obsolete aircraft, including Boeing P-26 "Peashooters," Seversky P-35s and Martin B-10s. (These images are from 8 mm movie stills.)

armed with outsize cannon and carrying bombs to drop on enemy formations. The Berliner-Joyce P-16 and Consolidated P-30 two-seaters filled this role, but neither remained long in squadron service. The multi-place idea reached its peak in the Bell XFM-1 Airacuda, a twin-engined heavy fighter with a five-man crew, armed with two .30- and two .50-caliber machine guns, two 37 mm cannon, and twenty 30-pound bombs. After extensive testing, sanity prevailed and the Airacuda never saw operational service.

More conventional development led to the Boeing P-26 "Peashooter" becoming the standard Air Corps fighter for most of the 1930s. A chubby little monoplane with a spatted, fixed undercarriage, braced wings and an open cockpit, the P-26 could manage 235 mph in level flight, but this was a speed soon exceeded by Boeing's own B-17 and, more significantly, by the bombers of Mitsubishi and Heinkel.

In the late 1930s, pursuit aviation advanced with the Seversky P-35 and the Curtiss P-36, both radial-engined single-seaters with closed cockpits and retractable undercarriages. Maximum speeds were close to 300 mph for the first time, and both aircraft were rugged and agile, but neither could match the performance of fighters being produced in Europe. As war drew ever closer, uncertainty about the role of the fighter and the lack of a suitable in-line engine left the Americans without an aircraft capable of ensuring superiority in the air battle.

REGIONAL WARS
The Chaco Boreal

In the late 1920s, a border dispute arose between Bolivia and Paraguay in a vast wilderness area known as the Chaco Boreal, which was believed to be blessed with valuable oil and mineral deposits. Armed clashes escalated into full-scale war in 1932, and by the following year both sides were making use of aircraft. Neither air force was large, but both operated a variety of machines and relied to some extent on foreign mercenary pilots. The much smaller and less well equipped of the two was the Paraguayan, but it could count on the help of an Italian Military Mission. Starting with Potez 25 reconnaissance aircraft, the Paraguayan Air Force acquired from Italy Bergamaschi A.P.1 monoplane and Fiat C.R. 30 biplane fighters, Caproni Ca.101 bombers and Breda Ba 44 transports. The Bolivians flew Curtiss Falcon and Curtiss-Wright Osprey general-purpose aircraft,

Curtiss Hawk 1A fighters, and a few Junkers W.34 bombers. In three years of intermittent warfare in which some 88,000 men were killed, most air operations were flown as bombing or reconnaissance missions, but there was occasional air fighting, and each side lost about thirty aircraft in combat. On the whole, however, air power was poorly employed, and had little influence on the outcome. By mid-1935, both nations were economically exhausted, and a truce was arranged. A settlement gave most of the Chaco to Paraguay, but the earth's riches have yet to be uncovered, so it was for little obvious gain.

Mussolini Imperator

Hitler's political skills and his willingness to take risks carried him through the bloodless occupation of the Rhineland, the first overt step on the road to WWII, and later brought him similar success in Austria and

Hawks Over China, *by Roy Grinnell. Chinese Curtiss Hawk IIIs turn in to attack a formation of Japanese Mitsubishi G3M bombers.*

Czechoslovakia. However, Fascist ambition was not to be pursued entirely without bloodshed. In 1935, Mussolini set out to extend his African empire by avenging the Italian defeat at Adowa forty years before and reasserting Italian control over Ethiopia.

Italian troops crossed the Ethiopian frontier on October 3, 1935, to begin a bitterly fought campaign lasting seven months. Although Ethiopian soldiers were often badly led and were outmatched in terms of sophisticated weapons, they proved tenacious warriors, especially when operating as infantry in rugged country where it was difficult for the Italians to use aircraft and armor effectively. Imperial Ethiopian Aviation could muster only a handful of outdated aircraft and these did not last long. The Regia Aeronautica therefore operated unopposed in the air with some 320 aircraft. Over 70 percent were bomber/transports, mostly Caproni Ca.101s, together with smaller numbers of Caproni Ca.111s/133s and Savoia-Marchetti S.M.81s. The remainder were Fiat C.R.20 fighters and armed reconnaissance aircraft such as the IMAM Ro.37.

The Italian commanders, first Marshal De Bono and later Marshal Badoglio, used air power extensively from the outset, with the brunt of the air campaign being borne by the trimotor bomber/transports, which bombed Ethiopian troop concentrations. Occasionally, to clear the defenders from difficult terrain, the trimotors were used to drop mustard gas, despite condemnation by world opinion. In their transport role, they played an important part in resupplying the ground forces, once moving 385 tons forward in one three-week period. Fighter and reconnaissance aircraft were used mostly for low-level operations, clearing the way ahead of advancing Italian columns with machine guns and antipersonnel bombs, and then attacking the Ethiopians as they retreated. Badoglio repeatedly refers in his memoirs to the devastating effect of these attacks, and to the thousands of casualties they inflicted. Once when a strafing fighter caught up with a fleeing column, the Ethiopian commander, Ras Mulugeta, was among those killed.

One-sided though these engagements appeared, they were not entirely so. The Regia Aeronautica was given ample evidence that aircraft could be vulnerable to ground fire. Ethiopian troops used their rifles and a few Oerlikon cannons against their aerial tormentors, and they were sometimes successful. Only sixteen of the Italian aircraft losses during the campaign were attributed to ground fire (three Ca.101s, two Ca.111s, two Ca.133s, two S.M.81s, five Ro.1s, one Ro.37, and one C.R.20) but a postwar American intelligence study pointed out that "on certain missions of ground strafing, all planes participating were reported struck by fire from the ground. During the ground strafing in the Mai Mescic valley following the battle of Amba Aradam, all planes participating [S.M.81s and Ca.101s] were hit by fire from the ground, one of them nineteen times. One plane was lost." In Ethiopia, Italian airmen were prepared to gamble. Flying against more heavily armed opposition in later conflicts, they learned to curb their flamboyance and become more discreet.

Given the organization and equipment of the respective ground forces engaged, the outcome of Mussolini's assault on Ethiopia was never in doubt, but it would have been a much more drawn out affair without the benefit of air power. Troops fighting without air cover and subjected to continual harassment from the air were shown to be at a severe disadvantage, and some useful lessons were learned about joint air/ground operations in difficult country. On the other hand, for those who cared to take note, there was a warning about the dangers involved in low-level attacks, even against an unsophisticated enemy.

Clashes in China

In the 1930s, Japan's developing military muscle, especially in the air and at sea, was reported on by various military attachés and observers, and was made apparent in actual combat on the Asian mainland. The signs were largely disregarded or misread, although the evidence of growing Japanese military and technical competence was plain to see.

The first Sino-Japanese clashes involving aircraft were relatively short-lived and occurred late in 1931 over Manchuria and during 1932 over Shanghai. In Manchuria, the Japanese were essentially unopposed in the air, and their

> *"In the air we shall of course be supreme. It is a manly weapon, a Germanic art of battle."*
>
> ADOLF HITLER, 1933

The Mitsubishi A5M was the Japanese Navy's first monoplane fighter and the first to be fitted with landing flaps. This is an A5M2a, the variant introduced with outstanding success as an escort fighter during the Japanese raids on Nanking in 1937.

army aircraft were able to concentrate on the close-support mission. Among the light bombers used was the first successful aircraft designed and built in Japan for the Imperial Japanese Army, the Kawasaki Type 88. The Type 88 inflicted heavy casualties on Chinese forces and helped to ensure the rapid imposition of a Japanese protectorate over Manchuria, subsequently known as Manchukuo. It was not quite so easy at Shanghai. After Japanese troops landed there in January 1932, the resistance of the defenders on the ground proved stronger than expected, so naval aircraft from the carriers *Kaga* and *Hosho* intervened. Some air-to-air fighting took place, but the Nakajima A1N3 fighters and Mitsubishi B1M3 attack aircraft had little difficulty in brushing the Chinese aircraft aside and operating more or less as they pleased. (Among those shot down by the Japanese was the prototype Boeing 218 [developed as the P-12E] flown by an American, Robert Short. In China to demonstrate the fighter, he charged into a formation from the *Kaga* and was killed in a dogfight with A1N3s.)

Both in Manchuria and Shanghai, the importance of having control of the air became clear to the Japanese, and the subsequent progress of military aviation in Japan was

rapid. If there was a problem, it was that Japanese interservice rivalry was bitter, so the air arms of the army and navy developed as separate air forces (IJAAF and IJNAF), with little if any cooperation over roles, missions or types of aircraft.

In the 1930s, the Japanese aircraft industry produced a rush of new designs for evaluation. Although stopgaps, they allowed the IJAAF and IJNAF, as well as the manufacturers, to expand and gain experience. Among the types to reach naval squadrons were the Nakajima A4N1 fighter, the Aichi D1A1 dive-bomber, and a land-based long-range bomber, the Hiro G2H1. At the same time, the Japanese began development of aircraft with better performance, including the Mitsubishi A5M fighter, Nakajima/Yokosuka B4Y1 attack bomber, Aichi E10A1 reconnaissance floatplane, Mitsubishi G3M1 land-based bomber, and Kawanishi H6K1, the first Japanese four-engined flying boat.

Ambitious though this production program was, it was followed by still more and even better designs which some years later were to make their mark on the Pacific War. While the IJNAF was thus engaged, the IJAAF pursued a development program of its own. New types appeared at a brisk pace — the Nakajima Ki-27 fighter, Mitsubishi Ki-30 light bomber and Ki-21 heavy bomber, Nakajima Ki-34 transport, Tachikawa Ki-36 army cooperation aircraft, Mitsubishi Ki-51 reconnaissance/close-support machine, Kawasaki Ki-48 light bomber, and Mitsubishi Ki-15 reconnaissance aircraft, a version of which surprised Western observers in April 1937 by flying from Tokyo to London in under 94½ hours (less than 57½ hours flying time).

In July 1937, all this effort was put to the test when the rumbling Sino-Japanese confrontation erupted into full-scale war. Japan invaded northern China and supported ground operations with intense air activity. The Japanese entered the conflict with some 500 aircraft available for combat. Over 250 of them were based on three aircraft carriers and tasked with operations in central and southern China; army aircraft looked after the north. The Japanese forces were well-trained, tightly controlled professionals, flying modern aircraft made in Japan. They were faced by Chinese units flying a bewildering variety of types from several countries, operating under fragmented control. The Central Government's air arm, directed by Chiang Kai-shek, was the largest Chinese air force, but the provinces of Kwantung and Kwangsi ran air forces of their own. Military missions from Italy and the United States gave advice, and Chiang Kai-shek's aircraft included Curtiss Hawks, Boeing P-26s, Martin 139s (B-10s), Northrop Gammas, and Douglas O-38s from the U.S.; Fiat C.R.32s, Breda Ba 27s, Caproni Ca.111s and Savoia-Marchetti S.M.72s from Italy; Heinkel 111s from Germany; and Blackburn Lincocks and Vickers Vespas from the U.K. Kwangsi also owned a number of British types, and the Kwantung Air Force added a collection of Russian aircraft. When the fighting began, no more than 100 of the fighters among these assorted machines were ready for combat with the invaders, many of them flown by foreign mercenaries.

Despite these various shortcomings, things did not go entirely Japan's way in the air. In three early raids on Nanking, the JNAF learned hard lessons about sending bombers on unescorted missions, losing a total of fifty-four. Japanese landings at Shanghai on August 11, 1937, strongly supported by aircraft from the carriers, were fiercely opposed. The fighting in the air over the city was intense, and the IJNAF suffered heavy losses, including eleven out of twelve bombers from one of the *Kaga* squadrons. The reaction of the Japanese commanders to these alarming events was swift. The carriers withdrew to reequip with Mitsubishi A5M2 fighters, which first restored the IJNAF's air superiority in the Shanghai area, and then began escorting the G3M bombers on their raids. The benefits from the change were not long in coming. During an engagement over Nanking on September 18, the A5M2s claimed eleven out of sixteen intercepting Chinese fighters shot down.

The Chinese were just as quick to seek improvements on their side. Sino-Soviet relations had been strained during Chiang Kai-shek's assault on the Chinese Communists, but the two nations now found common cause in their opposition to Japanese ambitions on the mainland of Asia. On August 29, the Chinese Nationalists signed a non-aggression pact with the Soviet Union and this was followed by the delivery of 400 Soviet aircraft to China, most of them Polikarpov I-15 and I-16 fighters. Four of the fighter squadrons and two Tupolev SB-2 bomber squadrons came complete with Soviet crews. Although these reinforcements made a difference, and the Chinese Air Force scored occasional successes, Japan's general superiority in the air could not be countered and, as the Japanese Army fought its way into most of China's eastern ports and cities during the next two years, Chinese air power was effectively destroyed.

The elusive goal of compelling Chiang Kai-shek's government to capitulate and recognize Japan's hegemony on the East Asian mainland remained out of reach, however, as the apparently fragmented Chinese society demonstrated impressive moral unity and will to resist. Japanese forces were still mired in the morass of a seemingly endless Chinese war when the government in Tokyo began turning its attention to Japan's position in the wider world and the creation of the proposed "Greater East Asia Co-Prosperity Sphere."

Manchurian Maneuvers

Besides the strain of carrying on the never-ending struggle in China, the Japanese had problems further north, on the poorly defined frontiers of Manchukuo with Mongolia and Siberia. Largely overlooked in the West because of tensions closer to home, the bitter clashes that occurred in 1938/39 involved large battles between Japanese and Soviet/Mongolian forces. Fighting first broke out near the mouth of the Tumen River, where the Soviets had fortified

Changkufeng Hill, commanding the point at which Siberia, Manchukuo and Korea came together. On July 11, 1938, the Japanese, outnumbered on the ground and in the air, tried to oust Soviet troops from their positions. The fighting was fierce but short-lived, with neither side able to score a conclusive victory. The opposing air forces each claimed hundreds of victories, more for domestic political reasons than from any wish to record the facts. The Soviets held on to the hill, and the battered Japanese attackers withdrew. A truce was signed on August 10, but resentments between the combatants smoldered on and the blaze was rekindled further west just nine months later.

After several incidents on the border between Manchukuo and the easternmost tip of Outer Mongolia, Soviet/Mongolian troops in a disputed area near Nomonhan in May 1939 were attacked by units of the Japanese 6th Army, strongly supported by aircraft of the IJAAF. Initially, events favored the Japanese, especially in the air. In the early fighting, the Soviet I-15 and I-16s were consistently outflown by the Nakajima Ki-27 and Kawasaki Ki-10 fighters of the IJAAF. These aerial successes were

followed up in June with damaging attacks on Mongolian airfields by Mitsubishi Ki-21 and Ki-30 bombers, together with some Fiat B.R.20s. The air battles were often huge, and several Japanese pilots began to amass sizeable scores, among them Warrant Officer Shinohara, who claimed four kills on May 27 and six more the next day. Shocked by Japanese successes, the Soviets moved in strong reinforcements and prepared for a counteroffensive under the command of General (later Marshal of the Soviet Union) Georgi Zhukov.

It was apparent that control of the air was going to be of vital importance to the outcome of the campaign. The Soviet Air Force flew in additional fighter squadrons equipped with I-16s and I-153s. Toward the end of June, the Soviets became more active, and dogfights on an impressive scale became common, often with over 100 aircraft locked together in combat. During one such action, on June 26, Major Zabulev, the commander of the 70th Fighter Squadron, was forced to bail out behind Japanese lines. His deputy, Major Gritsevets, risked landing his I-16 in open country nearby. Zabulev joined Gritsevets and, in a memorable rescue, the little

The Nakajima Ki-27 first flew in October 1936 and was the Japanese Army's first fighter with an enclosed cockpit. Ki-27s made their combat debut in 1938 against the Red Air Force near Nomonhan on the Manchurian border with Mongolia. They scored heavily in combat with Soviet I-15s.

fighter took off under fire, one Russian sitting on the lap of the other and the two of them bulging from an open cockpit that had dimensions barely adequate for one.

As Soviet strength in the air continued to increase, the air fighting intensified and Japanese pilots, flying four or five combat sorties per day, began to show signs of strain. Shinohara continued to pile up his score, setting a record on June 27 by claiming eleven victories during the day. On the ground, Zhukov's aggressive offensives inflicted heavy casualties on the Imperial Japanese Army. At the same time, the totals of aircraft destroyed, which had been to Japan's advantage in May and June, started to shift in favor of the Soviets. Russian pilots, changing their tactics, avoided being drawn into dogfights with the agile Ki-27s if they could, preferring to use the I-16's higher top speed to hit and run. The Soviets also gained from having their aircraft fitted with armor, whereas the Japanese fighters carried no protection, having been built as lightly as possible for

maximum maneuverability. Shinohara became a victim of that policy on August 27, when he was shot down in flames. With fifty-eight victories to his name, he was the highest scoring fighter pilot of the interwar years.

On August 20, Zhukov launched a formidable ground offensive spearheaded by 800 tanks and supported by a massive artillery bombardment. In a coordinated air and armored assault, 100 bombers and 150 fighters struck Japanese positions. Zhukov later wrote: "The strike of our air force and artillery was so powerful and successful that the enemy was morally and physically suppressed..." The outnumbered Japanese forces did indeed seem stunned by the impact of the attack, and Zhukov's troops made rapid progress. The IJAAF tried to respond against Soviet airfields, and Japanese pilots still fought tenaciously, but fatigue and the loss of too many experienced airmen began to tell. By mid-September, the Japanese commanders were ready to brush aside the reality of their losses and think of launching a counteroffensive. However, in both Tokyo and Moscow, events in Europe intervened to provide other preoccupations for the governments, and a ceasefire was agreed upon on September 16, 1939.

A Spanish Republican I-16 Type 5 Mosca single-seat fighter. This type was called Rata (or sometimes Boeing) by the Nationalists.

FIAT C.R.32

The Fiat C.R.32 was a biplane fighter of excellent quality, greatly admired by its pilots for being agile, reliable and easy to fly. The cockpit of the C.R.32 was neat and functional, and the fighter was powered by a 600-horsepower Fiat A.30 RAbis in-line engine. A distinctive feature was the prominent circular radiator, which formed a chin beneath the metal propeller. In August 1936, C.R.32s were sent to Spain to form La Cucaracha Squadron. More followed and, marked with the black cross on the rudder, a total of 377 saw combat during the Spanish Civil War, constituting by far the largest fighter element of the Nationalist air forces. This restored C.R.32 is in the collection of the Italian Air Force Museum at Vigna di Valle, north of Rome.

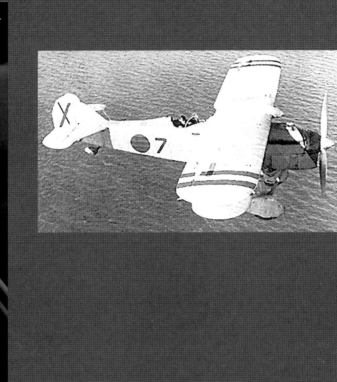

The Nationalist fighter leader Joaquin Garcia-Morato of Spain flew the Fiat C.R.32 and was the leading ace of the Spanish Civil War, with a total of forty aerial victories.

It can be argued that the IJAAF performed better than its Soviet opponents in the air war. Although the impressive claims for aircraft destroyed by each side need to be viewed with caution, it does seem that Soviet losses were higher than the IJAAF's. (The JAAF admitted losing 168, and claimed 1,260 Soviet aircraft. The Soviets admitted losing only 207, while claiming 660. The common fault of over-claiming is probably accentuated by the distortion of prop-aganda in arriving at these figures. The truth lies somewhere between the two sets.) Certainly, the intensity of operational flying undertaken by the Japanese pilots pro-duced some remarkable personal performances. Over fifty were recognized as "aces" during the four months of fight-ing. Their achievements may have helped to beguile their commanders into believing that the doctrines underlying Japanese air power were basically correct. The problems of the campaign were put down to lack of numbers and to unavoidable pilot fatigue. The idea that it might be worth considering the production of faster aircraft fitted with protective armor for aircrew and fuel tanks, even at the sac-rifice of some maneuverability, was put to one side. However, the campaign as a whole was recognized as having

been a defeat for Japan, an experience that the Tokyo gov-ernment was not anxious to repeat. From then on, Japan tried to ensure that there would be no further conflict with the Soviet Union, a fact that became known to Stalin and led him to judge that there would be little risk of having to fight wars against Germany and Japan at the same time. For their part, the Soviet military emerged from the Nomonhan battles with the soundness of their developing strategies confirmed. The combination of massive combined arms ground assaults and strong close-air support had been effective, and the advantage of having armored protection for aircraft proved. The differing military perspectives of the two nations would have considerable influence on events in the coming World War.

Rehearsal in Spain

Factional differences in Spain became increasingly polar-ized after the creation of the Spanish Republic in 1931. By the spring of 1936, following years of civil unrest and the effective destruction of Spanish democracy, a left-wing coalition government was doing its best to neutralize right-wing opponents by posting dangerous army generals to remote garrisons. They succeeded only in spurring the officers into a conspiracy to replace the Republic with a military dictatorship. Support for this Nationalist revolution came both from the monarchists, who had been promised that the king would return, and from the Fascists, who had been assured that fascism would prevail.

On the night of July 17–18, 1936, the Spanish Army of Africa rose against the government, and the next day General Francisco Franco arrived from the Canary Islands to take command. Within hours, there were uprisings all over Spain. By July 21, Nationalist forces controlled the greater part of northern Spain and the region round Seville in the south. Success for the rebels was by no means assured, however, since the coup had failed in most of central and southern Spain, and in the capital city, Madrid.

Ships manned by Republican "Loyalist" crews blocked the Straits of Gibraltar, and Franco's troops could not reach mainland Spain in any strength. Seville's airfield offered a possible solution, but the aircraft available were few and inadequate. One Fokker F.VIIa, three Fokker F.VIIbs, and a Douglas DC-2 began flying small groups of soldiers across from Morocco, and two Dornier Wal flying boats joined in, delivering twelve soldiers at a time to Cadiz harbor. The urgency of the situation was not lost on Franco, and he sent emissaries to Hitler and Mussolini with requests for help in the shape of aircraft. The response from the dictatorships was immediate, and Franco was given even more aid than he asked for, the initial wave including not only aircraft, but also crews, weapons and maintenance support. Most significant of the early arrivals were twenty Junkers Ju 52/3ms.

LEFT *The Junkers Ju 86D was one of the bomber types sent by Germany to Spain in 1937 to be evaluated in combat conditions. (The others were the Dornier Do 17E and the Heinkel He 111B.) Only four of each were sent initially, and the Ju 86D proved the least effective, convincing the Luftwaffe that it was inadequate as a frontline bomber.*

BELOW *Disturbed by the dominance of Soviet fighters over the Condor Legion's Heinkel He 51s, the Luftwaffe began sending Messerschmitt Bf 109Bs to Spain in 1937 to redress the balance. In July 1937, during the Battle of Brunete, fast monoplane fighters confronted each other for the first time when the Bf 109Bs fought I-16s. The tactics of air combat began to change from that moment.*

LEFT *One of three Junkers Ju 87As sent to Spain in January 1938. Adorned with a pink sow emblem on their "trousers," these aircraft were the first to evaluate the role of the dive-bomber under combat conditions, taking part in the Battle of Teruel and in the Nationalist drive through Aragon.*
BELOW *In moving nearly 14,000 troops to Spain across the Straits of Gibraltar during the first three weeks of August 1936, Junkers Ju 52/3m transports secured the future of the Nationalist cause in the most decisive air operation of the Spanish Civil War.*

Flying repeated shuttle trips across the Straits, the German trimotors delivered nearly 14,000 troops and their equipment to Spain during the first three weeks of August 1936. It was the first major airlift of troops ever attempted and, since the Nationalist cause could hardly have prospered without them, it was arguably the most decisive single operation of the Spanish Civil War. Not for the last time, air transport units, perhaps lacking the glamorous public appeal of front-line combat squadrons, had nevertheless demonstrated the crucial importance of their role in military aviation.

From Madrid, meanwhile, the Republican government had also called for help, seeking aid from the ruling left-wing coalition in Paris. Sympathetic though the French Premier was, his response was constrained by other considerations, not least the strong British objections to outside intervention in the Spanish conflict. By the beginning of September, an International Agreement of Non-Intervention had been signed by most European governments. Despite its provisions, there continued to be substantial international involvement in Spanish affairs, with men and material finding ways of joining the war as long as it lasted. The principal difference initially was that aid for the Nationalists was given openly, while that for the Republicans was not. As a result, by the end of September Franco's forces had received more than 140 aircraft of all types ready for operations; the Loyalists, on the other hand, had accumulated about thirty assorted French aircraft, without benefit of crews, spares or even armament.

In mid-July, before the uprising, there were some 550 aircraft of all types in Spain and Spanish Africa. Most

Spanish combat units were equipped with obsolete biplanes in varying states of disrepair, mostly CASA-Breguet 19s or Hispano-Nieuport 52s. In the week following the uprising, Franco's forces were able to appropriate no more than 20 percent of the total number for their use, and so were badly in need of help in the air. With foreign intervention, the character of the respective air forces began to change. Besides the Junkers Ju 52/3ms, the Nationalists received a few Heinkel He 51 fighters from Germany in August. Initially, the German aircraft were to be flown only by Spanish pilots, but that directive was soon rescinded and German pilots were in action before the month was out. On August 14, a German-flown Junkers Ju 52/3m bombed and disabled the Republican battleship *Jaime 1*. At the same time, the Italian response to Franco's request began to arrive in the shape of Fiat C.R.32 fighters and pilots. By the end of 1936, the Germans and Italians had built up their strengths to such a degree that they had been formed into separate organizations and the Nationalist air force had become three distinct entities — the Arma de Aviacion, the

Aviazione Legionaria, and General Hugo Sperrle's Legion Condor. Between them, during the course of the war, they made use of more than 1,600 aircraft, over 1,400 of which came from Germany and Italy.

On the Republican side, the Aviacon Militar and the Aeronautica Naval retained separate identities until mid-1937, and there were also two other air forces operating independently for the first few months, in Catalonia and the Basque/Asturian zone. In addition, the international volunteers and mercenaries (mainly French, British and American) formed squadrons of their own, at least to begin with, calling themselves the Escadre Espana and, in a conscious effort to revive past glories, the Escadrille Lafayette. Because of the conspicuous indiscipline of these units, they were soon placed under the command of Spanish officers, and later volunteers went directly into Spanish squadrons. In October 1936, the Soviet Union decided to counter the intervention of Germany and Italy and began sending aircraft, crews and technicians to Spain. The first to arrive were squadrons of Tupolev-designed SB-2 bombers and Polikarpov I-15 fighters, which, until the Legion Condor was reinforced, began to wrest the tactical initiative from the Nationalists. Before the war ended, some 1,200 aircraft had joined the Republicans from other countries, and more than 200 more had been built in Spain.

Altogether, about 3,500 aircraft of all types, civil and military, were flown in Spain during the Civil War. Given the length and scale of the conflict, that may not seem a remarkable total. On the other hand, the number of types involved was extraordinary. Over 280 types and variants were used. Although the Germans, Italians and Soviets bore the brunt of the problem with relatively few types, it can nevertheless be imagined what nightmares of maintenance and supply, and miracles of improvisation, lie behind that figure. Over 160 types flew as one-of-a-kind in Spain, and many of these had interesting, if short, careers.

An ageing Lioré et Olivier 213, unarmed and with unserviceable bomb-racks, was acquired by the international bomber squadron toward the end of August 1936. Mechanics did their best with unpromising material, rigging homemade bomb-racks inside the fuselage, and fitting two machine guns, one in the tail and the other in the dorsal position. Their exertions were poorly rewarded, however, as the lumbering LeO, operating under the dubious protection of an escorting de Havilland Dragon Rapide, was intercepted and shot down by Fiat C.R.32s on its first operational sortie. Hardly more fortunate was a Lockheed 9D Orion, originally built for the England-to-Australia air race in 1934 and later acquired by the French government. It was used in July and August 1936 for a number of diplomatic missions between Madrid and Paris, the last including among the passengers the photographer Robert Capa. After a forced landing in a remote part of Aragon, the Orion passed into the care of the local militia, who were instructed to transport it to Madrid. The aircraft was loaded on two linked ox carts, and they began the journey. They had gone no further than the first village when a problem arose. It was found that the Orion's wings would not pass between the houses. The militia commander, whose knowledge of aircraft was limited, had discovered that his valuable charge was principally of wooden construction, so he sent for the village carpenter and had him saw the wings off. With them roped alongside the fuselage, the cavalcade moved on, the commander well satisfied with his decisive handling of a difficult situation.

The protruding exhaust stubs and scissor-linked tail wheel identify this as a Messerschmitt Bf 109C, one of only five sent to Spain during the Spanish Civil War.

casualties and were instrumental in forcing the mostly Italian ground forces to withdraw in disorder. Guadalajara was significant because it was a major battle in which victory over an army on the offensive could be attributed mainly to the use of air power.

The defeated Nationalists took the lessons of Guadalajara to heart. In subsequent campaigns, the Legion Condor's able chief of staff, Wolfram von Richthofen (cousin of Manfred, WWI's "Red Baron"), made sure that air attack was closely coordinated with infantry and artillery action. During Franco's northern offensive in 1937, at the battles of Bilbao and Brunete, when the fighting on the ground sometimes became a desperate, see-saw affair, it was the intensive operations of the Nationalist air force that made the difference. The Heinkel He 51 squadrons often flew as many as seven sorties in a day, bombing and strafing as close as 50 yards from their own soldiers. They used fragmentation bombs and, in a step that foreshadowed the development of napalm weapons, fused fuel tanks. These attacks inflicted heavy losses on Republican forces and often forced the demoralized survivors to flee the field.

In the months after the arrival of the Soviets, their fighters had proved too much for the Nationalist's He 51s and Fiat C.R.32s. The He 51s suffered such heavy losses that they were relegated to ground-attack duties for the rest of the war. In the spring of 1937, the situation began to change with the appearance of the first Messerschmitt Bf 109s, but it was not until July that they saw serious action, at Brunete. During that operation and from then on, the Bf 109 units engaged in their primary duty of maintaining air superiority, but also flew as bomber escorts and on ground-attack missions and offensive sweeps.

Squadron commander Günther "Franzl" Lützow left a

The German, Italian and Soviet units involved in the war were generally well organized and professional, but even they had problems to solve. Although their interventions were politically driven, it was not long before the respective commanders perceived that the conflict offered rare opportunities to test untried equipment and doctrines under combat conditions. As had been seen in the later stages of WWI, the importance of commanding the air over the battlefield was soon demonstrated. An attempted invasion of Nationalist-held Majorca in August 1936 by a strong Republican force failed because locally based Italian aircraft pounded the invading troops and kept Republican aircraft from interfering. An American report was explicit: "For two days aviation harassed the landing force, inflicting heavy losses, and finally forced a precipitate withdrawal."

At Guadalajara in March 1937, the boot was on the other foot. A formidable Nationalist force of some 50,000 men, equipped with tanks and artillery, advanced on the city. Unfortunately for them, they paid scant attention to ensuring air support. The Republican air force in the area was superior in numbers and was operating from permanent airfields on the plain. Nationalist air force units nearby could use only poorly drained dirt fields at higher elevations, where low cloud often prevented them flying. Intensive air attacks over several days by Soviet SB Katiuska bombers, Polikarpov R-Z Natacha attack aircraft and I-15 biplane fighters, covered by I-16s, inflicted heavy graphic account of the air superiority struggle: "Mostly it was Ratas and Curtisses against my small formation. Seven against forty! There was no time to aim carefully. It was turn, attack, aim at the red circle, press the buttons, pull out, gain some height, turn back, get the next one in front of one's guns — hold it; this time too many are behind me — dive down and break away for a moment to get one's breath back." (Many airmen on the Nationalist side believed that the Soviet aircraft were of U.S. design. Hence, they often called the I-15 Chato [Snub-nose] a Curtiss, and the I-16 Mosca [Fly] or Rata [Rat] a Boeing.)

Brunete was the battle in which fast monoplanes first clashed in earnest, with Bf 109Bs tackling the Republican I-16s. Below 10,000 feet, the I-16 could not match the Messerschmitt in a dive, but it was more maneuverable, had a better rate of climb, and was as fast as the Bf 109B in level flight. Above that height, the advantage favoured the Bf 109B as the power of the I-16's M-25 engine (a license-built Wright Cyclone R-1820) declined. The German pilots found it to their advantage to use their aircraft's superior performance at altitude in claiming the "high ground," so dictating the terms of any engagement and avoiding turning dogfights by diving down on their enemies in slashing high-speed hit-and-run attacks.

More fundamentally, the higher speeds of the opposing fighters enlarged the scale of the action, so that air battles often covered hundreds of square miles instead of being the kind of concentrated affairs resembling swarms of gnats seen in WWI. This in turn led the Luftwaffe to devise new tactics. (In fact, they rediscovered the system devised by Oswald Boelcke in WWI. He led open formations that fought as a team, the relatively small distances between aircraft determined by the turning radius of his Albatros.) The close "vic" formation of three aircraft (*kette*) was found to be impractical for the new fighters, and the basic fighting unit became the much looser *rotte*, a pair of aircraft comprising a leader and a wingman flying perhaps 200 yards apart. Two *rotte* made up a *schwarm* (commonly known now as "finger four"), and a *staffel* in the air was usually made up of three *schwarm*. The development of these tactical arrangements in the closing months of the war in Spain

> *"Could any life be as good as death like this?"*
>
> OLOFF DE WET, REPUBLICAN GROUND-ATTACK PILOT, SPAIN, 1937

was led by Werner Mölders, who took over a squadron from Adolf Galland as it converted to Bf 109Cs and Ds in the summer of 1938. His efforts and his later reports on the success of the tactics, highlighting improvements in flexibility and in mutual support, established the practice in the Luftwaffe. In so doing, Mölders set a pattern for fighter combat that was eventually adopted as standard operational procedure by every air force worldwide. (Mölders also ended the war as the most successful German fighter pilot, with fourteen victories. Mario Bonzano from Italy had fifteen, and the Russian A.K. Serov, sixteen. Joaquin Garcia-Morato, the Nationalist fighter leader, shot down forty, almost all while flying the Fiat C.R.32.)

The most notorious use of air power in Spain took place during the campaign in the north. On April 26, 1937, the Legion Condor attacked Guernica, one of the fortified towns standing in the way of a Nationalist advance on Bilbao. Waves of He 111s and Ju 52/3ms bombed Guernica's center to destruction and He 51s strafed the roads out of the town. The town fell to the Nationalists two days later. The reaction to the raid, both in Spain and internationally, was one of horror, and the psychological impact immense. Guernica heightened worldwide public fear of the bomber and reinforced the commonly held conviction that it was air power, used against centers of civilian population, that would be decisive in future wars. These impressions were confirmed early in 1938 by a series of raids on Barcelona led by the fast Italian S.M.79s, which inflicted several thousand casualties, and by Republican reprisals against Valladolid and Seville. The outrage expressed around the world at these assaults on civilians, and those of the Japanese against Chinese cities carried with it the underlying fear of what might be in store for other populations in any wider conflict.

Victory in the north in 1937 allowed Franco to concentrate on the Republican strongholds to the east. In bitter fighting at Teruel, in Aragon and at the Ebro, Republican strength was steadily eroded, and the Nationalist air force became increasingly dominant in the air battle. In the latter stages of the war, the opposition faced by the Luftwaffe units stiffened for a while as later model I-16s appeared, more heavily armed and fitted with high-altitude versions of the Wright Cyclone engines. Bf 109 losses increased, but the essential preeminence of Messerschmitt's fighter was never seriously challenged.

It was at the River Ebro in 1938 that Nationalist air power truly came of age. After a strong Republican offensive had been blunted, Franco's forces set out to crush the opposition. In a combined arms counteroffensive, the Nationalist air force flew sorties against the enemy at a prodigious rate. Between August 15 and 19, more than 200 aircraft (a mixed bag of forty S.M.79s, thirty He 111s, thirty Ju 52/3ms, twenty S.M.81s, eight Do 17s, nine Ba 65s, and seven squadrons of He 51s) kept up incessant attacks on Republican positions, dropping an average of 10,000 bombs per day. The He 51 pilots involved had perfected a continuous chain diving attack that kept the target forces under almost uninterrupted fire. This led to their being given the nickname of *Los Cadenas* — "the Chains." The suggestion that steep dive-bombing, particularly by Junkers Ju 87s, was a significant technique employed during the final stages of the Spanish Civil War may have rung true for those who endured such attacks at first hand, but the fact is that it was a rare event. Three of the new Junkers Ju 87As were deployed to Spain in December 1937 to test their capabilities under operational conditions. The results were encouraging enough that five Junkers Ju 87Bs were sent to Spain for similar testing in October 1938. These five aircraft were flown successfully in combat, demonstrating that they could place their bombs with remarkable accuracy. Indeed, their mere appearance seemed to have a marked effect on the troops being attacked. They thereby added another element to the developing German doctrine of close air support and were assured of an important role in future military operations.

By the time of the Ebro campaign, the Nationalists enjoyed complete air supremacy, and once the initial Republican offensive had ground to a halt, it was clear that the end of the war could not be far away. The Soviets had seen what was coming, and had withdrawn in the early summer of 1938, leaving considerable numbers of their aircraft in Spanish hands. Losses during the year were heavy, however, and, of the fighters, only some thirty-five I-16s remained on the Ebro front by the autumn. Barcelona fell in January 1939, and Franco was able to concentrate all his forces against Madrid. By the end of

March, the Republican leaders had fled into exile and Franco became the head of state.

The Spanish Civil War lasted for the better part of three years, and the airmen who fought in it believed they had learned important lessons. Indeed they had, but some of them were misleading. Of the nations involved, Germany and the Soviet Union took the most trouble to interpret their wartime experiences for their future benefit. The Italians did very little and seemed content just to have taken part. The relative success of the Fiat C.R.32 fighter, and their pilots' addiction to aircraft with high maneuverability and open cockpits, delayed the development of more powerful and faster monoplane fighters with heavier armament. Italian bombers, too, had done their job well (particularly the fast-flying S.M.79), and the Aviazione Legionaria saw no reason to change either the equipment or their doctrine.

For the Germans, the positive effects of their Spanish involvement seemed all too obvious. The development of *schwarm* fighter tactics alone must have been worth their commitment. It was recognized, too, that modern fighters needed to be able to fly faster, climb higher and carry more firepower. The higher speeds of air-to-air fighting offered fewer opportunities to bring guns to bear, and it was important both to be able to dictate the terms of an engagement and make the first burst count. The general adoption of *schwarm* tactics and the appearance of the cannon-armed Messerschmitt Bf 109E were indications that the Luftwaffe's fighter arm was pointed in the right direction. So, evidently, was the transport force. The ability to move troops and equipment rapidly by air had been amply demonstrated, and the Junkers Ju 52/3m enshrined as a vital air power tool.

The same could not be said of the paths followed in the close-support and bomber fields. The value of providing strong support for ground troops had been verified, and von Richthofen had introduced an admirable system of command and control to ensure its effectiveness, including the establishment of air liaison officers both at army headquarters and at the front. However, the Junkers Ju 87's contributions and the importance of dive-bombing had been exaggerated. The relatively benign air environment in Spain was not taken fully into account. As a result, Udet's dive-bomber bias was strengthened, and the

Junkers Ju 87 was built in large numbers, even though it was a slow, specialized aircraft with light defensive armament, unsuitable for adaptation to other roles. Its acquisition distorted the Luftwaffe's front line, taking men and resources that could have gone to more useful machines, and its vulnerability would eventually be exposed when it faced modern fighters.

If anything, the Luftwaffe's blind spot over its heavier bombers was worse. The general success of the He 111s and Do 17s in evading interception and reaching targets fathered assumptions that they did not need much fighter escort, could dispense with the weight of more comprehensive defensive armament, and might be expected to drop their bombs accurately. It also seemed that heavy bombing did demoralize civilian populations. These conclusions confirmed the predictions of air war theorists, and reassured the Luftwaffe's leaders. The realization that no attacking force, whether close support or bomber, could operate effectively without air superiority, and that civilian populations could be surprisingly resistant to bombing, would dawn later, with lessons being learned the hard way by both the Luftwaffe and its opponents.

The Soviets had both gains and losses to balance after the Spanish Civil War. They became even more convinced about the value of providing massive air support for their ground forces, and they correctly assumed that bombers would need to operate in conditions of air superiority achieved by fighters. Their development therefore continued to emphasize air power as an element of the land battle, and plans were laid which would bear fruit some years later, in the shape of the armored Ilyushin Il-2 Shturmovik, probably WWII's best attack aircraft, and the fighters produced by Yakovlev, Mikoyan-Gurevich, and Lavochkin. The down side came with Stalin's purges of the Soviet military leadership, at least some of which followed from his perception that the Communist effort in Spain had failed. His political sensitivity and ruthless nature combined to remove many of the most experienced and dedicated officers from the Red Air Force — a house cleaning for which the Soviet Union would later pay a high price.

As the dust settled on the Spanish Civil War, airmen all over the world began to consider what had been learned about aerial warfare. Many air force planners tried to decide what course of action they should take to ensure the future effectiveness of their various services. Some saw that conventional theories about air power needed to be revised in the light of experience; others may have seen that not all the lessons of Spain would apply in a wider conflict; but there were also those who had the authority to act on their conclusions who took a selective approach, choosing those elements which most conveniently supported already held convictions. Shock and disillusionment inevitably followed when the severity of WWII challenges proved many of those convictions ill-founded.

The first ship to be designed and built from the outset as an aircraft carrier was HMS Hermes, *which entered service with the Royal Navy in 1923.* Hermes *served principally in the Far East and Pacific until sunk by Japanese naval aircraft off Ceylon in 1942. Here* Hermes *is seen off Honolulu in 1924.*

THREE-DIMENSIONAL SAILORS
RIP RNAS

With the formation of the independent RAF in April 1918, the progress of British naval aviation slowed considerably. Placed as it now was in direct competition with its larger land-based counterparts within a single service, it was almost inevitable that the requirements of the former Royal Naval Air Service would be given less priority than before, especially when the fighting stopped and defense spending was cut back. Having once been the unchallenged leaders in devising ways of taking aircraft to sea and operating them successfully, Britain's naval aviators began to feel like poor relations. Although they still had contributions to make, it became clear well before WWII that the leading nations in building naval air power would be the United States and Japan.

Pacific Power Play

The island nation of Japan was quick to appreciate the potential of being able to project air power in the vast spaces of the Pacific. Alarmed by the extent of Western penetration in the part of the world they perceived as their sphere of influence, the Japanese looked for ways to command the ocean from the air. They considered the numerically superior U.S. fleet their primary strategic problem in the post-WWI period; they needed to be able to defeat it if it approached Japan. The Pacific island chains mandated to Japan after the defeat of Germany offered useful bases from which to attack a fleet at sea, and this inclined the Imperial Japanese Navy, more than other navies, to think about developing and operating long-range landplanes. Nevertheless, they laid down their first aircraft carrier in 1919.

The *Hosho* was a small ship, less than 7,500 tons displacement, but it was a start. Soon after construction began, the Japanese asked for assistance from Britain in building a naval air arm. A British mission, led by ex-RNAS officers, was duly dispatched to Japan. Details of British carrier design were freely given, and naval aircraft provided for evaluation. Doubtless much to the benefit of the British balance of payments, many of these aircraft were then manufactured in Japan under license and with the guidance of teams from British companies. Nakajima gained experience by making Avro 504Ks; Aichi built Felixstowe F.5 America flying boats with technicians from Shorts; and Mitsubishi engaged the services of Herbert Smith, former chief designer at Sopwith's. Included in the deal were Gloster Sparrowhawk naval fighters, but it was not long before the first generation of naval aircraft designed in Japan began to appear. By 1923, the Mitsubishi 1MF fighter and 2MR reconnaissance aircraft were reaching operational units. They were followed by the Mitsubishi B1M, which could be used in the bombing, reconnaissance and torpedo attack roles. True to their Sopwith roots, all three and their variants performed well, the 1MF serving in the front line until the end of the decade (when replaced by the Nakajima-built Gloster Gambet), and the B1M remaining in carrier service until 1938.

British experience also sparked American interest in carrier aviation. Relations between the two fleets were close after the United States entered WWI in 1917, and a number of U.S. officers served with the Royal Navy. They observed at first hand early British carrier trials and operations and several became influential in the subsequent development of naval aviation in the U.S. To help further, the British naval construction engineer, S.V. Goodall, was sent on loan to the USN's Bureau of Construction and Repair, and

he took with him details of British carrier designs. Convinced about the importance of naval air power, the USN's airmen pressed their case for building large, capable carriers. Personal enthusiasm and the help of friends are not always sufficient, however. The postwar Congress was not inclined to spend money on unproven ideas, and refused to authorize funds for new construction. All they were prepared to accept was the conversion of the slow collier USS *Jupiter* to the experimental carrier *Langley*. After extensive remodeling, the *Langley* emerged from the Norfolk yards as the first U.S. aircraft carrier (CV1) on March 22, 1922.

The *Langley* was not the answer to a naval aviator's dreams. Still fitted with collier's machinery, her top speed was only 14 knots, far too slow to allow the ship to stay with the fleet, and the limitations of the small flight deck severely restricted operations. With an eye on what the Japanese were doing, the U.S. Navy continued to push for better

ships. Politicians, concerned about the costs, became nervous about the possibility of a naval arms race. To prevent matters getting out of hand, the United States called for an international conference to discuss naval armaments and the situation in the Far East. At a conference held in Washington, D.C., in 1921 and 1922, the naval questions were tackled by representatives of the U.S., Britain, Japan, France and Italy. On February 6, 1922, the Naval Armaments Treaty was signed; it established the ratio of capital ship tonnages allowed to the five states. In effect, the United States and Britain were each restricted to a total of 525,000 tons, Japan to 315,000 tons, and France and Italy to 175,000 tons. Within

F2F-1s of VF-2B joining formation over San Diego in 1939.

these figures there was a limit of 27,000 tons for each aircraft carrier, and restrictions on total carrier tonnages of 135,000 tons for the U.S. and Britain, and 81,000 tons for Japan. The smaller Japanese totals were argued on the grounds that the interests of Japan were confined to the Pacific, whereas the other two major naval powers needed to cover all the world's oceans.

Carrier Forces Take Shape

The reaction of the three powers to the conditions of the treaty included converting superfluous battle cruisers to carriers. Indeed, both the United States and Britain moved in that direction before the treaty was signed. Making the most of a concession clause that said that the signatories might complete two carriers of 33,000 tons each if they were converted from capital ships now liable to be scrapped, the U.S. chose the intended battle cruisers USS *Lexington* and *Saratoga*. The Japanese began working on *Amagi* and *Akagi*, but earthquake damage to *Amagi* meant the almost completed battleship *Kaga* was used instead. Britain set about converting two smaller ships, HMS *Courageous* and *Glorious*, which had seen fleet service as large cruisers in WWI.

The small size of the British ships made it possible for the Royal Navy to operate six carriers and still stay within the treaty requirements. That force — HMS *Furious, Argus,*

Hermes, Eagle, Courageous and *Glorious* — remained numerically the largest carrier fleet afloat until the 1930s. However, the ships all suffered to some extent from their WWI origins, and could handle only relatively small aircraft complements. The Royal Navy also continued to emphasize reconnaissance over all other roles for the Fleet Air Arm (the former RNAS), seeing its aircraft and their ships primarily as supporting the actions of the conventional surface fleet. As long as the RN's battleship guns were still considered the most important weapons for establishing sea power, it was difficult to promote the idea that aircraft carriers could operate separately from the battle line and become the core of major striking forces in their own right. Such was not the case with either the U.S. or Japan.

Although strongly influenced by British advisers in their early days, the Japanese soon became interested in using fast carriers for long-range strikes. They believed that carriers occupied both ends of the scale in terms of naval capability, as they carried the potential to deliver crushing blows on their enemies, yet were extremely vulnerable. Battleships were still important to them, but they recognized that opposing carriers could be a major threat, and believed that any fleet action would have to start with the elimination of the opposition. In keeping with these beliefs,

The Professionals, *by Jim Dietz. Boeing F4B-4s of VF-2 on board the USS* Lexington. *VF-2 was a unique U.S. Navy squadron — all of the pilots were enlisted men.*

The last biplane fighter to fly with the U.S. military, the Grumman F3F joined the fleet in 1937 and at one time equipped seven Navy and Marine Corps squadrons. The aircraft on display at Pensacola is in the markings of VMF-2, the unit it was assigned to when ditched off the Californian coast by 1st Lieutenant Bob Galer in 1940. Galer survived to be awarded the Medal of Honor in WWII, and his aircraft was recovered from the sea in 1990.

the aircraft complements on Japanese carriers became biased toward strike aircraft (dive and torpedo bombers) and fighters for local defense. Most reconnaissance duties were entrusted to floatplanes mounted on heavy cruisers. At the same time, principally because they feared losing a lot of ships at once in a confrontation with the USN, the IJN preferred to split up its fleet into task forces that separated the carriers from other big ships.

For their part, the Americans began viewing the carrier as an offensive weapon almost from the start. The concept was given a boost when the large, fast carriers *Lexington* and *Saratoga* became available. Their capacity to take many more aircraft than other ships, and their superior speed, reinforced the idea that they should operate independently with cruiser escort. By the early 1930s, the doctrine of the independent carrier task force was well established in the U.S. Navy.

ABOVE *The U.S. armed forces overwhelmingly favored radial engines for their aircraft in the 1920s and 1930s. Here the rugged innards of a radial are exposed in a cutaway.*

OPPOSITE *The Goshawk (BFC-2) was intended for the U.S. Navy's fighter-bomber role. It could carry four 112-pound bombs under the wings or one 500-pound bomb beneath the fuselage on a swinging crutch. Only fifty-seven Goshawks were built and they were the last Curtiss fighters accepted for service with the U.S. Navy. BFC-2s were delivered to the VF-1 "High Hat" Squadron in 1933, and the Goshawk at Pensacola carries that unit's insignia.*

The U.S. Navy's first monoplane was the Douglas TBD Devastator, which reached Torpedo Squadron VT-3 in 1937. When it was ordered, the Devastator could claim to be one of the best torpedo aircraft anywhere; by the time of the Japanese attack on Pearl Harbor, it was outclassed. At the Battle of Midway in 1942, the Devastators of VT-3, VT-6 and VT-8 suffered the greatest loss rate of any U.S. aircraft. Thirty-five of the forty-one launched were destroyed. VT-6 from the USS Enterprise *(seen here) lost nine of the squadron's fourteen Devastators during the attack on the Japanese carriers.*

American Aircraft Aboard

The world's navies necessarily procured their aircraft to counter threats that they were likely to face in war. As independent carrier operations became accepted in the USN, and the job of scouting and spotting for the battle line was undertaken by aircraft catapulted from battleships and cruisers, carrier complements were heavily biased toward fighters and attack aircraft. The U.S. Marines exerted their influence, too, representing the need for effective dive-bombers and close-support aircraft. The dive-bomber also drew favor from naval attack pilots for its ability to deliver bombs so accurately that even a maneuvering ship could not guarantee to escape. Taking the various requirements into account, and bearing in mind the imminent commissioning of the *Lexington* and *Saratoga*, the 1926 Morrow Board investigating service aviation recommended a five-year program for the construction of a 1,000 aircraft force for the USN. By 1931, U.S. Naval Aviation (including the Marine Corps) had expanded to twenty-seven squadrons operating over 950 aircraft. More than 200 further aircraft were on order, together with a new light car-

rier, the *Ranger*. The aircraft included Boeing F3B and F4B fighters, Curtiss O2C and Chance Vought O2U/O3U observation planes, Martin T4M torpedo bombers, and the Curtiss F8C Helldiver. Interesting but impractical sidelines were the experimental programs in which a tiny Parnall Peto biplane was housed on a submarine, and those that involved a Vought UO-1 and several Curtiss F9C Sparrowhawks hooking onto and releasing from USN airships in the air, both by day and night.

During the post-WWI period, the USN encouraged a number of trail-blazing and record-breaking flights, gaining favorable publicity for its air arm. The first aircraft to complete a transatlantic crossing, via the Azores, was the USN's NC-4 flying boat in 1919. Polar exploration began in 1925 with Loening amphibians and a Vought UO-1, and continued the following year when Admiral Richard Byrd set off for the North Pole in a Fokker F.VIIa-3m. In 1923, a Curtiss CR-3 floatplane won the Schneider Trophy for the United States, and USN pilots took the first two places in the Pulitzer race with Curtiss R2C-1s. At that time, the USN held twenty-three of the seventy-eight official aviation world records. (See Chapter 2, The Aerial Adventurers.)

The USN, as concerned as the Japanese about the carrier's vulnerability to air attack, developed scout squadrons whose tasks would include seeking out the enemy's fleet and, in those pre-radar days, serving as aerial pickets to report enemy aircraft. To fill this role initially, Curtiss F8Cs were redesignated for observation duties as O2Cs. By 1935, with the Japanese already set to acquire an all-monoplane force, the USN was still a biplane service, typified by the Boeing F4B-4, Curtiss BF2C-1 and Grumman FF-1/F2F-1 fighters; Vought SBU-1 scouts; Martin BM-1/2 and Great Lakes BG-1 dive-bombers; plus Grumman J2F and Consolidated P2Y-1 amphibians and flying boats. The USN's Bureau of Aeronautics had long since decided that it would accept only air-cooled radial engines for its aircraft, and knew that the monoplane's time was coming. However, naval aviators preferred the low-speed handling characteristics of biplanes for carrier operations, and their useful life in the front line was extended by employing such technological advances as stressed-skin construction, tightly cowled engines, enclosed cockpits and retractable landing gear.

The next period of U.S. naval aviation expansion began with the launching of the *Yorktown* (CV-5) and *Enterprise* (CV-6) in 1936. In the same year, the keel of the smaller *Wasp* (CV-7) was laid down. Monoplanes were not far behind, but the first monoplane fighter to enter USN service did not arrive until June 1939; it was the Brewster F2A Buffalo, a tubby little aircraft which, like many trail-blazers, was destined to gain a poor operational reputation (except during the Winter War against the Soviets in 1940, when the Finnish Air Force achieved great success with the F2A). It was preceded by other monoplanes, notably the Douglas TBD Devastator torpedo bomber in 1937. The Devastator is not fondly remembered either, but at the time of its entry into service it was one of the best carrier attack aircraft in existence, and it set the fashion followed by torpedo bombers for over a decade. Such aircraft were necessary stepping stones to those that carried most of the burden in the Pacific during WWII, such as Grumman's TBF/M Avenger and "Cat" fighter series, and the Douglas SBD Dauntless. In non-carrier aviation, the Consolidated PBY Catalina, first flown in 1935, was an exceptional performer and gave sterling service throughout the war.

In spite of many protestations to the contrary about the inevitability of war, the U.S. administration was not blind to political events, and in 1938, the previously modest expansions of USN naval air strength were succeeded by more forceful measures. Congress approved an increase to 3,000 naval aircraft and a program of building additional air stations was begun, both in the United States and on a number of Pacific islands.

The 822-foot-long carrier USS Lexington *(CV-2) in the late 1930s. On deck are some of the ship's complement of eighty biplanes.*

ABOVE *The last biplane fighter flown by the RAF, the Gloster Gladiator was the first to have an enclosed cockpit and four forward-firing guns. It entered service in February 1937 with No. 72 Squadron, and continued in production until April 1940. Over 700 were built. The world's last flying example of a Gladiator (L8032) is maintained by the Shuttleworth Collection at Old Warden Airfield in England. When photographed in 1999 by Dan Patterson, L8032 was wearing Norwegian Air Force markings. Parked alongside was a Tiger Moth.*

RIGHT *Apart from the standard panel in the center, the Gladiator's instruments were not arranged very logically. The engine instruments are scattered about on both sides. Unusually for a British fighter, the cockpit was roomy, but it was advisable to hold on to maps and pencils tightly, since there was no floor and anything dropped was likely to be lost for the rest of the flight.*

OPPOSITE *The Grumman F4F-3 Wildcat on display at the National Museum of Naval Aviation, Pensacola, is in the markings of VF-72 (Fighting Wasps) when the squadron was assigned to CV-7, USS Wasp, in December 1941. At the Battle of Santa Cruz in 1942, VF-72 flew from USS Hornet, claiming twenty-eight Japanese aircraft shot down for the loss of ten Wildcats and five pilots.*

The Blackburn Skua was the Fleet Air Arm's first naval dive-bomber and the first deck-landing aircraft to have flaps, retractable landing gear and a variable-pitch propeller. It reached squadron service in 1938, but was already obsolescent. Nevertheless, it made its mark in aviation history. Skuas were the first British aircraft to shoot down a German aircraft in WWII, and Skuas sank the first large warship sunk by Allied forces in the war, the German cruiser Koenigsberg.

Japanese Aircraft Appear

The Imperial Japanese Navy, as convinced as the USN of the need to develop powerful carrier striking forces, had by the early 1930s begun weaning itself away from foreign aircraft. The launching of the *Akagi* and *Kaga* in 1927–28 encouraged the IJN to sponsor competitions for indigenous combat aircraft, but the results were disappointing and foreign designs were used to establish air wings on the new carriers. In 1930, however, the growing pool of Japanese aeronautical engineers began to have an effect. The Nakajima A2N fighter took its place afloat, and the front line took delivery of two reconnaissance floatplanes (Nakajima E4N1, Kawanishi E5K) and a flying boat (Hiro H3H). By 1932, the trend was more marked and Japanese industry produced the first of the 7-Shi series of aircraft (named for the seventh year of the imperial Showa house). The results were not overly impressive, and only two of the series were approved for production, both for reconnaissance — the Kawanishi E7K floatplane and the twin-engined Hiro G2H landplane. To improve the striking power of the forces at sea, the Heinkel He 50 dive-bomber was modified and manufactured as the Aichi D1A.

To ensure that the most could be made of the IJN's growing power in the air, the Japanese began construction of a small carrier, the *Ryujo*, in 1929, but then decided that they could not live within the restrictions of the Washington Naval Treaty, formally renouncing the terms in 1936. Two more carriers, *Soryu* and *Hiryu*, were begun. Work on the 9-Shi aircraft series started, but as insurance against further failures, foreign aircraft evaluations continued. The Dewoitine D.510 monoplane was considered a promising fighter, and provisional orders for it were placed. However, the Japanese surprised themselves. In comparative trials, the Mitsubishi A5M1, designed by the talented Jiro Horikoshi, proved to be superior, and the French order was canceled. Horikoshi's machine, developed as the A5M2 (Allied code name Claude), went to sea as the world's first operational naval monoplane fighter, and was available to intervene in the fighting for Shanghai in 1937.

By the mid-1930s, the Japanese were convinced that biplanes were being overtaken by events, and when, in 1935, the IJN issued requests for new carrier-borne aircraft, the specifications were for all-metal, low-wing monoplanes. The results included the Nakajima B5N (Kate) torpedo bomber and the Aichi D3A (Val) dive-bomber. At Mitsubishi, Horikoshi, far from resting on his laurels with the A5M, moved on to work on a far more impressive fighter, the A6M Zero. IJN operations away from the carriers were taken care of by the Kawanishi H6K (Mavis), an excellent four-engined flying boat, and a modern twin-engined bomber, the Mitsubishi G4M (Betty), was on the way. As the inevitable Pacific conflict grew closer, these were the principal aircraft with which the IJN would face the Allies. Many of their characteristics reflected the Japanese concern for the vast distances of the Pacific and others were drawn from Japan's experience in the war with China. Range was considered paramount, and the fighter pilots preferred maneuverability to speed. A horizontal bombing capability was thought important, too, probably because the IJN had been so heavily involved in striking at Chinese land targets. Those operations had also convinced the Japanese of the value of fighter escort for day bombers, a conclusion not yet clearly established in air force minds elsewhere. To meet the requirements of range and maneuverability with the available engine power, and keeping in mind the limitations on size and takeoff performance

imposed by the carrier itself, designers had to dispense with weight where they could, preserving fuel and minimal turning radius at the expense of protection for the crew and the fuel tanks. These shortcomings notwithstanding, the aircraft of the IJN in the late 1930s were at least comparable, and in some aspects superior, to their likely opponents. They would deliver some brutal shocks and destroy more than a few complacent attitudes in the West when the war in the Pacific began.

Fleet Air Arm Fumbles

Among the most irksome problems for British naval aviation during the interwar period was that the RAF was responsible for providing pilots and procuring aircraft. This resulted in the lack of strong aviation representation in the senior ranks of the RN and, with funds so short, in naval aviation being given low priority relative to the needs of the RAF itself. The curious command arrangements led to confusion about the roles naval aircraft could best fulfill, and that did not help when it came to ensuring that the FAA's aircraft were adequate for their tasks. With the "battleship navy" still very much in evidence, carriers were viewed as ships operating in support of the fleet, and, even though there were six RN carriers by the end of the 1920s, they were small. After *Glorious*

The Mitsubishi A5M Claude was the Imperial Japanese Navy's principal fighter in the war with China during the late 1930s. It was the IJN's first monoplane and was at first regarded with suspicion by the pilots, but its demonstrated superiority in combat with both Chinese and Soviet fighters soon overcame their distrust. This example is an A5M4, a longer range variant introduced in 1939.

AIRCRAFT FLYING OVER H.M.S. ARK ROYAL.

A formation of Fairey Swordfish torpedo bombers over the Royal Navy's aircraft carrier HMS Ark Royal. In May 1941, this potent combination ensured the destruction of the Bismarck by preventing the German battleship from reaching the safety of a French port.

and *Courageous* were commissioned, the total aircraft strength of the FAA, spread across six ships, was still only some 150 machines, a number that could have been comfortably accomodated by just two of the USN's carriers. Taking these things together, it is hardly surprising that the Royal Navy was slow to make the most of the aircraft that accompanied its ships to sea, or that the FAA developed a different concept of operations from other naval air arms.

In the 1930s, the Royal Navy quite reasonably saw its principal threat coming from Germany across the narrow northern seas of Europe. The German Navy had no aircraft carriers — two German carriers, *Graf Zeppelin* and *Peter Strasser*, were being built in 1939, but neither was completed — however, it was recognized that the Luftwaffe's land-based bombers could be dangerous, particularly for lightly armored ships. This drove the RN toward carriers with armored decks, and led to a bias against deck parks, in the belief that aircraft should be protected in hangars between sorties. Inevitably, operating rates were slow, since each aircraft had to be struck down below before the next one landed. This meant that the carrier's capacity was limited to the number of aircraft

> *"I wish for many reasons that flying had never been invented."*
>
> STANLEY BALDWIN, BRITISH PRIME MINISTER, 1935

that could be accommodated in the hangars. The USN's practice of settling for unarmored decks and using deck parks increased their carriers' vulnerability, but allowed them to operate more aircraft more expeditiously. The RN's inability to accommodate many aircraft per ship also posed the problem of how best to carry out the roles of naval air warfare. Given the available space, the ideal solution — having specialized aircraft — seemed impractical, and so imprudent compromises were sought. Requirements for new aircraft tried to combine several roles in one, and, since it was thought that single pilots could not be counted on to navigate away from the ship, there had to be at least two seats. All this, together with the low procurement priority for the FAA's aircraft, combined to produce machines of poor performance. When it came to the defense of the fleet, hindsight suggests that this was bad judgment, but British sailors of the day seemed content to rely more on AA guns and armor than on aircraft for defense against air attack.

Things did improve for Britain's naval air power in 1937, when the Admiralty regained control of the Fleet Air Arm. A hasty expansion was begun to ensure that the seven new carriers on order in the late 1930s could be properly provided for. Aircraft such as the Fairey Swordfish, and Blackburn's Skua and Roc were brought into service, but even though they gave occasionally valuable service, they could hardly have been described as outstanding performers. Like the Fairey Flycatcher of earlier years, they were no match for most of their land-based counterparts. (The Fairey Flycatcher was the FAA's principal fighter for nearly a decade, from 1923 to 1932. It was fun to fly, but its maximum speed was 133 mph and it was hardly ever allowed to operate out of sight of the ship.) Apart from the Swordfish, they did not long survive in the front line when war came, and even the Swordfish, affectionately known as the "Stringbag," continued only in the absence of a reasonable alternative.

Other Naval Air Arms

Besides the big three naval powers, a number of other nations found it prudent to develop at least a modicum of naval air expertise between the world wars. Only France, however, operated an aircraft carrier, the *Bearn*, a converted battleship with a complement of only twenty-five aircraft and a top speed of just 21 knots. There was also a French seaplane carrier, the *Commandant Teste*. The Italians had no carriers but operated a strong force of maritime aircraft. Elsewhere, countries as diverse as the Soviet Union, Argentina, Brazil, Colombia, Peru, Greece, the Netherlands,

Norway, Portugal, Yugoslavia, Australia and Canada either formed small naval air services or flew maritime aircraft, but restricted themselves to aircraft launched from conventional warships or to those operating from shore stations and harbors, mostly for maritime reconnaissance duties. The Royal Danish Navy's air service was very small, but it did complete a major scientific program during the 1930s. Using three Heinkel He 8 floatplanes and a Dornier Wal flying boat, the Danes carried out the first photographic survey of Greenland. This vast project occupied the summer months for seven years, and was of immeasurable value to the Allies when they came to set up mid-Atlantic bases for aircraft delivery and convoy protection during WWII.

THE LIGHTS BEGIN TO DIM IN THE WORLD THEATER

As the decade of the 1930s drew to a close, it became increasingly obvious that world conflict was at hand and that military aviation would have a large, if poorly understood, part to play in the battles to come. Air power theories had been expounded, air force budgets increased, service expansions begun, new equipment procured, essential research encouraged, and political alternatives exhausted. The rehearsals had been conducted in Spain, China and elsewhere, and the leading characters of the drama were waiting nervously in the wings. In Europe, it was time for the curtain to rise on the first act.

A Danish Dornier Wal. Photographic surveys of Greenland completed by this aircraft proved invaluable in setting up Allied mid-Atlantic bases in WWII.

CHAPTER 2

The Aerial Adventurers

*"The pioneering is over,
but the perfecting is yet to be done."*

CHARLES LINDBERGH, 1927

By THE END OF WWI, just fifteen years had passed since Kittyhawk, but the progress made by aviation in that brief time had been dramatic. It had come in two distinct periods, the first marked by the trials and errors of individuals probing the unknowns of a new dimension, and the second by the challenges of aerial combat. Supremely different though they were, both periods helped to establish the public impression that aviators were courageous daredevils, flamboyant characters who enjoyed taking risks and were quite prepared to meet their maker to experience the rapture of human flight. The coming of peace did little to alter that perception. Most people still looked on aviators as a race apart, and regarded flying as a dangerous occupation undertaken by those for whom thrill-seeking was a way of life. It was ranked with such activities as motor racing and circus acts. This was understandable, given that little had been done to develop aircraft that could be useful to the general public. In the 1920s and 1930s, flight's Golden Age, attitudes began to change, but while that was happening there was still room to embellish the image of the daring flier, and no shortage of adventurous men and women who, inspired by the appeal of flying to the human spirit, were ready to test the limits — their own and that of their machines. Airborne trail-blazers and record-breakers often featured in the world's headlines during the interwar years, bringing touches of romance and excitement to the lives of the earthbound.

As some blazed the trails, so others followed, and when it was no longer possible to be the first to fly somewhere, to experience the thrill of original discovery, aviators found excitement in striving to get there faster, go higher, fly further or for longer than those who had gone before. Indeed, for many fliers, the urge to be at the forefront of at least one aspect of aviation was more important than anything else. Between the wars, the names of many fliers were known worldwide, their exploits making them as celebrated as film stars. They were a select few at the pinnacle of a still hazardous occupation, and not all of them survived to enjoy their celebrity in later years.

*OPPOSITE PAGE
Artifacts from the
U.S. Army Air Corps
1924 flight round the
world in Douglas
World Cruisers are
preserved in the
USAF Museum,
Dayton, Ohio.
Among them are
Leigh Wade's jacket,
helmet and gloves,
and John Harding's
bible, diary and
cigarette case. Erik
Nelson is represented
by a pennant given
to him by a rival
round-the-world
airman, Antonio
Locatelli of Italy.*

THE CROSSING OF THE POND

In 1793, the French aeronaut Jean Pierre Blanchard first demonstrated balloon flight in the United States. From then on there were people who dreamed of being able to reach Europe by air. Numerous proposals were put forward for transatlantic balloon flights in the 19th century, and at least three serious if short-lived efforts were begun by American balloonists. (The *New York Sun* newspaper of April 13, 1844, announced that: "The Atlantic has been actually crossed in a balloon!" The report detailed a flight from Wales to South Carolina, but it proved to be a flight of imagination by Edgar Allan Poe, one of the *Sun's* correspondents.) By 1910, the problems of steering lighter-than-air craft were being solved. In that year Walter Wellman's airship *America* spent almost 72 hours in the air and managed to travel 1,000 miles from its starting point in New Jersey (but only 400 miles off the U.S. coast) before coming to grief.

Lord Northcliffe of the *Daily Mail,* a leading sponsor of aviation, ignited public excitement in 1913 by offering £10,000 for the first nonstop flight between the British Isles and North America. At the time, no aircraft was capable of covering the 1,800 miles separating Newfoundland and Ireland, nor could engines be counted on to keep running for 20 hours or more. Lord Northcliffe's promotion was disparaged by many on the grounds that he was inviting people to risk their lives in pursuit of the impossible. It was noted also that the prize had been announced on April Fools' Day, and other newspapers responded by offering huge sums for flying to the Moon, Mars and Venus. Lord Northcliffe, however, was not fooling. He believed in stimulating aeronautical advance by setting goals beyond current capabilities, and it was not long before his challenge was accepted. Two companies, Martin and Handasyde (later Martinsyde) in Britain and Curtiss in the United States, designed and built aircraft for the Atlantic crossing. The death of the Martinsyde's pilot and the onset of war prevented the attempts being made.

Lord Northcliffe had a reputation as a visionary, but he surprised people when, in July 1918, with the issue on the Western Front still far from settled, he announced in the *Daily Mail* that the transatlantic prize would be renewed, excluding only airmen and aircraft of the soon-to-be defeated Central Powers. With the signing of the Armistice in

November, aviators on both sides of the Atlantic were quick to turn their attentions to conquering the ocean barrier. Preparations were underway by the spring of 1919, with aircraft from Handley Page, Vickers, Boulton-Paul, Fairey, Shorts, Sopwith and Martinsyde among the British entries. In the United States, a floatplane designed by the Witteman-Lewis Company and flown by the Swedish pilot Hugo Sunstedt was being readied, and the U.S. Navy decided to make an official transatlantic effort. The Navy, however, declined to be drawn into the mercenary world of the *Daily Mail's* competition, declaring that it would be ethically improper for the USN to enter the contest when backed by all the resources of a national exchequer. They elected instead to continue with a wartime project already in hand and to be content with "the immortal honor of being first."

The Navy by Stages

The aircraft chosen by the U.S. Navy was a Curtiss flying boat, conceived for maritime patrol duties in European waters but produced too late to see wartime use. Four NC class flying boats (Navy Curtiss, generally known as "Nancies") were built. They were large biplanes with unequal wings, the upper wing spanning 126 feet and the 96-foot lower wing carrying a 45-foot hull. A triple-finned tail was mounted well aft at the end of skeletal booms. Designed for three engines, the final configuration chosen had four 400-horsepower Liberty engines in three nacelles, the center one housing two of the Liberties in a push-pull partnership. Crew comfort was not a priority. One passenger who flew in NC-1 on an eight-hour flight remarked on its slow cruising speed and grumbled about being exposed to the elements in the open cockpit: "It was cold and windy almost beyond endurance for so long a time. No lunch either."

The intention had been for the NCs to be flown to Europe for wartime operations, and a refueling base at Trepassey Bay in Newfoundland had been selected as the starting point for an Atlantic crossing. The end of the war removed the requirement, but the Navy remained interested in establishing an aerial transatlantic link. Preparations for the crossing were entrusted to Commander John Towers, who planned a route from Newfoundland to England via the Azores and Portugal. The NC's fuel capacity of 1,610 gallons gave a cruising range of 1,470 miles, which ruled out a nonstop flight. Determined to succeed, Towers left nothing

In May 1919, the Curtiss flying boat NC-4, commanded by Lieutenant Commander Albert Read, was the first aircraft to complete an Atlantic crossing, staging through the Azores.

to chance. Three aircraft were made available to attempt the crossing. Each would carry a crew of six, and would have both radio and radio direction-finding equipment on board. The plan included the deployment of an armada of sixty-six USN ships stationed along the intended track all the way from Long Island to southwest England, available to give weather reports, provide navigational assistance, and carry out rescues.

On May 8, 1919, NC-1, NC-3, and NC-4, commanded respectively by Lieutenant Commander Patrick Bellinger, Commander Towers, and Lieutenant Commander Albert Read, set out from Long Island for Trepassey Bay. NC-4 was forced down on the sea by engine trouble on the way, and Read's crew spent several uncomfortable hours taxiing for 80 miles to reach Chatham, near Cape Cod. It seemed that NC-4 must be out of the running, but on May 15, with the other two aircraft making final preparations to leave, Read rejoined the formation at Trepassey Bay. On the same day, another USN transatlantic effort arrived in the bulbous shape of the airship C-5. The hopes of the lighter-than-air contingent were dashed that evening, however, when the C-5 tore loose from its moorings in a squall. The three men on board jumped for their lives and the airship was whisked out to sea, surprising the inbound NC-4 before disappearing over the horizon, never to be seen again.

The three flying boats lifted off on the first leg of their epic flight, 1,300 miles to the Azores, on the evening of May 16. Bad weather soon enveloped them. They flew on separately, but heavy clouds and low ceilings denied them a sight both of the sea and of star-shells fired by ships as a tracking aid. With the weather worsening, both NC-1 and NC-3 were forced to exchange one unfriendly element for another, each splashing down into rough seas and suffering damage. After five hours of drifting, the men from NC-1 were rescued by the Greek freighter *Ionia*, but their aircraft was abandoned to a watery grave. Commander Towers in NC-3 was determined to reach the Azores. Drifting and taxiing for some 200 miles in the next 53 hours, he at last struggled into Ponta Delgada on the island of Sao Miguel, steadfastly refusing the offer of a tow from the destroyer *Harding* over the last few miles. Missing both wing pontoons, most of the lower wing fabric and part of the tail, the battered NC-3 would go no further.

Meanwhile, NC-4 had battled through the storms and survived the worst the weather could do. On the morning of May 17, a relieved crew sighted the island of Flores. The weather was still appalling, so Read, well short of the intended destination of Ponta Delgada, put his aircraft down at Horta on the island of Fayal. The NC-4 had covered 1,380 miles in 15 hours and 13 minutes, an average speed of 90 mph. Compared with the drama of the first leg, the rest of the crossing was anticlimactic. Read moved on to Ponta Delgada when conditions improved and then, after a few days rest for man and machine, took NC-4 to Lisbon, touching down on the Tagus River on May 27, 1919, after a flight of 9 hours and 44 minutes. The Atlantic had been crossed by air for the first time. Four days later, Read's crew and their flying boat arrived in Plymouth Sound, near where the Pilgrim Fathers set sail from England in 1620. They had covered 4,320 miles since leaving Long Island and had spent 53 hours and 58 minutes in the air. It was a memorable achievement, a tribute to the commitment of the U.S. Navy and to the determination of a thoroughly professional crew of naval airmen.

C.G. Grey wrote in the British aviation magazine *The Aeroplane:*

> There is pure poetic justice in the victory being won by the Americans. After all, the first people to fly were the Wright brothers in 1903, on a machine of their own build with an engine of their own make . . . and the first flying boat was designed and built by Glenn Curtiss in 1913, again with a home-built engine. Who therefore has a better right to be first across the Atlantic than an American crew on an American flying boat with American engines? . . . The American victory was the deserved result of great personal gallantry, great skill in the design, preparation, care and handling of the machine and her engines, and great ability in seamanship and airmanship. But above all it was a triumph of organization — which is just where we in this country fail so constantly.

Originally designed in WWI as a counter to the threat of German U-boats, the Curtiss NC flying boats gave the U.S. Navy the chance to attempt an Atlantic crossing by air. Four were built, of which three were prepared for the flight (NC-1, 3 and 4). Storms over the Atlantic in May 1919 forced both NC-1 and NC-3 down, but NC-4 survived to complete the crossing to Plymouth, England, via the Azores and Lisbon. The NC-4 is preserved in the National Museum of Naval Aviation, Pensacola. With a wingspan of 126 feet, the size of the flying boat is impressive. Even powered by four 400-horsepower Liberty engines, the NC-4 could not drag its bulky frame along faster than 85 mph.

The Curtiss NC-4 in flight. The wings and tail seem to have been added as an afterthought to a boat. Note the crew exposed to the elements in open cockpits and the large fabric wing-fences. The two central Liberty engines are mounted in the same nacelle, one pulling and one pushing.

Atlantic Nonstop

The Atlantic had been conquered in stages, but the *Daily Mail* prize still had to be won. It was about to be settled, and in a way that would help to counter C.G. Grey's criticism of his countrymen. Of all the hopefuls lining up to tackle the ocean, only two crews managed to mount a serious challenge. First away were Harry Hawker, Sopwith's Australian test pilot, and his navigator, Lieutenant Commander Kenneth Mackenzie-Grieve. They had been champing at the bit since mid-April, but had been held back by atrocious weather. Two days after the U.S. Navy's NCs set off, Hawker could wait no longer. The weather was still not encouraging, but his patience was at an end and he thought it would be worth trying to beat the American flying boats to the British Isles. His aircraft was the Sopwith Atlantic, a development of the company's B.1 bomber, powered by a 350-horsepower Rolls-Royce Eagle. The varnished top-decking of the aircraft behind the cockpit disguised a detachable dinghy, built in to provide some insurance against the ultimate emergency.

On the afternoon of May 18, Hawker dragged the heavy Sopwith into the air from Glendennings Farm near St. Johns, Newfoundland, using almost every inch of the 400 yards available. After takeoff, he jettisoned the undercarriage, a ploy that added some 7 mph to his cruising speed. Soon the Sopwith was wrapped in heavy cloud, lashed by rain and buffeted by turbulence. Hawker climbed to 15,000 feet, but was still in cloud. Five and a half hours out, Hawker was alarmed to see the coolant temperature rising to a dangerously high level. He reduced power and dived to increase the rush of cooling air through the radiator. The maneuver gave only temporary respite. Within an hour the temperature was back up to 175 degrees Fahrenheit. With the coming of daylight, the engine began missing, and then stopped altogether. Hawker managed to get it started again with the Sopwith just above the waves. Accepting the inevitable, he turned south for the shipping lanes. It was two and a half anxious hours later before the little Danish steamer *Mary* was sighted. Hawker ditched the Sopwith close by and then helped Mackenzie-Grieve to launch the dinghy so thoughtfully built into the fuselage. The surging seas made rescue difficult and so it was over an hour before they were safely on board. Once there, they found that the *Mary* had no radio. As far as the rest of the world was concerned, they had disappeared without trace.

Assumptions of disaster seemed justified when the wreckage of the Sopwith, complete with a bag of mail containing a letter from the Governor of Newfoundland to King George V, was recovered by an American ship, the *Lake Charlotteville*, on May 23. The next day, the King sent letters of condolence to the crew's relatives. It was May 25 before the *Mary* was off the coast of Scotland and able to signal details of the rescue to the Butt of Lewis coastguard. Public reaction to the news was ecstatic. Hawker and Mackenzie-Grieve were received with all the honor and rejoicing that the British perversely reserve for sensational failure, especially when its pain is relieved by miraculous survival. Massive crowds welcomed them to London, the King awarded each of them the Air Force Cross, and the *Daily Mail* presented a consolation prize of £5,000. Back in Newfoundland, John Alcock, the pilot of the waiting Vickers Vimy, muttered: "Their hands are so blistered from clapping Harry Hawker that we'll be lucky to get even a languid hand."

Captain John Alcock was only twenty-six, but he was a seasoned airman. He learned to fly in 1912 by placing his hands over those of his instructor and following their movements. After two hours of this he was deemed ready and was sent solo in a Farman Longhorn; within a week he had won his first air race. Two years later, he had accumulated an impressive number of flying hours, and when war broke out, he joined the RNAS. He first was retained as an instructor, but later operated in the eastern Mediterranean, where he flew against the Turks, destroying seven of the enemy to earn the Distinguished Service Cross before being shot down himself and taken prisoner. During his captivity, he often spoke about his intention to fly across the Atlantic, and upon his release he presented himself at the Vickers factory to talk about doing just that. His experience and his enthusiasm were suitably impressive, and he was hired for the Atlantic attempt.

A few weeks later, Arthur Whitten "Teddy" Brown turned up at Vickers looking for a job. Born in Scotland of American

> *"Since flight is not a natural function of man; since it has been won by centuries of effort; since it has been climbed to arduously, not simply stumbled upon; since it has been slowly built, not suddenly discovered, it cannot be suspended as the word 'freedom' is suspended in the mind. It rests, firmly supported, on a structure of laws, rules, principles — laws to which plane and man alike must conform. Rules of construction, of performance, of equipment, for one; rules of training, health, experience, skill, and judgement, for the other."*
>
> ANNE MORROW LINDBERGH

parents, he was six years older than Alcock. He had served with the RFC as a B.E.2c observer on the Western Front and he, too, had been shot down behind enemy lines, suffering a serious leg injury that had left him lame. While a prisoner, he had mastered the art of navigation with the aid of books from the Red Cross, and had given a lot of thought to the problem of navigating an aircraft across the Atlantic. He and Alcock discovered their shared ambition and teamed up. By May 13, 1919, they were in Newfoundland to prepare for their Atlantic flight. At this stage, because of their late arrival, they and their Vickers Vimy were the outsiders. The departure of the USN flying boats did not concern them, since the NCs were not crossing nonstop, but Hawker's Sopwith was ready to go, as was a Martinsyde aircraft flown by Freddie Raynham and navigated by Fairfax Morgan, who claimed to be a descendant of Henry Morgan, the notorious pirate. Not far behind was a Handley Page team busily putting together the largest entry, a massive V/1500 bomber powered by four Rolls-Royce Eagle engines. Alcock and Brown were impatient spectators as first Raynham crashed on takeoff and then Hawker disappeared in mid-Atlantic. The V/1500 had problems and did not seem to be in a hurry to leave.

The Vickers Vimy, like its huge rival, was a converted bomber, but was only half its size. Its wingspan was 67 feet and it was pulled along by two Rolls-Royce Eagles fitted with four-bladed propellers. Armament and bomb-racks had been removed to allow for extra fuel tanks, bringing the capacity up to 865 imperial gallons, enough for 2,440 miles. Facilities in Newfoundland were primitive, and the Vimy had to be reconstructed in the open, inadequately protected from the often unfriendly weather by a few canvas screens. While the aircraft was being assembled, Alcock searched for a takeoff field. Eventually, a meadow owned by a Mr. Lester was decided on. Barely 400 yards long, it was cleared of rocks and trees by enthusiastic helpers.

A Newfoundland working song encouraged their efforts: "Oh! Lay hold Jackie Alcock, lay hold Teddy Brown, lay hold of the cordage and dig in the groun'. Lay hold of the bowline and pull all you can, the Vimy will fly 'fore the Handley Page can."

By June 8, Lester's Field was clear, but the weather was not. Gales and rain frustrated the waiting airmen until June 13, and then, when it seemed that they might get off at last, a shock absorber broke as the Vimy was being fueled. Mechanics worked all night on the problem and, on June 14, 1919, everything was ready. Alcock and Brown were at the field before dawn, getting weather forecasts, loading navigation instruments and provisions, and accepting bags of special mail. The fuel had been strained through chamois leather, and the radiator water boiled and filtered to ensure against the sort of failure that, it was thought, had defeated Hawker. To make doubly sure, Alcock and Brown carried their lucky mascots, two stuffed toy cats, Lucky Jim and Twinkletoes. After eating lunch under the Vimy's wing, they climbed into the cockpit and started the engines.

The Vimy was positioned as near the end of the field as possible, and Alcock had arranged for men to stand in front of the wing, holding the aircraft back as he opened up to full power. One of these improvised brakes later recalled that at Alcock's signal "we all sat down on the ground and the plane shot forward." The Vimy lumbered into the air at 16:13 GMT. For a few moments, the anxious onlookers held their breaths as Alcock kept the nose down to gain airspeed and the aircraft sank out of sight into a valley. All was well, however, and the Vimy crossed the coast at 1,200 feet, heading out over the open sea.

As they settled on a heading for Ireland, the wind-driven generator supplying power to the radio failed. Soon after that, Brown's electrically heated jacket failed, too, and the starboard engine's exhaust manifold broke away, the resulting uninhibited roar making cockpit conversation impossible. Once the coast was left behind, Brown took his

On display in the History of Flight gallery at London's Science Museum is the Vickers Vimy in which John Alcock and Arthur Whitten-Brown made the first nonstop crossing of the Atlantic in June 1919. The fabric on the left side of the fuselage has been removed to reveal the additional fuel tanks fitted for the 16-hour transatlantic flight from Newfoundland to Northern Ireland.

The Vickers Vimy's blunt nose and its forest of struts and wires did not help its aerodynamics. The two 350-horsepower Rolls-Royce Eagle engines had to work hard to pull the converted bomber along at a cruising speed of 90 mph.

first sextant shots and measured the Vimy's drift, but it was not long before they were sandwiched between banks of cloud and sea fog and further observations became impossible. They had been flying for eight hours when Alcock broke through the clouds and gave Brown a chance to fix their position. He calculated that they were close to their intended track and had covered 850 miles at a healthy ground speed of 106 mph. He later described that period of the flight: "An aura of unreality seemed to surround us as we flew onward towards the dawn and Ireland. The distorted ball of the Moon, the weird half-light, the monstrous cloud shapes, the fog, the misty indefiniteness of space, the changeless drone, drone, drone of the motors."

The first light of dawn came accompanied by solid walls of cloud across their path. With no alternative, Alcock plowed into the murk. The Vimy was thrown about by severe turbulence, while ice formed on the wings and blocked the pitot tube, rendering the airspeed indicator and altimeter useless. The art of instrument flying was still in its infancy and airmen still believed in the notion that it was

possible to "fly by the seat of your pants," but, deprived of the basic blind flying instruments, Alcock soon became disorientated. As he remembered it: "We lost our instinct of balance. The machine, left to its own devices, swung, flew amok, and began to perform circus tricks." In fact, the Vimy probably stalled before entering a spiral dive, losing height rapidly and breaking clear of the low cloud-base frighteningly close to the sea in a steeply banked descending turn. Given visual reference points, Alcock recovered to level flight and brought the aircraft back onto an easterly heading. Brown's impression was that he could almost have reached out and touched the wave tops.

That scare behind them, Alcock and Brown still had battles to fight. The weather became even worse. There were few breaks in the cloud and Brown got little opportunity to use his sextant. Climbing to find clear air, Alcock often had to move the controls briskly to break loose the ice that threatened to jam the ailerons. The fuel-flow gages outside the cockpit iced over and several times Brown had to stand up in the teeth of the biting gale to scratch them clear. Struggling up to 11,000 feet, they at last saw the sun, and Brown was able to estimate that they were only 80 miles from land. Ice then built up in the engine intakes, and the starboard engine lost power. They had to descend again into warmer air, going down to 500 feet before the engine regained its ear-shattering roar. Less than half an hour later, the ordeal was almost over. They sighted the small islands of Eashal and Turbot off the coast of Galway, and soon after saw the masts of the Clifden radio station. Still faced by appalling weather and exhausted by over sixteen hours in the air, Alcock decided to land, although there was enough fuel left in the tanks to take them to London. He selected what appeared to be a smooth, grassy field and settled the Vimy onto its surface, only to find that he had chosen an Irish bog. The wheels sank into the morass and the aircraft came rapidly to rest, its nose buried deep in the soft mud. With its tail in the air and its nose pressed to the earth, the Vimy seemed to be kissing the ground in gratitude for its safe arrival on the eastern side of the great ocean. Its Rolls-Royce Eagles had kept them in the air for 16 hours, 28 minutes (15 hours, 57 minutes coast to coast), hauling the angular airframe along for 1,890 miles at an average of 118 mph.

Alcock and Brown had carved their names into aviation history as the first to fly the Atlantic nonstop. The hands that welcomed them were anything but "languid." Crowds cheered them at every railway station on their way to London, and their drive to a Royal Aero Club lunch in their honor became a triumphal procession. Winston Churchill, then Secretary of State for War and Air, was there to present them with their cheque from the *Daily Mail*, and the next day they were knighted by King George V. Wrapped in the nation's adulation, the airmen did not forget those who made their flight possible: £2,000 of the prize money was set aside to be shared out among the ground crew.

John Alcock (left) and Arthur Whitten-Brown (right) in uniform after their epic flight across the Atlantic. Both were knighted for their exploit by King George V. Alcock did not enjoy his fame for long. He was killed on December 18, 1919, when his Viking amphibian crashed in France during an attempted forced landing in fog. The car is a 10-horsepower Humber, and the man in the middle is Leonard Davies of the Humber Car Company.

It seemed that Alcock and Brown had assured their futures in aviation, but the fates decided otherwise. Six months later, Sir John Alcock was killed in a flying accident. Sir Arthur Whitten Brown must have felt that the demands of the Atlantic crossing had been enough to last a lifetime. Although he lived for another quarter of a century, he never flew again.

A Ship of the Air

Less than three weeks after the Vimy arrived in Ireland, crossing the Atlantic by air was rendered almost commonplace. Between July 2 and 6, the British airship R 34 flew sedately from East Fortune in Scotland to Mineola, Long Island, with thirty-one people on board. By any standards, the R 34 was a colossal machine, nearly 650 feet long with a capacity of two million cubic feet of hydrogen. Powered by five Sunbeam Maori engines of just 250 horsepower each, this immense creation was not very swift. Its top speed was only 65 mph, and on its into-wind east-to-west crossing it averaged little more than 30 mph, taking a tedious 108 hours for the flight. Compared to Alcock and Brown, however, the passengers traveled in comfort, and enjoyed the luxury of the first in-flight entertainment system — jazz music played on a gramophone. They also had the thrill of discovering two stowaways en route; the first was William Ballantyne, one of the airship's regular maintenance men, and the second was a kitten smuggled aboard for luck by one of the crew. The wind-assisted return flight, made between July 9 and 13 from Mineola to Pulham in England, took a relatively rapid 75 hours. Again, the R 34 carried thirty-one people, but three of those on the outbound trip had been replaced by new faces, leaving twenty-eight who could claim to have completed the double crossing.

By the end of 1919, aircraft had made the Atlantic Ocean look much less formidable as a barrier. Forty-two people had crossed the Atlantic by air and, while transoceanic air travel was still a hazardous undertaking, it could be foreseen that it would become a feasible proposition in the not too far distant future. Blériot's flight across the Channel had shocked the British into realizing that their country was no longer surrounded by an unbridgeable moat. Now it seemed that even the great divide between the New World and the Old was beginning to assume less forbidding proportions.

Slowly Southward

After the excitement of 1919, a three-year lull settled over the Atlantic. The focus then shifted to the south. In 1922, the Portuguese set about linking themselves by air with Brazil via the island chain across the South Atlantic. The route chosen was Lisbon to Canary Islands to Cape Verde Island, and St. Paul's Rocks to Fernando Noronha to Recife to Rio de Janeiro. Modified Fairey IIID floatplanes were used in what became an undertaking of epic scale. At the first attempt, with Commander Sacadura Cabral as the pilot and Rear Admiral Gago Coutinho navigating, the flight ended at St. Paul's Rocks, where the aircraft damaged a float on alighting and had to be abandoned. It had, nevertheless, been an extraordinary achievement. The leg from Cape Verde Island to St. Paul's Rocks consisted of nearly 1,000 miles over the sea. In an open cockpit with no radio, the admiral hit a target only 650 feet across and a few feet high after eleven hours out of sight of land. There was less than a gallon of fuel left at touchdown. A second Fairey IIID was prepared and sent out by ship, only to suffer engine failure soon after getting airborne. It duly joined its sister in the depths. With laudable determination, a third Fairey IIID (and the last in Portugal) was shipped to the crew, and this time they were successful. The saga of the first South Atlantic crossing, accomplished in stages, lasted for eighty days. Portugal and Brazil had been linked by air, and the world of aviation applauded Cabral and Coutinho for their remarkable persistence.

Across Two Oceans

In 1924, four more names were added to the list of Atlantic fliers. Once the Atlantic was conquered, airmen began to think of flying round the world. In the United States, the effort was led with professional thoroughness by the Army Air Service. Preparation included shipping spare parts and tools to various points along the route, getting clearances from the foreign governments involved, positioning rescue ships, and dispatching officers to collect local information and arrange for supplies. The machines selected were designed by Donald Douglas, based on his rugged Liberty-engined DT-2 Navy floatplane. Five were ordered, four to make the flight plus one spare. The Douglas World Cruiser (DWC) was a big, two-seat, open-cockpit biplane with a fuel capacity of 450 gallons, enough for over 1,000 miles in

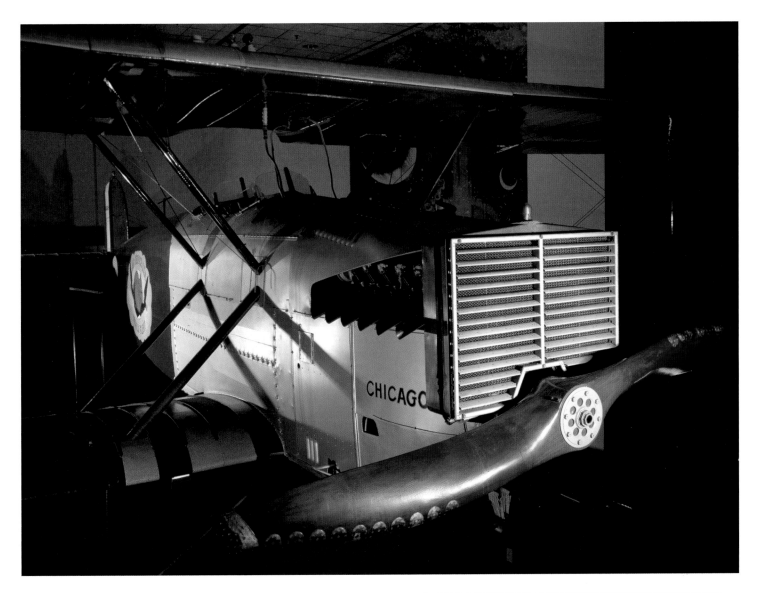

In 1924, one of the great milestones in aviation history was passed when the U.S. Army's aviators became the first to fly round the world. Four Douglas World Cruisers set off west from Seattle on April 6 and two of them (Chicago and New Orleans) returned to close the global circle on September 28 after conducting a meticulously planned and executed flight. One (Seattle) crashed in Alaska, and a second (Boston) was lost in the Atlantic. (That crew, Wade and Ogden, resumed the flight in Boston II after crossing the Atlantic by ship.) On display at the National Air & Space Museum, Washington, D.C., Chicago is a tribute to the sturdiness of Douglas construction. Strength and reliability were more important on this flight than high speed and long range. In six months of flying, the World Cruisers were airborne for more than 360 hours in covering over 26,000 miles. They averaged 72 mph and landed at seventy-five destinations on the way. RIGHT Chicago's pilot, Lowell Smith, is welcomed back to the east coast of the United States.

For the long, overwater legs of the round-the-world flight, the Douglas World Cruisers could exchange their wheels for floats. Here Chicago *shows off her oceangoing gear.*

still air. Since the DWC's cruising speed was not much more than 80 mph, it was clear that the Army was prepared to take its time over the venture.

Led by Major Frederick Martin, the formation of four DWCs (*Seattle, Chicago, Boston* and *New Orleans*) left Seattle on April 6, 1924, and headed for Alaska. There they suffered a grievous blow when *Seattle* crashed into a fog-obscured mountain on the long Alaskan Peninsula. Martin and his mechanic survived, and the flight continued with three aircraft, now led by Lieutenant Lowell Smith, a pioneer of aerial refueling. The route took them from Alaska via the Aleutian chain to Japan, China, India, Iraq and Turkey, and across Europe to the U.K. After refitting for the Atlantic crossing, Lieutenant Leigh Wade's *Boston* was lost when the engine failed on the way to Iceland. Rescued by the USS *Richmond*, Wade and his mechanic were able to rejoin the flight in Newfoundland, where the spare DWC, now named *Boston II*, was waiting. However, that meant that only the crews of *Chicago* and *New Orleans* completed the first east-to-west heavier-than-air staged crossing of the Atlantic. Lieutenants Lowell Smith and Erik Nelson succeeded in closing the global circle on September 28, 1924, arriving back at Seattle 175 days and over 360 flying hours after they began. The 27,553 miles had been covered at an average speed of 74 mph. Meticulous preparation combined with the professionalism and determination of the crews had brought the U.S. Army Air Service the honor of recording the first round-the-world flight.

Thirty-Eight More

Zeppelin LZ 126 carried thirty-one people, including its captain, Hugo Eckener, from Friedrichshafen, Germany, to Lakehurst, New Jersey, in October 1924. Delivered to the

U.S. military, LZ 126 became the *Los Angeles* and remained in service until 1939. Two more southern crossings were completed in 1926, and the international flavor of oceanic aviation was intensified with airmen from Brazil (Ribeiro de Barros, Negrâo, Braga, and Cinquini in a Savoia Marchetti S.55) and Spain (Ramon Franco, de Alda and Rada in a Dornier Wal). Ramon was the brother of Francisco, later General Franco, the Spanish dictator. By the beginning of 1927, eighty-six people had crossed the Atlantic by air, including sixty-five in three airship flights. So far, the heavier-than-air attempts had been few and far between, and the aircraft used were pushed to the edge of their capabilities. In the year that followed, as aircraft of greater potential were conceived and long-distance air travel became more feasible, more pilots began to believe that they could join the transatlantic club, and more passengers trusted them to make the trip.

The Orteig Prize

In 1919, Raymond Orteig, a French-born hotel owner in New York, sent a letter to the Aero Club of America announcing his intention to award a prize of $25,000 "to the first aviator of any Allied country crossing the Atlantic in one flight, from Paris to New York or New York to Paris." The required distance was twice that between the coasts of Newfoundland and Ireland, and particular points of departure and arrival were specified. By 1926, aircraft and cockpit instruments had improved sufficiently to generate interest in the challenge, and a number of airmen began making plans to relieve Orteig of his money. In September of that year the competition opened when the Sikorsky S.35 trimotor was wheeled out of its hangar at Roosevelt Field, New York. Its crew of four was led by the famous French ace, René Fonck, and flight tests suggested that it was an excellent aircraft. Lightly loaded for its intended role as an airliner, the S.35 flew very well. Fueled with the 2,380 gallons needed to cross the Atlantic, it was 10,000 pounds above its designed weight. Fonck, delighted with the aircraft's handling and keen to be off, elected not to fly overweight tests scheduled by Sikorsky. On September 20, Fonck took his crew (Curtin, Clavier, Islamov) aboard and began a takeoff run on Roosevelt Field's mile long runway. The heavily laden aircraft never got airborne. It struck a gully at the edge of the airfield and burst into flame. Fonck and Curtin scrambled clear, but Clavier and Islamov were burned to death. They were the first to die for daring to challenge the Atlantic by air, but they would not be the last. Another French tragedy followed in May 1927, when a Farman Goliath set out over the South Atlantic from Senegal. Neither the Goliath nor its crew of three (Saint-Roman, Mouneyres, Petit) were ever seen again.

In the early months of 1927, two more crews, one Italian (de Pinedo, del Prete, Zacchetti) and one Portuguese (de Bieres and Castilho), crossed the South Atlantic in stages. The Italians, flying Savoia Marchetti S.55 *Santa Maria*, achieved far more than a South Atlantic crossing. Starting from Rome, they circled the Atlantic via Morocco, Senegal, Brazil, the West Indies, Cuba, Louisiana, Texas, New York, Chicago, Newfoundland, the Azores, Portugal, and back to Rome. In Texas, the *Santa Maria* was burned out and replaced by *Santa Maria II*. To reach the Azores the crew endured being towed for three days after running out of fuel 180 miles from the islands. The epic journey covered 25,300 miles and took over four months. The Portuguese crew originally numbered four, but because of takeoff difficulties with a full load, the copilot (Dovalle Portugal) and the mechanic (Manuel Gouveia) were left behind in Portuguese Guinea. This brought the number of successful transatlantic fliers to ninety-one — not counting the cat.

L'Oiseau Blanc — the Levasseur PL-8 flown by Charles Nungesser and Francis Coli in their attempt to fly the Atlantic from east to west. They left Le Bourget, near Paris, on May 8, 1927, with 40 hours of fuel and confident of success, and there were reports of their aircraft having passed overhead as far away as Newfoundland and Maine, but they were never seen again.

The growing total cloaked the fact that there had not been a nonstop crossing by a heavier-than-air machine since 1919. However, several of those with their eyes on the Orteig Prize appeared to have the aircraft and the ability to follow Alcock and Brown. With Fonck eliminated, there were five principal contenders. This was reduced to three during two disastrous weeks in the spring of 1927. On April 26, Noel Davis and Stanton Wooster were killed when their overweight Keystone Pathfinder crashed on takeoff from Langley Field, Virginia. Two weeks later, the French crew of Charles Nungesser and Francois Coli attempted the first nonstop east-to-west crossing of the North Atlantic in their Levasseur PL-8 *L'Oiseau Blanc*. Their ill-fated flight is one of the Atlantic's most intriguing mysteries. After taking off from Le Bourget, near Paris, and jettisoning the under-carriage to improve the Levasseur's performance, they were seen crossing the French coast. Then there was news of them over Ireland. Later still, there were reports of them being sighted over Newfoundland and Boston, and enthusi-astic French newspapers came out with headlines reading "Nungesser est arrive." Sadly, they were wrong. The truth was that Nungesser and Coli had disappeared. No reliable trace of *L'Oiseau Blanc* was ever found.

Most observers now believed that the race for the Orteig Prize lay between two of the three remaining aircraft and crew combinations. Either of those two had the capacity to succeed, and one of them gave ample proof of that over Long Island in April. Clarence Chamberlin and Bert Acosta kept the Bellanca W.B.2 *Columbia* flying in circles for more than 51 hours to establish a new world's unrefueled endurance record. It was the equivalent of 4,080 miles in a straight line and more than enough to capture the Orteig Prize. The other

team was led by Commander Richard Byrd, USN. Only months before, he had flown a Fokker F.VIIa-3m during a series of polar flights and claimed to have been the first to fly over the North Pole. Impressed by the Fokker's performance, Byrd recommended a similar aircraft for the transatlantic flight, and the result was the Fokker F.VIIb-3m *America*. Byrd and his sponsors insisted that they were not influenced by the Orteig Prize. Their flight, they said, aimed to gather informa-tion about the problems to be overcome in establishing future commercial transatlantic services. That statement notwithstanding, their active preparations made them com-petitors in the eyes of everyone else.

Ninety-Second and Still First

The third remaining contestant actively preparing a transatlantic bid was a comparatively unknown young man named Charles Lindbergh who proposed to take on the daunting challenge solo. He had made his way in aviation as a barnstormer and air mail pilot and was no beginner, but his Ryan aircraft was an unknown quantity and his chal-lenge seemed little short of foolhardy. Ryan Airlines occu-pied part of a San Diego fish cannery and was no better known than was Lindbergh. Nevertheless, Claude Ryan's company had built a modified version of their M-2 mail plane to Lindbergh's specifications in just sixty days. In acknowledgment of his backers, it was named *Spirit of St. Louis*. It was very much Lindbergh's aircraft. He had kept a close eye on its construction, insisting on perfection at every stage and saving weight by eliminating any item he considered less than essential. He had no radio, which saved 90 pounds, and the instrument panel was as basic as it could be, without such luxuries as fuel gauges. Having care-

LEFT *Charles Lindbergh's Ryan NYP, on display at the National Air & Space Museum, Washington, D.C., was based on a standard Ryan M-2. The wingspan was increased by 10 feet (to 46 feet) and certain structural features were redesigned to take account of the greater fuel load. The fuselage was lengthened by 2 feet and the enlarged fuel tank installed at the center of gravity. The cockpit was moved to the rear, behind the fuel tank, and the engine moved forward for balance.*

BELOW *Those companies that supported Lindbergh's transatlantic flight were happy to use their association in advertising. Standard Oil's Red Crown Aviation Gasoline got a huge boost, and Mobiloil promotions carried the following message from Captain Lindbergh: "In my flight from New York to Paris my engine was lubricated with Gargoyle Mobiloil B and I am happy to say it gave me every satisfaction. My engine functioned perfectly." Note that the aircraft is being refueled by can and funnel. To the right of the tall figure of Lindbergh is Donald Hall, Ryan's chief engineer.*

fully observed the performance of the Ryan's single Wright Whirlwind radial, he thought he could calculate the fuel used by knowing the engine rpm and keeping track of time in the air. Lindbergh even dispensed with a parachute (a piece of equipment that Lindbergh had already had to use on four occasions) and kept his rations to a bare minimum, just five sandwiches and a canteen of water being thought sufficient to sustain him for what was likely to be a flight lasting a day and a half. The weight saved was converted into fuel, 2,500 pounds of which was squeezed into an aircraft totaling little more than 5,000 pounds fully loaded. Most was in a huge tank placed between the engine and the cockpit, filling the fuselage from top to bottom and denying the pilot the benefit of any forward view.

If anyone doubted Lindbergh's serious intent, that doubt was dispelled on the afternoon of May 12, 1927, when the *Spirit of St. Louis* landed at Curtiss Field, Long Island, having flown from San Diego with one stop at St. Louis to show the Ryan to his backers. The newspapers greeted his arrival with a mixture of skepticism and astonishment, one labeling him the "Flyin' Fool." Lindbergh avoided them as much as possible and made final preparations for the flight. On the way to Long Island he had discovered that the Whirlwind engine was susceptible to carburetor icing, so he had a heater installed. An earth inductor compass was added to provide accurate headings. Worries about the limitations of Curtiss Field were overcome by a generous gesture from Richard Byrd, who offered the use of the long runway at Roosevelt Field. The ever-present problem of the weather remained. Lindbergh checked with meteorologist James Kimball twice a day for a week before getting a favorable forecast. On the evening of May 19, Kimball reported that high pressure over the Atlantic promised clear skies for most of the route.

Lindbergh retired to his hotel for a few hours sleepless rest, but was back with his aircraft before sunrise to see it towed through drizzling rain to Roosevelt Field, where the fuel tanks were filled to capacity for the first time. The heavy load and the soft, wet ground caused some anxiety, but Lindbergh did not show his concern. At 7:40 A.M. he started the engine and got ready to go. Recalling the moment, he later wrote: "I glance down at the wheels. They press deeply, tires bulging, into the wet, sandy clay. There is in my plane this morning more of earth and less of air than I've ever felt before."

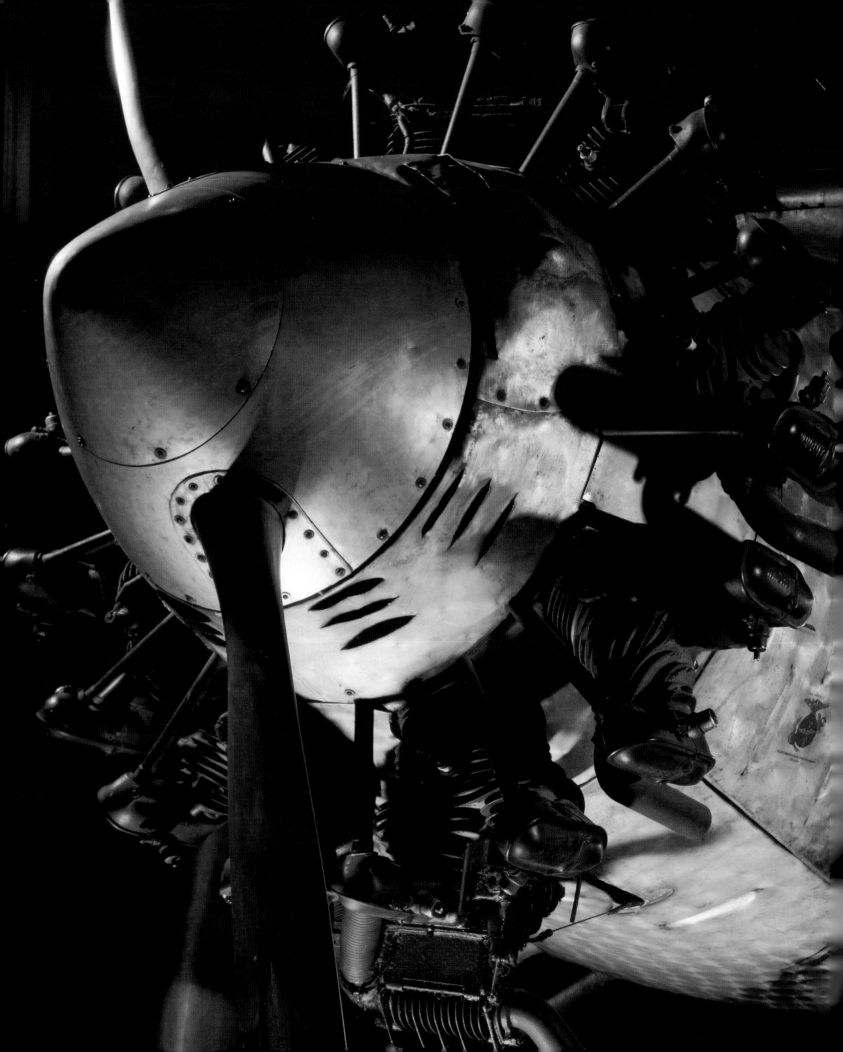

In the Spirit of St. Louis, *the engine and the 450-gallon fuel tank filled the front half of the fuselage, leaving no room for a windscreen. The pilot could see directly forward only through a periscope. A Wright Whirlwind J-5C engine supplied the power.*

Designed by Charles L. Lawrance, the Whirlwind was the most reliable aircraft engine of its time. In 1927, the year that Lindbergh crossed the Atlantic, the Collier Trophy, America's most prestigious aviation award, went not to the pilot but to Lawrance as the engine designer who made it possible. The nine-cylinder J-5C Whirlwind was simple and easily maintained, and developed 220 horsepower for a weight of only 510 pounds. It was the engine of choice for most of the trail-blazing aviators of the late 1920s.

The aircraft registration number for the Spirit of St. Louis, *N-X-211, appears at the top of the fin. Below it, on the rudder, is the manufacturer's designation — Ryan NYP, chosen as an acronym for New York to Paris.*

The cockpit of the Spirit of St. Louis *was notably Spartan. Lindbergh did not want to carry an ounce of weight that was not absolutely essential, so cosmetic refinements such as paneling were not fitted. There was no parachute, no radio — not even a fuel gauge on the instrument panel. The weight saved by dispensing with such "luxuries" was converted into fuel for a flight expected to last a day and a half.*

*In the absence of a fuel gauge, Lindbergh intended to calculate the fuel remaining by knowing the rate at which the Whirlwind consumed fuel and keeping a record of hours flown. The rough pencil marks he made on the plywood instrument panel as the hours passed are still there (*UPPER LEFT*), as is the lightweight wicker chair he sat in while he fought off the urge to sleep (*UPPER RIGHT*).* OPPOSITE *As each hour passed, he turned the valves in the piping below the instrument panel to select a different fuel tank. The periscope was viewed through the hole at the upper left of the panel. The lever that moved the periscope into position is to the left of the hole, and the periscope itself can just be seen outside the window.* LEFT *At the National Air & Space Museum: Seen from the front, the fuselage of the Spirit of St. Louis is hidden by the Wright Whirlwind engine. To either side are the legs of the landing gear, modified to a much wider track than the standard Ryan M-2 on which the NYP design was based.*

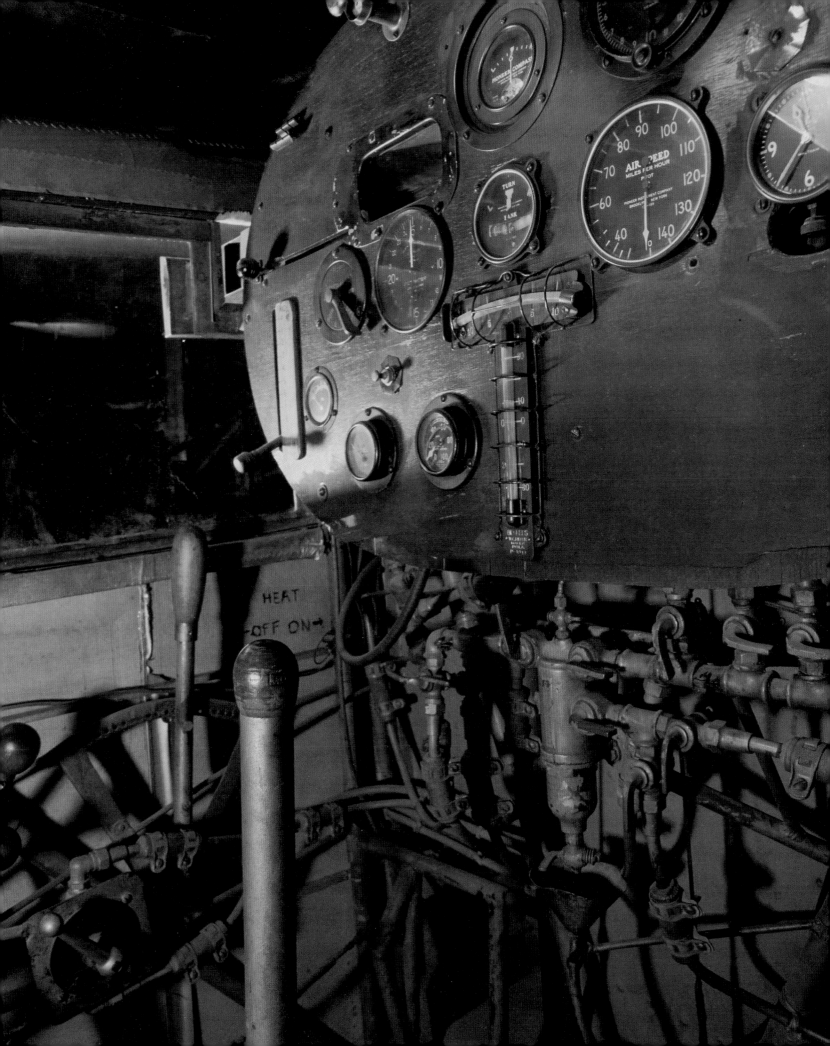

ABOVE *Often overlooked by visitors to the Musée de l'Air et de l'Espace at Le Bourget is a statue commemorating Lindbergh's landing there on May 21, 1927.*

TOP LEFT *Looking toward Paris, these hangars on the far side of the Le Bourget airport were built in the early years of aviation history. Thousands of spectators filled this space with anticipation, looking toward Paris the evening that Lindbergh was approaching. Le Bourget was used by the Germans in WWII and these same buildings were used by the occupiers to service Luftwaffe aircraft.*

LEFT *A smiling Lindbergh stands in front of the* Spirit of St. Louis *and draws attention to a Keep Out notice modified to add "of the water."*

At 7:52 A.M. on May 20, 1927, the *Spirit of St. Louis* began to move. Agonizingly slowly, it gathered speed. The tail was up at the halfway point and the aircraft hopped once or twice before lifting to clear the telephone wires at the edge of the airfield by 20 feet. Lindbergh coaxed the *Spirit of St. Louis* up to cruising speed, throttled back to 1,750 rpm, and settled down to the monotony of flying in long straight lines while sitting still behind the unchanging

The Spirit of St. Louis *in Dayton, Ohio, clean and unadorned by the flags and insignia of the countries and military organizations later visited by Lindbergh.*
LEFT *Orville Wright, accompanied by an Army Air Corps officer, came to meet Lindbergh at McCook Field on June 22, 1927.*

roar of a radial engine. In the hours that followed, his principal enemy was not the weather, it was his own body. By mid-Atlantic, he had hardly slept for two days, and the need to close his eyes was almost irresistible: "Every cell of my being is on strike, sulking in protest, claiming that nothing, nothing in the world could be worth such effort; that man's tissue was never made for such abuse. My back is stiff; my shoulders ache; my face burns; my eyes smart. It seems impossible to go on longer." Overcome by fatigue, he stopped keeping his log and became confused over when to make the heading changes needed to keep him on his great circle track. "For the first time in my life," he wrote, "I doubt my ability to endure."

At last, after more than twenty-four hours, Lindbergh saw fishing boats. Seeking assurance, he flew low and circled them, calling out fruitlessly for directions to Ireland. Soon after leaving them, he was revived by the sight of land. It was Dingle Bay, and, despite his dozing, he was only 3 miles off his intended track. He pressed on over southwest England and reached Cherbourg at dusk. As darkness fell, he picked up the gleam of airway beacons and followed them to Paris. Shortly after 10 P.M., the *Spirit of St. Louis* circled the Eiffel Tower before heading northeast to look for Le Bourget airfield. It was not immediately obvious. Lindbergh finally decided that it must be a large dark area

Only two weeks after Charles Lindbergh landed at Le Bourget, Clarence Chamberlin and passenger Charles Levine flew a Bellanca Skyrocket from New York to Eisleben, just 40 miles from Berlin. This was the aircraft favored by Lindbergh before he approached Ryan. At the Virginia Aviation Museum, Richmond, is an aircraft that was originally a Bellanca CH-300 Pacemaker, powered by a 300-horsepower Wright J-6 radial. After it was salvaged from an Alaskan glacier in 1962, it was restored with a 450 Pratt & Whitney and painted to represent the Bellanca CH-400 Skyrocket Columbia of Chamberlin and Levine. The Columbia featured standard Bellanca traits — airfoil-shaped struts and a contoured fuselage, which added extra lift and allowed a higher payload.

ringed by car headlights. Now, exhausted and with no forward vision, all he had to do was to put his aircraft down safely on an unfamiliar airfield in the dark. "Back on the throttle. Bank round for a final glide. The wheels touch gently. The tailskid, too. Not a bad landing. I start to taxi toward the hangars, but the entire field ahead is covered with running figures!"

It had occurred to Lindbergh that the world might be watching his progress, but he was astonished by the exuberance of the welcome he was given by the French. The waiting crowd flattened a steel fence and surged forward. He was pulled from his cockpit and passed from hand to hand over the heads of the mob. Souvenir hunters began ripping fabric from his aircraft. When an American newspaper correspondent was mistaken for him after appropriating his flying helmet, Lindbergh was smuggled to the safety of a hangar and then taken to the American Embassy where he borrowed a pair of pyjamas from the ambassador and fell asleep for the first time in more than two and a half days. He had achieved what few had thought possible, a solo flight from New York to Paris — 3,610 miles in thirty-three and a half hours.

Orteig Also-Rans and Others

Clarence Chamberlin must have found Lindbergh's success hard to take. The Bellanca *Columbia* he planned to fly to Paris with Bert Acosta was ready at the beginning of May. However, the aircraft's owner, Charles Levine, could be difficult to deal with, as first Acosta and then his nominated replacement, Lloyd Bertaud, discovered. Each in turn was summarily removed from the crew by Levine. Acosta went off to join Richard Byrd's team, but Bertaud was so upset that he obtained a court injunction that, for a while, barred the Bellanca from leaving without him. The argument raged on and *Columbia* sat in her hangar while Lindbergh arrived from San Diego, made his preparations and left for Paris. Thus denied his chance of the Orteig Prize by petty argument, Levine had no intention of giving up. The injunction removed, Chamberlin supervised the preparation of the Bellanca early on the morning of June 4. Up to the last minute, it seemed that he would be making another solo flight with the aim of surpassing Lindbergh's distance record. He climbed in and started the engine. Levine, dressed in a business suit and a leather jacket, walked up to the aircraft, apparently to say farewell. Instead, he climbed

aboard and told Chamberlin to take off. Shortly after 6 A.M. on June 4, 1927, *Columbia* set course for Europe, carrying Charles Levine as the first transatlantic heavier-than-air aircraft passenger. Nearly forty-three hours later, Chamberlin touched down in a field near Eisleben, about 100 miles southwest of Berlin. In her wanderings, *Columbia* had covered more than 3,911 miles, which was the officially recognized distance between takeoff and landing. Chamberlin found some consolation for following Lindbergh in holding the record for the greatest distance flown nonstop between two points on the Earth's surface. It was cold comfort, however, for that record would soon be claimed by others and Chamberlin's achievement would slip into obscurity, while Lindbergh's solo flight would be forever remembered.

Richard Byrd's preparations went on until June 29, 1927. He and his crew (pilots Bert Acosta and Bernt Balchen, and radio operator George Noville) then took off from Roosevelt Field in the Fokker C-2 *America* and set off for Paris. The contrast with Lindbergh's effort could hardly have been greater. The multiengined *America* weighed some 15,000 pounds, carried a crew of four, and was lavishly equipped with navigation aids, long-range wireless, survival gear and emergency rations. There were problems, however. When they ran into cloud over the Atlantic, Acosta's limitations as a pilot were revealed. He had no instrument flying experience and became disorientated. Balchen had to take over and from then on was the pilot in control whenever instrument flight was necessary. The luxuries of radio and navigation aids notwithstanding, when they sighted land it was not Ireland. They were some 250 miles south of their intended track near Brest on the French coast. Pressing on into bad weather, they passed over Paris in darkness and were heard at Le Bourget, but they could not see the ground. Frustrated, Byrd turned back to the coast and clearer skies. With the fuel supply dwindling and no airfield in sight, the *America* was ditched close to the shore by the light of drift flares, having been in the air for forty-two hours. The crew launched a dinghy and paddled to the beach, leaving the *America* to the mercy of the waves and the beachcombers. Their spirits sadly dampened, the airmen reached Paris by rail the next day, where they were somewhat revived by the warmth of the Parisian welcome.

These successes having been recorded, the remaining months of 1927 saw several more transatlantic ventures, all

A German card commemorating the first aerial crossing of the Atlantic from east to west by a heavier-than-air machine in 1928. The aircraft was a Junkers W.33 powered by a water-cooled in-line engine. Note that the two German members of the crew are featured, but there is no mention of James Fitzmaurice, the Irish copilot.

but one of them doomed to failure. Before the year was out, four more aircraft and their crews had disappeared into the gray wastes of the ocean. (Lost in a Fokker F.VII were Minchin, Hamilton and Princess Lowenstein-Wertheim; in a Fokker F.VII, Bertaud, Hill and Payne. A Stinson Detroiter went down with Medcalf and Tully; and a Sikorsky amphibian, with Omdal, Goldsborough, Schroeder and Frances Grayson.) The Atlantic demanded a high price for the passage of a favored few. The one success came from William Brock and Edward Schlee, who crossed from Harbor Grace, Newfoundland, to Plymouth, England, in a Stinson Detroiter named *Pride of Detroit*. It was one leg of what began in Detroit as an attempt to fly round the world in fifteen days. After leaving England, they flew on via Munich, Belgrade, Athens, Constantinople and Baghdad, before crossing India, Burma and China to reach Japan. In Tokyo, caution prevailed and they abandoned plans to take on the Pacific. They had covered over 18,400 miles in 191 flying hours.

In 1936, Beryl Markham, flying a borrowed Percival Vega Gull, became the first woman (and the second person) to complete a solo flight across the Atlantic from east to west. She left London at 8 P.M. on September 4, facing a strong headwind, low clouds and blustery weather. Ice in a fuel line threatened Markham with disaster, but she survived a forced landing in Nova Scotia. Her book, West With the Night, *is a classic of aviation literature.*

Against the Wind

A notable feature of the 1927 successes over the North Atlantic was the performance of the Wright Whirlwind radial engine. With minor variations, it had powered the *Spirit of St. Louis, Columbia, America* and *Pride of Detroit*, and had hardly missed a beat. However, an in-line design led the charge from east to west. The 310-horsepower Junkers L.5 six-cylinder engine was boosted to 350 horsepower for the Atlantic attempt by the Junkers W.33 monoplane *Bremen*. That was barely sufficient. At takeoff from Baldonnel, Ireland, on April 12, 1928, the *Bremen* weighed nearly twice its designed all-up weight. It carried a three-man crew, two Germans and an Irishman: pilot Hermann Köhl, copilot James Fitzmaurice, and Baron Gunther von Hunefeld, a rich aviation enthusiast. Baldonnel's runway was higher in the middle than at the ends and getting the overloaded *Bremen* free from the grip of the soft grass was a stimulating experience for them all.

Köhl's description recalls the hazards: "I could feel the wheels sinking into the moist ground and it almost

looked as if the feeble engine would fail to drag the four tons behind it up the slope…. We started to race two ambulances up the slope. At the time it almost looked to me as if they would reach America before we did. The top of the airfield ran quite smoothly. Now we began to win the race. The last third sloped gently downward. We needed to reach 75 mph to leave the ground and the airspeed indicator was hovering around 68 mph. I felt success in my grasp when Fitz suddenly shouted in my ear. The next moment he snatched the controls. A sheep had walked out onto the runway."

The *Bremen* hopped over the sheep and sagged back onto the ground, bumping several times before finally struggling into the air. Once there it refused to climb. The undercarriage dragged through treetops at the edge of the airfield, and then, during a desperately low gradual turn to avoid high ground, the wingtip clipped a hedge. These excitements survived, Köhl set course for America.

The next thirty hours or so were relatively uneventful, but progress was slow because of strong headwinds. Some 400 miles from land, they were enveloped by cloud and fog, and their compass began to wander. They kept heading what they hoped was generally westward, encountering first sleet and then snow as they were unwittingly carried far to the north of their planned track. In the middle of a blizzard, they caught sight of land for the first time, but had no idea where they were. Concerned about the fuel state, Köhl elected to land on a small island covered in ice and snow. The Junkers was brought to an abrupt halt by jagged blocks of ice, its propeller smashed and undercarriage damaged. It was not the triumphant arrival in New York they had intended, but they were glad to be down safely on Greenly Island, Labrador. The opposing winds had not been kind. Covering 2,125 miles had taken the *Bremen* over 36 hours, resulting in an average speed of only 58 mph, a rate of progress almost as pedestrian as that of the R 34 in 1919. Nevertheless, slow and wayward though their flight had been, they had completed the first heavier-than-air crossing of the North Atlantic from east to west.

The engine of choice for most trail-blazing pilots of the 1920s — the 220-horsepower Wright J-5 Whirlwind. It kept going for over 33 hours on Lindbergh's transatlantic flight.

The Continuing Challenge

By the time the *Bremen* arrived in Labrador, doubts about the feasibility of transatlantic air travel were diminishing. However, it remained a hazardous undertaking, challenging to the stamina of men and machines alike. In both 1928 and 1929, eleven attempts were made to fly across the North Atlantic. Just two were successful in each year. After that, the ratio of success to failure began to improve, but the grim Atlantic continued to exact its toll. As late as 1939, when commercial crossings had become a regular event and aircraft were considerably more capable and reliable than they had been in the 1920s, three aircraft and crews disappeared into the gray waters of the ocean after leaving North America.

The *Bremen's* achievement did not close the list of notable Atlantic flights, nor even of "firsts." Amelia Earhart later put her name in the record books twice. In 1928, she became the first woman to fly across the Atlantic as a passenger in the Fokker F.VIIb-3m *Friendship*, flown by Wilmer Stultz and Lou Gordon. Of the five women who had tried to precede her, three had died in the attempt. In 1932, Amelia Earhart moved to the pilot's

In September 1930, French aviators recorded a notable transatlantic success. Dieudonné Costes and Maurice Bellonte, flying a Breguet 19 Super TR named Pointe d'Interrogation *(a large "?" was painted on the fuselage), flew from Paris to New York in 37½ hours. They landed with only 99 of their original 1,137 gallons of fuel left.*

seat and joined the immortals when she flew her Lockheed Vega solo from Newfoundland to Northern Ireland. The Frenchman Dieudonné Costes, celebrated for his record-breaking performances in modified Breguet 19s, was the pilot for the first direct crossing of the South Atlantic, from Senegal to Brazil, in 1927. More notably, in a flight that stirred French emotions and recalled the tragic loss of Nungesser and Coli, Costes and his navigator-mechanic Bellonte flew back along Lindbergh's path from Paris to New York, landing at Curtiss Field on September 2, 1930, after nearly 37½ hours in the air. Their Breguet 19 Super TR was called *Pointe d'Interrogation* and carried a large white question mark on its bright red fuselage.

In August 1932, Britain's Jim Mollison completed the first solo crossing from east to west, flying a D.H. Puss Moth named *The Heart's Content* from Ireland to New Brunswick. The first solo east-to-west crossing by a woman followed in September 1936, when Beryl Markham flew a Percival Vega Gull named *Messenger* between Abingdon, England, and Cape Breton Island. In between times, Benito Mussolini used the Atlantic for a politically motivated spectacular, intended to demonstrate the power of Fascist Italy in the air. General Italo Balbo led a formation of twenty-four Savoia-Marchetti S.55X flying boats to the 1933 Chicago World's Fair. It was an impressive display of professional airmanship and, in the ease with which the formation completed the various stages, it also showed how far the state of the art had advanced since the struggles of the U.S. Navy's NC flying boats in 1919.

One other solo Atlantic crossing deserves to be singled out, if only for sheer audacity. In 1927, Douglas Corrigan was a mechanic working on Lindbergh's aircraft at the Ryan factory. Lindbergh's success inspired Corrigan with the idea of transatlantic flight. Eventually he bought a used Curtiss Robin for $325 and fitted it with new instruments, extra fuel tanks and a Whirlwind engine. By 1937 he was ready, and he applied for permission to attempt a transatlantic flight. Inspectors were not impressed by the Robin, telling him that he could fly from Los Angeles to New York but no further. When he reached New York he was granted a license for his return flight to California. On the evening of July 16, 1938, Corrigan took off from Floyd Bennett Field and was seen about an hour later heading east. The next day he landed near Dublin, Ireland, expressing surprise that he was not in California and explaining that "the compass must have been wrong." Skeptical officials on both sides of the Atlantic were not amused, but Corrigan stuck to his story. He was nicknamed "Wrong Way Corrigan" and was later made an honorary member of the Wisconsin Liars' Club.

Lindy's Legacy

Momentous though these flights were in their own right, they all stood in the shadow of Charles Lindbergh and the *Spirit of St. Louis.* Lindbergh's accomplishment caught the popular imagination more than any other in aviation during the interwar years. To people of many more nations than his own, Lindbergh represented an ideal. His modest demeanor and steadfast determination, combined with the magnitude of what he had achieved, aroused universal admiration. To most people he seemed an unassuming Midwestern American, and they felt that they could identify with him, vicariously experiencing the thrill of becoming suddenly a world-famous figure, lionized by newspapers and paid tribute by heads of state. He was showered with honors and more than 15,000 gifts from sixty-nine countries. On his return to the United States, the welcome he was given by New York City was unprecedented, with four million citizens cheering him home in a parade worthy of a Roman emperor. He was the "Lone Eagle" or "Lucky Lindy," the inspiration for a crop of popular songs, lapel buttons and advertising slogans. His flight touched the daily lives of ordinary people in hundreds of ways. These consequences were remarkable enough in themselves, but the impact of Lindbergh's achievement on the aeronautical world was even more significant. The transatlantic flight of the *Spirit of St. Louis* did more to raise public awareness of aviation's potential than any other of the 1920s and 1930s. Interest in the possibilities of air travel increased sharply, and the aviation industry surged as the demand for aircraft, both commercial and

private, rose. Flying schools expanded to cope with thousands who wished to emulate their hero by learning to fly.

Richard Mock, an aircraft designer studying aeronautical engineering at New York University, had personal experience of Lindbergh's impact: "In the early days of 1927 we were aware that in the graduating class of the year before, only one student had got a job in aviation...so there was great apprehension about how we were going to get our bread and butter. I wrote letters to some thirteen companies...all the ones I thought counted. Then Lindbergh's flight was completed successfully...the net result was that *all* the companies I had written to wrote offering me a job."

Lindbergh's later life was marred by tragedy and controversy, but his influence on aviation stands as an aeronautical milestone. Ninety-one people had preceded him across the formidable Atlantic barrier by air, but the airships had not inspired public confidence, and the other aircraft had bridged the gap between remote, inaccessible places. None of the heavier-than-air fliers before Lindbergh had linked major cities, nor even announced their exact destination beforehand. It may be claimed that others could have done these things. True enough, but he was the first — and he did them alone.

In the summer of 2000, Dan Patterson photographed the Pointe d'Interrogation *under restoration at Le Bourget. The white "?" had been repainted on the red fuselage and the normally hidden massive fuel tank was revealed.*

In 1919, Australian Prime Minister Hughes offered a £10,000 prize for the first Australians to fly from England to Australia in thirty days or less. The winners were four members of the Australian Flying Corps in a converted Vickers Vimy bomber, The pilots were brothers Keith and Ross Smith (here in peaked caps), with Jim Bennett and Wally Shiers as mechanics.

AUSTRALIAN ODYSSEY

Prime Minister Billy Hughes of Australia occasionally revealed that he was a farsighted man. Shuttling between London and Paris by air during the Paris Peace Conference in 1919, he became convinced that aviation was vital to Australia's future development. He saw it as essential for linking the cities and outposts of his vast nation, and for bringing Australia closer to the industrial centers of Europe and North America. At the time, there were few Australian pilots and even fewer aircraft. To change the situation, Hughes proposed a £10,000 prize for the first Australians to fly from England to Australia in thirty days or less. Several crews announced their intention to take part and the competition took on the character of a race. Not all were

accepted. Charles Kingsford-Smith and his crew were rejected on the grounds that their navigational knowledge was inadequate, and Bert Hinkler because it was believed that his solo bid was impractical. Determined to make their mark, neither man would be denied for long, and both would later force their way into the aviation record books. Kingsford-Smith made his forthright views on his rejection known, saying: "I don't know when or exactly how yet, but I'm going to make that bloody Hughes sit up and take notice of me…and I *am* going to fly to Australia."

Six aircraft were accepted as entrants for the 1919 England-to-Australia air race. A seventh, a Caudron G.IV crewed by Etienne Poulet and Jean Benoist, took off from Paris on October 14, well aware that they were not eligible for the prize but keen to capture the headlines and show that French aviation still led the world. They survived engine trouble and a forced landing in Persia, then malaria in Karachi, only to be overtaken by the winning crew at Akyab, Burma, and stranded near Rangoon with a cracked cylinder. The six from England suffered varying misfortunes. One crashed after takeoff, killing the crew, and another was lost off the island of Corfu in the Mediterranean. A Blackburn Kangaroo bomber crash-landed in Crete, and a Sopwith Wallaby struggled on for five months until suffering a similar fate on the island of Bali. The fifth was still in England long after the race was over.

Success for the Smiths

The sixth official entrant was a Vickers Vimy, crewed by four members of the Australian Flying Corps. Ross Smith and his brother Keith were the pilots, and Jim Bennett and Wally Shiers the mechanics. The civilian registration of their converted bomber was G-EAOU, which they said stood for "God 'Elp All Of Us." Ross Smith got the Vimy airborne from London on November 12, 1919, beginning a flight that faced one challenge after another. Heavy ice-forming clouds over France gave way to torrential rain in Italy and sandstorms in Iraq. A faulty oil gauge forced a landing in the desert on the way to Allahabad, and a tree-stump-covered airstrip in Malaya shattered a tail-skid. Jim Bennett manufactured a new one on a borrowed lathe and they set off for Singapore, where the "runway" proved to be part of a racetrack and on the short side for an aircraft without brakes. To ensure that the maximum amount of down force was applied during the landing, Bennett climbed out of the cockpit just before touchdown and slid along the fuselage to the tail, adding his weight where it was most needed, above his new tail-skid. At Surabaya in the Dutch East Indies, the Vimy sank up to its axles in boggy ground, and a takeoff was managed only by creating a runway from hundreds of bamboo mats contributed by the local people. During the last leg of the journey, from Timor to Darwin, it was apparent that the Vimy was

Bert Hinkler was an accomplished Australian pilot, but he preferred to fly alone. In 1928, he realized a long-held ambition when he flew an Avro Avian from England to Australia, becoming the first person to accomplish the feat solo.

showing signs of wear and tear, and the crew began to wonder if they would fall at the final hurdle, but at 3:40 P.M. on December 10, Ross Smith put the bomber down on Australian soil. As Wally Shiers put it: "We almost fell into Darwin." It was twenty-eight days after their departure from England, and the £10,000 prize was theirs. Knighthoods were conferred on the Smith brothers, while Bennett and Shiers were awarded Air Force Medals. More important, the purpose of Prime Minister Hughes' competition had been accomplished. Britain and Australia had been linked by air, and, to judge by their enthusiastic reaction, the interest of the Australian people in aviation had been thoroughly aroused.

Hinkler Alone

Others followed in the wake of the Smiths, but it was more than eight years before anyone flew from Britain to Australia alone. After being denied the opportunity in 1919, Bert Hinkler took a job as a test pilot with A.V. Roe and Company and saved his money. In 1920, he bought the prototype Avro Baby, a tiny machine powered by an

engine producing only 35 horsepower. He set off for Australia in it on May 31, 1920, but got only as far as Rome before the unsettled situation in the Middle East prevented further progress. The dream was postponed for four more years, by which time Hinkler had accumulated enough money to acquire an Avro Avian. He was so reticent about his plans that only a handful of spectators saw him leave from Croydon, near London, on February 7, 1928. Reports of his progress soon attracted attention, however, especially when he arrived in Basra, Iraq, after only five days, half the time it had taken the Smiths. The Avian was no faster than the Vimy, but Hinkler pushed himself to keep going through long days of flying and punishing nights of maintenance. He always claimed that his most important piece of equipment was his alarm clock. He reached Darwin on February 22, just fifteen days after leaving England, almost two weeks quicker than the Smiths. Australian officialdom acknowledged his achievement by awarding him a special prize of £2,000 and saying: "[Hinkler's] was not a stunt or a freak flight; it has reestablished Australia in the eyes of the world."

It was not the last time that Hinkler would earn headlines. In 1931 he flew a D.H.80A Puss Moth, powered by a 120-horsepower Gipsy III engine, from Toronto, Canada, to London via Brazil. Flying from Port Natal to Bathurst, Gambia, an overwater leg of 1,760 miles that took some 22 hours, he recorded the longest nonstop flight and first transatlantic flight by a light aircraft, and the first west-to-east crossing of the South Atlantic by any aircraft. Little more than a year later, on January 7, 1933, Hinkler set out alone from London in an attempt to lower the flying time to Australia once more. He was not heard from again, and his body was not found until April 28, close to the wreckage of his Puss Moth in the Pratomagno range southeast of Florence.

PACIFIC PIONEERS

If the Atlantic was a trial for pioneer aviators, the Pacific offered an even more formidable challenge. Its unbroken expanses of water are greater, its storms at least as fierce, and its landfalls no more than tiny dots in the limitless ocean. Even so, there were those who believed that an aerial Pacific crossing was feasible as early as 1919. Australia's Charles Kingsford-Smith, fuming at being rejected for the 1919 England–Australia air race, turned up in California

seeking backers prepared to acquire a Vickers Vimy for a transpacific project that would allow him to make good his promise, "I *am* going to fly to Australia." Disillusioned by his failure to raise the necessary money, Kingsford-Smith went home in December 1920, and had to wait seven long years before another opportunity arose.

The first linking of the Americas to the Orient by air is often overlooked because it happened in the course of achieving the far larger goal of a round-the-world flight. In 1924, the U.S. Army Air Service's Douglas World Cruisers took a route across the northern Pacific that hugged the coast of Alaska before hopping along the Aleutian island chain to Japan. It was not a simple affair. As Lieutenant Lowell Smith said, "We knew the trans-Pacific leg would be the worst of our flight, but it was ten times worse than we expected. Fog, snow, hail, wind, and more fog conspired to prevent us crossing the Pacific." From Seattle to the Japanese home islands took more than five weeks and involved massive support from vessels of the U.S. Navy and Coast Guard. Besides providing wonderful publicity for Army aviation, it was a stated aim of the flight "to point the way for all nations to develop aviation commercially." To some extent, this may have been done. However, the experimental nature of the flight was apparent from the time taken and the short stages planned over the unfriendly northern route, and from the size of the supporting cast. It would be many years before aircraft acquired sufficient range, reliability and comfort to convince passengers that air travel was the preferred means of being transported between continents.

Naval Follies

At a time when Billy Mitchell seemed to be intent on promoting U.S. Army air power by destroying the U.S. Navy's credibility, American admirals were not happy at the favorable publicity attracted by Lowell Smith and the Douglas World Cruisers. In looking for ways to draw attention to naval aviation, the U.S. Navy began thinking about flying from California to Hawaii. In 1924, navigating an aircraft to a small island across 2,400 miles of open ocean was a daunting challenge. The U.S. Navy's best flying boat, the Naval Aircraft Factory PN-7, did not have the range to get halfway to Hawaii. New aircraft, capable of flying for thirty hours at 80 mph, were ordered from the Naval Aircraft

Factory and Boeing. Gambling that the hope would beget the fact, the Navy rashly announced that the flight would take place by the end of August 1925. Engine problems seriously delayed the testing of the NAF PN-9 and Boeing PB-1 and it seemed the Navy would suffer the public embarrassment of not meeting the target date. Severe vibration put the PB-1 out of the running, and by August 30 neither of the two PN-9s available had completed their flight tests, most significantly those involving fuel consumption rates. Nevertheless, fear of humiliation led to orders that the flight must proceed. Accordingly, two PN-9s struggled away from San Francisco Bay and set off in the general direction of Hawaii, aiming down a line of ten USN ships strung out at 200-mile intervals along the intended track.

Only 100 miles beyond the first guard ship, one PN-9 was forced down with a serious oil leak caused by severe vibration. After six hours of wallowing in heavy seas,

they were taken in tow and endured twenty-nine hours of buffeting before arriving back at San Francisco. The surviving PN-9, captained by Commander John Rodgers, flew on until it became obvious that there was insufficient fuel to reach Hawaii. (John Rodgers was only the second USN officer trained to fly and was a cousin of Calbraith Perry Rodgers, the flamboyant transcontinental flier.) Given an incorrect bearing from the nearest guard ship, Rodgers "flew down a radio bearing, and chased around for about an hour, following different radio bearings, and finally the gasoline gave out, so naturally the engines wouldn't run any more and we came down."

The subsequent search was concentrated too far south, and days passed without the PN-9 being sighted. Now Rodgers showed his skill as a seaman: "We stripped the fabric off the lower wing and rigged it up for sails between the wings." A course was set for Oahu and progress was made at

The Curtiss H series of WWI (seen here is an H-16) were the forerunners of a family of U.S. Navy flying boats built by Curtiss or the Naval Aircraft Factory to the same basic design until the end of the 1920s. In 1925, Commander John Rogers and the crew of the PN-9 attempted to fly from San Francisco to Hawaii. They ran out of fuel and went down in the Pacific short of their objective, but made sails from wing fabric and sailed the rest of the way.

some 50 miles per day. Oahu was seen on September 9, eight days after the fuel ran out, but, to the despair of the crew, it was too far to the south. Rodgers then aimed for Kauai, the most northerly island of the Hawaiian group and their last remaining chance of a landfall. On the next day, Kauai was seen dead ahead, but Rodger's epic feat of sailing ended soon thereafter. When the PN-9 was within 20 miles of shore, it was sighted and towed to safety by the USN submarine *R-4*.

Commander Rodgers and his crew emerged from their ordeal with honor, which was more than could be said for the U.S. Navy. Desperate to improve the image of their service, the admirals had allowed ten men to undertake the longest overwater flight yet attempted, using equipment that was not up to the task. The aircraft were not fully tested, carried insufficient fuel, and flew with a number of known problems. It was hardly surprising that the fiery Billy Mitchell was driven to voice accusations of "incompetence, criminal negligence and almost treasonable administration," and to add: "All aviation policies, schemes and systems are dictated by the non-flying officers of the Army and Navy, who know practically nothing about it. The lives of the airmen are being used merely as pawns in their hands." It was a savage indictment, but it had a ring of truth.

"Tragedy in pioneering breeds caution, and too much caution in hazardous undertakings is never possible."

EDITORIAL, *HONOLULU ADVERTISER*, AUGUST 28, 1927

Seagoing Soldiers

The U.S. Navy, having suffered the consequences of acting in haste, then suffered the chagrin of watching while U.S. Army airmen showed the way to Hawaii in a landplane. On June 28, 1927, only five weeks after Lindbergh crossed the Atlantic, Lietenants Maitland and Hegenberger flew the Fokker C-2 *Bird of Paradise* the 2,400 miles from San Francisco to Oahu in 25 hours, 50 minutes. The advances in capability since 1925 were marked. Radio beacons were installed at the points of departure and arrival, and the C-2 had improved radios, an earth inductor compass, four magnetic compasses and a drift sight. Lindbergh commented that it was "The most perfectly organized and carefully planned flight ever attempted." The meticulous preparations meant little to the sensation-seeking press,

and newspaper reports dramatized the risks of the flight and the daring of the pilots. Hegenberger went out of his way to contradict the headlines: "Contrary to popular opinion, the significance of the Hawaiian flight was not the personal hazard involved but the triumph of careful preparation of the plane and equipment." He drew attention to the Army's emphasis on flight safety and pointed out that the *Bird of Paradise* had fuel reserves sufficient for another 800 miles when it landed at Wheeler Field, Oahu.

The Dole Disasters

Two weeks after the Army's success, a civilian crew made the crossing, too. Ernest Smith and Emory Bronte flew their Travel Air *City of Oakland* from San Francisco to the island of Molokai, where the fuel ran out and the engine stopped. With little choice in the matter, Smith put the aircraft down as best he could among trees close to the coast. The *City of Oakland* was a write-off, but the two fliers walked away with mere cuts and bruises and were given a welcome fit for heroes. While the end result was less satisfactory than the Army airmen's, it seemed to confirm the developing promise of aviation, particularly when viewed in conjunction with the other long-distance flights of 1927. In any event, it was a far better achievement than some of those that followed.

While the U.S. Army and Ernest Smith were completing their Hawaiian epics, others were intent on pursuing the same end. Within days of Lindbergh's Atlantic crossing, the Hawaiian pineapple magnate, James Dole, was encouraged by Honolulu's *Star Bulletin* newspaper to join the accelerating aviation bandwagon by offering "$25,000 for the first flier and $10,000 to the second flier to cross from the North American continent to Honolulu in a non-stop flight within one year after the beginning August 12, 1927." Besides promoting his pineapple empire, Dole also wished to bring closer the day when air-mail services would reach Hawaii from the U.S. mainland. Explaining the reasons for his aviation prize in the *Star Bulletin* of May 26, 1927, he acknowledged the influence of Lindbergh's achievement: "The flight of Captain Lindbergh is an evidence of the startling progress being made in aeronautics. It seemed obvious that a flight from the mainland should be the next order to have the future of aviation brought nearer to the present." Dole invited Lindbergh to take part in his competition, but the invitation was declined. What he got instead was a collection of hopeful adventurers who were generally ill-qualified and poorly prepared for such a demanding flight.

The generous prize for the Pacific Air Race (or "Dole Derby") attracted a curious assortment of barnstormers, stunt fliers, mail pilots and the like, all anxious to free themselves from the hand-to-mouth existence of their daily lives. Their aircraft were equally eccentric, most of them hastily adapted from standard models rather than specially built for the task, with crammed-in extra fuel tanks raising their gross weights to levels far above anything they were designed to lift. The one common item chosen was the Wright Whirlwind, the same engine used in the *Spirit of St. Louis*. It was a sensible choice. For the time, it was exceptionally reliable, averaging forty hours running between repairs.

Fifteen entrants announced their intention to be at Oakland, California, the chosen departure point, by race day, August 16. By then, the event had been somewhat upstaged by the U.S. Army and Ernest Smith, but their early departures made them ineligible for the Dole prize, and so much public interest had been aroused that it was decided to continue. Of the original fifteen, six were out before the starting date — two failed to make an appearance, one retired, and three crashed, killing three men. It was an inauspicious beginning. Another aircraft was disqualified on race day when officials found it had insufficient fuel to reach Hawaii. That left eight. Two of those crashed on takeoff, and two more retired after setting course, one (Travel Air *Oklahoma*) with engine trouble and the other (Swallow *Dallas Spirit*) because it was peeling fabric. Of the remaining four, only two reached Wheeler Field near Honolulu.

The winner of Dole's prize was a Travel Air named *Woolaroc*, flown by Arthur Goebel and Bill Davis. (Travel Air was formed by Walter Beech, Clyde Cessna and Lloyd Stearman, all later founders of aircraft companies in their own names.) The official time for the flight was 26 hours, 17 minutes and 33 seconds. Second place went to the

In June 1927, U.S. Army Air Corps pilots Maitland and Hegenberger flew the Fokker C-2 Bird of Paradise *from California to the island of Oahu, a distance of 2,416 miles in 26 hours, 49 minutes. Their arrival over Wheeler Field was welcomed enthusiastically by local soldiers. The Secretary of War was "proud that the perils of another great span of the air have been conquered by the skill, courage and daring of officers of the Air Corps." (The Wright Whirlwind engine on page 131 is all that remains of this aircraft.)*

Breese *Aloha,* flown by Martin Jensen and Paul Schulter.

Jensen acknowledged that he was fortunate to survive. He revealed the limitations of his airmanship when he said: "The altimeter registered 100 ft above sea level, which I had held for some hours. Perhaps the density in mid-Pacific was different and caused an error, for no doubt I must have been actually no more than five or ten feet above the water. I hit the top of a wave and the spray ripped a long slit in the stabilizer fabric. The fact that I never once took my hands off the throttle or stick saved us. I had instant control and climbed immediately to 500 ft." Bedeviled during the night by vertigo and driven off course by changing winds, Jensen eventually landed *Aloha* at Wheeler Field with only four gallons of fuel remaining.

Lockheed Vega *Golden Eagle,* flown by Jack Frost and Gordon Scott, reputed to be the best prepared aircraft and the prerace favorite, was never seen again after passing San Francisco's Golden Gate. Nor was the Buhl Airsedan *Miss Doran,* the only aircraft that carried three people — John "Augy" Pedlar, Vilas Knope, and a young schoolteacher, Miss Mildred Doran, who had been the center of press attention before the race. She was described by the aircraft's owner as its "captain" and by one reporter as "the prettiest little pigeon on wings." It was believed she was on board to attract publicity. Keen enough to go at first, she was affected by seeing the takeoff accidents and was in tears when *Miss Doran* returned with engine trouble soon after the start. While repairs were carried out, she was urged not to go, but she insisted. As reported by the San Francisco *Bulletin:* "She was scared to death when she entered the little cabin of that plane on the last trip. But no one was going to call her a quitter. She wouldn't stay behind." Mildred Doran paid for her fear of being humiliated with her life.

The Dole drama was not yet over. The Swallow *Dallas Spirit,* its peeling fabric repaired, left for Hawaii two days later. Bill Erwin announced that he would be searching along the route for the missing aircraft. Equipped with a radio from the wrecked *Pabco Pacific Flyer,* the *Dallas Spirit* made several transmissions in the early hours of the flight. When darkness fell, the messages became alarming. The lighting on the instrument panel failed and Erwin apparently succumbed more than once to vertigo. The final signal, suggesting that the aircraft was spinning, ended abruptly, probably when the *Dallas Spirit* hit the sea.

The Dole Derby had resulted in the loss of eight aircraft and the lives of ten people. Suddenly the press

The Breese Aloha *finished second in the disastrous race from California to Hawaii sponsored by James Dole, the pineapple king.* Aloha *was airborne for 28 hours, 16 minutes, and had used all but four gallons of the fuel available. Aircrew Martin Jensen and Paul Schluter shared a $10,000 prize.*

Winner of the 1927 "Dole Derby" was the Travel Air Woolaroc, *which landed in Hawaii after 26 hours and 18 minutes in the air. The $25,000 in prize money was split between pilot Arthur Goebel and navigator W.C. Davis.* Woolaroc *was the only aircraft in the race with a radio that could both transmit and receive. (The name is a contraction of "Woods, lakes and rocks.")*

was not amused. Newspapers that had been keen to build up the drama and excitement of the race were quick to join the public clamor criticizing the organizers and expressing abhorrence of inherently dangerous staged spectacles. Mr. G.O. Norville of Standard Oil wrote to the National Aeronautic Association with a blunt condemnation: "The progress of aviation has been retarded to such an extent that it will take at least two years of conscientious effort to place it again in the position it held on August 1, 1927."

Equally somber judgment was passed by *The Aircraft Year Book*, a publication of the Aeronautical Chamber of Commerce of America: "The event was marked by unnecessary crashes and loss of life, due in part to a scramble to win prize money, in some instances without proper preparations and without regard for the fitness of equipment." Indeed, the phrase "in some instances" might have been dispensed with, since none of the Dole Derby entrants had prepared with the care taken by Lindbergh, Byrd or Maitland. It had been an object lesson in the hazards faced when aircraft and aircrew are stretched beyond their capabilities, but it would not be the last time that aviators would point their machines in new directions, relying more on luck than professionalism to see them through.

"I Am Going to Fly to Australia"

While the drama of Dole's Pacific Air Race was unfolding, Charles Kingsford-Smith was back in California seeking sponsors for a transpacific flight to fulfil the pledge he made in 1920. This time he had the money to buy a Fokker F.VIIb-3m named *Detroiter* used during Hubert Wilkins' 1926 Arctic expedition. However, the Dole disasters made finding a backer to fund his proposed flight more difficult than ever, and he was at the point of selling the Fokker to meet mounting debts when he met Allan Hancock, a millionaire shipbuilder. Hancock offered to buy the aircraft, now named *Southern Cross*, and then lend it back for the transpacific attempt. With the enterprise thus secured, Kingsford-Smith showed his qualities as a professional airman. The *Southern Cross* was modified at the Douglas factory in Santa Monica, and properly equipped to tackle the great ocean. The two standard compasses were joined by a master aperiodic compass and an earth inductor compass. There were sextants, two drift meters, and a blind flying panel fitted with the best instruments available.

Kingsford-Smith spent hours in the air with the altimeter and airspeed indicators covered, practicing basic instrument flying. The navigator, Harry Lyon, trained himself in

1. Sir Alan and Lady Cobham, on the Thames, about to start their 20,000-mile-around-Africa flight in the "Singapore."
2. The inauguration at Miami, Fla., of the first international passenger and mail service between the United States, Cuba and West Indies. Photo shows—L. to R., Assistant Secretary of Commerce for Aeronautics, MacCracken and Mrs. MacCracken, Miss Earhart, Postmaster General New and S. I. Glover, 2nd Assistant, in charge of air mails.
3. La Nina, the first international service air mail plane to arrive at Havana.
4. Lieut. Ben Eielson and Capt. Sir George Hubert Wilkins, who flew over the Arctic, at City Hall, New York.
5. Commander Byrd—A close-up.

6. L. to R. Oscar F. Grubb, mechanic, and Capt. Hawks at Los Angeles, about to begin their successful trans-continental flight to New York—18 hours, 22 minutes, beating Art Goebel's record by 36 minutes.
7. Lieut. James H. Doolittle, U. S. Army Pilot, winner Schneider cup race.
8. Art Goebel, first prize winner of $25,000 Dole Air Derby, Oakland to Honolulu.
9. The Southern Cross.
10. Crew of the Southern Cross flight, San Diego to Australia. L. to R. Capt. Lyon, Capt. Kingsford-Smith, Lieut. Ulm, James Warner.
11. Amphibian Biplane arriving in New York with mail from the Ile de France from which the plane took off 500 miles at sea.

the use of a bubble sextant by taking shots while standing up in the back seat of a speeding open car on the coast road near San Francisco. The copilot, Charles Ulm, later described the measures taken to cope with the ultimate emergency: "We fitted a dump valve which would drop the bulk of our gasoline load in 50 seconds. We carried steel saws that would enable us to cut off the outboard motor and steel fuselage and turn the wing into a raft. In the wing we placed emergency rations, a still to condense water, and a watertight radio transmitter. Four gas balloons were carried to lift the aerial of this transmitter."

On May 31, 1928, they were ready. At Oakland airport, the tanks of the *Southern Cross* were filled with 1,200 gallons of fuel, and Kingsford-Smith assured reporters that "Nothing has been left to chance." Good luck charms of a silk Australian flag and a silver ring that had belonged to Alvin Eichwaldt of the *Dallas Spirit* were pressed into his

hand, and then they were off — but not without a scare. In the middle of the takeoff run, the center motor ran down to idle and "Smithy" had to close the throttles on the other two and try again. Copilot Ulm had inadvertently let the center fuel mixture control slip back, causing the engine to lose power. A few minutes later, the *Southern Cross* was safely airborne and climbing out over San Francisco Bay on the first leg to Honolulu. Twenty-seven hours later, it was welcomed to the Hawaiian Islands by an aircraft escort that included the *Bird of Paradise*, flown by Lowell Smith of the U.S. Army's round-the-world flight. An incident shortly before they reached Hawaii offered some insight into one of the perils facing oceanic fliers. A small island was reported to the left of the aircraft's track. It should not have been there and it suggested that Lyon's navigation was off the mark. They altered course, only to find that the "island" was a cloud and its shadow. How many other aviators, searching desperately for a landfall, had been, and later would be, led by cloud illusions into chasing shadows until the fuel ran out?

The second leg of the flight was to Suva in the Fiji Islands, a formidable 3,200 miles away. To give Kingsford-Smith the longest possible takeoff run with a full fuel-load of 1,300 gallons, the *Southern Cross* was ferried across to the 4,500-foot runway of Kauai's Barking Sands. He got the aircraft airborne with 1,000 feet to spare but then took six minutes to struggle up to 300 feet. Storms made things uncomfortable for several hours, particularly for the pilots, drenched by torrential rain in their open cockpit. Ulm's log recorded his feelings: "The storm seems all round us now. Smithy is at the controls. Thank God he is

the flier he is. Rain bloody rain all around and that rip-snorter of a wind!" Battered by turbulence and slowed by strong winds, after more than 30 hours in the air they were exhausted and wondering if they had enough fuel to reach Fiji. That anxiety was allayed an hour or so later when the first island appeared on the horizon, but another concern took its place. The *Southern Cross* was the first aircraft to approach Fiji and, tired as he was, Kingsford-Smith had to land the big trimotor on a hastily prepared 1,300-foot strip on a playing field. Without brakes, he did well to bring the aircraft to a stop with a deliberate ground loop at the end of the landing roll. The *Southern Cross* had been in the air for 34½ hours, and there were just 30 gallons left in the fuel tanks.

The crew of the Southern Cross, *the aircraft that completed the first crossing of the Pacific by air in 1928. From left to right: Harry Lyon (navigator), Charles Ulm (copilot), Charles Kingsford-Smith (pilot), and James Warner (radio operator).*

The Southern Cross *was a Fokker F.VIIb-3m, originally owned by the Arctic explorer Hubert Wilkins and named* Detroiter. *Extensively modified with the best instruments available and carrying comprehensive survival gear, the* Southern Cross *was better prepared for long over-ocean crossings than any aircraft had ever been.*

The final leg of the flight was supposed to be the easiest. Fiji to Brisbane is only 1,900 miles, and Lyon felt that even an amateur navigator could find Australia. It was to prove more of a challenge than they thought. Taking off from another beach, Kingsford-Smith was soon battling the worst weather he had ever experienced: "The visibility dwindled to a mile, then to a few yards, then to nothing. Torrential rain began to drum and rattle on the windshield…. Raking gusts jolted the plane so that we had to hold on to our seats." The awful conditions persisted for most of the flight, and by the time they abated, Lyon had no idea of their position. Testing his belief that Australia was too big to miss, he suggested steering due west. They crossed the Australian coast more than 100 miles off course. Their welcome when they landed at Brisbane's Eagle Farm airport was suitably ecstatic. The first crossing of the Pacific by air had occupied more than eight days and taken 83 hours and 15 minutes flying time.

Being the first to fly across the Pacific (and "make that bloody Hughes sit up and take notice") was reward enough, but the icing on the cake came in a congratulatory message from their American benefactor, Allan Hancock. His cable included news of a remarkable gesture: "I am delivering to the California Bank of Los Angeles for transmission to the Commercial Banking Company of Sydney a bill of sale transferring to Kingsford-Smith and Ulm the *Southern Cross* together with release and discharge of all your indebtedness to me." For the moment, the two Australian airmen were on top of the world. It would not always be so, nor would their first crossing be the last time they challenged the Pacific.

Like other aerial firsts, the flight of the *Southern Cross* gained a place in the record books. It was also a promise that the time was coming when aircraft might be expected to fly great distances regularly. However, that time was still not in the immediate future. Reliability was not yet adequate, and the machines were still incapable of carrying a useful payload very far, needing to use most of their lifting capacity to give them sufficient fuel. Then there was the question of providing ground facilities — airfields, navigation aids and so on — that would make the journey less of an adventure. Before these things could appear, there was a lot more adventuring to do, and Kingsford-Smith and Ulm did their share.

The Cruel Sea

In the years after the *Southern Cross* flight, Kingsford-Smith and Ulm tried to launch Australian National Airlines, but when that enterprise failed they went their separate ways. Charles Ulm concentrated on becoming known in his own right and set out to introduce air mail and passenger services across the Tasman Sea and the Pacific Ocean. His proposed Pacific route ran via New Zealand to Fiji, Fanning Island and Hawaii, and in 1934 he decided to carry out a proving flight from the United States, using the occasion to break the transpacific record and gain publicity for his forthcoming airline at the same time. The aircraft chosen was the new Airspeed Envoy, a sleek little six-seat airliner powered by two 350-horsepower Armstrong Siddeley Cheetahs. With the passenger cabin converted to take overload fuel tanks, it was capable of 3,100 miles cruising at 170 mph. Ulm named it *Stella Australis*. Flight tests confirmed that the aircraft would have no trouble covering the 2,400 miles of the first leg, so on December 3, 1934, Ulm and his crew, George Littlejohn and Leon Skilling, took off from Oakland, California, and set heading for Hawaii. Among those waving goodbye was Amelia Earhart. Radio messages, transmitted in Morse code, were picked up at intervals thereafter, both by shore stations and ships. For the most part, they reflected the crew's confident assurance that the flight was going well. "Making speed, weather perfect, engines sweet" was typical. Sixteen hours out, the *Stella Australis* called the liner *President Coolidge*, saying "We are about over you now." The airmen could see the lights of a ship and were happy to have a fix just 400 miles from their destination. Later, the ship's radio officer recalled wondering why, if the aircraft was close to overhead, the incoming signal was so weak.

At about the time when the *Stella Australis* should have arrived over Hawaii, the character of the signals changed. "We do not know whether we are north or south of the islands — weather bad" was followed by others such as "Very little petrol left" and "We are just going to the water." At last

came a final message: "Come and pick us up. The plane will float for two days." Then came a six-minute stream of SOS signals before the transmissions were cut off.

A massive air and sea search was launched, but it may be that much of it concentrated on the wrong areas in the belief that the aircraft had come down short of Hawaii. That changed with the appearance of the S.S. *Maliko*. The captain suggested that Ulm and his crew had mistaken his ship for the *President Coolidge*, causing them to think that they were 150 miles further from Hawaii than they actually were. That would have made them overfly the islands, hidden in cloud, and brought them down to the west. No trace of the *Stella Australis* or its crew was ever found. Charles Ulm and his dreams of a Pacific airline were lost. His former partner was soon to follow.

In October 1930, Kingsford-Smith knocked more than five days off Bert Hinkler's time from London to Australia, flying an Avro Avian over the route in nine days and 22 hours. In November 1934, P.G. "Bill" Taylor was his copilot in a Lockheed Altair christened *Lady Southern Cross* when they became the first to cross the Pacific by air from west to east, reversing the track of six years before to reach San Francisco via Fiji and Hawaii. None of these achievements brought Kingford-Smith the fortune to match his fame. Showered with honors, including a knighthood for services to aviation, he was still trying to raise funds in 1935, when he took the *Lady Southern Cross*

Airspeed Envoy VH-UXY Stella Australis, *minus wings, being loaded on board the Cunard liner* Ascania *at Southampton in November 1934. Charles Ulm and his navigator, George Littlejohn, joined their aircraft for the transatlantic voyage to Quebec, then flew it across the continent to the west coast before attempting the fatal flight to Hawaii.*

to England for yet another attempt to beat the England-to-Australia record, which was down to just 71 hours. He and his mechanic, Tommy Pethybridge, left London on November 8, and two days later vanished into the Bay of Bengal. Sir Charles Kingsford-Smith, the indestructible "Smithy," was gone. Tributes came from all over the world, including one from his American contemporary, Jimmy Doolittle: "[Smithy] was a pioneer who made great contributions to the progress of aeronautics. He is truly one of the outstanding names in the history of aviation. His loss is a tragedy, not only for Australia, but for the world."

Travels from Tokyo

In July 1927, galvanized by Lindbergh's heroics over the Atlantic, Japan's Imperial Aeronautics Association announced to the world that a Japanese pilot flying a Japanese manufactured and owned aircraft *would* make the first nonstop flight between Japan and the United States. The Kawanishi Company was asked to design and construct the necessary machine. When the Kawanishi K12 appeared, it looked like an inflated version of Lindbergh's Ryan. Unfortunately, scaling up the design did not produce the required increase in performance. Tests revealed both that the aircraft's gross weight greatly exceeded its design limit and that its fuel capacity was insufficient. Eventually, the Japanese government refused to register the aircraft and

withdrew support for the flight. Kawanishi found itself stuck with a very expensive and utterly useless machine, which was finally hung up in the company's assembly shop, bearing the sad inscription: "How Not to Design or Build a Special-Purpose Aircraft."

During the next three years a number of transpacific attempts ended in failure, usually because the aircraft chosen were inadequate for the task. The one successful crossing, made by the German airship *Graf Zeppelin* from Tokyo to Los Angeles in 1929, was accomplished with disarming ease but had no bearing on the problem confronting heavier-than-air aviators. To encourage further efforts, the Imperial Aeronautics Association offered a prize of 200,000 yen (then $100,000) for the first person to fly from Japan to a point in North America south of Vancouver Island. The Tokyo newspaper *Asahi Shimbun* added 100,000 yen if the successful flight was made by a Japanese pilot, or half that amount for a foreigner, and a group of Seattle businessmen weighed in with another $28,000 for a flight ending in their city. Such rich pickings brought on a rash of attempts, but it seemed that 1931 would pass without the prizes being claimed.

Then two Americans, Clyde Pangborn and Hugh Herndon, reached Tokyo in August in the course of a failed bid to break Wiley Post's round-the-world record, and were immediately in trouble with the authorities for landing in Japan without proper clearances. Detained for two months

The Lockheed Altair Lady Southern Cross *flown by Kingsford-Smith and Bill Taylor in the first west-to-east crossing of the Pacific by air in 1934. This was the aircraft in which Kingsford-Smith and his mechanic, Tommy Pethybridge, disappeared over the Indian Ocean in November 1935.*

The Bellanca Skyrocket Miss Veedol *was designed for flying long distances. It had fuel tanks holding 735 gallons and provision for fuel to be added in flight from 5-gallon cans carried in the cockpit. In October 1931, Clyde Pangborn and Hugh Herndon flew* Miss Veedol *from Sabishiro, Japan, to Wenatchee, Washington State, to become the first airmen to cross the Pacific by air nonstop.*

and fined for their transgressions, they spent the time planning to compete for the prizes. Pangborn believed that the range of *Miss Veedol*, their Bellanca Skyrocket, might just be adequate for the flight, but he added insurance by modifying the undercarriage so that it could be jettisoned after takeoff. The reduction in drag, he estimated, would add approximately 15 mph to the Bellanca's airspeed and give them as much as 600 additional air miles.

Miss Veedol lifted off from Sabishiro Beach near Tokyo on October 2, 1931, the 915 gallons of fuel aboard raising the gross weight to 3,500 pounds above the aircraft's design limit. Once on course, Pangborn jettisoned the wheels and was concerned to see that two bracing rods had not dropped away. Nevertheless, now 300 pounds lighter, *Miss Veedol* began a steady climb to 17,000 feet, where tailwinds gave her a helpful push. In smooth, clear air, Pangborn then handed over to Herndon and did something about the offending rods. Pangborn had made his name as a stunt pilot and wingwalker and he put his barnstorming skills to good use, twice climbing out of the cockpit to stand on the struts supporting the wing while he worked the rods loose. Herndon's contributions were less impressive. He twice forgot his responsibility to top up the main fuel tanks from the auxiliaries by using a hand-operated pump. On the second

occasion, the engine stopped and they lost 13,000 feet before it could be persuaded to fire again. Later, when Pangborn needed to sleep after 30 hours at the controls, Herndon allowed the aircraft to wander off track, missing both Vancouver and Seattle, a fact which became evident only when they confronted Mount Rainier. Weather denied them access to the airfields of Boise and Spokane, so Pangborn turned round and made for his home town of Wenatchee, Washington State, where he put *Miss Veedol* down on her belly early on the morning of October 5, 1931, after more than 41 hours in the air.

Pangborn was poorly compensated for his considerable efforts. Herndon's mother, a Standard Oil heiress, had financed the flight. She claimed both the *Asahi Shimbun* prize (*Miss Veedol* was not eligible for the others) and the cash realized from the sale of the aircraft. Pangborn received $2,500 for his services. For him, more lasting rewards came in the form of the prestigious Harmon Trophy, the Imperial Aeronautical Society's White Medal of Merit, and a gift of apples. Just before taking off from Japan, Pangborn had been touched by a gesture from a small Japanese boy, who had given him five apples from his father's orchard. He did not forget. The mayor of Wenatchee was asked to send five cuttings from Washington's Richard Delicious apple trees to Misawa City, near Sabishiro Beach. They were successfully grafted onto local trees, and the apples are now grown all over Japan.

Although the nonstop crossing of the Pacific had been accomplished, the Japanese were still keen to see their airmen do the same thing. The *Hochi Shimbun* newspaper provided three aircraft for 1932 — a Saro Cutty Sark flying boat, a Bellanca Skyrocket called *Rising Sun*, and a Junkers W.33. Both the Saro and the Bellanca crashed before reaching Japan, and the Junkers disappeared somewhere near the Aleutians while on the great circle track for the United States. In a strange postscript, plans to reduce the Pacific crossing to the level of a relatively minor achievement by embarking on the even greater challenge of flying directly to New York from Tokyo were actively pursued in 1940, even though a Pacific war threatened. The *Asahi Shimbun* asked the Tachikawa Aircraft Company to design a special long-range aircraft for the flight. The result was the Tachikawa A-26, powered by two 1,000-horsepower Nakajima engines, a remarkably streamlined aircraft with long, high aspect-ratio wings. After the Japanese attack on Pearl Harbor, the idea was shelved and the aircraft put into storage, but in 1942 it was thought that the A-26 might be useful for special long-range missions, so flight tests were conducted. In 1944, with U.S. forces already on Saipan and B-29s regularly attacking targets in the Japanese homeland, it was decided, possibly as a matter of honor, to demonstrate that the A-26 could indeed have flown from Tokyo to New York. A closed circuit over Manchuria was mapped out and the aircraft droned round it for 57 hours and 11 minutes, landing on the evening of July 4, 1944, after covering 10,248 miles, over 3,000 miles more than the great circle distance to New York. Enough fuel for another 1,000 miles was still in the tanks. Honor had at last been satisfied.

OVER THE FROZEN WASTES

There were two principal reasons why aviation pioneers turned their eyes to the far frozen north after manned flight became a practical proposition. The first was simply the lure of the unknown. It was to be expected that among such an adventurous group as the early aviators there would be some for whom the main attraction of the aircraft was that it promised access to regions largely uncharted or previously

beyond the reach of earthbound humans. The Arctic offered an awesome but irresistible challenge for aerial explorers. The immense scale of the polar area, the ferocity of its storms, the lack of landmarks on its icy surface, the absence of human beings, the risk of being lost without trace following a forced landing — all these things excited those who sought the ultimate experience of going where others had never been. Then there was the second reason: airmen knew that the most efficient way of linking two places is to travel along a great circle track, curving across the globe's surface to follow the shortest possible route. If commercial air travel was ever to be established on a regular basis between Europe and North America or the Far East, that meant flying over the Arctic, and even over the North Pole itself.

To the Top of the World

The first to mount a serious aerial assault on the North Pole was Roald Amundsen. The celebrated Norwegian traveler had reached the South Pole on foot in 1911, but even as early as that he was beginning to believe that the most effective way to explore the frozen regions at the ends of the Earth would be by air. He obtained Norway's first pilot's licence in 1912 and bought a Farman biplane in 1914 with the intention of flying it in the Arctic. WWI intervened, but in 1922 he began again with a Junkers F.13. That attempt ended when the aircraft was severely damaged during trials. Amundsen's limited resources were strained by the failure, and it was not until 1924 that he met Lincoln Ellsworth, a wealthy businessman willing to fund an expedition to fly from Spitsbergen to Alaska via the North Pole. The proposed flight was beyond the capabilities of the aircraft available, but Amundsen had a solution to that problem. He planned to use two aircraft to get one across the Arctic. Both would fly to the Pole, where one would be abandoned once its remaining fuel had been transferred to the other. Two Dornier Wal flying boats fitted with twin Rolls-Royce Eagles were chosen. They were known to be as reliable as the 1924 state of the art could make them, and they had a useful range of 1,500 miles, just 200 miles short of the total distance to be covered.

Amundsen's expedition gathered at Kings Bay, Spitsbergen, in the spring of 1925, aiming to take advantage of the short Arctic summer, when cracks might develop in the interminable fields of ice and leads could appear offering sufficient open water to allow flying boats to operate. The Dorniers were loaded with 1,000 pounds of supplies each, including enough rations and fuel for a month's survival on the ice. On May 21, 1925, a break in the Arctic weather gave the explorers the opportunity they were looking for, and both Dorniers, numbered N-24 and N-25, got airborne heading north. After eight hours, Amundsen, anxious to check their position from the surface, spotted a wide lead and elected to put the N-25 down. On the descent, one of the engines died before the Dornier splashed into the slush-covered water. A broken air intake needed repairing before the aircraft could fly again. Ellsworth in the N-24 flew past and came down in a lagoon some 3 miles away, only for the crew to find that the hull was leaking so badly that the flying boat was in danger of sinking. What was more, the exhaust system of the N-24's rear engine was burned out. Both crews were stranded on the ice at 87 degrees, 44 minutes north, 150 miles from the Pole.

For several days, the crews struggled to repair their aircraft. It became clear that the N-25 could be made airworthy, but the N-24 would have to be abandoned. However, the two groups were not in contact, separated as they were by deep drifts of snow and by ice that was a tangled mixture of massive floes, creaking and groaning from their endless shifting. This constant erratic movement proved to be the expedition's salvation. After two days, the distance between the two groups had halved and they communicated by signal flags. By May 26, they were only half a mile apart across a lead covered with thin new ice. Ellsworth and his crew decided to risk a crossing and succeeded in reaching Amundsen only after two of them had fallen through the ice and been rescued from the freezing water. The reunited party then had to wait for an open lead to appear, long enough for the N-25 to attempt a takeoff with a double crew on board. By June 6, with their rations dwindling, they were still waiting, so they looked for a floe large enough to offer a runway — and found one half a mile away. The next

In the late 1930s, several record-breaking long-distance flights were carried out by Japanese airmen in Mitsubishi G3M1-L twin-engined transports. J-BEOA flew from Tokyo to Teheran; J-BEOC flew from Tokyo to Rome; and J-BACI, named Nippon *(seen here), flew round the world between August 29 and October 20, 1939 — 32,850 miles in 194 flying hours. The G3M1-L was a civil airliner version of the Japanese bomber that would become familiar to Allied forces in the Pacific as Nell.*

week was spent in hacking a way through to the chosen floe, flattening the surface, and hauling and taxiing the N-25 to the takeoff point. Exhausted by their efforts on what were now starvation rations, they were ready to go by June 14. That evening, an attempted takeoff failed because mushy ice refused to let go of the N-25's hull, but early the next morning, after a hard freeze overnight, they tried again and lifted off, heading for Spitsbergen. They had been marooned on the ice for three and a half weeks.

Having come tantalizingly close to the Pole, Amundsen and Ellsworth were determined to try again. Although they had shown that flying boats could be operated in the Arctic, they decided to use an airship. As they got ready, they found they had competition. American explorer Richard E. Byrd was equally determined to be the first over the North Pole. Both expeditions began gathering at King's Bay, Spitsbergen, in April 1926.

Amundsen and Ellsworth had acquired the *Norge*, an Italian airship piloted by its designer, Umberto Nobile. Nearly 350 feet long and powered by three 230-horsepower Maybach engines, it had a range of 3,500 miles, enough to allow a reserve of 1,000 miles after completing a flight from Spitsbergen to Nome, Alaska, via the Pole. Byrd, backed by such impressive sponsors as Edsel Ford, John D. Rockefeller, and Vincent Astor, had purchased a Fokker F.VIIa-3m powered by the ubiquitous Wright Whirlwinds. In honor of the chief patron's daughter, it was christened *Josephine Ford*. Byrd announced that his intention was not merely to reach the Pole, but "to explore unexplored areas and discover new land if it is there" and to "give an impetus to commercial aviation." Amundsen, too, emphasized the scientific nature of his enterprise. Regardless of these protestations, the world's press soon represented the efforts of the two groups as a race to the Pole, and there was a degree of tension in the atmosphere at King's Bay as final preparations were made. By May 7, 1926, both parties were ready and waiting for favorable weather. Byrd and his pilot, Floyd Bennett, were the first to move. In the early hours of May 9, the heavily laden Fokker lumbered into the air and turned to the north, settling down at 2,000 feet and 90 mph. Eight hours later, Byrd's instruments told him that they were over the Pole, although there was nothing to see that differed in any way from the icy wastes they had been crossing. They circled the spot for a while, taking various readings for confirmation,

and then flew back to Spitsbergen. Fifteen hours after takeoff, they were back at base, being warmly welcomed and congratulated by their competitors.

The Pole had apparently been reached by air, but the Arctic had still not been crossed. (Byrd's flight log and charts were verified by the National Geographic Society, but his claim was later questioned. Was 15 hours long enough for a Fokker Trimotor to complete a round-trip to the Pole?) On May 11, the *Norge* left its moorings to attempt the crossing. Traveling at its sedate pace, it took 15 hours before the airship transmitted a triumphant message: "North Pole, Wednesday, May 12 — we reached the North Pole at 1 A.M. today and are now lowering flags for Amundsen, Ellsworth and Nobile." Some hours later, the *Norge*, pressing on for Alaska, ran into worsening weather. For more than two days, ice on the radio aerials prevented transmissions reaching the outside world. It was not until they had been airborne for over 70 hours that Nobile brought his airship down at the little coastal village of Teller, Alaska, 3,180 miles from King's Bay. (Nobile later reported that a local boy had implored his father to shoot down "the flying seal.") The first ever transarctic flight had been completed, and the North Pole had been reached by air twice within a few days.

It remained for the Arctic to be crossed by a heavier-than-air machine, and that was done in 1928 by Australian adventurer Hubert Wilkins and his pilot, Carl Ben Eielson, an American pioneer of Alaskan bush flying. In 1926, they had wrecked two aircraft at Fairbanks in landing accidents, both Fokker aircraft, a trimotor and a single-engine machine. (The trimotor was later repaired and sold to

OPPOSITE *In May 1926, Italian Umberto Nobile piloted the first aircraft of any kind to fly from Europe to North America over the North Pole. The airship* Norge *left Spitsbergen on May 11 and reached Teller, Alaska, some 70 hours later. The Italian Air Force Museum at Vigna di Valle, north of Rome, preserves a collection recalling Nobile's achievements. In front of a plaque commemorating the* Norge's *flight are a number of items that belonged to Nobile, including his jacket, barometer, telescope, flare pistol, and navigational instruments. Also displayed is the pilot's wheel from the* Norge. *The charts are those showing the weather at the time of the loss of Nobile's airship* Italia *over the Arctic in 1928. (See Lighter than Air, in the fourth book of this* Aviation Century *series.)*

N-24 was one of two Dornier Wal flying boats acquired by Roald Amundsen for his 1925 Arctic expedition. The Wal had insufficient range to complete the intended crossing of the Arctic from Spitsbergen to Alaska, but Amundsen planned to abandon one aircraft at the North Pole and transfer its remaining fuel to the other. Mechanical problems and weather combined to defeat the expedition, and N-24 was left behind on the Arctic ice with a burned-out rear engine.

Kingsford-Smith, who named it *Southern Cross* and used it for the first transpacific flight in 1928.) In 1927, they did it again, barely surviving an arduous trek across the ice after crash-landing their Stinson Detroiter some 65 miles north of Point Barrow. Undeterred, Wilkins made more plans, and in California he saw the new Lockheed Vega on its maiden flight. It was the aircraft of his dreams. A cantilever-winged monoplane with a streamlined, plywood-skinned semi-monocoque fuselage, the Vega could fly at 135 mph and could be fitted with extra tanks that increased its range to over 2,000 miles. He ordered one, and, painted bright orange and fitted with skis, it was flown to Point Barrow in March 1928. Wilkins and Eielson set out on their 2,200-mile flight to Spitsbergen on April 15. The route they followed crossed vast unexplored regions, going from Point Barrow to the northern end of Ellesmere Island and then passing north of Greenland to reach Green Harbor in Spitsbergen. They were in the air for over 20 hours before a storm forced them down on a deserted island just 5 miles from their destination. Five days later, the storm finally abated and they were able to complete their epic journey. It was greeted with universal acclaim, and Amundsen went so far as to say: "No flight has been made anywhere, at any time, which could be compared with it."

Cold Commerce

The air explorers had shown that the Arctic could be crossed, and the airlines began sponsoring flights to pioneer possible great circle routes across the top of the world. In August 1930, the German company Luft Hansa helped to fund a flight from Germany to North America by the distinguished airman Wolfgang von Gronau. He reached New York from the German island of Sylt in a series of relatively short hops, via the Faeroes, Reykjavik, Ivigtut on Greenland's west coast, Cartwright in Labrador, and Halifax. The flight, in a Dornier Wal flying boat, took 47 flying hours spread over eight days. Brushing aside congratulations on his achievement, von Gronau said that he had merely undertaken "a training flight cruise with a flying boat which is somewhat out of date," and that any commercial enterprise would need to use more powerful and efficient aircraft able to carry payloads other than their own fuel. He was back in the Arctic the following year, this time taking a more northerly and hazardous track over the ice cap and mountains of Greenland on his way to Hudson Bay and Chicago. He expressed his conviction that great circle mail and passenger flights between Germany and the United States were feasible, but again warned that his trail-blazing efforts were no real indication of immediate commercial viability, saying that establishing a regular service "would take a lot of money."

At an early stage of his second transarctic flight, von Gronau exchanged waves with two American airmen going the other way. Parker Cramer had already tried to conquer the Greenland barrier twice. In 1928, he and his partner, Bert Hassell, had to abandon their Stinson Detroiter on the ice cap after running out of fuel, and in 1929 Cramer's Sikorsky flying boat sank in rough seas off Labrador. He set off for a third try in 1931, leaving Detroit just before von Gronau took off from Germany. Flying a Bellanca Pacemaker floatplane sponsored by Trans America Airlines, with Oliver Pacquette as his radio operator, Cramer became the first airman to overcome the perils of Greenland on August 5, and a few days later crossed paths with von Gronau in the Faeroes. On August 9, the Bellanca left the Shetland Islands for Copenhagen and carried its crew into the depths of the stormy North Sea.

Von Gronau flew the Dornier Wal between Germany and the United States again in 1932, but on that occasion he kept going. Leaving the island of Sylt on July 22, he reached Chicago on August 2, and announced that he would continue west. At a leisurely pace, the Dornier proceeded via western Canada, Alaska, Japan, China, Hong Kong, the Philippines, Borneo, Java, India, Persia, Greece and Italy, arriving back at Sylt on November 23. For Von Gronau, it was a vindication of his belief that flying boats would replace ocean liners as the means of linking the continents.

A Sirius Excursion

While the various Greenland adventures were unfolding, the Lindberghs were off to the other side of the world, sponsored by Pan American Airways. Charles and his wife, Anne, chose a Lockheed Sirius floatplane named *Tingmissartoq*, powered by a 600-horsepower Wright Cyclone, to challenge the northern route to Asia. Taking North Haven, Maine, as their starting point, they completed the first leg to Ottawa on July 31, 1931. From there they flew in short stages to the settlement of Baker Lake in Canada's Northwest Territories, and then crossed 1,000 miles of tree-less wilderness to the village of Aklavik before reaching Point Barrow, Alaska, the most northerly point of their journey. Anne Lindbergh was impressed by the starkness of the surroundings and the unfriendly nature of the Arctic's summer weather: "Here a cloud and there a drizzle, here a wall and there, fast melting, a hole through which gleamed the hard metallic scales of the sea." Leaving Point Barrow on August 10, the Lindberghs were forced by fog and approaching darkness to set the Sirius down in an Alaskan inlet, where they spent the night huddled in the cockpit. They reached Nome the next day and the island of Karaginski, Siberia, on August 16. At Petropavlovsk they rested before taking on the fog-shrouded Kuriles, en route to the home islands of Japan. The Kuriles lived up to their reputation, and Lindbergh was forced to make another unscheduled landing, splashing down hard into the waters of Ketoi Island and buckling the spreader bars of the float-plane's pontoons. The Sirius was repaired with the help of Japanese sailors, and the Lindberghs reached Tokyo on August 23. They had linked the east coast of the United States to Japan by air in three and a half weeks and a total of 83 flying hours. Charles Lindbergh described the flight as "a pleasure trip." It is doubtful whether many prospective airline passengers would have agreed with such a description.

> "We were told that one of the Eskimo boys had taken the airship for a flying seal and had shouted to his father 'Dad! Shoot it down!' Fortunately for us, his father did not take his advice."
>
> GENERAL UMBERTO NOBILE DESCRIBING THE ARRIVAL OF THE AIRSHIP *NORGE* AT TELLER, ALASKA, 1926

Arctic ANTs

Soviet aviators had been surprisingly quiet as their Western counterparts pioneered in the Arctic, but in the late 1930s they undertook a series of spectacular transpolar flights to the United States. By then, they had an aircraft with truly remarkable performance. The ANT-25, designed by Andrei Tupolev, was a pencil-slim monoplane resembling an over-grown powered sailplane. (The ANT-25's shape bears comparison with the Lockheed U-2 of the 1960s.) It was only 44 feet long, but its 25,000-pound gross weight was carried on high aspect-ratio wings spanning 112 feet. The single M-34R twelve-cylinder water-cooled engine of 960 horsepower drove a three-bladed propeller, and the fuel capacity of 2,000 gallons gave it a range of more than 6,000 miles. After

The Tupolev ANT-25 of the mid-1930s was like a gigantic powered sailplane. The 112-foot wings lifted a 25,000-pound aircraft, more than half of which was fuel. ANT-25s had a range of over 6,000 miles, which in 1937 enabled them twice to fly from Moscow over the North Pole to the west coast of the United States.

a nonstop flight from Moscow to Kamchatka in 1936, the Soviets were ready to be more internationally dramatic. On June 18, 1937, an ANT-25 bearing the inscription *Stalinskiy Marshrut* (Stalin's Route) left Moscow and turned north. Stalin had chosen pilot Valery Chlakov, copilot Georgi Baidukov, and navigator/radio operator Alexander Beliakov for this flight. Twenty-seven hours into the flight, they flew over the Pole. Baidukov was not impressed by the icy wastes below: "The Pole does not mean a damned thing to an airman. We have passed over it and that is that." Approaching North America, the Soviet airmen faced menacing cloud barriers. Concerned about icing and concealed mountains, they climbed to nearly 20,000 feet in an attempt to stay on track for Oakland, California, but as their oxygen supply diminished, they turned toward the coast and the safety of lower altitudes. On June 20th, 62½ hours and 5,507 miles from Moscow, the ANT-25 landed at the U.S. Army airfield near Vancouver, Washington State, and was welcomed by the base commander, Brigadier General George C. Marshall, the future Army Chief of Staff and Secretary of State.

Less than a month later, the Soviets underlined their success by doing it again. This time an ANT-25 piloted by Mikhail Gromov did rather better, getting as far as overhead San Diego before fog forced him to turn back and land near San Jacinto, 90 miles east of Los Angeles. Although Gromov was in the air for slightly less time than Chlakov, he touched down 6,262 miles from his takeoff point, a new world record. Encouraged by these achievements, the Soviets planned more. On August 12, an ANT-4 set out to fly from Moscow to Fairbanks, Alaska, and then to New York. The ANT-4 was a very different machine from its stablemate. Designed as a bomber, the huge four-engined aircraft was modified to carry up to twenty-five passengers and had a fuel capacity of 6,000 gallons. It was flown by Sigismund Levanevsky, often referred to as the Russian Lindbergh and known in the U.S. as the man who had rescued American James Mattern in Siberia during an ill-fated 1933 attempt to fly round the world. Radio transmissions from the ANT-4 indicated that it was over the Pole only 19½ hours after takeoff and all was well, but 300 miles

Tingmissartoq, on display at the National Air & Space Museum, Washington, D.C., is the Lockheed Sirius used by Charles and Anne Morrow Lindbergh on their 1931 flight from Maine to China via the Canadian Arctic, Alaska, Siberia and Japan. Lindbergh described the flight as one with "no start or finish, no diplomatic or commercial significance, and no records to be sought." The Sirius acquired its name, Tingmissartoq *("one who flies like a big bird"), in Greenland during an airline survey flight to Europe, Africa and South America in 1933.*

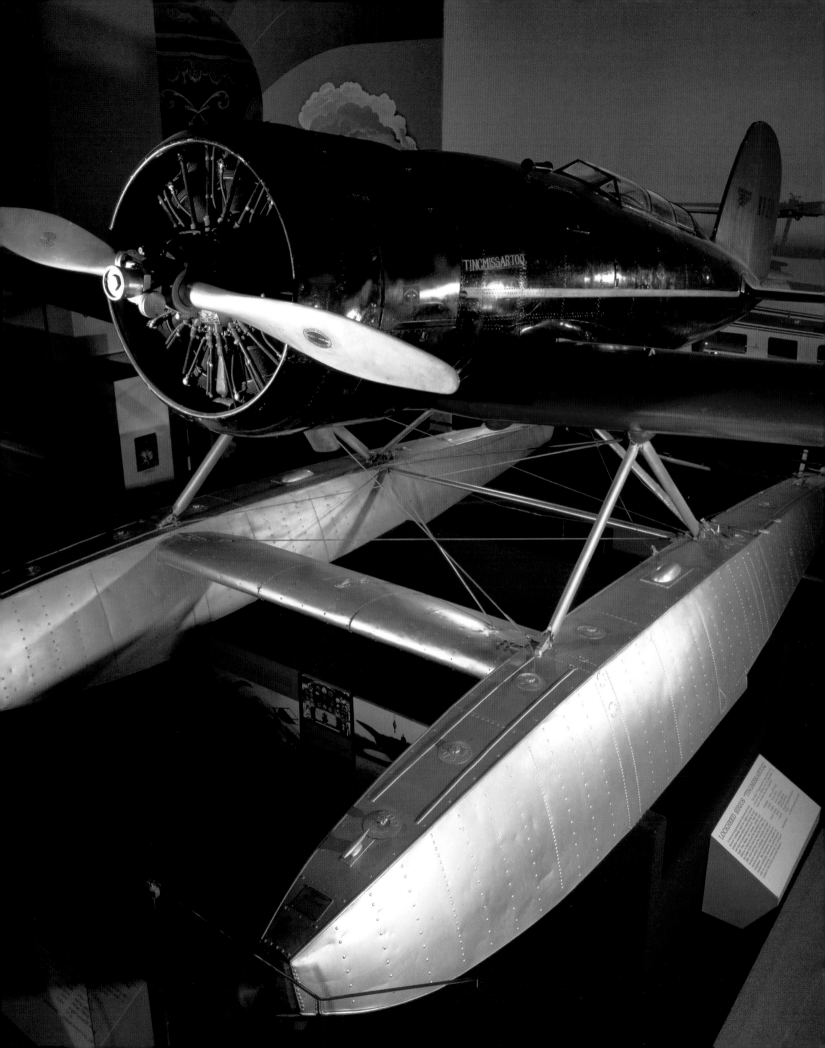

TINGMISSARTOQ

LOCKHEED SIRIUS "TINGMISSARTOQ"

further on came news that an engine was failing. This was followed by a message that the aircraft was losing height and was going to land. Then came silence. Exhaustive searches, many led by Hubert Wilkins, roamed the Arctic ice for more than six months, but no trace of the ANT-4 or its crew was ever found.

In the course of carrying out the searches, hundreds of thousands of square miles of the Arctic, nearly all in areas never before covered, were combed from the air. By the time it was over, Arctic flying had become almost commonplace. The aircraft in use were vastly more robust and reliable than their predecessors. They were equipped with better instruments and the techniques of navigating over the featureless Arctic in regions near the magnetic pole's deviations were more fully understood. Shortwave radios kept aviators in touch with the outside world, and meteorology had improved, too, reducing the risk of flying unwittingly into destructive storms. The knowledge gained would prove invaluable as Arctic traffic increased during WWII.

To the Ends of the Earth

There were no prospects of future air routes to underwrite aerial ventures over the great southern continent. The Antarctic drew those who sought the pure satisfaction of discovery, of going where none had ever been and seeing sights human eyes had never seen. The first to turn south were Richard Byrd and Hubert Wilkins. Both led expeditions to Antarctica in 1928. Byrd, backed by funds from Rockefeller, Ford, the National Geographic Society and the *New York Times*, among others, was sumptuously provided for. Eighty-three men made up the Byrd party, and they traveled south in four ships, together with ninety-four sled dogs, mountains of supplies and the latest scientific equipment. There were three aircraft — a Fokker Universal and a Fairchild FC-2W named *Stars and Stripes*, both single engine, and a Ford Trimotor 4-AT named *Floyd Bennett* in honor of Byrd's North Pole pilot, who had died of pneumonia the year before. The expedition reached the Ross Ice Shelf in December and set about establishing a base camp that came to be known as Little America.

Wilkins had already arrived and set up his more modest camp at Deception Island, over 2,000 miles away from Byrd. His party numbered three — Wilkins, plus Alaskan pilot Ben Eielson and engineer Joe Crosson. They began flying locally before the end of November, using two Lockheed Vegas, either of which could be fitted with wheels, skis or floats. The first exploratory flight over Antarctica was made on December 20 by Wilkins and Eielson. It lasted ten hours and

The Ford Trimotor 4-AT used during the 1928 Byrd expedition to the Antarctic was named Floyd Bennett *in memory of Admiral Byrd's pilot in the Arctic, who had died of pneumonia. On November 28, 1928, the* Floyd Bennett, *piloted by Bernt Balchen, became the first aircraft to fly over the South Pole.*

took them the length of the Graham Land peninsula, past features that Wilkins named in honor of his sponsors — Lockheed Mountains, Mobiloil Bay and Hearst Land among them. In February 1929, faced with deteriorating weather, Wilkins withdrew, vowing to return for the next brief summer season. Return he did, more than once, but his dreams of flying more deeply into uncharted territory himself were not to be fulfilled. His efforts in 1930 were defeated by bad weather and by the news that his pilot, Ben Eielson, had been killed in a flying accident off the Siberian coast. He was back again in 1934, but as expedition manager for Lincoln Ellsworth rather than as his own master.

At Little America, after a few short exploratory flights, the Byrd expedition settled down to wait out the winter of 1930, occupying themselves with geological and meteorological studies. Just before the long Antarctic night fell they lost an aircraft. On March 7, pilot Bernt Balchen took geologist Lawrence Gould 200 miles to the Rockefeller Mountains to collect samples. While on the ground, they were overtaken by a fierce storm, which persisted for days, battering them with winds of over 100 mph. The Fokker was torn from its moorings and carried half a mile, being destroyed in the process. It was March 22 before Byrd was able to complete a rescue with the Fairchild.

When Byrd started flying again he was soon in trouble. He and pilot Dean Smith took the Ford Trimotor halfway to the South Pole on November 18 to set up a supply dump at the edge of the Queen Maud Range. On the return trip, the engines sputtered and died 100 miles from base and Smith did a dead-stick landing on the ice. Their radio transmitter had failed, too, so they could not call for help. Within hours, however, Balchen appeared in the Fairchild with more fuel. Inspection revealed that the Trimotor's engines had been fitted with oversize carburetor jets, resulting in a higher fuel consumption than expected. Relieved to have discovered the fault before committing himself to long flights, Byrd made his mind up to go for the Pole. As his crew for the historic flight, he chose Balchen as pilot and Harold June as radio operator. Recording the achievement would be photographer Ashley McKinley. The Trimotor left Little America on November 28, 1929, aiming for a pass in the Queen Maud Range. As they approached the mountain barrier at nearly 10,000 feet, it began to look as though they might not have the height to clear the pass, and they frantically dumped supplies overboard. At the last minute, updrafts gave them help and they cleared the glacier by some 500 feet. They were through to the polar plateau with about 300 miles to go to.

The South Pole was reached 9 hours and 45 minutes after takeoff. Balchen circled while McKinley took photographs and Byrd confirmed his navigational computations. As a gesture to his former pilot, Byrd dropped an American flag wrapped round a stone from Floyd Bennett's grave. Satisfied that they had achieved what they set out to do, Byrd instructed June to transmit a radio message: "My calculations indicate that we have reached the vicinity of the South Pole. Flying high for a survey. The airplane is in good shape, crew all well. Will soon turn north." The flight back, with a one-hour stop at the supply cache, was uneventful, and the *Floyd Bennett* touched down at base after 17 hours and 26 minutes in the air.

The cover of Highlights of the Byrd Antarctic Expedition, *a collection of photographs published in 1930 by the Tide Water Associated Oil Company.*

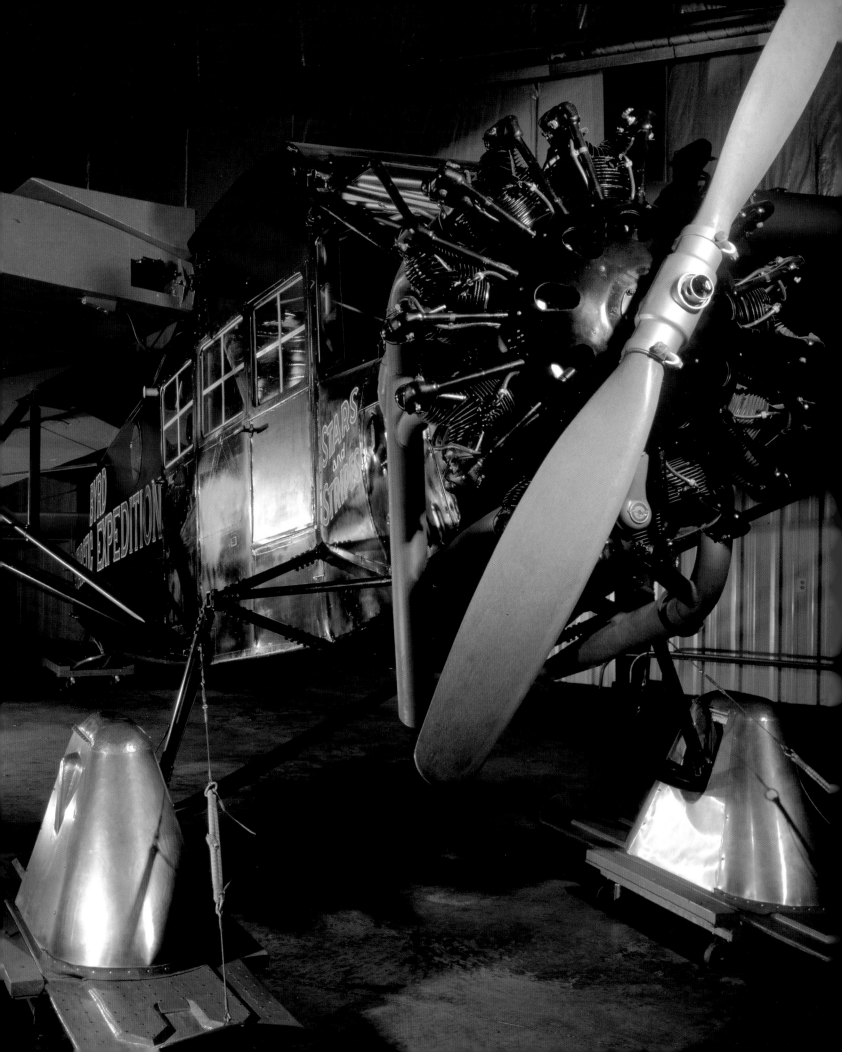

ADMIRAL RICHARD BYRD'S
FAIRCHILD STARS AND STRIPES

On display in the Virginia Aviation Museum, Richmond, is the Fairchild FC-2W2 *Stars and Stripes,* one of three aircraft taken to the Antarctic for the 1928 Byrd Antarctic expedition. In January 1929, it was the first of the three to take to the air, and on the 27th of that month, Richard Byrd, with pilot Bernt Balchen, began to explore in earnest when they took off from the base they called "Little America" and flew over the frozen continent for five hours. Powered by a 450-horsepower Pratt & Whitney Wasp, *Stars and Stripes* could cruise at 110 mph. The cabin had been modified for the expedition to carry a pilot, navigator, radio operator, fuel tank, writing desk, cameras, drift meter and survival gear. The wings could be folded for transit aboard ship or for storage, and broad skis were fitted for operations from the ice.

When Byrd left Antarctica in January 1930, *Stars and Stripes* was buried, wings folded, in a snow hangar. He did not return until December 1933, when the aircraft was dug out of its icy tomb and restored to flying condition.

ABOVE *Hubert Wilkins and Carl Ben Eielson took two Lockheed Vegas to the Antarctic in 1928. In December of that year the Vegas became the first aircraft to fly over the Antarctic continent.* LEFT *A young Bernt Balchen standing beside an aircraft he would come to know well. He was thoughtful man and a great aviator. His stone marker in Arlington Cemetery carries his own words: "Today goes fast and tomorrow is almost here. Maybe I have helped a little in the change. So I go on to the next adventure looking to the future but always remembering my teammates and the lonely places I have seen that no other man saw before."*

The public reaction in the United States to Byrd's feat offered confirmation of people's irrepressible hunger for heroics and their eagerness to applaud extraordinary achievement. Presidential congratulations and lavish praise from the press preceded the Byrd expedition's arrival in New York, where the party was welcomed with a ticker-tape parade along Broadway in the city's biggest celebration since Lindbergh's return in 1927. Byrd did not sail back to the Antarctic until December 1933. Then, during the early part of 1934, he restricted his activities to survey flights and scientific observations around Little America. Lincoln Ellsworth, however, still had ambitions to realize in the Antarctic.

Ellsworth also traveled south in 1933, reaching the edge of the Ross Ice Shelf on January 1, 1934, with his ship, the *Wyatt Earp*. He planned to cross the Antarctic by air from Little America to Graham Land, primarily just to be the first to do so, but also to determine whether there were two land masses or one beneath the ice. His aircraft was a Northrop Gamma named *Polar Star*, a monoplane capable of carrying fuel sufficient to give a range of 7,000 miles, and his team included experienced polar explorers. Hubert Wilkins was expedition manager and Bernt Balchen was principal pilot. Ellsworth's careful preparations did not guarantee success, however. Within days of setting up camp, he was headed back north. A freak wave had buckled the ice on which the *Polar Star* was standing, dropping the aircraft between grinding floes, causing so much damage that a rebuild was needed. It would be another year before Ellsworth could try again, and his second attempt was hardly more successful, bedeviled as it was by poor weather, aircraft unserviceabilities and a personality clash with Balchen.

Determined not to give up, Ellsworth changed both his team and his starting point. The *Wyatt Earp* arrived at Dundee Island, off the tip of Graham Land, on November 12, 1935. Little more than a week later, Ellsworth and his new pilot, Canadian Herbert Hollick-Kenyon, were ready to go. On two successive days, they took off but were turned back by mechanical problems and weather. At the third attempt, on November 22, Ellsworth refused to be denied. He insisted that they should press on despite radio failure and then land rather than turn back when clouds barred their way. They had been airborne for more than 13 hours and were disappointed to find that they had been flying into the teeth of strong headwinds that had reduced their average ground speed from an expected 155 mph to no more than 100 mph. They were still 670 miles from Little America. Only two short hops were possible in the next five days, both defeated by weather. After their second try, a blizzard pinned the two explorers to the ice for another week. When the weather at last cleared and they could dig out *Polar Star*, they flew to within sight of the Ross Ice Shelf only to run out of fuel and be forced to land on the ice short of their destination. A ten-day snowshoe trek brought them to Little America on December 15. There they had to stay, secure in Byrd's old camp, until mid-January, when men from the Australian ship *Discovery II* accomplished their rescue. It had been anything but easy, but Ellsworth was at last able to retire from the field, his ambition to fly across Antarctica (almost) fulfilled.

Lincoln Ellsworth first took the Northrop Gamma Polar Star *to the Antarctic in 1934, with Bernt Balchen as pilot. A plan to fly between the Bay of Whales and the Weddell Sea was thwarted when the aircraft fell through the ice and had to be returned to the United States for repairs. Later that year there was further frustration because of a broken connecting rod. It was not until November 1935 that Ellsworth and his pilot Hollick-Kenyon succeeded in flying the* Polar Star *across Antarctica. Even then they were forced down by fuel exhaustion and had to walk the last 25 miles to Byrd's abandoned Little America camp.*

In 1920, a flight began that would have significant impact on aviation in South Africa. The prize was £10,000, offered by the Daily Mail, *for the first flight from London to Cape Town. Lieutenant Colonel Pierre van Ryneveld (left) and Major C.J. Quintin-Brand, piloting Vickers Vimy* Silver Queen, *took off from Brooklands on February 4. On February 11, that Vimy was wrecked in a forced landing south of Cairo. Undeterred, the crew pressed on in Vimy* Silver Queen II, *only to destroy that one at Bulawayo. They borrowed a D.H.9 from the South African Air Force to finish the flight.*

FLIGHTS INTO THE UNKNOWN

The initial impetus for the penetration of Africa by air was given largely by British imperial ambition. The dream of an unbroken corridor stretching from the mouth of the Nile to the Cape of Good Hope entirely through British-controlled territory proved impossible to realize on the ground. Dense bush, tropical forest and arid desert rendered long surface journeys hopelessly difficult. Aircraft, however, offered the promise of leaping over obstacles while surveying the impenetrable regions from above. In 1918, three teams operating under the auspices of the RAF were sent to Africa to explore sections of a possible airway. They were instructed to seek the cooperation of local authorities in finding and clearing sites for a chain of forty-three landing grounds roughly 150 miles apart along a route from Egypt to South Africa. By the beginning of 1920, the job was done, and in February three Vickers Vimys and a Handley Page O/400 left Cairo at intervals to fly to the Cape. None made it, but one crew — South Africans Pierre van Ryneveld and

Quintin Brand — refused to be beaten and used three aircraft in reaching their goal. Their original Vimy, the *Silver Queen*, was wrecked in a forced landing south of Cairo, and their second, *Silver Queen II*, survived a number of forced landings before coming to grief during an overweight takeoff at Bulawayo, Southern Rhodesia. Quintin Brand later told of the strong vertical currents over Uganda: "On one of our downward thrusts, a large *wingless* black ant was forced on to Pierre's lap. We were at an altitude of 8,000 feet at that time. Pierre placed this ant in a match box…" Brand and van Ryneveld completed the route in a D.H.9, *Voortrekker*, supplied by the South African Air Force. The flight through Africa had taken three weeks and almost 73 flying hours.

Cobham's Continent

Of all the aviation pioneers who tackled the African continent, none made a greater contribution than Alan Cobham. He learned to fly with the Royal Flying Corps in WWI and managed to keep flying by giving joyrides to the public before joining the de Havilland Aircraft Company, where he became an air taxi pilot. In December 1921, he was hired by a wealthy American, Lucien Sharpe, who wished to study "the traces of Arab migration and the relics of the Roman Empire." In the weeks that followed, Cobham flew a converted D.H.9C through Spain, Morocco, Algiers and Tunisia, often giving the local people their first look at a civil aircraft. On another tour with Sharpe in 1923, Cobham flew 12,000 miles in North Africa, the Middle East and the Nile valley. The next year, he took Britain's Director of Civil Aviation, Sir Sefton Brancker, on a survey flight to Rangoon. These flights were admirable tests for aircraft and engines operating in severe conditions and gave Cobham valuable experience in flying into districts where aviation facilities were rudimentary at best. They also stirred his interest in promoting the development of aviation links between Britain and the Empire, especially in Africa. He wanted, he said, "to knock the stunt out of flying; to try and make people realize that aviation was coming and that it was a practical proposition. That you could set out in an aeroplane, fly to Africa and back again, and all you wanted was improvement in aircraft and the making of airways."

In 1925, Alan Cobham undertook his "Empire League Imperial Airways Survey," flying from London to Cape Town and back in a D.H.50 powered by a 385-horsepower Armstrong Siddeley Jaguar engine. He took with him a de Havilland engineer, A.B. Elliott, and a Gaumont Film Company cameraman, B.W.G. Emmott. Cobham intended to complete the outbound journey in twenty-one days, but he had not bargained for the interest shown in the flight, and consequently the need for him to meet people and give

Alan Cobham half out of the de Havilland D.H.50 he flew from London to Cape Town and back in 1925. Standing alongside is Air Vice-Marshal Sir Sefton Brancker, Britain's Director of Civil Aviation.

speeches, nor had he made allowance for Emmott's film work. Ninety-four days passed between leaving London and reaching Cape Town, even though the D.H.50 had been in the air on only twenty-seven of those days and had accumulated fewer than 100 hours flying. Worn out by weeks of spreading the word about aviation, Cobham was nonetheless satisfied: "Our job of survey over and with a complete knowledge of the route and the allocation of our supplies, we determined to do our utmost to make a speedy flight home." As it happened, there was competition to add encouragement. The day that Cobham took off from Cape Town coincided with the sailing of the Union Castle steamer *Windsor Castle*, and an unofficial race developed. Flying back up the eastern side of Africa, Cobham coped with waterlogged airfields in Rhodesia, sandstorms over the Nile, and gales in the Mediterranean, but he landed at Croydon, near London, on March 13, 1926, fifteen and a half days after leaving the Cape. The *Windsor Castle* docked at Southampton on March 15. It was an early long-distance success for aircraft over ships, but it had been close, showing that flying machines still had some way to go before they could offer a serious challenge to ocean liners as a means of intercontinental travel. Nevertheless, Cobham hoped he had demonstrated that flying was "not a fool's game but a practical proposition."

Three months later, Cobham was off again, this time to Australia. The D.H.50 had been fitted with floats for the trip, and he was once more accompanied by A.B. Elliott. The flight itself, via the Middle East, India, Malaya and the East Indies, was well planned and executed and Cobham touched down on London's River Thames on October 1, 1926, having covered some 26,000 miles. Elliott, however, was no longer with him. In a bizarre incident, he had died after being hit by a rifle bullet fired from the rifle of a Beduoin tribesman when the D.H.50 was between Baghdad and Basra.

Two by Water

In 1927, Cobham's African trail-blazing was followed by a Swiss airman, Walter Mittelholzer, flying a Dornier Merkur floatplane. He wanted to show that it was not necessary to prepare special landing grounds; stretches of open water were more convenient. It was also true that Mittelholzer was more of a pure explorer than Cobham, less interested in the commercial possibilities of aviation in Africa than in its capacity to carry him into the unknown, both for the sake of adventure and for scientific research. Even so, most of the time, staging from one stretch of water to the next meant following Cobham's route fairly closely, flying up the Nile, across the central African lakes and down the coast from Beira to Cape Town. Mittelholzer nevertheless wandered whenever he could, taking side trips into remote regions of Kenya, Tanganyika and Rhodesia to make contact with the local people.

By January 1928, Cobham (now Sir Alan, knighted for services to aviation) was back in Africa to conduct the "Wakefield Flight of Survey round Africa." His aircraft was a 10-ton metal flying boat, the Short Singapore, powered by two Rolls-Royce Condors of 700 horsepower each. Between January and May, Cobham flew the Singapore down the now familiar east coast route to Cape Town before returning to the United Kingdom via the west coast, touching down along the way on the rivers and harbors of Southwest Africa, Angola, Belgian Congo, French Congo, Nigeria, Gold Coast, French West Africa, Sierra Leone, Gambia, the Canary Islands and Morocco.

Most of the places visited by Cobham had never handled a flying boat before, and the facilities for coping with aircraft were often primitive. Just how difficult that could make things was pointed out by Henry Shaw, the manager of the Shell-Mex Oil Company's aviation department:

We had laid down supplies for one of Alan Cobham's flights…to South Africa. They had to go [to Lake Kivu] from the coast by road. Then where there were no roads they had to be carried by natives, each of the natives carrying two cases. Each case held two four-gallon tins. We had the signal that these supplies were in position, but it happened that one of the Shell inspectors was traveling near there on one of his annual visits and thought he should inspect the stock. He opened one of the tins and was horrified to find that it was full of water and not petrol. He opened several more and they were all full of water. We found out that one of the natives who did the last hundred miles carrying these packages had dropped his tin and out of it flowed what he considered was water. He must have thought, "Why carry all this stuff to Lake Kivu, where there is lots of water?" So they made a pinprick in the bottom of the cans and a pinprick in the top and let all the fuel flow out. When they got near home, they put all these tins in the river, let them fill up with water, and then sealed the pinholes with clay. Very smart indeed. We found out just in time to get a new supply there two days before Cobham arrived.

On Safari

By 1933, aircraft were no longer unusual in Africa. Some regular airline services had been established and most regions had been flown over by someone. Even so, there were still adventures to be had by aviators prepared to get off the beaten track. Among those to do so were Martin and Osa Johnson from Kansas, a couple who had a reputation for producing entertaining books and films about travels in wild places. Early in 1933, they set out on an African safari by air, basing themselves in a northern Kenyan valley. They had two Sikorsky amphibians, an S-39C painted in a giraffe-like pattern and named *Spirit of Africa*, and a much larger S-38B called *Osa's Ark*. The *Ark* was striped like a zebra and its lavish furnishings included beds, a bathroom and a kitchen. The Johnsons flew their Sikorskys all over East Africa, from Lake Rudolph to Tanganyika's Serengeti Plain, filming little-known tribes, wild animals and spectacular scenery wherever they went. To their surprise, many tribesmen who had never seen a flying machine before seemed unimpressed. Turkana men near Lake Rudolph were less than enthusiastic even when taken for a short flight, refusing to acknowledge either the wonders of the machine or the changes in perspective offered by a new vantage point. One man dismissed the idea that they could be flying over trees: "You look up to see a tree, and you can walk under a tree," he said. "That is not a tree."

In the summer of 1934, the Johnsons returned to the United States with thousands of feet of film. The movies they produced were often decried for their artless travelogue style, but there was no denying that Martin and Osa Johnson were true aerial adventurers. They used their Sikorskys to take them where no aviators, and not too many Western travelers of any kind had been before. They were also the first to use aircraft to compile a documentary record of adventurous travel. The movies of their aerial safaris were popular and helped to educate people not only about life in Africa but also about the possibilities of using aircraft to reach areas generally thought of as impossibly remote.

> *"Cobham has told me about flying to India and back in a week. When I send a despatch to India, I thank God I can't get a reply in under two months. Now Cobham is going to have a reply in a week. Life is going to be unbearable. We don't want airlines."*
>
> BRITISH GOVERNMENT MINISTER COMMENTING ON ALAN COBHAM'S IMPERIAL AIRWAY SURVEY, 1925.

Lost Horizons

Explorers everywhere had begun to realize in the 1920s that aircraft would allow them to reach and map parts of the Earth's surface that had been considered inaccessible. Expeditions intended to penetrate the polar regions and Africa usually drew a good deal of attention and were well covered by the Western press, but there were others that did not get the coverage they deserved. Vast stretches of South America fascinated but frustrated those who sought to unlock the continent's secrets. Alexander Rice, a Boston surgeon, had failed in six attempts over some twenty-five years to resolve the mystery of the River Orinoco's source. In August 1924, he set out again, up the Negro river from Manáos, with an expedition of over 100 men, but this time he had with him a Curtiss Seagull flying boat, powered by a 160-horsepower Curtiss C6 engine. (See *Aviation Century The Early Years.*)

The crew of the Seagull were U.S. Navy pilot Walter Hinton and U.S. Army pilot and photographer Albert Stevens. As the main party made slow progress up the Negro and its tributaries on the surface, the Seagull flew

The Sikorsky S-38B amphibian Osa's Ark, *painted in zebra stripes, was one of two aircraft flown by Martin and Osa Johnson in East Africa during 1933 and used in producing their popular travelogues.*

ahead, establishing the course of various rivers, spotting villages, and setting up supply bases. In March 1925, Hinton and Stevens took a four-hour flight over the Sierra Parima into the canyon of the Parima River. Flying where no white explorer had ever been, they established both the source of the Parima and its separation from the Orinoco. By the time the expedition left South America, Hamilton's Seagull had completed an aerial survey of over half a million square miles, and had settled questions about many of the region's rivers.

Two years after Hamilton's explorations, the Italian pilot Francesco de Pinedo arrived in South America during his epic sweep through the New World. In his Savoia-

Marchetti S.55 flying boat, he headed north from Buenos Aires toward Manáos, at the junction of the Amazon and Negro Rivers. During the flight he had to dare a crossing of the Mato Grosso. As he described, he flew over "solid, dense, dark green vegetation so unbroken that I had to steer my way across it by compass, as I did across the sea." Given the lack of clear areas for forced landings, accurate maps, adequate radios and even other aircraft for search and rescue, it says a great deal for the reliability of the S.55 and for Pinedo's nerve that the flight was successful. Impressed by his own achievement, Pinedo led a thanksgiving procession to a service in Manáos cathedral before setting off for the Caribbean and North America.

On the other side of the Pacific, jungles as impenetrable as those of South America hid the interior of New Guinea from explorers. In 1926, an expedition sponsored by the Dutch government and the Smithsonian Institution, led by Californian Matthew Stirling, used an aircraft in New Guinea's Nassau Mountains. It was a rugged Breguet 14 floatplane powered by a 400-horsepower Liberty engine. On May 15, 1926, Stirling and pilot Hans Hoyte flew into the highlands to establish a supply base. They alighted on a stream and went ashore, to discover that the natives were not always friendly. Attacked by tribesmen in canoes as they unloaded their supplies, they beat a hasty retreat: "Hoyte jumped onto the wing to crank the motor while I cut loose the line and stood on shore

A Sikorsky S-39C single-engined amphibian named Spirit of Africa *was the smaller of two safari-themed aircraft used by explorers Martin and Osa Johnson on their 1933 African flights. This beautiful replica of the Johnson's giraffe-patterned machine took part in the 2003 National Air Tour round the United States.*

Meticulously restored by Dick Jackson of Rochester, New Hampshire, this S-39C was brought to life using parts from five S-39s. Painted to represent Spirit of Africa, *the Sikorsky amphibian flown in 1933 by the Johnsons for their African safaris, it was photographed here by Dan Patterson, flying over Ohio during the 2003 National Air Tour. In honor of its designer, the restored aircraft is called* Spirit of Igor.

holding the plane by hand. The first arrows slithered over our heads or swished into the river short of us. One arrow ripped through the wing and at the same instant the motor roared. With throttle wide open Hoyte headed the plane's nose toward midstream while I crawled along the wing back to the cockpit…. The Papuans, paralyzed by astonishment, stood like ebony statues in their canoes. Then they leaped into the river in panic."

> *"I had no option but to fly by dead reckoning and trust in God."*
>
> SQUADRON LEADER HOWARD-WILLIAMS, COMMENTING ON RUDIMENTARY MAPS USED FOR A FLIGHT FROM KHARTOUM TO BATHURST, GAMBIA, 1930

Later, long after peaceful relations had been established, the Papuans still shot arrows at the aircraft, explaining that they were "trying to kill the big bird with the terrible voice that frightens us."

Even with the help of aircraft, New Guinea remained reluctant to reveal its secrets. It was not until 1938, that the crew of a Consolidated Catalina, part of an expedition led by biologist Richard Archbold, crested a ridge in north-central New Guinea and saw a cultivated valley populated by a people whose existence was unknown to the outside world. It was a sensational find, the last major discovery of a significant primitive society, and it was made possible because aircraft could cross physical barriers that defied ground-borne explorers.

Westlands Over Everest, by Michael Turner. Two Westland biplanes, a PV-3 and a Royal Air Force Wallace, become the first aircraft to fly over Mount Everest, on April 3, 1933.

OVER THE TOP

Aviation pioneers were drawn to the challenge of high mountains as moths to a candle flame. It felt almost godlike to look down on places that mountaineers might take weeks and suffer terrible privations to conquer. However, surmounting the higher peaks often demanded performance that early aircraft could not deliver. The first aerial crossing of the Alps in Europe, by Georges Chavez in 1910, ended both in triumph and tragedy when his Blériot XI succumbed to the stresses of mountain flying as he tried to land at Domodossola, Italy, and he was killed in the ensuing crash. The first crossing of the Andes, by Luis Candelaria flying a Morane-Saulnier Parasol, was more happily completed in April 1918. U.S. Army Captain Albert Stevens

looked down on the Andean peak of Aconcagua in 1930, remarking as his Fairchild began its descent: "How good the air feels at 19,000 feet. It seems like sea level by comparison with the air a mile above us."

During his time in Africa in 1930, the Swiss airman, Walter Mittelholzer, and his fellow pilot, Alfred Kunzle, became the first to see Kilimanjaro's craters from high above them. Mittelholzer used the updrafts from the mountain to help in raising his trimotor Ford to over 21,000 feet for an eagle's-eye view. Operating in rarified air without oxygen, he and Kunzle were afflicted by fierce headaches, tunnel vision and labored breathing, but counted themselves blessed by such an awesome experience.

Of all the world's mountains, Everest (29,028 feet) posed the severest challenge. In March 1933, a British expedition gathered at Purnea, near the Nepalese border in northeast India, aiming to fly over the world's highest peak. Besides the stated intention of performing a valuable scientific service by conducting a photographic survey of Everest and its environs, the flight was seen as a flag-waving exercise, promoting British aeronautical achievement. The aircraft were two almost identical biplanes, a Westland PV-3 (later known as the Houston-Westland) sponsored by a fervently patriotic eccentric, Lady Houston, and flown by the Marquess of Clydesdale and Lieutenant Colonel Stewart Blacker, and a Royal Air Force Westland Wallace, flown by Flight Lieutenant David McIntyre and cameraman Sidney Bonnet.

At the beginning of the 21st century, when thousands of people fly far higher than the Himalayas every day in the pampered security of winged metal cocoons, it is hard to envisage the difficulties faced by the Everest challengers. Crew comfort was not among the Westlands' qualities, nor was their performance at altitude more than barely adequate for the task at hand. Both machines had been modified from the RAF's Wallace general-purpose aircraft. They were large, open-cockpit biplanes, powered by supercharged Bristol Pegasus engines driving oversize propellers. To allow the fliers to survive the freezing cold blast of the rarified atmosphere above 30,000 feet, there were heated flight suits and goggles, and oxygen came through heating units to their masks. The equipment was tested in an altitude chamber simulating 39,000 feet. The large mapping cameras carried were heated too, but, to be safe, the film was tested for cracking in a refrigerated room.

Preparations were complete by the end of March 1933, and the crews then waited for favorable weather. On April 3, the mountain tops were clear, but the wind at 30,000 feet was estimated to be almost 60 mph. This was stronger than desirable, but the decision was made to go. The biplanes were airborne at 8:25 A.M., climbing northward into heavy haze. They reached 19,000 feet before they cleared the haze layer and saw the peaks of Makalu, Kanchenjunga and Everest ahead of them, towering into a clear blue sky. Everest's icy plume streamed away to the east, suggesting that the wind was stronger than reported.

It was a struggle to get sufficient altitude, but Clydesdale managed to achieve 31,000 feet before Everest's notorious currents took hold of the aircraft: "Down we went irresistibly in this current, although the throttle was wide open and the machine still at its maximum climbing angle." The biplane dropped 2,000 feet before entering an updraft just as powerful: "We now rose directly over the summit of Everest and cleared it comparatively comfortably by about 500 feet." To Blacker, looking through a trapdoor in the bottom of the Houston-Wallace, it did not seem that comfortable: "The crest came up to meet me as I crouched peering through the floor, and I almost wondered if the tail skid would strike the summit."

McIntyre had even more difficulty. The movie cameras he carried made his aircraft heavier than Clydesdale's and he had to make several attempts before he rode the updraft high enough to get over the crest. Elated by success, the crews turned for base after staying near Everest for some fifteen minutes. McIntyre, however, still had cause for alarm. Bonnet had collapsed after inadvertently rupturing his oxygen tube by stepping on it, and McIntyre was not sure if his cameraman was alive or dead. He was much relieved when, somewhere below 10,000 feet on the descent, he saw Bonnet reappear, white-faced and shaken but otherwise unharmed.

The aerial conquest of the world's highest peak was complete, but the intended mapping survey had been defeated by the dense haze. Ignoring orders to return home, the expedition's airmen decided to defy authority and finish the job. An unauthorized second sortie was flown on April 19, and this time the mapping cameras did their work. The press was euphoric, the *Times* of London adding comments such as "a piece of magnificent insubordination" to its congratulations. Clydesdale played the whole affair down, claiming with aristocratic understatement that the flight "was really nothing. It was very much like performing an ordinary Royal Air Force duty." In Clydesdale's eyes, perhaps that was so, but public opinion acknowledged his flight over Everest as a milestone in the progress of aviation. It climaxed an era in which aircraft had taken human beings to the most inaccessible spots on Earth. Flying over the densest jungles, the polar ice caps and the highest mountains, aviators had seen places and people as yet unknown to the rest of mankind.

method of flying in the weather or at night, and the aviation world was a safer place because of his efforts.

After Doolittle's coast-to-coast success, ambitious long-distance flights by U.S. military aircraft established routes and examined possibilities for deploying aircraft both within and beyond the limits of the continental U.S. In 1922, Lieutenants Oakley Kelly and John Macready prepared to fly the coffin-shaped Fokker T-2 across the continent nonstop. On their first attempt, they took off from San Diego, but could not coax the heavily laden T-2 over the hills to the west. Not wishing to waste the occasion, they settled down to break the world's endurance record. They landed over 35 hours later, having broken the record by almost 9 hours. After modifying the aircraft at McCook Field, they tried for endurance again in April 1923, and set a world mark of 36 hours, 4 minutes, 34 seconds. The following month, they took off for another transcontinental attempt, this time in the opposite direction, from Roosevelt Field on Long Island. A little less than 27 hours later, they landed in San Diego, exhausted but jubilant. The Air Service acclaimed the feat, declaring that Kelly and Macready had shown the feasibility of moving men, ammunition and supplies from one coast to the other in one day during a national emergency. The statement perhaps erred toward fantasy, since the crossing was achieved by two carefully prepared pilots, and the specially modified T-2 had so much trouble lifting its own fuel that it could not have carried cargo, but at least the flight offered a promise for the future.

The T-2's endurance record did not last long. The problem of staying airborne for long periods had been exercising airmen's minds for some time and General "Hap" Arnold's engineering officer at Rockwell Field believed he

TREND SETTERS AND RECORD BREAKERS
Jimmy Doolittle and Friends

In aviation's record books, Jimmy Doolittle left his mark on many pages. In September 1922, after months of preparation, during which his DH-4 was modified to extend its range, he became the first man to cross the United States in less than a day, flying from Pablo Beach, Florida, to San Diego in 22 hours, 35 minutes, including a stop of 85 minutes at San Antonio. He used a Curtiss P-1 in 1927 to become the first pilot to complete an outside loop. The year 1928 saw him heading a blind flight laboratory at Mitchel Field, New York, from where he completed perhaps his greatest contribution to aviation. By September 1929, he had evolved a panel with three new instruments — an accurate altimeter, a directional gyro, and an artificial horizon — and radio aids had been developed by which an aircraft could be homed onto a runway. On September 24, Doolittle flew a modified Consolidated NY-2 through a complete flight, from takeoff to landing, while "under the hood" and unable to refer to anything outside the cockpit. "It was," he said, "the first time an airplane had taken off, flown over a set course and landed on instruments alone." The *New York Times* greeted the achievement with prematurely euphoric headlines: "Blind Plane Flies 15 Miles and Lands — Fog Peril Overcome." Premature certainly, but the achievement was real enough. Jimmy Doolittle's work pointed the way to a had a solution. As Arnold himself reported: "There were no precedents to follow. The idea itself was simple — send up one plane and send up another when needed, carrying gas, oil, water or food to be transferred to the duration plane." After a couple of false starts, Lieutenants Lowell Smith and John Richter succeeded in a DH-4B on August 27, 1923. The servicing aircraft, a second DH-4, flew above trailing fuel or oil hoses, or a rope for food and messages. Richter's job was to grab the hose or rope while Smith held the aircraft steady. It was crude, but it worked and the DH-4B stayed in the air for 37 hours, 15 minutes. The endurance record was theirs, but more significantly, they had demonstrated the basics of a technique that would become immensely important to military aviation.

Nineteen twenty-four was another year for epic distance flights. Lieutenant Russell Maughan had been inspired by Doolittle's continental crossing in 1922. After victory in the Pulitzer Trophy races that year, it occurred to Maughan that it should be possible for a Curtiss aircraft to beat the sun across the continent. Preparatory work and false starts out of the way, he left Mitchel Field, New York, half an hour after official twilight on June 23 and, with stops at Dayton, St. Joseph, North Platte, Cheyenne and Salduro, passed over Crissy Field, San Francisco, with one minute to spare before the official time of dusk.

The Fokker C-2 turned to endurance flying in 1929. On New Year's Day, the talented U.S. Army Air Corps crew of Major Carl Spatz, Captain Ira Eaker, Lieutenant Harry Halverson, Lieutenant "Pete" Quesada, and Staff Sergeant Roy Hooe, got airborne from Los Angeles in a C-2A with a large question mark painted on the fuselage. The question was, how long could they stay in the air? Using the techniques developed for the DH-4s in 1923, they completed thirty-seven contacts with their refueling aircraft and stayed aloft for 150 hours, 40 minutes, landing on January 7, 1929. They were well satisfied, and Spatz noted in his report that, with aerial refueling, a bomber's radius of action "has scarcely any limit at all." In New York, the *Post* said the flight had opened "a new chapter in the history of aviation," and the *Washington Star* predicted it would lead to a nonstop flight round the world. (Twenty years later, in February 1949, a Boeing B-50 named *Lucky Lady II* circled the globe in 94 hours, refueled by KB-29 tankers four times on the way.) All the publicity for the "*?*" led to a rush of competitors. By the end of 1929 there had been over forty attempts on the record, and the year closed with a small private aircraft known as the *St. Louis Robin* in the prime spot, after a flight of 420 hours, 21 minutes. (The *St. Louis Robin* was a Curtiss Robin powered by a 170-horsepower Curtiss Challenger engine and flown by Dale Jackson and Forest O'Brine. In 1930, they flew again and set a new mark of 647 hours and 28 minutes.) The contest had assumed the status of a circus act, and the Air Corps was no longer interested. "Tooey" Spatz and the "*?*" had proved the concept of aerial refueling and offered a glimpse of military aviation's future.

TOP *The Fokker T-2 flown nonstop across the United States in May 1932 by Lieutenants John Macready and Oakley Kelly.*
BOTTOM *On January 1, 1929, a Fokker C-2 appropriately emblazoned with a large question mark took off from Los Angeles to answer the question "How long can an aircraft stay airborne?" After it was refueled thirty-seven times by a team of DH-4Bs, the answer was, over 150 hours. The crew included three men who would go on to hold great responsibilities as generals in WWII — Carl Spaatz, Ira Eaker and Pete Quesada.*

Lady from Kansas

Of all the American aviators who gained celebrity between the wars, none stirred the emotions more than Amelia Earhart. Nor was anyone more effective in promoting flying as an activity everyone might enjoy. In May 1923 she was the first woman given a pilot's certificate by the National Aeronautic Association, and in 1930 became the first president of a women's flying association. Known as "The Ninety Nines" after the number of charter members, the association aimed to promote flying and to expand the role of women in aviation. Earhart fought against sex discrimination, but still espoused feminine values. Flying was evidence of her liberation, but she shied away from the idea that she was a "superwoman." She flew in shirt and slacks rather than in formless flight suits and shielded her eyes with sunglasses instead of goggles, preferring to appear as unexceptional as she could. By so doing, she helped to establish the idea that flying was an everyday event, and not necessarily dramatic or hazardous.

In June 1928, Earhart became the first woman to fly across the Atlantic. She was not entirely happy with her role, however, because she did so only as a passenger in the ex-Byrd Fokker F.VIIb-3m, now named *Friendship* and flown by Stultz and Gordon. After landing in Wales, she gave all credit to her pilots, but adding pointedly: "I do not believe that women lack the stamina to do a solo trip across the Atlantic." Four years later, she proved it. On May 20 and 21, 1932, Earhart flew a Lockheed Vega from Harbour Grace, Newfoundland, to a Northern Ireland cow pasture in 14 hours, 54 minutes. Within three months she became the first woman to fly nonstop from Los Angeles to New York. She was rewarded for her achievements with the Gold Medal of the National Geographic Society and in the United States was voted Outstanding Woman of the Year.

Amelia Earhart is America's most famous woman aviator. Her aviation achievements were many, but she is particularly remembered for two events: in 1932 she became the first woman to fly solo across the Atlantic, and in 1937 she disappeared into the Pacific during an attempt to fly around the world.

Earhart returned to the headlines in 1935 with long-distance flights in her Vega, becoming the first ever to fly from Hawaii to San Francisco and from Mexico City to New Jersey. She also began making plans to become the first woman to pilot an aircraft round the world. The chosen aircraft was a modified Lockheed 10 Electra. After a takeoff accident in Hawaii forced her to abandon a westabout attempt, she decided to go the other way, but it seemed that she was beginning to tire of the effort. "I have a feeling that there is just about one more good flight left in my system," she said, "and I hope this trip is it. Anyway, when I have finished this job, I mean to give up long-distance 'stunt' flying." She left Miami with her navigator, Fred Noonan, on June 2, 1937, heading east over the Caribbean. All went well across the Atlantic, Africa and Asia, and by the beginning of July they were in New Guinea. When they took off from Lae on July 2, Earhart and Noonan were aiming for Howland Island, over 2,500 miles away and only 2 miles long. The Electra was loaded with some 1,000 gallons of fuel, enough for close to 21 hours flying. Nineteen and a half hours after takeoff, the coast-guard cutter *Itasca*, standing by near Howland Island, received a message: "KHAQQ calling *Itasca*. We must be on you but cannot see you…gas is running low." A final radio transmission, giving an estimated position, was made three-quarters of an hour later, and then came silence. A two-week search by nine naval vessels and

The bright red Lockheed Vega 5B flown by Amelia Earhart on her 1932 Atlantic crossing is on display in the National Air & Space Museum, Washington, D.C. The 450-horsepower Pratt & Whitney Wasp allowed the Vega to cruise at 140 mph, and she covered the distance between Newfoundland and Northern Ireland in just under 15 hours.

sixty-six aircraft found no trace of the Electra or its crew. Amelia Earhart and Fred Noonan had disappeared into the limitless horizons of the Pacific.

Throughout her career, Amelia Earhart was guided by the belief that she should do all she could to further women's emancipation. Aviation gave her the opportunity to champion that cause by showing that women could match the achievements of men. In one of her last letters to her husband, George Putnam, she set down the essence of her creed: "Please know I am quite aware of the hazards…. I want to do it because I want to do it. Women must try to do things as men have tried. When they fail their failure must be but a challenge to others."

Waving the Union Jack

While American trail-blazing was being led by Amelia Earhart, Wiley Post and others, pilots from Britain and what was then the British Empire were following in the footsteps of Charles Kingsford-Smith and Bert Hinkler, concentrating principally on routes joining the "mother country" to some of the larger Commonwealth nations — India, Australia and South Africa. They flew lighter aircraft than those of the Americans, with single engines rarely exceeding 120 horsepower. Prominent among them was Amy Johnson, an intensely independent woman who shared Amelia Earhart's determination to promote equality of the sexes. Johnson was the daughter of a fishmonger and earned her living as a typist. She was fascinated by aviation and spent her spare money on flying lessons. She also showed considerable technical aptitude, and was the first British woman to gain an aircraft ground engineer's certificate. She acquired her pilot's licence in 1929 and immediately began thinking of doing more than local flying. In 1930, she bought a de Havilland D.H.60G Gipsy Moth, powered by a 100-horsepower Gipsy engine, which she named *Jason*. Inexperienced though she was, Amy Johnson promptly announced that she meant to fly this frail little biplane to Australia in an attempt on Bert Hinkler's record.

Johnson took off from Croydon, near London, on May 5, 1930, heading for Vienna. Her departure attracted little attention, but by the time she reached Karachi she was two days ahead of Hinkler's time and had become an overnight celebrity. From there, things did not go so well. In Burma, she damaged a wing landing on a sports field and had to improvise repairs with fabric strips torn from shirts. After forced landing on Timor, ant hills had to be leveled before she could take off again. *Jason* reached Port Darwin on May 24, nineteen and a half days after leaving London. Hinkler's record was intact, but Johnson's failure to beat his time was ignored by an ecstatic public. She had flown a light aircraft nearly 10,000 miles over some of the world's most rugged country and that was more than enough. That a young woman with Amy's humble background could bring off such a staggering achievement endeared her to people everywhere and brought her congratulations from kings and commoners all over the world.

The public attention given to Amy Johnson encouraged others to follow in her slipstream. Later in 1930, Kingsford-Smith, in an Avro Sports Avian, reduced the outbound record to less than ten days, but that did not stand for long. In 1931, it was beaten twice more, first by C.W.A. Scott in a D.H.60M Moth and then by C.A. Butler in a tiny Comper Swift, who reached Australia in 9 days, 2 hours and 29 minutes, an astonishing performance in an aircraft powered by a 75-horsepower Pobjoy engine. For the return journey, first Scott and then Jim Mollison, both in D.H. Moths, set the fastest time, Mollison reaching the south coast of England 8 days, 19 hours and 25 minutes after leaving Australia. Between 1935 and 1938, Jean Batten of New Zealand joined in with her Percival Gull Six and competed with H.F. Broadbent

Amy Johnson was determined to show that women could be as competent as men in male-dominated activities. In 1929 she gained her pilot's license and became a licensed aircraft engineer. She then determined to set a record for flying from England to Australia. With only 85 hours of solo flying experience, she set off from Croydon on May 5, 1930, in a D.H. Gipsy Moth (G-AAAH) named Jason *and landed in Darwin on May 24. She was the first woman to fly solo to Australia.*

ABOVE *Amy Johnson's Gipsy Moth today hangs in the London Science Museum's History of Flight gallery.* Jason *is a small, unsophisticated aircraft, powered by a 100-horsepower Gipsy 1 engine that gave it a cruising speed of 85 mph. It was relatively cheap and had an easily maintained wood-and-fabric structure. Amy Johnson said of her audacity in flying such an aircraft halfway round the world:* "The prospect did not frighten me, because I was so appallingly ignorant that I never realized in the least what I had taken on."

LEFT *Amy Johnson in Australia in her D.H.60 Gipsy Moth.*

for the fastest times over the England to Australia route. By the end of the 1930s, Jean Batten had reduced the time from Australia to England to 5 days, 18 hours and 15 minutes, and Broadbent, flying a Percival Vega Gull with a 205-horsepower Gipsy Six, had gone the other way in 5 days, 4 hours and 21 minutes.

While the England-to-Australia competition usually drew the biggest headlines, there were plenty of other records to tackle, and women were prominent among long-distance fliers. In 1931, Amy Johnson flew her Puss Moth *Jason II* to Tokyo and back. Australian Lores Bonney, who in 1933 was the first woman to fly from

Australia to England, became the first pilot to reach South Africa from Australia via South Asia and the Middle East in 1937. She used a Klemm Eagle in covering 18,200 miles. Beryl Markham grew up in what is now Kenya and, between 1931 and 1936, she flew an Avro Avian and a D.H. Leopard Moth all over East Africa, carrying passengers, mail and supplies. In September 1936, Markham secured her place in aviation history when, in her Percival Vega Gull named *Messenger*, she became the first woman, and the second person, to fly the Atlantic solo from east to west. (Beryl Markham's book *West With the Night* is one of the classics of aviation literature.)

numerous lights were more than my eyes could stand." He believed that he could not make a safe landing in the face of the lights and decided to land on the beach near Cape Town docks. It sloped more than he could judge in the dark, and he lost control of the aircraft during the landing run. "She turned down the slope and, in spite of my efforts, ran four or five feet into the sea and completely turned over." Mollison kicked out a window and dragged himself ashore, where he hailed a taxi and went dripping to the airfield. His arrival there was duly noted, and his official time from the U.K. recorded as four days, 17½ hours — a new and hard-won record.

The Mollisons

Beryl Markham was preceded across the North Atlantic by Jim Mollison in 1932. He was by then a well-known airman, having flown from England to both Australia and the Cape of Good Hope only months before. His flight to the Cape had been particularly exciting. Flying a D.H.80A Puss Moth, he left England in the early hours of March 24, 1932, intending to cross the Sahara at night. Unfortunately, the French authorities in Algeria refused him permission and he had to wait until dawn before going further south. Nearing Niamey, French West Africa, in darkness, he landed on a mud bank alongside the Niger River and spent a disturbed night keeping inquisitive villagers off his aircraft. By the time he approached Cape Town, he was exhausted and his vision was affected. "I was suffering acutely from duplicated vision owing to my extreme fatigue and when I circled round the aerodrome the revolving beacons and

Among those there to congratulate Mollison was Amy Johnson. Four months later, they were married. It seemed a marriage made in aviators' heaven, and the press made it appear so. However, they were competitive people, intent on establishing solo records. Within weeks of their union, Amy announced that she was "going to try to beat Jim's Cape record — just as a sporting effort." Avoiding the hazards which had bedeviled her husband, she knocked more than ten hours off his time. On her return flight she experienced some engine problems, but still managed to post a record, breaking the one held previously by C.D. Barnard and the redoubtable Mary, Duchess of Bedford. (In 1928, another titled woman, Lady Mary Bailey, flew a D.H. Moth to the Cape via East Africa and returned by the west coast, becoming the first woman to fly solo to and from South Africa.)

The Mollisons went on setting records throughout their

marriage. Flying his Puss Moth in 1933, Jim made the first solo east–west crossing of the South Atlantic, and, in 1937, he posted a time of 13 hours, 17 minutes for the North Atlantic west–east passage in a Bellanca 28-90 named *The Dorothy*, taking only 10 hours between coastlines. Amy completed a series of flights to and from South Africa, competing with Tommy Rose for the best times. In February and March of 1936, Rose snatched both records with a Miles Falcon Six, but by the end of the year Amy had taken them back with her Percival Gull. Although the Mollisons tried some joint ventures, the strains of a marriage between self-sufficient people proved too much and they divorced in 1938. Amy joined the Air Transport Auxiliary and ferried military aircraft in WWII. In January 1941, caught by bad weather and low on fuel, she bailed out of an Airspeed Oxford and was lost in the frigid waters of the Thames Estuary.

The Navigator

In the years 1966 and 1967, the sixty-five-year-old Francis Chichester sailed his yacht *Gipsy Moth IV* single-handed round the world and was knighted for his efforts by Queen Elizabeth II. He is principally remembered as a sailor and navigator, but before he went to sea he was a pioneering air-

man. Born in Britain but brought up in New Zealand, he traveled back to England in 1929 and took a flying course. Once awarded his pilot's licence, he bought an 85-horsepower D.H.60G Gipsy Moth. He named it *Mme Elijah* and, after broadening his experience with several landing accidents, set off for Australia. He left Croydon on December 20, 1929, reached Darwin in five weeks and then flew on to Sydney. He crossed the Tasman Sea to New Zealand by ship, but then wondered if he could fly across in *Mme Elijah*. Given the limited range of his Moth, that required him to stage via two tiny specks of land, Norfolk and Lord Howe Islands. *Mme Elijah* was fitted with floats, and on March 28, 1931, Chichester left Auckland, aiming a few degrees to one side of Norfolk Island. He had devised what he believed was a foolproof method of finding small patches of land after crossing hundreds of miles of open sea. He argued that anyone heading directly for an island would be at risk if it did not appear close to the estimated time of arrival. Variable winds might have carried the aircraft to one side or the other. Which way to turn? By deliberately inducing an error to the left or right, a pilot would know which way. Using a sextant, it was only necessary to fly to the sun line on which the target stood and then follow that line to a safe landing.

LEFT *Lady Mary Bailey flew a D.H.60 Moth from the U.K. to South Africa and back in 1928. (Presumably without the hat.) Her outward journey was bedeviled by aircraft and health problems, and it took her seven weeks to reach the Cape. On her return flight she chose a route that followed the west coast of Africa and became the first person to fly from South Africa to Dakar in French West Africa.*
RIGHT *Mary, Duchess of Bedford was born in 1865. She flew solo in 1930 and gained her pilot's license in 1933. Before becoming a pilot in her own right, she shared the controls with other pilots on a number of record flights in light aircraft, including from England to India and back (1929) and to the Cape and back (1930).*

He proved his point by touching down in Norfolk's Parengarenga Harbor a little less than six hours after leaving Auckland. He reached Lord Howe on April 1 and then suffered one of nature's practical jokes. Squalls that night capsized and sank *Mme Elijah*. In the nine weeks that followed, using only local unskilled labor and improvised tools, the aircraft was salvaged, dismantled, repaired and rebuilt. Chichester flew it to Sydney on June 10, 1931.

Having got started, Chichester could not bring himself to stop. He planned to complete a flight round the world, making for Britain via New Guinea, Japan, Alaska, Canada, Greenland and Iceland. He left Sydney on July 3, 1931, and got as far as southern Japan. Just after taking off from Kitsugura Bay for Tokyo on July 17, *Mme Elijah* hit steel cables and fell vertically to crash beside the harbor wall. Chichester was seriously injured and his aircraft damaged beyond repair. His round-the-world ambitions were put to one side for thirty-five years and were accomplished in a very different vehicle.

Quickest to the Cape

In November 1937, the records between England and the Cape appeared to have been put out of everyone's reach by Arthur Clouston and Betty Kirby-Green flying a de Havilland Comet, although the solo records remained intact. (See Chapter 3. This was the victorious Comet from the England-to-Australia air race in 1934.) The Comet lowered the times to one day, 21 hours and 2 minutes out, and two days, 9 hours and 23 minutes back, using the route down the eastern side of Africa both ways. They were dramatic improvements over existing figures and seemed untouchable. However, Alex Henshaw did not think so. He began considering an attempt on the record in the summer of 1937 and the Comet's times did not discourage him. In 1938 he flew a survey flight with his father in a Percival Vega Gull, going south along the west coast of Africa and north along the east coast. By early 1939, he was ready. His aircraft was a tiny Percival Mew Gull fitted with a 205-horsepower Gipsy Six engine, long-range fuel tanks and an

BELOW *A record-breaker from the 1930s, Percival Mew Gull G-AEXF, in which Alex Henshaw made his epic flight from London to the Cape and back in 1939. The record he set was still intact over sixty years later. Dan Patterson photographed the Mew Gull, minus spats, outside the Shuttleworth Collection hangars at Old Warden Airfield in 2000.*
LEFT *The cockpit of the Mew Gull is tiny, and is not improved for the pilot by large compass on the right, nor by the reserve fuel tank fitted under the instrument panel for the flight. Alex Henshaw spent nearly 31 hours here during his record flight.*

ABOVE Alex Henshaw in 1938, holding the King's Cup, which he won that year in his Mew Gull with a fastest speed of 236.25 mph. LEFT Alex Henshaw survived the century at least as well as his Mew Gull. The last of the great record-breaking pilots of the 1930s, he is also celebrated as one of the only two pilots to have flown every variant of the Spitfire.

extra oil tank in a saddle over the engine. A reserve fuel tank of 6 gallons was added in the cockpit, making a cramped space even smaller.

Henshaw took off from Gravesend, England, in the early hours of February 5, 1939, aiming to follow the shortest possible route to the Cape. He refueled at Oran, Gao, Libreville and Moçâmedes on his way to Wingfield Aerodrome, Cape Town, arriving there in the incredible time of 39 hours and 25 minutes — 6,419 miles at an average speed of 209.6 mph. Nearly 31 hours had been spent in the air, and Henshaw was weary from lack of sleep and the demands of flying and navigating accurately. He slept for 14 hours before starting back. On the flight home, he suffered a recurrence of malaria contracted the previous year, and has described himself as "worn out with blind flying, fever and cramp in the stomach." On the final leg, his nose began to bleed badly and when he landed at Gravesend his appearance — bloody, oil-stained and obviously exhausted — alarmed the welcoming crowd. Bathed and rested the following day, he found that his return flight had taken only 11 minutes longer than the outbound trip. It was an astonishing solo achievement, and a triumph of careful planning, accurate piloting and personal determination. The records to and from the Cape were his, and they still were more than sixty years later. Alex Henshaw, his Mew Gull and his solo light aircraft records were all intact at the end of aviation's first century, rare survivors of flying's Golden Age.

ALL THE WAY

It is a truism to say that the aviators of flight's Golden Age relished a challenge. Throughout the 1920s and 1930s, fliers of many nationalities pushed their aircraft and themselves to and beyond their limits as they vied with one another in achieving the seemingly impossible. The crossing of oceans and continents was a severe test for the machines of the time and for anyone who flew them. But perhaps the greatest challenge for those wishing to write their names in the record books was to fly round the world.

Who Needs Lots of Horses?

There were aviators who did not feel driven to post faster times than anyone else. Often pilots of smaller aircraft, for them the flight itself was reward enough. Many were inspired by the pure joy of flying and the thought of traveling by air to exotic places. Perhaps the best example of this was one of the first, a young German who left home in the summer of 1929 with no intention of flying round the world, but kept finding that he had to see what was over the next hill.

Baron Koenig-Warthausen was twenty-one years old when his father bought him a light aircraft. It was a Daimler-Klemm that cruised at 70 mph, powered by a 20-horsepower two-cylinder engine. When he had accumulated the grand total of 17 hours solo in this machine, the young baron announced that, in an attempt to win the Hindenburg Cup, awarded for significant achievements in sports flying, he was going to make a nonstop flight from Berlin to "as far as Moscow, if possible." Carrying a passport, basic

En Route for the Cape Record, *by Michael Turner. Alex Henshaw taking off at night from Gao, French West Africa, during his record-breaking flight from England to South Africa in February 1939.*

tools, a toothbrush and a Thermos of hot tea, Warthausen left Tempelhof on the evening of August 29, 1929, and headed east. He had never been in the air for longer than 40 minutes before and had never flown at night. Fourteen hours later, he landed in a rainstorm near a Russian village and learned that he was only 10 miles from Moscow. The 1929 Hindenburg Cup was his.

Success whetted Warthausen's appetite and he decided to fly a little further before returning to Germany. From Moscow, he turned south and followed the railway line to Baku, clearing the mountains by hauling the little Klemm to 12,000 feet. Persia beckoned next, where he stayed for a

BELOW *The little Daimler-Klemm that in 1929–30 took twenty-one-year-old Baron Koenig-Warthausen around the world at a gentle pace, giving him the opportunity to have tea with the RAF in India and to collect a cat from the King of Siam.*
LEFT *The Baron's Daimler-Klemm was powered by an opposed two-cylinder engine that delivered just 20 horsepower.*

month, fully intending that he and his aircraft should travel back from there to Germany by rail. When he found that the nearest railroad was over 600 miles away, he reasoned "Since I had to fly, why not fly on?"

Several forced landings introduced him to the desert people of southern Persia, who helped him on his way to Karachi, where he was a guest of the Royal Air Force. He reached Calcutta on December 23, once again thinking that he would turn back and start for home, this time by ship. The lure of the Orient was too strong, however, and he flew on to Rangoon. Wherever he landed, it was difficult to restrain curious crowds, who "sometimes made holes in the wings. If glue and other repair materials were unobtainable, I was forced to employ my handkerchiefs as patches and stick them

on with the white of an egg." In Bangkok, he met the King of Siam and was presented with "a rare and valuable specimen of Siamese cat." At Singapore, he decided to keep going east round the world, via China and Japan, flying where he could and using ships when he could not. A Japanese ship carried Warthausen, his Klemm and his cat across the Pacific to San Francisco, where he found that he was something of a celebrity. A serious car accident in El Paso put him in hospital for a while, but he recovered and during his recuperation waved to the *Graf Zeppelin* as it passed overhead on its own round-the-world journey. He reached New York at the end of October and boarded the liner *Bremen* for Bremerhaven on November 15. From there he flew to Hanover, but bad weather prevented him from flying the final leg to Berlin.

Arriving home by train on November 24, 1930, he learned that he had been awarded the Hindenburg Cup for the second time, "for having circled the globe in a light plane with no accidents and no thorough overhauling."

Although he did not fly the whole way round the world, Warthausen's feat deserves to be remembered. A novice when he set out, he flew for 450 hours solo (apart from the cat) in covering more than 20,000 miles over some of the most inhospitable places on Earth in an aircraft that was little more than a motor glider. He made no long-term plans, had no supporting organization and solved problems himself as they arose. Never knowing where he was going next, he was drawn on by his enthusiasm for flying and the places it could take him. The young baron was one of aviation's true adventurers. (Mrs. Victor Bruce, a British housewife, completed a similar epic in 1930. With only 40 hours in her logbook when she started, she flew a single-engine, open-cockpit Blackburn Bluebird round the world, using ships to cross the Pacific and Atlantic.)

One-Eyed Wiley

An oilfield accident led to the loss of Wiley Post's left eye, but that did not prevent him from becoming one of the great names of aviation's Golden Age. Indeed, his eye-patch gave him a dashing look that complemented his achievements in the air. As the personal pilot of oilman F.C. Hall, he became associated with a Lockheed Vega named after the oilman's daughter, *Winnie Mae*. Post believed that such an outstanding aircraft could be used for setting aviation records, and in this he was encouraged by Hall. It particularly rankled with Post that the fastest global circumnavigation had been accomplished by the *Graf Zeppelin* rather than a fixed-wing aircraft, so in 1930 he began planning to fly round the world. The *Winnie Mae* was modified with a 420-horsepower Wasp engine, extra fuel tanks and better instrumentation for the record-breaking flight, and Australian Harold Gatty was hired as the navigator. Post prepared himself physically for the flight by practicing relaxation and, in an early

Wiley Post standing up in the cockpit of the Lockheed Vega Winnie Mae. *He flew this aircraft round the Northern Hemisphere twice, the second time solo and over a day faster than the first.*

Wiley Post with Harold Gatty, who was the navigator for Post's first round-the-world record flight in 1931. They completed the global circuit in less than nine days, having spent 107 hours in the air to cover 15,474 miles.

attempt to counter the problem of crossing time zones, by sleeping at different times each day.

Post and Gatty took off from Roosevelt Field, New York, on June 23, 1931, aiming to circle the globe via Berlin, Moscow, Novosibirsk, Irkutsk, Blagoveshchensk, Khabarovsk, Nome, Fairbanks, Edmonton and Cleveland. There were some disturbing incidents along the way. Taking off from a soft sand beach near Nome, the *Winnie Mae* nosed over and the propeller tips were bent. Post improvised a repair with a hammer, a wrench and a large rock, and then ran the engine to test for vibration. Both he and Gatty were suffering from fatigue and may have been less careful than normal. Gatty, standing near the nose when Post cranked the engine, was struck on the shoulder by the propeller. Fortunately his injuries were no more than a severe bruise and a sprained back, and they were able to continue. At Edmonton, however, the airfield was soggy from rain and Post was wary about taking off from another soft surface. In a remarkable gesture, the city authorities authorized him to use Edmonton's paved main street, and arranged for the removal of power and telephone lines to make it possible.

Slowed by these events and by a couple of brief unscheduled stops when they were uncertain of their position, Post and Gatty nevertheless had no difficulty in obliterating the *Graf Zeppelin's* time, landing back at New York on July 1, 1931, eight days, 15 hours and 51 minutes after leaving. The *Winnie Mae* had spent just over 107 hours in the air while traveling 15,474 miles. By any standards, it was a great achievement and the two airmen received worldwide praise for their flight. Still not satisfied, Post, began to talk about the possibility of doing it all again — by himself.

As a first step, Post acquired the *Winnie Mae* from F.C. Hall. He was planning to improve the aircraft's equipment when fate stepped in and nearly killed him, in the process giving him the opportunity to undertake a major rebuild. He was taking off from an airport near Mexico City to demonstrate the *Winnie Mae's* new Sperry autopilot to a friend when the engine cut at 50 feet. The aircraft plunged into a peach orchard and was extensively damaged, but the occupants survived. Teenagers had siphoned fuel out of the tanks for their car. In putting the *Winnie Mae* back together, Post made a number of changes. Larger fuel tanks were installed in the wings and rear cabin, raising the total capacity to 645 gallons. A transfer system allowed Post to pump from one tank to another to compensate for shifts in the center of gravity as fuel was used. The compression ratio of the Wasp engine was increased and a controllable pitch propeller fitted. The *Winnie Mae* emerged a much improved and more efficient aircraft, capable of flying further and faster. Post planned to use the Vega's better performance to

Mirroring Wiley Post's efforts, Bill Odom flew this Douglas A-26 round the world twice, and he was solo and faster the second time, covering 19,645 miles in 73 hours and 5 minutes.

make only five refueling stops, at Berlin, Novosibirsk, Khabarovsk, Fairbanks and Edmonton.

Several round-the-world challengers surfaced while Post was busy with his preparations, but their plans came to nothing. James Mattern actually set off twice, both times coming to grief in the Soviet Union. At last, his test flights complete and a favorable weather report at hand, Post dressed in a business suit and climbed into the *Winnie Mae's* cockpit. He took of from New York on July 15, 1933, and landed at Tempelhof, Berlin, 25 hours and 45 minutes and 3,942 miles later. He was the first to fly directly between the two cities. Delighted Germans offered him food and beer, but Post was too tired and declined all hospitality: "I don't want to eat, I don't want to shave, I don't want to bathe, I just want to clear out of here. I flew here on tomato juice and chewing gum and that's enough for me." He was on the ground for only 2 hours and 15 minutes.

Post's tiredness now led to errors. He left his maps of the Soviet Union behind and had to land at Königsberg, East Prussia. While there, he discovered a leak in the autopilot's oil-supply line and arranged to stop at Moscow for repairs. Distracted by the change in plans, he left Königsberg without his luggage. More autopilot trouble forced him down at

Irkutsk, and he made another unplanned Siberian landing at Skovorodino. Over Alaska, Post got lost and landed on a short dirt airstrip at the little town of Flat. Unable to stop before the end of the runway, he ran into a ditch, damaging the right undercarriage leg and bending the propeller. All was not lost, however. Alaskan aviators came to Post's rescue, flying in a mechanic with a new propeller. By the time he had taken some much needed rest, the *Winnie Mae* was ready to go. Still very tired, on the leg from Edmonton to New York he dozed as the autopilot flew on. To prevent himself falling into a deep sleep, he held a wrench in his hand and tied it to one of his fingers. If he slept, the wrench fell and jerked him awake.

Some 50,000 people gathered at Floyd Bennett Field to welcome Wiley Post back to New York. When he touched down, the official timers of the National Aeronautic Association stopped their watches at seven days, 18 hours, 49½ minutes. He had beaten his previous global mark by more than 21 hours. Besides claiming a new round-the-world record, Post was the first to fly round the world twice and the first to do it alone.

Convinced that he could break more records by flying in the strong winds at high altitude, Post became involved in developing pressure suits. In 1935, he took the *Winnie*

Mae above 30,000 feet and recorded a ground speed of 340 mph. Later that year, he and his friend Will Rogers, the American humorist, took a trip to Alaska in a Lockheed Orion-Explorer. Against the advice of the Lockheed engineers, he added pontoons so that he could operate from Alaskan lakes. On August 15, the aircraft stalled just after takeoff and crashed into a lake near Point Barrow. Both Post and Rogers were killed, and a shocked America mourned the loss of two great national figures.

In Wiley's Wake

Wiley Post's round-the-world mark stood for five years before it was reduced by a thirty-three-year-old millionaire named Howard Hughes. In the mid-1930s Hughes had set a number of aviation records. Flying the Hughes H-1 he raised the world speed record for landplanes to 352.4 mph, and later crossed the continent from Los Angeles to Newark in only 7 hours, 28 minutes. By 1938, Hughes had decided that the Lockheed 14, suitably modified, would be ideal for a global flight. Two 1,100-horsepower Wright Cyclones were fitted, and the cockpit furnished with a full blind flying panel, plus an autopilot and the latest navigation and radio equipment, much of it described as "revolutionary." The press took to calling the aircraft "The Flying Laboratory," and Hughes insisted that the flight would be undertaken primarily to test the equipment in various challenging environments. The elaborate survival gear for the crew of four included dinghies, parachutes and 250 orange markers. Special food containers and 20 gallons of drinking water were loaded aboard as the time for takeoff drew near.

Hughes lifted the Lockheed 14 away from Floyd Bennett Field on the evening of July 10, 1938, and made just six refueling stops on his way round the Northern Hemisphere — Paris, Moscow, Omsk, Yakutsk, Fairbanks and Minneapolis. (In 1959, the FAI decreed that the minimum distance for a round-the-world record should be equal to or greater than the length of the Tropic of Cancer — 22,859 miles / 36,788 kilometers.) Delayed more than eight hours in Paris by repairs to the tailwheel, Hughes still managed to land back in New York after only three days, 19 hours and 17 minutes.

In a speech afterward, Hughes emphasized his concern that America should strive to lead in aeronautics: "The

speed record for seaplanes is held by Italy, the speed record for landplanes is held by Germany, the altitude record is held by England, and Russia, with its magnificent flight [over the North Pole] of last year will probably hold the distance record for a long time to come. If this flight has demonstrated to Europe that American engineers and American workmen can build just as fine and just as efficient an airplane and its equipment as any other country in the world, then I feel it has been well worthwhile."

During WWII, long-range flying by large aircraft became commonplace, and there were several round-the-world flights, notably one by the Pan American Boeing 314 *Pacific Clipper* that began while the Japanese were on their way to Pearl Harbor. Caught on a scheduled service from San Francisco to Auckland, New Zealand, as the Japanese attacked, the big flying boat was ordered to pick up passengers from Noumea, New Caledonia, and take them via Australia to New York. In a journey lasting more than a month, the *Pacific Clipper* touched down on the waters of five continents, crossed the equator six times and spent 210 hours in the air. Pan American felt justified in bragging about its staff: "As a test of ingenuity, self-reliance and resourcefulness," said the company magazine, "the flight has no equal in aviation history."

Nine years after the Hughes flight, Milton Reynolds, a millionaire pen-maker, bought a surplus Douglas A-26 and had it modified to promote his pens internationally by breaking records. His pilot, William Odom, took it round the world in record time twice, the second time solo. Denied permission to use Soviet air space, his route was more than 5,000 miles longer than that flown by Hughes, going from Chicago via Gander, Paris, Cairo, Karachi, Calcutta, Shanghai, Tokyo, Adak and Edmonton. A period of wandering around over Canada after falling asleep used up fuel and forced an extra stop at Fargo, but even so, Odom posted a time of three days, one hour and five minutes.

Within months of Odom's flight, the United States Air Force demonstrated an active interest in global operations. In July 1948, as international tensions increased, the USAF revealed the strategic capabilities of its bombers when two Boeing B-29s (*Lucky Lady* and *Gas Gobbler*) flew round the world. This flight was followed in 1949 with another, aiming both to emphasize the global reach of Strategic Air Command and to gain the publicity of an aviation first for the USAF. On February 26, 1949, a B-50 named *Lucky Lady II* took off from Carswell Air Force Base, Texas. It landed back at base 94 hours and 23,452 miles later, having been refueled in the air four times by KB-29 tankers. For the first time, an aircraft had circled the Earth nonstop. The Secretary of the Air Force called the achievement "an epochal step in the development of air power," and the crew was awarded the Mackay Trophy for the most meritorious Air Force flight of 1949.

The USAF found reasons to girdle the globe nonstop twice more, both times with B-52s. Not long after its arrival on operational squadrons, SAC chose to show the world what the B-52 could do. Within a year of its introduction, a B-52 dropped a thermonuclear weapon with a yield of almost four megatons at Bikini Atoll. Then the reach of the huge bomber was demonstrated in January 1957 when three B-52s of the 93rd Bomb Wing, supported by KC-97 tankers, flew from California via Labrador, Morocco, Ceylon, the Philippines, Guam and Hawaii to complete a nonstop round-the-world flight of 24,325 miles in 45 hours and 19 minutes. The captain of the leading B-52, *Lucky Lady III*, was Lieutenant Colonel James Morris, who had been the copilot of the B-50 *Lucky Lady II* on SAC's 1949 global epic. In just eight years, Morris had seen the round-the-world record reduced by better than half. Twenty-three years later, in March 1980, B-52s of the 410th Bomb Wing operating from Michigan repeated the nonstop performance, refueling nine

times in the course of a mission that included photographing units of the Soviet Navy in the Arabian Gulf. They were back at base in 42½ hours to win another Mackay Trophy for SAC.

Small but All Round

The first aircraft to fly right round the world powered by engines of less than 500 horsepower were two Piper Super Cruisers. In 1946, Clifford Evans and George Truman, flying instructors at College Park airport, Maryland, dreamed of flying round the world in light aircraft, both for their own satisfaction and to show that it could be done. The Piper Aircraft Company agreed to support the project by supplying and modifying two almost-new Super Cruisers. Lycoming supplied the engines for $1 each. Evans and Truman left Teterboro, New Jersey, on August 9, 1947. Bad weather dogged them almost everywhere and they were never free of financial concerns, but they stuck to their task and arrived back at Teterboro on December 8, having covered the 25,612 miles of their route in 122 days, 23 hours and 4 minutes. Truman was modest about their achievement: "There are probably a hundred thousand pilots in this country who could do what we have done if they are careful. That's about all we were trying to prove."

Evans and Truman showed the way, but it was some years before other private aviators followed, flying aircraft of greatly improved performance and fitted with better instrumentation and navigational equipment. In 1951, Congressman Peter Mack of Illinois flew a Beechcraft Bonanza on a world tour aimed at promoting friendship with the United States. He was in no hurry and took three and a half months to visit thirty countries. Peter Gluckman, on the other hand, wanted to break records. Flying a Meyers 200A, he left San Francisco on August 22, 1959, and in spite of several

Francis Chichester's D.H.60G Gipsy Moth Mme Elijah *fitted with floats for his crossing of the Tasman Sea in 1931. The navigation system he used for this flight became generally accepted as the best method for finding small islands in a vast sea.*

On March 19, 1964, Jerrie Mock left Columbus, Ohio, flying a 1953 Cessna 180 named Spirit of Columbus. *She was back 29 days, 11 hours and 59 minutes later, having covered 23,103 miles and become the first woman to fly round the world. On May 4, President Lyndon Johnson presented her with the Federal Aviation Administration's Exceptional Service Decoration. The* Spirit of Columbus *is preserved in the National Air & Space Museum, Washington, D.C.*

delays for unserviceability was back there in a little less than thirty days, having flown 23,765 miles. Gluckman did not have long in which to relish his success. Later in 1959, he and his aircraft disappeared after taking off from Tokyo.

Max Conrad was an airman who enjoyed his flying for longer than most. By the time he died at the age of seventy-six, he had more than 53,000 hours in his log book, accumulated over half a century. In the 1950s, he gained a reputation as a pilot who flew light aircraft very long distances. He crossed the Atlantic twice in a Piper Pacer in 1950, and in 1953, to commemorate the 50th anniversary of powered flight, visited the capitals of the forty-eight states in fourteen days. In 1959, Conrad set a number of records, including one in which he flew a Piper Comanche nonstop from Casablanca to Los Angeles, a distance of 7,668 miles. Over the Christmas weekend of 1964, at the age of sixty-one, he topped that by flying a Piper Twin Comanche 7,778 miles from Cape Town to St. Petersburg, Florida. In between times, Conrad decided to tackle the round-the-world record. With Richard Jennings along as the official observer for the National Aeronautic Association, he set off westward from Miami in a Piper Aztec and called at Long Beach, Honolulu, Wake Island, Guam, Manila, Singapore, Bombay, Nairobi, Lagos, Dakar, Amapa (Brazil), Atkinson (Guiana) and Trinidad. The Aztec was back at Miami after eight days, 18 hours and 36 minutes. Only 50 hours and 2 minutes of that time had been spent on the ground.

Globetrotting Women of the 1960s

After Amelia Earhart disappeared in 1937, it was more than a quarter of a century before another woman took up the challenge of flying round the world. In the spring of 1964, Geraldine "Jerrie" Mock of Columbus, Ohio, became the first woman to pilot an aircraft in a complete circumnavigation. Her machine was neither new nor particularly striking. It was a 1953 Cessna 180 modified to take 65 gallons of fuel in the wings and another 178 gallons in the rear of the cabin. A full load was enough for 25 hours flying. She left Columbus on March 19, 1964, and flew the first leg to Bermuda. Her in-flight diary reveals not only the care with which she planned the flight but also her self-deprecating sense of humor. Recording her arrival at Casablanca, she wrote: "[The city] is quite pretty from the air. Bounced on landing as usual." By the time she reached Tripoli, the Cessna needed to have its brakes repaired, "but no one has parts. They all say the next place. It is like mañana." At Cairo, she discovered that she had landed at the wrong airfield when "three truck loads of soldiers drove out to see who I was." At Dharan, "they kept watching for the man pilot to climb out." On the approach to Karachi, air traffic control was amazed when they asked for her occupation and were told "house-wife," and Saigon asked "if I had a man aboard." Nearing Honolulu after taking $16\frac{1}{2}$ hours to come from Guam, the reaction was different: "Some radar man complained that I was twelve miles south of course. I'd like to see him do better with small plane equipment." The final entries in the diary, made after she landed at Columbus on April 17, 1964, sum up her down-to-earth view of an aviation milestone: "It was a nice easy trip. I'm glad to be home."

At the same time that "Jerrie" Mock was on her way, Joan Smith was airborne, too. She planned to fly her Piper Apache over Amelia Earhart's route and therefore further than Mock. Smith did not have an easy time of it. Bad weather, fuel leaks, hydraulic failure, electrical faults, and a revolution in Brazil combined to make for a difficult flight, but Smith stuck to her task, and arrived back in Oakland on May 12, 1964, to become the second woman to fly solo round the world. She was, however, the first to do so at the equator and, until Sheila Scott's flight in 1966, she held the record for the longest solo flight in history — 27,750 miles in 56 days. She was followed in 1967 by Ann Pellegreno, who set out to mark the 30th anniversary of Amelia Earhart's death by flying a Lockheed 10 Electra like Earhart's over the pioneer aviator's route and dropping a wreath on Howland Island, the intended destination when she disappeared. Pellegreno and her crew took off from Oakland on June 9, 1967. Their beautifully restored Electra performed perfectly and they reached Lae, New Guinea, Earhart's last stop, on July 1. After some diligent searching, they found Howland Island and dropped their tribute, before pressing on to reach Oakland on July 7, where they

were welcomed by Vivian Maata, who had been Earhart's secretary and had hoped to be there to meet her Electra thirty years before. In 1997, for the 60th anniversary, Texas businesswoman Linda Finch paid her respects to Earhart's memory by doing it again in another restored Electra. Even in an ageing design, it was still an achievement, but the passage of time was apparent in the aircraft's cockpit, where computer displays and a global positioning system replaced the simple instruments of 1937.

Britain's Sheila Scott was another record breaker of the 1960s, and more prolific than most. From 1965 on, flying a Piper Comanche named *Myth Too*, she took every opportunity to set or break records. Most memorably, in May and June 1966, she completed the longest solo flight in a single-engine aircraft ever attempted by any pilot anywhere. Leaving London on May 18, Scott flew round the world with stops at Rome, Athens, Damascus, Bahrain, Karachi, Jaipur, Delhi, Calcutta, Rangoon, Butterworth, Singapore, Bali, Darwin, Mount Isa, Brisbane, Sydney, Auckland, Norfolk Island, Fiji, Pago Pago, Canton Island, Honolulu, San Francisco, Phoenix, El Paso, Oklahoma City, Louisville, New York, Gander, Lajes and Lisbon. She was back in London on June 20, having flown 31,000 miles in 189 flying hours. In the process she had added eight Class C1c inter-city records to her impressive collection. As the 20th century ended, more than 100 point-to-point records were held in Sheila Scott's name, including class records between the United Kingdom and South Africa, and across both the North and South Atlantic. In June 1971, she flew a Piper Aztec over the North Pole, so becoming the first woman to complete a polar crossing and the first pilot to do so solo. Many of the hazards faced by pioneers such as Amy Johnson have become things of the past. A Piper Comanche is not a D.H. Moth, and international airports are not beaches or sports fields. Nevertheless, Sheila Scott's achievements showed that technological advances had not diminished the aviator's urge to fly and to be first.

Over and Under

It was not until 1949 that a pilot could say he had piloted an aircraft over both poles. By then, the Norwegian-born Bernt Balchen, Byrd's South Pole pilot in 1929, was a colonel commanding an Arctic Rescue unit of the USAF. In May 1949, he flew a Douglas C-54 transport from

As a polar airman, Bernt Balchen (seen at right in this photograph) had no equal. During WWII, Colonel Bernt Balchen commanded a base in Greenland and worked with the Norwegian underground to set up escape routes. In 1949, he pioneered commercial Arctic air routes, flying a DC-4 from Fairbanks to Oslo. His efforts were recognized when SAS, the Scandinavian airline, had its polar routes approved in the early 1950s. Balchen was the first man to pilot an aircraft over both Poles. Note that here, after his return to the USAF, he is wearing both USAF and Norwegian Air Force Wings.

Fairbanks, Alaska, on a routine mission over the North Pole to Greenland. It was after he landed when a query from a mechanic made him realize that he had accomplished something unique.

Two TWA pilots, Fred Austin and Harrison Finch, decided in 1965 that it was time for someone to fly round the world following lines of longitude rather than latitude. Sponsored by Rockwell-Standard, they leased a Boeing 707 from the Flying Tiger Line and called it *Polecat*. Starting from Palm Springs, California, they planned fly to Hawaii and then to stick as closely as possible to the zero and 180 degree meridians, with refueling stops in London, Buenos Aires and Christchurch, New Zealand. As it turned out, bad weather forced a diversion from London's Stansted Airport to Heathrow, where they took on a light fuel load, adding another stop in Lisbon to make up the difference. With the sixty-six-year-old Bernt Balchen on board, the polar flight was completed between November 15 and 17, 1965, covering the 26, 230 miles in 62 hours, 28 minutes.

The Flying Tiger association was there again for the first solo polar orbit in 1971. Captain Elgen Long, a pilot for the airline, felt he had the necessary experience to try for the ultimate "over and under." Besides his 25,000 hours as a pilot, he held ratings as a navigator, radio operator and FAA mechanic. Long aimed to cross four cardinal points during his flight — both poles, plus the junctions of the equator with the Greenwich meridian and the International Date Line. A Piper Navajo was the chosen aircraft, modified by Nystron Aviation with additional fuel tanks to give a range of 4,000 miles. The flight began from San Francisco on November 5, 1971, and went on through Fairbanks, Tromso, Stockholm, London, Accra, Recife, Rio de Janiero, Puntas Arenas, McMurdo Sound, Sydney, Fiji, Wake Island, Honolulu and back to San Francisco. The Navajo performed flawlessly throughout, apart from problems with the cockpit heating system that Long overcame by wearing

Voyager, *by Paul Rendel. The grace and apparent fragility of* Voyager *is captured in Paul Rendel's painting. Buffeted by storm clouds during the aircraft's nonstop round-the-world flight,* Voyager's *immensely long wings bend and flex in turbulent air.*

three sets of thermal underwear and all the survival clothing he could find. His only other concern was the overpowering feeling of loneliness during the interminable legs over the poles: "As you're going toward the North Pole, farther and farther away from everyone, you become a speck, and the immensity of the ice-cap starts to get to you…it's difficult to imagine its vastness and your smallness."

California to California, Nonstop

Until 1986, the longest nonstop flights recorded had been those of a USAF B-52H, which flew 12,532 miles from Okinawa to Spain in 1962, and, for piston-engined aircraft, the 11,235 miles covered by a U.S. Navy P2V-1 Neptune flying from Australia to Ohio in 1946. Given the problem of lifting enough fuel to get the job done, it seemed almost inconceivable that an aircraft could be built with the range to fly unrefueled round the world, but that is what designer Burt Rutan set out to do. The result was the *Voyager*, an unconventional two-place, twin-engined aircraft made of lightweight composite material, mainly a sandwich of honeycomb paper and graphite fiber, which kept the structural weight under 1,000 pounds. At takeoff, however, *Voyager* weighed well over 9,000 pounds. Most of that was fuel, more than 7,000 pounds of it in seventeen tanks. The lift was provided by 110-foot-span high aspect-ratio wings so flexible that the tips deflected upward some 5 feet in flight. Power came from two Teledyne Continental engines mounted in tandem, the one in front producing 130 horsepower and the one behind, 110 horsepower. Both engines were used together only for takeoff or for emergency maneuvering. In flight, the *Voyager* cruised on the rear engine alone. Efficient use of power was essential, since success could be guaranteed only if the aircraft could average 4 miles per pound of fuel (24 miles to the U.S. gallon).

The pilots chosen were Dick Rutan and Jeana Yeager. In taking on the flight, they knew that they would be sharing a compartment just 7.5 feet long and 3.5 feet across for more than a week. The *Voyager* cruised at not much more than 110 mph and there were over 24,000 miles to go. They took off on December 14, 1986, from Edwards Air Force Base,

California. The USAF's test center was used because of its exceptionally long runways, and on the day, *Voyager* took 14,200 feet to get airborne. During the two-minute takeoff roll, the tips of the fuel-filled wings dragged along the ground, damaging the winglets fitted to improve aerodynamic efficiency. The winglets broke off soon after, but the decision was made to continue the flight. From then on the principal challenge for Rutan and Yeager was to cope with the physical and mental strain of being confined for days on end in a coffin-sized space while flying in long straight lines and listening to the unchanging note of the rear engine.

For most of the trip, the weather allowed *Voyager* to hold desired headings and to fly at the optimum cruising altitude of 8,000 feet. In the Pacific, the fringe of a typhoon was used to boost the *Voyager's* groundspeed to 150 mph for a while, and thunderstorms over Africa forced the crew to start the front engine and climb to 20,000 feet. Off Brazil at night, a violent storm almost hurled the fragile aircraft onto its back, but perhaps the most alarming incident occurred on the last day when exhaustion was taking its effect on the crew. An air pocket developed in the fuel line to the rear engine and it stalled. Voyager fell some 5,000 feet before they could get the front engine started. With the aircraft climbing again, the blockage was overcome and the rear engine recovered. A few hours later, *Voyager* landed back at Edwards AFB, nine days, 3 minutes and 44 seconds after taking off. It had been a close run thing. Almost 99 percent of their fuel load was gone. The official distance flown by the *Voyager* was 24,986,727 statute miles at an average speed of 115.65 mph.

The last great milestone in atmospheric aviation was passed as Rutan and Yeager touched down in California. Almost as an afterthought, it was observed that, for the first time, the world records for distance in a straight line and over a closed circuit had been set at the same time. The *Voyager* lived up to its promise as a superb example of the aircraft designer's art and a splendid technological achievement, but it was a very specialized machine. It had not been intended to make major contributions to the mainstream development of aeronautics nor to drive for commercial success. *Voyager* was built because flying round the world nonstop had not been done, and someone had to be first.

CHAPTER 3

The Entertainers

*"Racing planes didn't necessarily require
courage, but it did demand a certain amount
of foolhardiness and a total disregard of one's skin."*

MARY HAIZLIP, PIONEER AIR RACER

THE AVIATION WORLD HAS always had room for people with a flair for showmanship — individuals who take delight in showing off their aerial talent or their extraordinary machines. From the earliest days, crowds were drawn to witness the spectacle of human flight, fascinated by the phenomenon of three-dimensional freedom and the fliers who dared to exploit it. Aviators generally reveled in the adulation. The Wright brothers were exceptions to the rule, working as they did in almost complete seclusion before competition drove them into the open and launched them on the world stage in 1908. Most other pioneers disdained the detached attitude of the Wrights, actively seeking the limelight and enjoying the headlines. It is no coincidence that an active promoter of aviation in its early days was a press baron, Lord Northcliffe of London's *Daily Mail*. He knew that flying exploits made good stories and that readers of his newspapers could not get enough of them. Given that aviation could generate such excitement, it was inevitable that flying machines and the general public would be brought together at an early stage in the history of heavier-than-air flight. Flying, it was realized, had the potential to become a major spectator sport, capable of being exploited for profit by sponsors, promoters and the aviators themselves.

Conceived in France, the first real air show was born at Reims in 1909, and every display since, from the barnstormers of the 1920s to the vast annual Experimental Aircraft Association's gathering of the aeronautical clans at Oshkosh, Wisconsin, traces its ancestry to that event. Changed though they may be in scale or detail, the character of air shows remains essentially the same. For aviators, they are welcomed as an excuse for getting together to swap yarns and examine each other's machines. A few brave visitors can go for joyrides, perhaps to experience flying for the first time. Often, the meeting performs the function of an aeronautical marketplace,

OPPOSITE PAGE *The USAF Museum's Boeing P-12, seen during its restoration at Wright-Patterson AFB, Dayton, Ohio. The vast majority of aircraft on display in the world's aviation museums and those flying as vintage machines at air shows for the pleasure of the general public have been painstakingly restored, often starting from piles of almost unrecognizable wreckage. The investment of time and money in these restorations is huge, and a debt of gratitude is owed to those whose dedicated efforts do so much to preserve the icons of aviation history.*

where aircraft and their accessories are demonstrated, bought and sold. Above all these things, however, air shows are occasions for the public to be thrilled by the sights and sounds of an aerial circus, and they offer pilots the irresistible chance of performing in front of an admiring audience on the world's greatest stage — an arena stretching beyond the horizon and encompassing the clouds.

The Reims Meeting

Aviation's first great gathering at Reims, in northern France, was held from August 22 to 29, 1909, promoted largely by the Champagne industry. The dramatic events of the twelve months since Wilbur Wright's first demonstrations at Le Mans had caught the public eye and huge crowds flocked to Reims to see the phenomenon of flying at first hand. Most people had never even seen a flying machine, and here was a chance for them to discover that the adventure of taking to the air was more than mere fantasy. Political and military leaders were among the distinguished guests who were duly impressed by the exhibition. Lloyd George, then Britain's Chancellor of the Exchequer, was astonished and perhaps alarmed by what he saw. His comments reflected the views of many politicians confronted at Reims with the realities of aviation for the first time. "Flying machines are no longer toys and dreams," he said, "They are an established fact. The possibilities of this new system of locomotion are infinite. I feel, as a Britisher, rather ashamed that we are so completely out of it." On the evidence, he was right to feel bad. Only one British pilot was present, George Cockburn, and he was flying a French Farman biplane.

A poster announcing the first Paris air show, held in the city's Grand Palais in 1909. Of the 333 exhibitors at the exposition, 318 were French.

Thirty-eight aircraft appeared at Reims, but only twenty-three flew during the eight days of the show. Of these, eight were monoplanes and fifteen biplanes. The monoplanes were four Blériots (two XIs, a XII and a XIII), two Antoinettes, and one REP (Robert Esnault-Pelterie). The biplanes were seven Voisins, three Henry Farmans, three Wrights, one Breguet and one Curtiss. More than 120 takeoffs were made and many records established in the course of competition. If there was a disappointment, it was that the Wright brothers did not attend, Wilbur scorning the idea of public display, but the presence of almost everyone else of note in aviation, and their performances in the air ensured the show's success.

Henry Farman had fitted an engine of new design to his aircraft. It was a Gnôme rotary, in which the seven cylinders rotated round a fixed crankshaft, producing 50 horsepower for a weight of 165 pounds. (The Gnôme was the ancestor of a family of rotary engines much in demand for the combat aircraft of WWI.) With it, Farman won the 50,000-franc ($10,000) grand prize for distance, flying 180 kilometers (111.8 miles) in 3 hours, 5 minutes. He also caused some excitement when he became the first ever to fly carrying two passengers at once. Hubert Latham shrugged off the effects of his recent unsuccessful attempts to fly across the Channel by setting an altitude record of 155 meters (509 feet) in his Antoinette. The highest speed of the meeting, 76.95 km/h (almost 48 mph), was recorded by Blériot in his Type XII, but the Gordon Bennett prize of 25,000 francs, awarded for the highest speed achieved over two laps of a closed circuit, went to Glenn Curtiss, the only American competing. His *Reims Racer* was a pusher biplane of his own design with separate ailerons set between the wings. It had been built especially for the Reims competition, and was powered by a Curtiss V-8 engine delivering 50 horsepower. On August 28, Glenn Curtiss completed the 20-kilometer course in 15 minutes, 50.6 seconds, an average speed of 75.76 km/h (47 mph). To the despair of the home crowd, he beat their hero, Blériot, by less than six seconds.

To add to the thrills of aerial achievement, the Reims meeting had several accidents, although no serious injuries. Both Louis Breguet and Henri Fourneau wrecked their aircraft, and Leon Delagrange carried out a forced landing when his propeller disintegrated. Blériot crashed twice, the second time burning his hands when his aircraft burst into flame after hitting the ground in a turn. Given

the frail nature of the machines and the lack of safety features, even seatbelts, it is remarkable that until after the Reims meeting there were few bad flying accidents and even fewer fatalities. (In powered flying machines, there had been only one, Lieutenant Selfridge at Fort Myer.) This was a blessed state of affairs that could not last long. Within a month, two of France's most prominent pioneers, Eugene Lefebvre and Ferdinand Ferber, were killed; Lefebvre when his Wright Type A suffered structural failure in the air, and Ferber when he taxied his Voisin at high speed into a ditch.

It would be hard to overstate the effect of the Reims meeting on aviation. It was profound, bolstering the growing public impression that flying was becoming a practical activity, that it was here to stay, and that it held great promise for the future. Aviation meetings and competitions grew increasingly popular, and the seeds of the aircraft industry

Early aircraft, such as this 1909 Blériot, were fragile creatures. Sunshine reveals their translucent character, the dark framework etched on delicate fabric. Blériots appeared in most of the early air shows, and this one is regularly a star of the show at the Shuttleworth Collection in England.

were sown. Many aircraft and engine designers basked in the warm glow of public interest after Reims, especially Blériot. Following his triumph over the Channel and his flamboyance at Reims, he received orders for over one hundred aircraft, and his Type XI, suitably modified, became well known in various parts of the world, remaining in service for several years and inspiring many imitators.

After Reims

The remarkable success of the Reims meeting prompted others to reproduce it and so reap the profits there for the taking in organizing an aviation spectacular. Before the end of 1909, hastily arranged competitive air shows had been mounted in Brescia, Berlin and at two towns in northern England, Doncaster and Blackpool. At none of them were the preparations so comprehensive as at Reims, and the competitions often descended into organizational farce, not helped by frequently unfriendly weather. The large crowds that turned out were for the most part rewarded by rain and very little flying, but since few people had ever seen an aircraft, they seemed well satisfied when even one machine took to the air. In Berlin they were thrilled to see the great Blériot, and he was content to receive some $4,000 for his efforts. If the meeting at Brescia, Italy, is at all memorable, it is perhaps because two writers were there and were influenced by what they saw. The young Franz Kafka recorded his impressions in a piece called *Die Aeroplane in Brescia*, and the hero of the Italian poet D'Annunzio's novel *Forse*

che si, forse che no (Perhaps Yes, Perhaps No) is an aviator who takes part in an international meeting at Brescia. The words of both writers convey a feeling of awe at seeing machines fly, and a deep admiration, approaching reverence, for the superhuman beings who perch at the controls, becoming the brain of the mechanical bird and directing its movements.

A useful "Aero Show" was held in London in March 1909, and similar events were repeated annually until 1914. They were indoor exhibitions, and the first one attracted eleven aeroplanes and several engine manufacturers, besides a number of aeronautical contractors. In September 1909, the French capitalized on the success of Reims and again scored a triumph with their much larger Exposition of Aerial Locomotion in Paris. There were 333 exhibitors who laid out their aeronautical wares in the imposing setting of the Grand Palais. The fact that 318 of them were French reflected to some extent of the home ground advan-

ABOVE *The stone marking the spot near Dover Castle where Blériot landed after crossing the English Channel in 1909 is in the shape of his aircraft. The inscription reads: "After making the first Channel flight by aeroplane Louis Blériot landed at this spot on Sunday 25th July 1909."* LEFT *Before WWI, Roland Garros took part in numerous air shows and races, and in 1912 became the official test pilot for manufacturer Morane-Saulnier, breaking the world altitude record in an MS monoplane.*

tage of the hosts, but more to the point, it emphasized the rapid rise of France to a position of very real dominance in the aviation world, only one year after Wilbur Wright had stunned the Europeans with his masterly flying at Le Mans.

The events of 1909 established the way in which aviation, its achievements and prospects, would be set before the public. Generally speaking, in this pre-WWI period, "meetings" were outdoor aerial circuses and "shows" were indoor static exhibitions. As the years went by, the distinction became less clear, until most large "air shows" later in the century productively combined the functions of entertainment and commercial promotion.

The year 1909 had opened the flood gates for aviation as public entertainment. Within months, it was hardly possible to find a weekend without a meeting or a show being held somewhere. The first organized meeting in the United States was staged by the Aero Club of California at Dominguez Fields, Los Angeles, in January 1910. Far smaller than the Reims meeting, it still had attractions enough to draw crowds, including appearances by Glenn Curtiss and the French airman, Louis Paulhan. Between them, they pocketed most of the available prize money, with $19,000 going to Paulhan, who set new marks for height (4,165 feet) and, with a flight of over 100 miles, for passenger carrying. Los Angeles got the year off to a flying start, and meetings proliferated, with major events in Europe at Paris, Bar-le-Duc, Cannes, Le Havre, Lyons, Nice, Rouen, Brussels, Barcelona, Berlin, Munich, Bologna, Florence, Milan, Geneva, Copenhagen, Budapest and St. Petersburg. Britain had displays at London, Bournemouth, Burton, Cardiff, Dublin and Lanark, and the Middle East joined in with one at Heliopolis, Egypt. In the U.S., Los

Angeles was followed by Boston and Belmont Park, N.Y.

Invariably, the number of people attending these displays, whatever the weather, was large. The novelty of the experience was part of the attraction, but it was also true that most spectators recognized flying as a hazardous occupation. The vicarious thrill of watching aviators risk their lives in frail machines was certainly a factor in drawing the crowds. In 1910, there were many occasions when those who paid their entrance fee expecting to see a crash were suitably rewarded. The first midair collision ever recorded happened at Milan, when an Antoinette collided with a Henry Farman, both pilots having the good fortune to survive. At Bournemouth, the Honourable C.S. Rolls (of the Rolls-Royce partnership) crashed and was killed when an auxiliary elevator fitted to his Wright biplane gave way during a diving turn. Besides such serious accidents, the early displays were full of lesser incidents, with wings being crumpled, propellers broken and undercarriages bent. The most serious damage was often that suffered by an aviator's pride, but there was no doubt that display flying was a dangerous business, and many fliers regarded their admiring audiences with cynicism. Ralph Johnstone, who flew for the Wright brothers and was killed in a crash in November 1910, wrote: "The people who go to see us want thrills. And, if we fall, do they think of us and go away weeping? Not by a long shot. They're too busy watching the next man and wondering if he will repeat the performance."

Another draw for the crowds was the star quality of the leading fliers, many of whom became internationally known and made small fortunes out of their celebrity status. High on the list in 1910 was the Englishman Claude

The air show at Brescia in September 1909 was significant in promoting the idea of aviation in Italy. Among the aviators were Louis Blériot and Glenn Curtiss, and spectators included Puccini and the poet Gabriele D'Annunzio. Curtiss flew his first passenger at Brescia — D'Annunzio, who later composed a poem about his experience of flying in the Rheims Racer. Writer Franz Kafka was there, too, and his first published work was an account of the air show at Brescia.

C.G.WHITE.
FLYING at HENDON SERIES. 216.

Grahame-White. A handsome, dashing figure, and already rich, Grahame-White was inspired by stories of Louis Blériot's Channel crossing. He went to the Reims meeting to see some flying and, impressed by what he saw, he bought a Blériot on the spot. Before 1909 was out, he had his pilot's certificate, and by February 1910 had established his own flying school at Pau in southern France with six Blériot XIs. Only five months after learning to fly, he was a household name, gaining enormous publicity from being the gallant loser in his race with Louis Paulhan from London to Manchester in April 1910. He was in constant demand to perform at air displays, and news of his prowess

spread across the Atlantic. Members of the Harvard Aeronautical Society, dazzled by his reputation, offered him the enormous sum of $50,000 plus expenses to fly in the air meet they were organizing for September 1910 at Squantum, near Boston. Once there, his good looks and charm, combined with his willingness to fly as often as asked, gained Grahame-White both social and financial success. Female admirers were frequently among those who paid $500 to fly round the field with him, and his 100-horsepower Blériot proved unbeatable in the competitions. (Military observers took note of Grahame-White's performance against a model ship target. He scored nine direct hits with "bombs" made of plaster.) By the end of the week, he had added prize money of $22,100 to his fee. He picked up another $50,000 for an appearance at nearby Brockton, before going on to New York for the biggest air meet in the United States so far, held at Belmont Park on Long Island from October 22 to 30.

Belmont Park was the site for the second Gordon Bennett Aviation Cup competition, which took place on the penultimate day of a week filled with air racing events and contests of piloting skill. Speeds had risen sharply in the year since Reims, many aircraft being capable of well over 60 mph. Competitors arrived from France and the U.K. to challenge the Americans on their home ground, and although the race was arranged as individual time trials, it promised to be a thrilling affair. In the end, it was not so. Crashes and mechanical problems removed most of the fastest aircraft, leaving Grahame-White in an unassailable position, having completed the 100-kilometer course in just over 61 minutes at an average speed of 98.25 km/h (60.9 mph). All would have been well had the meet ended there, but there was one more race to come. A prize of $10,000 was offered by New York financier Thomas F. Ryan for the fastest flight from Belmont to the Statue of Liberty and back again. Grahame-White posted the best time before the contest was declared closed and was hailed as the winner, but John Moisant, taking off late, was faster by 43 seconds. The judges deliberated, changed their minds about the contest being closed and announced that Moisant was the winner. Denied the chance of a rerun, Grahame-White lodged a formal protest with the Federation Aeronautique Internationale. More than a year later, the FAI upheld the protest and awarded the prize money to Grahame-White, together with some $500 interest. By then, John Moisant was in no state to regret his loss. He was killed when his Blériot crashed near New Orleans on December 31, 1910.

> *"Air racing may not be better than your wedding night, but it's better than the second night."*
>
> MICKEY RUPP, INDIANAPOLIS 500 DRIVER
> AND AIR RACER

Air shows and meetings had become well established as essential elements of the aviation calendar by the end of 1910, and the pattern was continued and expanded during the remaining years before WWI. Ever an astute business-man and consummate showman, Grahame-White took advantage of the aviation boom, using his considerable winnings to acquire a plot of land for an airfield at Hendon, northwest of London. There he promoted meetings with advertisements such as this one from 1912: "Racing every Saturday and holiday (weather permitting). Special exhibition flights every Thursday, Saturday and Sunday afternoon by well-known aviators. Admission to enclosures 6d, 1s and 2s/6d. Passenger flights from £2/2s." The crowds that gathered for the holiday displays often numbered more than

50,000, which assured Grahame-White of a comfortable profit on his investment and was an indication of the public excitement generated by display flying.

Of the proliferating air races, two emerged as major annual international events: the Gordon Bennett Aviation Cup, and the Coupe d'Aviation Maritime Jacques Schneider, commonly called the Schneider Trophy. For the most part, French machines dominated, filling the leader board at the Gordon Bennett and at most of the lesser events. The 1911 Gordon Bennett, run at Eastchurch in England, was won by a Nieuport monoplane at 126 km/h (78 mph). However, the pilot was the American Charles Weymann, so the 1912 competition was held near Chicago. This time, the French regained their composure, and the winner was Jules Vedrines flying a 160-horsepower Deperdussin at an average speed of 170 km/h (105 mph). In 1913, back at Reims, the French emphasized their superiority when Maurice Prévost won in another Deperdussin at 201 km/h (125 mph). In just four years the winning speed had risen to more than two and a half times that set by Curtiss in the first Gordon Bennett.

Taking to the Water

The first hydro-aeroplane contest ever held was at Monaco in March 1912. Since most of the contestants either crashed or could not take off, it was something of a farce, but the Belgian pilot, Jules Fischer, was judged to have won with a Henry Farman biplane. The tests included one that required aircraft to take off from water with a passenger, fly a selected course and return to harbor, landing both pilot

Italian flying boats such as the Savoia S.13 dominated the Schneider Trophy competition in the years after WWI. Only the unfortunate missing of a turning point in the fog at Bournemouth in 1919 prevented the Italians from winning three times in a row and so retaining the trophy in perpetuity after 1921.

and passenger without getting their feet wet. A second hydro-aeroplane meet, again at Monaco, was organized for April 1913. This was a much more elaborate affair, with various contests taking place over two weeks. The last day introduced the Schneider Trophy, an international event that grew to have unexpected consequences. Jacques Schneider believed that maritime aircraft held the future to international travel, and his original intention was to encourage the development of fast but practical aircraft, with a good payload and reasonable range, and capable of operating from the open sea. He had no wish to spawn a family of freakish racing machines. Alas for his principles, the turn of events after WWI made it inevitable that the competition should go to the swift rather than the practical.

The Schneider Trophy was an open international competition, and each nation choosing to compete was permitted to enter up to three aircraft. The trophy would be retained permanently by a nation that managed to win the trophy three times in five successive contests. In the 1913 competition at Monaco, French aviation dominance was readily apparent. All four competing aircraft were French, as were three of the pilots. Even the American pilot Charles Weymann was born in Haiti and brought up in France. It was a small beginning to an event that would later involve governments and affect national prestige.

The Schneider Trophy was not strictly a race. Aircraft started at intervals and flew round a closed-circuit course independently. In 1913, they had first to demonstrate seaworthiness by taxiing 5 kilometers before taking off to fly another 280 kilometers. Two of the French pilots were eliminated at an early stage, leaving Maurice Prévost and Charlie Weymann to fight it out. Prévost was first away and the first to finish, but, contrary to the competition rules, he made the mistake of landing short and taxiing to the finish. Weymann, meanwhile, was airborne and flying faster, so Prévost refused to take off again and fly over the line to record an official time. With the trophy seemingly in his grasp, Weymann was denied at the last by a broken oil-line, so Prévost decided that he would fly again after all. His winning speed was given as 45 mph, but it should have been 61 mph, if he had not wasted nearly an hour brooding over his premature touchdown.

The 1913 Schneider Trophy may have been a disappointment, but 1914 looked more promising. France, Germany, Switzerland, the U.S. and the U.K. were all represented at Monaco in April 1914. Once again, however, the machines proved generally unreliable. Only two aircraft completed the course, and the winner was a tiny British biplane called the Sopwith Tabloid, which averaged 87 mph to finish well ahead of a Franco-British Aviation flying boat entered by Switzerland. The French made the most of the fact that the Tabloid's engine was a 100-horsepower Gnôme rotary, but they were downcast at the failure of their Deperdussins and Nieuports to match the Tabloid's performance. The long-term effects of the result were more profound. The arguments of those who promoted the innate superiority of biplanes seemed to have been justified. For the time being, and until well after WWI was over, biplanes held the upper hand over their monoplane rivals. (See *Aviation Century The Early Years,* Chapter 1, Reservations.)

ROARING TWENTIES, NERVOUS THIRTIES

World War I imposed an interregnum on flying as sport or entertainment (although some airmen belittled the horrors of aerial combat by maintaining that it contained elements of each), but the end of hostilities led rapidly to a resurgence of both. Suddenly there were thousands of surplus aircraft available at knock-down prices, and lots of newly trained pilots who were reluctant to forgo their recently acquired skills and go back to the office or the farm. Eager though many were to stay in the cockpit, however, there were not nearly enough flying jobs to go round. The military air services were being savagely cut back and organized civil aviation was still embryonic. On both sides of the Atlantic the situa-

tion produced aviators who sought to make a living by flying for themselves. Nowhere did this become more apparent than in the United States, where the small towns and farming communities of the countryside experienced an aerial invasion of young men eager to earn their keep by introducing people to the exhilaration of flying. The phenomenon soon earned a name. It was called "barnstorming."

The Barnstormers

In Britain after WWI, the aircraft most used by often penniless pilots was the Avro 504, and in the United States it was the Curtiss JN-4 Jenny. The JN-4 was not a spectacular performer. Powered by its 90-horsepower Curtiss OX-5 engine, a new machine was flat out in level flight at 75 mph. However, it had two seats and, provided there was sufficient height, it was fully aerobatic. It could be bought for about $600, and, since some 10,000 had been built, spares were plentiful. An overhauled OX-5 could be had for $75, and recovered wings were only $30. Reconditioned ailerons,

ABOVE *Harold Johnson has been performing and flying in air shows across the country since the end of the barnstorming era. This portrait was made in 1979 when he was known as the "Flying Mayor," as he was the elected mayor of Moraine, Ohio. Johnson is also a past president of the National Aviation Hall of Fame.*
LEFT *Wingwalking was an early staple of the barnstormer's repertoire. Jimmy Dorsey, seen here at the end of the wing, at the bottom of the photo, has recreated some of the past century's most daring stunts. During an air-show performance with pilot Darrell Montgomery, he would walk and crawl all over the Stearman biplane. According to Dorsey, the first rule of wingwalking is "to not let go of what you're holdin' onto, until you get a hold of something else."*

Ormer Locklear was always willing to try a new stunt and would do almost anything with an aircraft that a movie script required. Here he scares the bad men off a church steeple by simply flying his Curtiss Jenny through it!

rudders and elevators cost no more than $2.50 each. Most of the young men who flew the Jennies did their own maintenance, learning the hard way as they operated from any open space available, usually a farmer's field near a town. Since the aircraft generally spent their lives in the open in all weathers, they needed constant attention, and pilots had to be able to dismantle and reassemble engines, patch worn and torn fabric, and repair broken struts and bracing wires, often under the eyes of an admiring local audience.

For many people in the American heartland, a barnstormer's Jenny was the first aircraft they had seen, and the man who emerged from it was necessarily a heroic and romantic figure. The young pilots fostered this image and dressed the part, appearing in leather jackets, silk scarves, gauntlets, riding breeches, shiny boots and begoggled helmets. A flamboyant mustache was an optional extra. The free and easy, devil-may-care nonchalance that went with the classic picture of the glamorous airman was often a bold front covering a hand-to-mouth existence in which pilots slept under the wings of their planes and sometimes had to offer flights in exchange for a meal, a bath or a gallon of fuel. In the early days, when barnstorming was a novelty,

things were not too bad. Arriving over a likely looking town, a barnstormer would fly low to attract attention and then land in a nearby field, hoping that the local people would be interested enough to follow. When they did, they would be offered a flight of ten minutes or so for perhaps $15. As time went by and people became more accustomed to aircraft, the price fell, reaching $3 or even less. Asked what he thought was the most dangerous thing about flying, one barnstormer answered, "The risk of starving to death." To revive waning enthusiasm, airmen had to add touches of the spectacular, putting on aerobatic demonstrations and offering their passengers the chance to fly upside down. It was haphazard and unpredictable, but barnstorming introduced Americans to aviation as nothing else could have done. Flooding across the country spreading the word of their flying gospel, barnstormers laid the foundations of air-mindedness on which was built the rise of the aviation industry. Local airfields, private aircraft, flying clubs, and the acceptance of the idea that aircraft could be used to transport mail and people from one place to another — barnstormers profoundly influenced these and many other facets of aviation's development.

On a Wing and a Prayer

As the barnstorming business became increasingly competitive, aviators banded together in groups to put on air shows, devising stunts that became ever more spectacular. Low-level aerobatics might be done as a synchronized team or in formation. A brave (or foolhardy) barnstormer sometimes flew with a partner and climbed out of the cockpit in flight to walk on the wing, unhindered by anything so craven as a safety harness. These nerveless individuals followed in the footsteps of the pre-WWI aviators for whom the challenge of being seen as the most daring performer in the air was irresistible, and their airborne antics were of a kind that truly deserved to be described as death-defying.

Typical of the barnstormers who were advertised as "dancing with death" was Ormer Locklear. While serving as a U.S. Army pilot in Texas, he began adding excitement to his flying by handing over to another pilot and then leaving the cockpit to wander around the aircraft, first on the lower wing and then on the upper. In 1919, he resigned to accept an offer from William Pickens, an entrepreneur who specialized in presenting spectacular acts to the public. Pickens said he was "willing to risk a generous dollar provided the other man would chance his neck." With performances that included handstands on the upper wing, and hanging from his Jenny's landing gear to drop onto an aircraft below, Locklear was in great demand. He knew he needed to keep his act fresh by adding to it, and was always willing to try something different. With two aircraft flying wingtip to wingtip, he changed planes in midair, stepping across the gap from one to the other. At a show in Erie, Pennsylvania, he stood up in a speeding car and grabbed a ladder hanging beneath a passing Jenny. Before long, Locklear was flying for Universal Films in Hollywood, performing his stunts in a silent epic called *The Great Air Robbery* and making more money than he had thought possible.

In August 1920, for 20th Century Fox's film *The Skywayman*, Locklear was hired to fly a Jenny at night, entering a spin during which he would ignite magnesium flares under the wings to simulate the aircraft's fiery demise. To help the cameras, the night sky was lit by five massive arc lights. All went well until the latter stages of the spin, when the lights seemed to blind and confuse the pilot. Locklear's Jenny hit the ground and exploded, bringing him the death he had so often courted. The shock of Locklear's passing was felt across the nation. Few airmen have gone to their graves with such ceremony. On the way to Los Angeles railway station, his casket was escorted by a military honor guard, a police band, a troop of movie cowboys and countless limousines. A formation of aircraft circled overhead. In Fort Worth, 50,000 people lined the streets to bid him farewell, and thousands more clustered round the church and in the cemetery where he was buried. The *Los Angeles Times* mourned his passing, but added that it was unlikely to discourage others from being as audacious.

The *Times* was quite right. Teams of wingwalkers such as the Lunatics of Love Field and the Flying Black Hats went on devising outrageous stunts to astonish the public. Men hung beneath aircraft by their teeth or their heels, and a man named "Bonnie" Rowe moved from one aircraft to another with one hand tied behind his back. Women, too, got into the acts and proved just as intrepid as their male counterparts. Gladys Ingle practiced archery while standing on one wingtip with a target on the other, and simulated playing tennis along the top wing against a male opponent. Buffalo

The Avro Tutor was a lively performer at air shows in the U.K., and sometimes had time to pick up handkerchiefs.

Bill's niece, Mabel Cody, danced on the wings and did transfers from speedboat to aircraft. Lillian Boyer hung by one hand beneath a Jenny, and Gladys Roy walked the top wing blindfolded. (Frank Hawks and Wesley May could be considered in-flight refueling pioneers since each of them did a stunt in which he crossed from one aircraft to another with a can of fuel to top up the second aircraft's tank.) There was a price to pay for this uninhibited behavior. In 1923, there were 179 barnstorming accidents in which 85 people were killed and 126 injured. Such carnage could not be allowed to continue, and in 1926 the U.S. Congress passed the *Air Commerce Act*, which included provisions for comprehensive licensing of pilots and mechanics, and registration and inspection of aircraft. "String and sealing wax" machines could no longer fly, and the free-for-all days of the individual barnstormer were effectively over.

The Flying Circus

A natural development of the barnstorming era was the flying circus, an organized traveling air show consisting of a number of aircraft performing in set pieces and featuring both men and women as pilots and wingwalkers. Among the most celebrated was the Gates Flying Circus, whose chief pilot was Clyde Pangborn, which by 1927 could expect to draw a crowd of 30,000 to each performance. (Pangborn was the first to fly across the Pacific nonstop. See Chapter 2, Travels from Tokyo.) Admission to the airfield for the show was usually $1, but that was not the main source of income.

As Duke Krantz, one of the star performers, explained: "The main thing was to put on wingwalking shows to draw the people. Then we would sell tickets and take people up for rides." A straight flight was offered at $5, and one with aerobatics for $10. Krantz included a transfer to another aircraft in his act. The second machine had a ladder hanging down from one wingtip. As it approached, he would "walk out past the outer strut and up on the upper wing, where there was a brace you could steady your leg against. That was the only thing you could hold on to at all." Then, as the ladder hanging from the second aircraft came closer, he would "reach for the last rung. Then it was only a matter of hanging on, because by that time the other ship was out from under you, leaving you in space."

The Gates Flying Circus team was not by any means the only one touring the United States. Between the wars, there were dozens of flying circuses — among them Jimmy Angel's Flying Circus, Cliff Rose Death Angels, Hunter Brothers' Flying Circus, Tidewater Air Circus, Doug Davis Baby Ruth Flying Circus, Flying Aces Air Circus, and (defying superstition) 13 Black Cats. Each team had its own style, but all included spectacular feats of daring in their shows. Walter Hunter of the Hunter Brothers hung by his knees from the undercarriage spreader bar of a low-flying Jenny before letting go and

ABOVE In their name and way of life, the members of the 13 Black Cats flying circus defied superstition and the norms of rational behavior. As their promotional material said, they were prepared to "do anything" that involved an airplane, a motorcycle or an automobile.

LEFT Even with an empty cockpit, some Black Cats preferred to hang about outside.

Air shows in the 1930s helped raise public consciousness about aviation while providing a spectacle for many and air experience for a few. RIGHT *In Britain, Alan Cobham's Flying Circus toured with groups of aircraft to put on shows and offer the opportunity for some people to get airborne. Here a Handley Page W.10 airliner is leading an Avro 504, a D.H. Gipsy Moth, a Miles Southern Martlet and a D.H. Tiger Moth to another venue.*
BELOW *The Avro 504 was cheap, stable, and easy to fly and maintain. These qualities made it a popular mount for Alan Cobham's wingwalkers.*

was $150, and a fight with one man being knocked off in midair cost $225. Looping with a man standing up on each wingtip needed $450, but a head-on collision with a car could be had for only $250. Curiously, crashing into more static objects, such as houses or trees, cost a great deal more — $1,200. At $1,500, blowing up an aircraft in midair while the pilot bailed out was understandably the most expensive item.

falling into a haystack. Occasionally the unexpected livened up the show. Jessie Woods of the Flying Aces has told of the time when she became "the world's first topless wingwalker." It was a hot day and she was wearing a light shirt, which was torn off by the slipstream while she was hanging from the landing gear. As she clambered back to the cockpit, she watched her young pilot's eyes widen as she revealed "skin, and then more skin, and then still more skin!" Much surprised, but very gallant, he passed her his own shirt before they landed to great applause. (At Florida's Sun 'n' Fun Airshow in 1991, at the age of 82, Jessie Woods relived the triumphs of her youth, standing on the top wing of a Stearman as it flew past the crowds!)

Among the best organized of the American Flying Circuses was 13 Black Cats. They established a fixed price list for their various stunts. To move from one aircraft to another was $100, and from a motorcycle to an aircraft, $150. Flying upside down with a man on the landing gear

In the United Kingdom, the most professional flying circus was run by Alan Cobham, who came back to display flying after making his name with international trailblazing flights. (See Chapter 2, Cobham's Continent.) In the early 1930s, Cobham set out on an aerial crusade to make Britons more air-minded. Starting with a flag-waving tour of the U.K., in a D.H.61 Giant Moth named *Youth of Britain*, he gathered together a dozen or so different types of aircraft, which he took to two or three towns every week during the summer, giving displays and passenger flights. He did not labor in vain. Many of the young men who rushed to join the RAF when war loomed in 1939 first experienced flying in an aircraft of Alan Cobham's Flying Circus.

Better organized though they became over the years, there was no denying the risks run by flying circus performers. Each season added more deaths and many close calls.

One of the closest came during a show put on by Gates Flying Circus. A young woman named Rosalie Gordon tangled the lines of her parachute in the undercarriage as she jumped from an aircraft's wing. She swung helplessly in the slipstream some 20 feet below the machine. Stuntman Milton Girton left the cockpit and reached the spreader bar but did not have the strength to pull the girl up. Pilot Clyde Pangborn knew that time was limited; he did not have much fuel. A second aircraft got airborne, and another stuntman, Freddy Lund, got on Pangborn's wing. Lund joined Girton, but even pulling together they could not reel in the helpless Rosalie Gordon. The slightly built Lund then climbed up to the cockpit and took over the controls, allowing the much bigger Pangborn to add his muscle to Girton's. Inch by painful inch they pulled her to safety, but they took her no further than they had to. Pangborn dragged himself back to the cockpit and landed the aircraft as gently as he could, with Girton and a very shaken Rosalie Gordon still perched precariously on the spreader bar. Many people in the audience thought it was all part of the act and went home suitably impressed.

Free-wheeling, "anything goes" teams such as Gates Flying Circus were gradually forced out of the business by increasingly restrictive regulations. By 1929, the Gates performers had given their last show. They were replaced as the leading circus in the U.S. by the Flying Aces, which was operated by Jimmie and Jessie Woods from 1929 to 1938. The Woods did not use government surplus equipment. Their aircraft were new Stearmans, Swallows and Travel Airs, and their maintenance practices were tightly controlled. The Flying Aces did their best to stay within the regulations, but even they were eventually worn down. By the time of the Civil Aeronautics Act of 1938, they knew it was pointless to go on. As Jessie Woods put it, "They did not want air shows any more, we were too sensational. All they wanted was to educate people to the safety of flight and encourage the growth of business aviation and airlines." The movement that had done as much as any to open the eyes of the American public to aviation had become an obstacle to organized progress. Like the frontiersmen of an earlier age, the barnstormers and their kin were overtaken by events. It was time for the settlers and developers to establish a more civilized society.

The tradition of barnstorming did not disappear entirely. Elements of its flamboyance, carefully controlled, can still be seen in modern air shows, and a few groups do their best to recreate the atmosphere of the 1920s and 1930s. In the U.K., a wingwalking team operates Stearmans under the unlikely banner of the Utterly Butterly Barnstormers, and at Bealeton, Virginia, the Flying Circus invites people to "relive the golden years of flight" watching wingwalkers, biplane dogfights, crazy flying, and parachuting. Hot-air balloons are often on show, too, and flights can be booked in both balloons and open-cockpit biplanes such as the Stearman. The performers dress the part in leather helmets and silk scarves, and vintage cars tour the area. It is very nostalgic, and a delightful reminder of the days when all fliers were superstars and flying was a breathtaking, eye-popping, pulse-racing adventure.

> *"The sudden feeling of crushing weight when the machine banked round in a turn at 300 mph was sheer nightmare horror."*
>
> VICTOR BURNETT, JOURNALIST, 1937

The Big Show

More formally organized, and more closely associated with a single venue than the flying circuses, were large air shows and air fairs put on to showcase the aircraft industry and let the public see the military aircraft their taxes were buying. Between the wars, the largest military display was given each year at RAF Hendon, the airfield originally established northwest of London by Grahame-White. The series was initiated by Marshal of the Royal Air Force Lord Trenchard at a time when the RAF was fighting to maintain independent status. He felt that a public display of the RAF's capabilities might gain publicity that would do the cause no harm, besides serving as a recruiting tool and raising funds for the service's Memorial Fund. The first of these annual events — successively known as the RAF Tournament, the RAF Pageant and, from 1925, simply as the RAF Display — was held on July 3, 1920. The crowd of 60,000 who paid admission and the thousands more who watched from nearby hills saw an impressive display of aerobatics, formation flying and mock bombing attacks that drew praise from a press that had not been overly supportive of the RAF's case for independence. In the years that followed, the show

Formation aerobatics have been a feature of air shows since the 1920s. The RAF biplane teams between the World Wars were provided by individual squadrons or units. They developed the use of smoke and sometimes made their entrance tied together. After WWII, RAF squadrons again formed aerobatic teams. They flew jet aircraft such as Vampires, Meteors and Hunters, and particular squadrons were selected to represent the RAF. In 1965, it was decided to form the Royal Air Force aerobatic team as a permanent unit, and so the Red Arrows came into being, initially equipped with Folland Gnats, but from 1980, with the British Aerospace Hawk. The Red Arrows fly with nine Hawks, but in parts of the show two aircraft split away to perform separately. The use of smoke has continued, often now in red, white and blue — but the jet teams have not revived the practice of tying aircraft together.

became more elaborate and representative of the RAF's roles. The 1920 setting of the Flanders battlefield was replaced in 1922 by a huge colonial fort, and by 1927 there were troops being rushed in by air to rescue women and children from hostile natives. When such colonial topics grew too sensitive in the 1930s, attacks were made on figures described in the program as "pirates."

The last RAF Display at Hendon was held on June 26, 1937, and it was a day to remember. The flying program began with a handicap race between such varied types as Bristol Blenheim, Fairey Battle and Hawker Hart bombers, Gloster Gladiator and Hawker Fury fighters, and a Supermarine Walrus amphibian. Then came individual aerobatics in a Hawker Fury, and a spot-landing competition. Six Gloster Gauntlets fired blank ammunition at a target towed by a Fairey Gordon, and in an air-to-air refueling demonstration, a Boulton Paul Overstrand received fuel at a rate of 80 gallons per minute. Three more Hawker types then took over the show, with Hinds showing off their dive-bombing accuracy, Demons indulging in air combat, and Hectors picking up messages from the ground with trailing hooks. With these curtain-raisers out of the way, the main events began. A stunned crowd saw a mass flypast of 250 aircraft, before being entertained by an "inept pupil" act in a Hart trainer, and formation aerobatics by five Gauntlets. Venerable Vickers Virginias bombed the airfield and were set upon by intercepting Gauntlets. To rousing cheers, one of the Virginias disappeared, going down with trailing smoke and erupting parachutes. An ancient Farman biplane carried a shotgun-armed big-game hunter in his bid to bag some monster balloons, and Central Flying School instructors demonstrated inverted formation flying. After a historic set piece in which Bristol Fighters, S.E.5s and a Sopwith Triplane launched themselves against WWI observation balloons, forcing one observer to bail out, Hawker Furies dealt with a band of river pirates in a captured steamer. The grand finale featured seven RAF squadrons in the air at the same time, with Vildebeestes flying through a balloon barrage and antiaircraft gunfire to torpedo a port's lock gates; Whitleys, Wellesleys and Blenheims on bombing runs; Hinds dive-bombing; and Gladiators and Demons doing their best to intercept the attackers. It was a spectacular show and great entertainment, but it was the last before WWII. Little of it was a realistic representation of modern aerial warfare, and it was time for the RAF to turn its attention to more serious matters.

THROTTLES WIDE OPEN
The Return of the Schneider

The rumble of guns had hardly died away at the end of WWI before air-racing enthusiasts were picking up where they left off in 1914. Once they got started, however, it sometimes seemed as though the results were hardly worth the effort. The annual Schneider Trophy contest was first away, resuming in September 1919, and until 1923 it appeared that Schneider's aim of promoting the development of intercontinental maritime aircraft would be maintained. The flying boats dominating his competition during those years did suggest that such machines might lead to others which would eventually span the globe. The problem was that the competitions were undeniably boring.

The 1919 event, held at Bournemouth on England's south coast, was a poorly organized affair, ill-advisedly

The British entry for the 1923 Schneider Trophy was the portly Supermarine Sea Lion III. It finished a distant third behind the the speedy Curtiss CR-3s of the U.S. Navy.

La Coupe d'Aviation
Maritime Jacques Schneider — the
Schneider Trophy, more colloquially known as
"The Flying Flirt." It was presented by Jacques
Schneider in 1912 to promote the development of
practical, reliable aircraft capable of operating from
the open sea and flying long distances. Schneider
believed that the future for commercial aviation lay
in intercontinental travel, and in 1912 it seemed
obvious that flying boats would provide
the most practical answer. He did not
wish to inspire high-speed freaks
useful only for racing. Competitive
pressures eventually defeated
Schneider's high ideals and
led to the freaks he so
wished to avoid,
producing unexpected
consequences in
WWII.

flown in foggy conditions. The lone finisher was an Italian Savoia S.13 flying boat, which was immediately disqualified for having consistently missed a turning point. No contest was declared, but in an attempt to smooth ruffled feathers, it was decided that the Italians should be invited to host the next event. Unfortunately, since it was generally accepted at the time that Italy built the best flying boats, the airmen of other nations were not very interested in going to all the trouble of trying to develop better aircraft and then traveling to Venice to compete. The events of 1920 and 1921 were therefore flown unopposed, the Italians doing their best to get excited about competing against each other. But for the disqualification in 1919, Italy would have won three in a row and had permanent possession of the Schneider Trophy, and they were favored to do just that in 1922. They were denied by the intervention of a solitary British private entry, a chubby little flying boat called the Supermarine Sea Lion II. Modified from an earlier design by a young man called R.J. Mitchell and flown by Henry Biard, it astounded the Italians by winning at an average speed of 146 mph. Had the Italians won, the Schneider Trophy would have been relegated to obscurity. Their failure saved the competition for greater things, which began to take shape in 1923 with the entry of a team from the United States. The American intervention brought about irreversible change, steering the competition away from Jacques Schneider's original concept and making it more about brute power and sheer speed.

Goodbye, Gordon Bennett

On the face of it, the Gordon Bennett Cup promised to be more rewarding for spectators than the Schneider Trophy. By their very nature, landplanes ought to be more exciting than flying boats, and the Gordon Bennett had no pretensions to being other than a race, uncluttered by regulations requiring such distractions as demonstrations of seaworthiness. For the 1920 competition, held south of Paris, there was an impressive list of entrants from France, the U.K. and the U.S. However, bureaucratic difficulties and mechanical problems destroyed British and American hopes, and the

> *"The utmost speed ever to be developed [would be] about 500 kilometers per hour."*
>
> SADI LECOINTE, WORLD SPEED RECORD HOLDER, 1923

French won, Sadi Lecointe's clipped-wing Nieuport-Delage NiD 29V averaging 168 mph. Having been the winners of two prewar races in the series, the French claimed the cup, and the Gordon Bennett competition came to an end.

To prolong the French air-racing tradition, the widow of a wealthy industrialist and patron of aviation, Henry Deutsch de la Meurthe, presented an international challenge cup (the Coupe Deutsch de la Meurthe), intending that it be competed for annually in an unrestricted speed contest. The first of these races was planned for October 1921, to be flown over the same course as the final Gordon Bennett. In France, it was expected that it would be another jewel to add to Sadi Lecointe's already impressive air-racing crown. He was flying a delightful Nieuport-Delage sesquiplane in which he became the first man to post a world speed record of more than 200 mph, recording 330.275 km/h (205 mph) just days before the race. The international opposition, a brutal Fiat R.700 and a Gloucestershire Mars I, were obviously quite fast, but it was not thought that they were fast enough. On the day, their speed proved irrelevant, as both of the visitors retired. Sadi Lecointe, however, crashed. There were only two finishers, and Georges Kirsch, in a second Nieuport-Delage, was declared the winner.

The following year produced a race that was almost a carbon copy of the first. The same two foreign entries retired and Lecointe crashed again! Fernand Lasne, flying the Nieuport 29V from the 1920 Gordon Bennett, won as the only contestant to finish. Given that so few non-French aviators had been attracted by the competition and that hardly any aircraft had completed the course, the hope that the Deutsch would become a thrilling international competition faded. Even so, the racing had been a valuable experience for designers. The aircraft flown had operated at or beyond world record figures, pushing both engines and airframes to their limits and expanding performance envelopes. The lessons learned would be applied to good effect in the future, but not in the Coupe Deutsch de la Meurthe. After just two races, it was thought not worth continuing with the competition.

Of all the nationalities involved in the Schneider Trophy, the Italians were the most imaginative in their aeronautical creations. For the 1929 competition, they excelled themselves. The Piaggio-Pegna P.c.7 was especially adventurous. To eliminate the drag of floats, small hydroplanes were fitted and the whole aircraft rested on the surface when stationary. The 970-horsepower engine drove a marine propeller to get things moving, and a clutch transferred power to the airscrew once the hydroplanes rose to the surface. It never managed to leave the water.

The Pulitzer

It was in 1919 that Ralph, Joseph and Herbert Pulitzer, with the approval of the U.S. government, established an international air race. The combination of pure speed and official government recognition was to have a powerful effect on the Pulitzer, and thereby on air racing elsewhere. Initially, it was awarded for cross-country racing, and the first winner was Captain Mansell James, a Canadian who flew a Sopwith Camel from Atlantic City to Boston to claim the trophy. Unfortunately he never returned to collect his prize money. In one of aviation's most baffling mysteries, James disappeared after refueling at Lee, Massachusetts, on his way back to Atlantic City. No trace of him or his Camel was ever found.

The next year, the Aero Club of America got Ralph Pulitzer to abandon the cross-country idea and accept the more easily managed formula of a closed-circuit race for the trophy. The rules for the competition were set by a committee that included several military representatives, and the list of forty-nine entrants for the 1920 race was dominated by U.S. Army Air Service, U.S. Navy and U.S. Marine Corps pilots flying military aircraft. The race was run from Mitchel Field, Long Island, on November 25, 1920, over four laps of a 29-mile course. Thirty-eight aircraft actually crossed the starting line and a commendable twenty-four survived to finish. The winner, at an average speed of 156.5 mph, was 1st Lieutenant Corliss Moseley, USAS, in the Verville-Packard that had failed so ignominiously in the Gordon Bennett Cup only two months earlier. He was chased home by Captain Harold Hartney in the second prototype of the Thomas-Morse MB-3. From every point of view, the Pulitzer was judged a great success. Over 40,000 people had come out to Mitchel Field, and they had seen a thrilling race, with large numbers of aircraft on the course at the same time. The glowing postrace reports had a positive effect on the American public's attitude to aviation. Glenn Curtiss was well content, giving it as his opinion that "The public, at last, is interested in the airplane."

In view of the enthusiasm shown in 1920, the entry list for the 1921 Pulitzer was disappointing. Just six aircraft took part in the race, and only four finished. Nevertheless, it marked a significant step forward in the creation of high-speed aircraft.

The U.S. Navy had been perturbed by its poor showing in the 1920 event. The Curtiss Aeroplane Company was therefore asked to produce two machines fast enough to restore naval pride. The Curtiss CR-1 was the result, a slim little biplane capable of over 180 mph. It was powered by the superb 400-horsepower Curtiss CD-12 engine. Based on a Charles Kirkham design, modified by Arthur Nutt, the CD-12 was a liquid-cooled, V-shaped 12-cylinder that produced one horsepower for every one and a half pounds of weight, a considerable achievement for the time.

At the eleventh hour, the U.S. armed services, concerned about their budgets, withdrew their support for the Pulitzer, and cancellation loomed. However, the Omaha Aero Club stepped in and offered to host the race in Nebraska. Without official military participation, the few entries were privately sponsored, although several military pilots were engaged to fly the aircraft. Curtiss actually had to borrow back one of the CR-1s from the U.S. Navy to compete. Bert Acosta, who had finished third in the 1920 Pulitzer, flew for Curtiss and saw to it that the CR-1 lived up to their expectations, winning at 177 mph. Second place went to Clarence Coombs in the Curtiss-Cox Cactus Kitten, a monoplane hastily modified to triplane form to reduce its brisk landing speed. Very fast in a straight line, the Cactus Kitten was an ill-disciplined tiger in maneuver and could not hold the CR-1 round the pylons.

In 1922, the military came back to competition with a vengeance. More money for aeronautical development was available, and air racing was encouraged by the services as a spur to the process. The site for the event was the home of the 1st Pursuit Group at Selfridge Field, near Detroit, and it was an elaborate affair, with the Pulitzer occupying pride of place in a week of aerial contests known as "The National Air Races." Concern about the imagined consequences of allowing designers to be completely uninhibited in their creation of racing aircraft caused the nervous organizers to introduce a rule mandating a 75-mph maximum landing speed for the Pulitzer. Despite this curious limitation, it was clear that race speeds were going to be much higher than in previous events. Rivalry between the services was intense, with Verville-Sperry, Loening and Thomas-Morse machines joining the Curtiss designs flown by both the Army and Navy.

At the time of the 1922 Pulitzer, the world speed record was still held by France's Sadi Lecointe, at 205 mph. A few days before the race, public appetites were whetted by the news that Lieutenant Russell Maughan had recorded an unofficial 220 mph in his Curtiss R-6. The R-6 was powered by Arthur Nutt's D-12 engine, a wetsleeve aluminum monobloc, a design that continued to exert a profound influence on high-performance aviation until the coming of the turbojet. Hearing the stories about Maughan's speed, the sailors began to regret that the U.S. Navy's entrants were flying Curtiss CR-2s, which were last year's CR-1s given a facelift and fitted with uprated engines. The modifications had made them faster, but it was feared they were not that fast. The fears were seen to be well founded on race day, October 14. A crowd of some 75,000 saw the Army's R-6s, flown by Russell Maughan and Lester Maitland, finish first and second. Maughan's winning speed of almost 206 mph was faster than the current world record. In those days, even pilots did not have a clear understanding of the effects maneuvering in

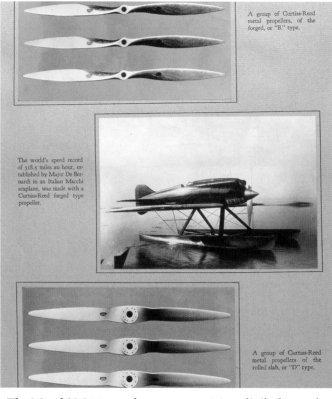

The Macchi M.39 was the response to Mussolini's decree that the Regia Aeronautica was to "win the Schneider Trophy at all costs." In the hands of Mario Bernadi, it did just that at Hampton Roads, Virginia, in 1926, winning at 246.5 mph.

high-speed flight could have on the body, and Maughan sounded unsure of what had been happening to him when he reported after the race that during a turn on the fourth lap he had been "whirled into unconsciousness for three or four seconds." He later added that he was "stunned more or less at each of the fifteen turns." Since he had to pull some 6G through about 120 degrees to stay close to the turning points, it was hardly surprising that he was experiencing the phenomenon of blacking out. The newspapers made the most of misunderstanding the problem, dramatically linking it to pure speed rather than centrifugal force, one correspondent writing that Maughan was traveling "at a speed so terrific he was unconscious at times."

In the 1922 Pulitzer, the Army's R-6s were in a class by themselves, but the racing was generally competitive, with seven of the eleven finishers posting race speeds higher than the recognized closed-circuit world records for distances up to 200 kilometers. Third and fourth were the Navy's CR-2s; fifth was a Verville-Sperry R-3; and sixth place went to the winners of 1920, but this time Lieutenant Moseley coaxed his Verville-Packard to 179 mph, almost 23 mph faster than two years earlier. With the racing excitement out of the way, General Billy Mitchell stepped forward to fly the victorious R-6 for the first time, and on October 18 he used it to capture the world speed record with an official average over a measured kilometer of 358.836 km/h (222.97 mph). For Curtiss and the U.S. Army Air Service, 1922 was a vintage year, and for Billy Mitchell, heavily engaged in his air power crusade, the Pulitzer and the world record were two more weapons for his armory.

The National Air Races of October 1923 were held in St.

Mario de Bernadi was a great Italian airman. He won the Schneider Trophy in 1926, and was the first man to push the world speed record to more than 300 mph in 1928. He died in the cockpit after landing from an aerobatic display in 1959.

Louis, and the Pulitzer was again the principal event. Over 100,000 spectators saw the Navy reverse the result of 1922. The Army had settled for flying its R-6s virtually unchanged and, although they raised their average speeds by some 10 mph, they could do no better than fifth and sixth, behind two Curtiss R2C-1s and two Wright F2W-1s. The winner was the R2C-1 of Lieutenant Al Williams, who averaged 243.7 mph, in the process setting new world records for closed circuits at 100 and 200 kilometers. A month later, he raised the outright world speed record to 266.59 mph. (The world speed record was not set by an American aircraft again until after WWII.) Like Maughan in 1922, Williams commented after the race about having trouble with the high speed turns: "I felt funny when it was all happening…somewhere in the third lap I went woozy. I felt like I was asleep. It was those turns that did it." The effect of sustained high G had become a regular experience for racing pilots, but they still found it puzzling.

After reaching the peak of St. Louis, the Pulitzer competition went rapidly downhill. In 1924, the U.S. Navy withdrew its support and the Army had nothing new to offer. The race, held near Dayton, was given an ominous curtain-raiser when Lieutenant Alex Pearson was killed. The Curtiss R-8 he was testing suffered structural failure. (The R-8 was the ex-Navy R2C-1 that finished second in 1923 and was then sold to the Army for $1.) To make things even worse, Captain Burt Skeel was killed when his R-6 (the ex-Maughan aircraft) disintegrated during his dive to the starting line. That left only three Army competitors flying, and the heart had gone out of the event. The winner, for what it was worth, was Lieutenant Harry Mills in a Verville-Sperry.

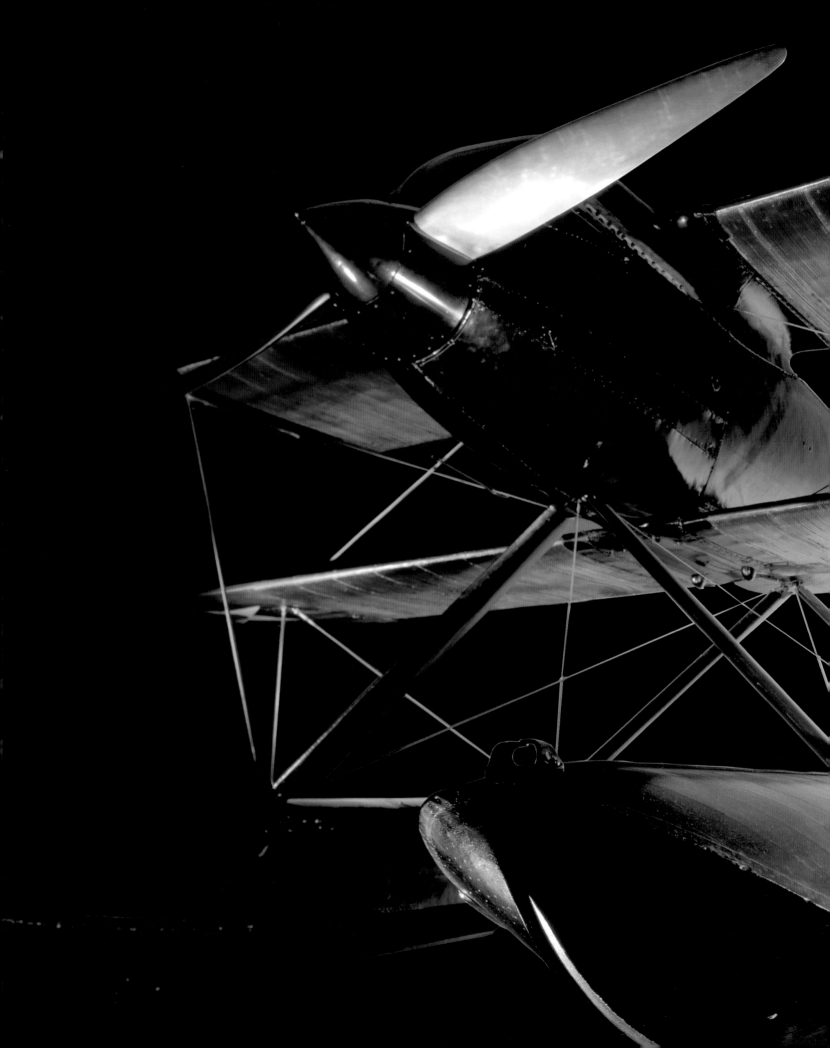

DOOLITTLE'S R3C-2

The Curtiss R3C biplane appeared in 1925 and was bought by both the U.S. Army and Navy. The landplane version was designated the R3C-1, and Lieutenant Cyrus Bettis flew it to win the Pulitzer Trophy race on October 12, 1925, at 248.9 mph. It was then fitted with streamlined single-step wooden floats and redesignated the R3C-2. On October 25, it won the Schneider Trophy race, piloted by Lieutenant James H. Doolittle. The next day, Doolittle flew the R3C-2 over a straight course at a world-record speed of 245.7 mph.

LEFT AND BELOW Doolittle's R3C-2 is now displayed in the National Air & Space Museum, Washington, D.C., still in the colors it wore during the 1925 Schneider Trophy competition. Note the extent of the radiators on the surface of the wings. With this and all subsequent Schneider Trophy aircraft, cooling the powerful racing engines was a problem, and radiators were made to cover more and more of the aircrafts' surfaces.

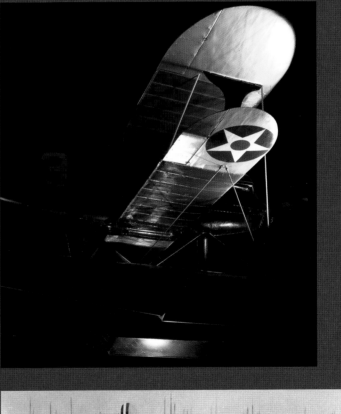

He was almost 30 mph slower than Williams in 1923, and in that race would have finished no better than sixth. The standard was raised again in 1925, when the Pulitzer went back to Mitchel Field, Long Island, but it was not an exciting race. There were only six entrants, and only two of those had any real prospect of winning. Al Williams was back for the Navy in a Curtiss R3C-1, and Lieutenant Cyrus Bettis was flying the Army's version of the same aircraft. In an unusual display of cooperative effort, the funding for the machines had been shared by the services. On the day, Bettis flew the better race, winning at an average speed of 249 mph. Although the fastest Pulitzer speed yet, even it was disappointing, since 270 mph had been predicted and there would not be another chance to take the competition to higher levels. The U.S. military announced that it had no further interest in using air racing as a means of developing pursuit aircraft. With that, the Pulitzer competition came to an end, and the National Air Races deteriorated, becoming little more than aerial events held as accompaniments to fairground entertainments. It would be years before they regained their lost glory.

Speed Comes to the Schneider

In the warm glow of success that followed the performances of the Curtiss racers in the 1922 Pulitzer, the United States announced that an American team would be competing for the 1923 Schneider Trophy. When the U.S. Navy was invited to form the team, the character of the competition was for-

ever changed. For the first time in the Schneider series, the air-racing pride of a nation would ride with aircraft and pilots directly supported by their government. From the moment the U.S. team arrived in the United Kingdom on August 25, 1923, it was apparent that amateurism was a thing of the past, as were the days of ponderous flying boats. The Navy airmen were experienced, disciplined pilots, and they were backed by a thoroughly prepared support organization. Their Curtiss CR-3s (CR-2s brought out of storage, refurbished and fitted with floats) were the technological wonders of the time, slim graceful creatures carrying the promise of awesome performance. All this professionalism knocked the hosts off balance and provoked reactions from the British press that ranged from the pompous and shortsighted to the poorly informed. An editorial in *The Times* disdainfully commented: "British habits do not support the idea of entering a team organized by the state for a sporting event." *The Aeroplane* magazine rightly regarded the CR-3s as "astonishing," but rival *Flight* published a graph for computing lap speeds that went up to only 170 mph, which was quite enough for the flying boat entries but would be rather inadequate for the Curtiss racers.

The entry list for the 1923 Schneider included teams from Italy and France as well as from the U.S. and Britain. The Italians withdrew the week before race day, and of the four French aircraft that arrived, only one was able to start. The French entry was not a factor in the race, since it retired

The Savoia-Marchetti S.65 was another of the Italian flights of fancy built for the 1927 Schneider Trophy race. It was powered by two 1,050-horsepower Isotta-Fraschini engines, one at either end of a slim central nacelle. The pilot was squeezed into a tiny cockpit between the two, and slender twin booms carried the tail, which was braced to the rear end of the floats.

on the second lap and was, in any case, too slow. One of the British entries, the Blackburn Pellet, crashed during the pre-race navigability trials, and the U.S. team lost the aircraft of its supporting cast, a Navy-Wright NW-2 that crashed during testing and a NAF TR-3A that could not be started for the race. That left only three competitors — the two CR-3s and Britain's Supermarine Sea Lion III, which was the 1922 winner updated. From the moment the CR-3s began their takeoff runs and the booming roar of their D-12s echoed across the waters of the Solent, it was clear that the race was theirs — if they stayed in the air. Henri Biard in the Sea Lion III did his best, but he was outclassed. Lieutenant David Rittenhouse won at an average speed of 177.3 mph, and he was followed across the line by Lieutenant Rutledge Irvine at 173.3 mph. Biard was some way behind, at 157 mph. For those Europeans who had been complacent about their aeronautical technology and had thought that claims made for American aircraft were exaggerated, the results were a rude shock. It was clear that U.S. aviation had made great strides and that the world's fastest aircraft were now being made on the western side of the Atlantic.

The Aeroplane was among the first to recognize that the United States had pointed the way to the future, urging that "the precedent of the U.S. government should be followed by other governments," and insisting that this would be for "the good of international relations and technology." It took a while for the lesson to sink in. Although Italy, France and Britain all meant to compete when the U.S. hosted the

1924 Schneider in Chesapeake Bay, their preparations were less than adequate. First the Italians and then the French found the time too short to develop new aircraft, and withdrew. In Britain, the Air Ministry ordered two new aircraft, one from Supermarine and one from Gloster, with the understanding that they would be lent back to the manufacturers so that they could compete under private arrangements. Only the Gloster II floatplane got as far as being tested, but porpoised violently on touching down from its first flight, turned over and sank. With the challengers eliminated, it remained for the U.S. team to fly over the course to claim their second victory, so setting themselves up for three in a row and permanent possession of the Schneider Trophy. Given the costly preparatory work done by the U.S., including the loss of an aircraft, the Europeans despondently assumed that the Americans would do just that. They were therefore astonished when the Baltimore Flying Club asked the National Aeronautic Association to cancel the race for that year. The Royal Aero Club at once cabled "our warmest appreciation for this sporting action." In the long run, it was much more than that. American magnanimity in 1924 joins Italian disqualification in 1919 as an action that prolonged the life of a dramatic competition to the point where it can justly be claimed that the developments it fostered had an indirect but significant effect on events in WWII.

With the priceless gift of time, the British and the Italians were able to get their acts together and travel to Baltimore in 1925. The evidence of the aircraft they took with them suggested that the British, at least, had learned something from their humiliation in 1923. The Air Ministry had again ordered new aircraft from Supermarine and Gloster, but official involvement in the race was still not thought appropriate. The responsibility of competing remained with the companies. Two Gloster IIIA biplanes were produced, which were refined versions of the ill-fated Gloster II. At Supermarine, however,

designer R.J. Mitchell started from scratch. Still only thirty years old and virtually self-taught in aerodynamics, Mitchell had been chief engineer at Supermarine for five years. Although he had specialized in flying boats, he showed himself to be full of innovative ideas, as his first venture into racing floatplane design revealed. The Supermarine S.4 was a beautifully proportioned little monoplane with an unbraced cantilever wing. With the drag of bracing wires removed and its frontal area reduced to the minimum necessary to enclose the 680-horsepower Napier Lion engine, the S.4 was undoubtedly fast. It set a new floatplane world record of 226.75 mph just before leaving for Baltimore, and it seemed to be capable of going even faster. However, after taking off for the navigability trials on the morning of October 23, pilot Henri Biard performed a few high-speed steep turns, during one of which he reported that he experienced severe wing flutter. The S.4 became uncontrollable and it crashed into Chesapeake Bay. Mitchell was watching from a rescue launch and was convinced that Biard must have been killed. He was therefore relieved to see a very vocal helmeted head surface among the wreckage, although with typical Anglo-

Saxon restraint he asked only, "Is it warm?"

On the day of the race, only one aircraft from each of the competing nations finished. The Italian Macchi M.33 flying boat, held back by the drag of its design and by an engine delivering less than full power, was by far the slowest at 168.4 mph. The Gloster III-A, creditably flown by Hubert Broad, fell just short of averaging 200 mph, which was considerably faster than the 1923 winning speed. The star of the day, however, was Lieutenant Jimmy Doolittle of the U.S. Army Air Service. He gave a masterly display in his Curtiss R3C-2, which had been the winning R3C-1 landplane in the Pulitzer only twelve days before. Doolittle won at 232.6 mph, setting world records for 100-kilometer and 200-kilometer closed circuits on the way. The next day he rubbed it in with a new world speed record for floatplanes of 245.7 mph. With U.S. superiority so emphatically confirmed, Americans looked forward to claiming the Schneider Trophy permanently in 1926. Alas for their hopes, the day of the biplane was over.

Marvelous Macchis

The problem was that the U.S. military authorities had said that they were no longer prepared to support the costs of development work on racing aircraft. The 1925 machines would be the ones to defend the Schneider Trophy in 1926. In Britain and in Italy, official circles were belatedly recognizing that the competition held such international prestige that it was worth winning, and that it had become almost impossible for private entries to succeed. It was also realized that it would be more sensible for the contest to be run every other year, allowing time for thorough development work. When this proposal was put to the United States, together with a request that the next race be postponed until 1927, it was rejected. With no more funds available and a winning team at hand, the U.S. wanted to get the competition over and done with. The race would be held as planned at Hampton Roads, Virginia, in November 1926.

The British, faced with preparing a challenge capable of wresting the Schneider Trophy from the Curtiss racers, stubbornly refused to believe that this was the last word, and held back, preferring to think about what they might do in 1927 — if the competition survived that long. In Italy, however, Mussolini saw an opportunity to show the world that nothing was too difficult for a Fascist state. He instructed the Italian aircraft industry and the Regia Aeronautica to "win the Schneider Trophy at all costs." In 1926, nobody in the aviation world gave the Italians, traditionally associated with flying boats, the remotest chance of success, but Il Duce's exhortations and government funds were wonderful encouragements.

With little time left to develop original ideas, the Italians sensibly set out to improve on work done by others. At Fiat they studied the Curtiss engines, and Macchi's designer Mario Castoldi drew on the lessons of the Curtiss racers and Supermarine's S.4. The resulting A.S.2 engine produced over 800 horsepower on the bench, and the M.39 airframe was a firmly braced monoplane with very clean lines. It looked promising, and early tests showed that the M.39 was very fast. However, the program was rushed and not without problems, among them the loss of the Italian team captain when he crashed into Lake Varese shortly after taking off on his first M.39 flight. Even after reaching Hampton Roads, the Italians were dogged by a series of oil-cooling and carburation snags that led to an engine failure and two fires. If anything, the U.S. team fared even worse, losing three aircraft and having two pilots killed in the run-up to the race. At this level of competition, where national pride was at stake, the cost was measured in more than mere money and materials.

Depressed as they were by loss of their comrades, the U.S. team still believed they could win. The Italians had mechanical problems, and the speeds of the competing aircraft seemed reasonably matched. Both teams had tactical plans. The Americans were going to fly two Curtiss R3Cs (Lieutenants George Cuddihy and Christian Frank) and a slower but reliable F6C (Lieutenant "Red" Tomlinson). The F6C was almost guaranteed to finish, and it would not be the first time that only one aircraft was left running at the end. The Italians countered by arranging for their first M.39 (Lieutenant Adriano Bacula) to conserve the engine by flying well below full power, but at a faster speed than the F6C could manage. The second M.39 (Captain Arturo Ferrarin) was to track the faster of the two R3Cs closely, aiming to do just enough to win, while the third M.39 (Major Mario de Bernadi) would be flown flat out, its true capabilities unveiled for the first time. As might have been expected with such high-strung machinery, all did not go according to plan. Ferrarin retired with a broken oil-pipe, and Cuddihy, with the finishing line in sight on his last lap and second place in his grasp, had his engine die from lack of fuel. Bernadi, his scarlet M.39 howling past the stands at full throttle, won comfortably at 246.5 mph. Against the odds, the Italians had achieved a minor miracle, and the Schneider Trophy series would continue. Bernadi sent a simply worded telegram back to Il Duce in Rome: "Your orders to win at all costs have been carried out."

Somewhat ironically, the intervention of a Fascist leader had provided the British with another chance to get properly organized. The Air Ministry reacted by ordering new high-speed aircraft from three companies — Supermarine, Gloster and Short Brothers. This positive step was followed by another; the Chief of the Air Staff, Lord Trenchard, swallowed his misgivings about allowing the RAF to become involved with racing and asked the RAF High Speed Flight to represent Britain in the competition. The stage was set for the final acts of the Schneider Trophy drama.

> *"Your orders to win at all costs have been carried out."*
> TELEGRAM TO BENITO MUSSOLINI FROM MAJOR MARIO DE BERNADI, SCHNEIDER TROPHY PILOT, 1926

And Then There Were Two

The last three races of the competition were held in 1927, 1929 and 1931, agreement having been reached that two years were needed between races. In the United States, many people felt that an attempt should be made to achieve the all-important third victory in five races, but neither the government nor the manufacturers were prepared to fund the project. Valiant efforts were made in all three years by groups of businessmen to provide Al Williams with an aircraft. The Kirkham-Williams floatplane was built, powered by a 24-cylinder Packard engine of 1,250 horsepower, but problems proliferated and Williams never succeeded in reaching the starting line. The U.S. never again raced for the Schneider Trophy.

The French, who since 1919 had managed to get only one aircraft as far as the second lap, could not compete in 1927. In 1928, the government ordered two racing floatplanes from the Bernard and Nieuport-Delage companies, and formed a racing flight of the Armée de l'Air. Much work was done, but the team was not ready in 1929, and the French finally withdrew in 1931 after crashes destroyed two aircraft, killing one pilot. It was left to the Italians and the British to fight it out.

They Fell by the Wayside

With both the British and Italian governments involved and development funds available, the final years of the Schneider saw a number of original designs developed. After producing another biplane for 1927 and noting its inferior performance, Gloster built a beautiful monoplane for 1929 but could not cure its engine problems and did not compete again. The Short-Bristow Crusader, Britain's only radial-engined entry, was not fast enough and was relegated to duty as a training aircraft. It crashed during precontest flying in 1927, but it had not existed in vain. The work done on its Mercury engine served as the basis for the great Bristol radials of WWII.

Italian designers were more adventurous, producing several startlingly imaginative machines. The most orthodox was Fiat's C.29, which followed Macchi's low-wing monoplane form but was smaller, cramming its 1,000-horsepower engine into a fuselage only 17 feet, 10 inches long. It crashed during trials in 1929. The Savoia Marchetti S.65 broke with convention by being twin-boomed and squeezing the pilot's cockpit into a slim center nacelle between two 1,050-horsepower engines, one pulling and the other pushing. It got as far as flight testing in 1930, but then crashed, killing its pilot. Most outrageous by far was the Piaggio-Pegna P.c.7, a high-wing monoplane fitted with hydrofoils. At rest, it floated with the wings on the surface of the water. The engine was intended to drive both a boat propeller aft and an airscrew in the nose. Clutches engaged one or the other, depending upon the medium being traversed. The P.c.7 did get as far as behaving like a boat, but it was never driven fast enough to allow its wings to spread.

> "[The 'R' engine of the Supermarine S.6] would have taken at least three times as long to produce under normal processes of development had it not been for the spur of international competition. There is little doubt that this intensive engine development will have a very pronounced effect on our aircraft during the next few years."
>
> R.J. MITCHELL (DESIGNER OF THE SPITFIRE), 1929

Superb Supermarines

As was to be expected, the principal standard bearers for Italy and Britain from 1927 to 1931 were Macchi and Supermarine. For the clash at Venice in 1927, Macchi drew on the success of the M.39 to produce the slightly smaller M.52 wrapped round a 1,020-horsepower Fiat A.S.3. The new engine was regarded as a design triumph, achieving 220 horsepower more than the A.S.2 by increasing the bore, stroke, capacity and compression ratio while reducing the frontal area. However, in boosting the A.S.2's performance, they ruined its digestion. The A.S.3 was more temperamental than its predecessor, and the M.52 was fast and good-looking, but unreliable. In Britain, R.J. Mitchell had taken the lessons of his ill-fated S.4 to heart. The S.5 wing was braced and lowered to the bottom of the fuselage to improve the pilot's field of view. Rather than risk a new engine, he decided to stick with the "broad-arrow" Napier Lion, which in 1927 was delivering 875 horsepower. (A broad-arrow engine carries its cylinders in three equal in-line banks. The Napier Lion had three banks of four cylinders each.) Helped by the use of flush-wing radiators and a more efficient propeller, Mitchell anticipated that the Lion would drive the S.5 along at 300 mph or so, some 70 mph faster than the S.4.

The business end of the Supermarine S.6B, winner of the final Schneider Trophy competition in 1931. The Rolls-Royce "R'" engine delivered 2,300 horsepower and was closely cowled to achieve minimum frontal area. The 9-foot, 1½-inch propeller was fixed pitch and was set to give maximum efficiency at speed. This meant it was nearly stalled at low speed and takeoff runs could be laborious. The huge floats housed fuel tanks in their midsections and had coolant radiators over almost their entire top surface.

SUPERMARINE S.6B

Supermarine S.6B S1595, designed by Leslie Mitchell, can be seen in the History of Flight gallery at the Science Museum in London. In a display case behind the aircraft is the Schneider Trophy the RAF won for Britain in 1931. S.6B S1595 completed the course at an average speed of 340 mph, and two weeks later the same aircraft, fitted with an uprated "R" engine of 2,600 horsepower, set a world speed record at 407.5 mph. It was the first time 400 mph had been exceeded. Given the drag of the floats, this was a remarkable achievement. (Jimmy Doolittle claimed the landplane record with the Gee Bee R-1 at 294 mph in September 1932 — over a year later and more than 100 mph slower.)

The slim line of the S.6B made the most of the "R" engine's 2,300 horsepower, rating it at 4,340 horsepower per square meter of aircraft frontal area. The engine's reliability was improved by using new sodium-cooled valves, developed in the U.S. The oil tank for the engine was in the fin and the fairing behind the pilot's head, and the oil was cooled by passing it down the length of the fuselage in parallel pipes, then cascading it inside the fin into a collector tank. All the aircraft's external surfaces were smooth and were assembled with countersunk riveting, an advanced technique at the time.

Hovering behind the S.6B in the Science Museum is the shape of things to come in the 1930s — the Spitfire, an aircraft designed by Leslie Mitchell using his experience of the Schneider Trophy racers. The Spitfire's Rolls-Royce Merlin was the descendant of the "R" engine. It was a combination of inestimable value to Britain in WWII.

When the teams faced each other at Venice, the S.5s justified their promise, while the M.52s were not quite as fast as their rivals and certainly not as reliable, all three of them retiring from the race with mechanical troubles. The RAF's Flight Lieutenant S.N. Webster completed the seven laps of the course with clockwork regularity, coming home the winner at an average of 281.6 mph, a speed achieved during a closed-circuit race yet exceeding the world speed record for any type of aircraft. (In December 1924, Florentin Bonnet of France raised the world speed record to 278.5 mph flying a Bernard V.2.) Cumbersome floats notwithstanding, intense competition had made racing floatplanes the fastest aircraft in the world. To underline the fact and recapture some lost Italian pride, Mario de Bernadi took a specially prepared M.52R to a world speed record of 296.84 mph in November 1927, and then did it again in March 1928, achieving 318.57 mph to become the first to post a world record above 300 mph.

Buoyed by these belated successes, the Italians made determined preparations for revenge in 1929. Mario Castoldi, remarking that Fiat had given him "donkey-power" in 1927 when he needed horsepower, turned to an 18-cylinder Isotta-Fraschini of 1,800 horsepower for his M.67. It was not a happy marriage. The big engines could not be made to run smoothly at full throttle and the pilots complained that they emitted dangerous levels of dense black fumes that were being sucked into the cockpit during turns. The team blamed the fumes when Giuseppe Motta's M.67 dived into Lake Garda and he was killed. Macchi disagreed, but installed special ventilating tubes in the cockpits of the remaining M.67s anyway.

Comparatively speaking, Mitchell's problems with his Supermarine S.6 were minor. He too decided to change engines, because he felt that the Napier Lion's potential had been exhausted. It had been the first choice for British competitors since 1919 and had performed nobly, boosted from 450 horsepower to almost 900 horsepower and providing two firsts, two seconds and a third in the Schneider Trophy along the way. Now Mitchell turned to Rolls-Royce for inspiration, unconsciously initiating a process that would lead eventually to the Merlin, perhaps the greatest in-line engine ever produced. The Rolls-Royce engineers built on their 12-cylinder, 825-horsepower Buzzard in developing the new engine, following Sir Henry Royce's principle: "Invent nothing — inventors go broke." The result was the

"R" engine, which was mostly constructed of Buzzard parts. It reached 1,850 horsepower in 1929, using a supercharger with a double-sided compressor and a special fuel cocktail devised by Air Commodore Rod Banks. (It was 78 percent Benzol, 22 percent aviation spirit, plus a dash of tetra-ethyl lead.) To accommodate the "R" engine, the S.6 was larger than the S.5, and covered with cooling panels to dissipate the great heat the new engine generated. Maintaining the correct operating temperatures was not an easy matter, and to ensure that the race distance could be flown, it was decided to fly at less than full power throughout.

On the night before the race, disaster threatened the British team. A mechanic changing the spark plugs on the primary S.6 noticed a tiny spot of white metal on a plug. Heat had begun to melt the face of a piston. The rules forbade an engine change after the aircraft had completed the preliminary tests, but allowed for the replacement of parts. A party of Rolls-Royce engineers had arrived in town to see the contest, and they were hastily summoned from their prerace celebrations. They rebuilt the engine overnight, and gave it a test run shortly after dawn. Not wishing to cause unnecessary anxiety, they said nothing to the RAF pilots. As it happened, their efforts could not have been better spent. Both M.67s were forced to retire, one because the pilot was choking on oily exhaust smoke, and the other when a radiator pipe burst, spraying scalding water into the cockpit. Italian hopes then rested on their third string, the M.52R that had set the world speed record. Flown with spirit by Dal Molin, its Fiat engine emitting an ear-splitting scream, it ticked off its laps without difficulty, and came closer to success than the Italians realized. Both S.6s were much faster, but the one flown by Flying Officer Richard Atcherley was disqualified for cutting a pylon on the first lap. The winner at a speed of 328.63 mph was Flying Officer H.R.D. Waghorn, flying the S.6 with the rebuilt engine. But for the sharp eyes of a mechanic and the efforts of the Rolls-Royce engineers, Dal Molin would almost certainly have won the race for Italy.

Private Funding Succeeds

Now, like Italy and the United States in earlier years, Britain had permanent possession of the Schneider Trophy within reach. However, to the astonishment of almost everyone, the British government followed the example of the U.S. and announced that further involvement of Britain in the Schneider Trophy would have to be left to private enterprise. Since the government of the day was socialist, there was a certain irony in the situation. Subjected to withering attacks from the press and public for its decision, the government stood firm. With at least £100,000 needed, it looked as though Britain would join the U.S. in walking away from the competition. When all seemed lost, a fairy godmother appeared. Dame Lucy Houston, the eccentric widow of a shipping millionaire, had two commodities in abundance — money and a hatred of socialists. In 1931 she sent a message to the British prime minister that read, in part, "To prevent the British government being spoilsports, Lady Houston will be responsible for all extra expenses beyond what can be found so that Britain can take part in the race." She made it clear that she would personally guarantee the entire £100,000. Perhaps embarrassed by such breathtaking generosity, the government authorized the RAF to represent Britain in the Schneider Trophy for the third time.

Meanwhile, the Italians concentrated their efforts behind Macchi alone. Mario Castoldi returned to Fiat for his engine and the result was dramatic. Two 12-cylinder A.S.5 engines were bolted back to back to form a single power unit 11 feet long. This supercharged monster, the A.S.6, produced 3,000 horsepower, and to house it, Castoldi designed the MC.72, the ultimate in racing floatplanes. To handle the enormous power, the A.S.5 elements drove separate coaxial propeller shafts turning contrarotating propellers. The combination ran beautifully on the ground, but in the air the MC.72 suffered tremendous backfiring at speed. The Italian team persisted in flying to try to pin down the trouble, and in the process lost two pilots when their aircraft blew up. (The deaths of Monti and Bellini in the MC.72 followed the loss of Dal Molin, who crashed in the twin-boomed SM.65

The RAF's fairy godmother, Lady Houston, who gave £100,000 of her own money to fund Britain's Schneider Trophy efforts in 1931 and so "prevent the British government being spoilsports."

during an attempt on the world speed record.) The MC.72 was very fast, but it was also lethal. In the circumstances, Italy joined France in submitting a formal request for a postponement. Britain, however, was committed. Lady Houston's generosity was not likely to be repeated in 1932. For Britain, it was now or never, so the request was denied. The two challengers sadly announced that they would not be competing in 1931. For the Italians in particular, that was a bitter pill to swallow.

In Britain, Mitchell modified his successful S.6 and asked the Rolls-Royce engineers to squeeze more power out of the "R" engine. They obliged by boosting the output to 2,300 horsepower. Initially, there were problems to be solved in getting this potent combination, designated S.6B, to leave the water. The massive torque once the throttle was opened tended to bury one float, and so the S.6B went round in circles. The solution, which involved carrying much more fuel in one float than the other, fitting a longer propeller, and developing handling techniques, allowed the pilots to get both S.6Bs (and two S.6As — the 1929 S.6s refined) into the air. However, flying any of the S.6 series was a challenge, and the British team lost Lieutenant Jerry Brinton of the Fleet Air Arm when he crashed on takeoff in one of the S.6As. Given the withdrawal of the challengers, it was decided that it would not be sensible to add unnecessary risk by allowing the RAF pilots to race against each other. One S.6B, flown by Flight Lieutenant John Boothman, would be flown round the course at a speed sufficiently higher than 1929 to be acceptable, while the other aircraft stood by. Assuming that all went well, the other S.6B, with Flight Lieutenant George Stainforth aboard, would then attack the world speed record over a straight 3-kilometer course.

One of the most beautiful aircraft ever built, the Macchi MC.72 exudes grace and power even when stationary. Today the ultimate in racing floatplane design sits, silent and magnificent, in the collection of the Italian Air Force Museum at Vigna di Valle, on Lake Bracciano, north of Rome. In 1934, its massive Fiat A.S.6 power plant howling, it hurtled over a measured course on Lake Garda to record a world speed record for any kind of aircraft of 440 mph. To keep the A.S.6 at a reasonable operating temperature, the MC.72 was covered in radiators — on the surface of the wings, the struts and the floats.

ABOVE *The open cockpit of the MC.72 is small and tucked into the long fuselage two-thirds of the way back from the nose. Since the aircraft was not intended to ever have to fly very far or for very long, the instrumentation was basic and was principally concerned with the engine. The pilot sat well down behind a steeply sloped windscreen, and his view was limited.*

BELOW *Francesco Agello was the pilot who mastered the dangerous MC.72 and took it to a world record. His jacket and helmet are preserved in the Italian Air Force Museum.*

The fine lines of the Macchi MC.72 and the immense length of the engine compartment are obvious in a view from the side. The 3,000-horsepower, 24-cylinder Fiat A.S.6 (below) is 11 feet, 6 inches long, and was created by bolting two A.S.5s together. The rear unit drives the foremost of the contra-rotating propellers and vice versa. In 1931, carburetion problems led to immense backfires during flight tests, destroying two MC.72s and killing their pilots. After extensive ground tests using a blower to provide ram air and simulate in-flight airspeeds, the problems were overcome.

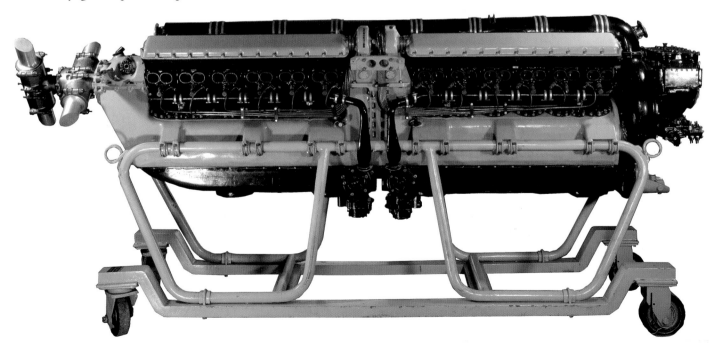

On Sunday, September 13, 1931, vast crowds packed the cliffs and beaches overlooking the Schneider Trophy course in the Solent. Boothman got airborne in his slim silver and blue S.6B (S1595) just after 1 P.M. and flew the required seven laps, the "R" engine's raucous song never faltering. He flashed across the finishing line to record an average speed of 340 mph and give Britain the Schneider Trophy in perpetuity. To cap the performance, George Stainforth sent everyone home happy by raising the world speed record to 379 mph. It was not quite what he had hoped for, so he tried again on September 29, by which time S.6B S1595 had been fitted with a sprint version of the "R" engine that, with the help of a Rod Banks fuel cocktail, gave 2,600 horsepower. This time, Stainforth became the first man to push the world record beyond 400 mph, reaching an average of 407.5 mph in four runs over the course.

Schneider's Legacy

Of the four principal nations involved in the Schneider Trophy, it was ironic that France, the parent nation, should be the least rewarded. The U.S. blazed briefly in the 1920s, only to face later disappointments. These were mollified by the knowledge that the Curtiss teams had fundamentally changed the character of the race and administered the shock that stimulated the advances made by the Italians and British. Italy gave the most in terms of passionate commitment. The Italians submitted the most race entries, their designs were the most imaginative, and they lost the most pilots — seven between 1922 and 1931. Their Schneider hopes dashed, they nevertheless persisted with the MC.72. They invited the British fuels wizard Rod Banks to work with them on the troublesome A.S.6. His advice on wind-tunnel bench testing and on fuel mixtures helped to solve the engine's problems, and on October 23, 1934, the MC.72, flown by Francesco Agello, reached a world record speed of 440.68 mph, a record later overtaken by propeller-driven landplanes, but one that still stands for floatplanes. Ironically, the development work on the superb Fiat engines was set aside, and in 1941 Castoldi had to turn to Germany to find a liquid-cooled engine for his fighters.

The British belatedly made the most of the Schneider Trophy experience. Mitchell's work on the aerodynamics of the low-wing monoplane form led to his superb Spitfire. The Rolls-Royce "R" engine fathered the famous Merlin,

For the first nine months of 1935, the diminutive French Caudron C.460 (22-foot wingspan, 370-horsepower engine) held the world landplane speed record at 314 mph. Despite that, Michel Detroyat was not given much chance of success when he arrived in the U.S. to fly the C.460 in the 1936 Thompson Trophy race. He won easily, and it was the only time a European entrant carried off the Thompson Trophy.

Roscoe Turner wore a uniform of his own design consisting of a powder blue coat, Sam Browne belt, beige riding breeches, shiny boots, white silk scarf and military cap. In 1929, he convinced Gilmore Oil to buy a Lockheed Air Express, Black Hornet, *to promote the company (and himself) by breaking speed records. Since the company's trademark was a lion's head, Turner acquired a five-month-old lion cub, named it Gilmore and flew with it as a mascot. Together they set several transcontinental speed records.*

which powered not only the Spitfire, but also the Hurricane, Lancaster, Mosquito and the P-51 Mustang, all of which made powerful contributions to Allied air power in WWII. The evolution of superchargers and the use of high-compression fuels were other aspects of high-performance flight that were markedly advanced. In the end, Jacques Schneider's ideals may not have been closely followed, but as his competition developed, it spurred the progress of aviation as much as any other peacetime initiative in the 20th century.

With the end of the Schneider Trophy series, the phenomenon of international closed-circuit air racing passed into history. While it was there, the Schneider had to be won, but once it was gone, there was an almost official sigh of relief that the traumas of the competition no longer had to be suffered. Air racing continued, but in more nationally focused forms.

The Thompson

In the United States, the National Air Races were rejuvenated by a promoter called Cliff Henderson. In 1929, at Cleveland, he turned the event into a highly publicized air fair, including commercial demonstration flights and barnstorming as well as an air-racing program. The principal contest, sponsored by industrialist Charles Thompson, was a closed-circuit race for the Thompson Cup. It was an unlimited, free-for-all event expected to be won by one of two Curtiss fighters — an Army P-3A and a Navy Hawk. If anyone else had a chance, it was thought to be Roscoe Turner flying a Lockheed Vega. Adding interest was a dark horse in the field of eleven, Douglas Davis in the new Travel Air "R" monoplane. Davis kept his aircraft well hidden, so it earned the nickname "Mystery Ship." The mystery was solved on the day of the race when the little black and orange Travel Air "R" left the competition, military and civilian, struggling in its wake. The result caused an uproar in the press, which found in the military's humiliation a reason to attack the U.S. government's lack of sponsorship for competitive flying. The Army and Navy were embarrassed, and resolved to stay away from free-for-all contests. It was not thought to be a good idea to draw attention to privately owned aircraft that could run rings round the nation's defenders.

The success of his event in Cleveland encouraged Charles Thompson to go further and sponsor an annual closed-circuit contest. The Thompson Trophy, first run in 1930 at Chicago, was intended to boost the development of faster landplanes. It was an open competition, with no restrictions on the aircraft used by competitors, and it became the principal event of the annual National Air Races. The Greve Trophy for aircraft with an engine displacement of less than 550 cubic inches was an accompaniment to the Thompson from 1934. From 1931 until 1939, the Nationals were held in Cleveland, except for 1936, when they were in Los Angeles. Official invitations to participate were sent to the governments of several nations, but in a Depression-burdened world, there was little official enthusiasm.

The Travel Air "R" had shown that a small company could build an aircraft to take on the best in the aircraft industry and beat them. This was the heyday of intuitive designers and backyard builders, many of whom operated on a shoestring and had learned about structures and aerodynamics by barnstorming in a Jenny. It was remarkable how often the aircraft they produced flew off with air racing's prizes, including the Thompson Trophy. Perhaps the most notable of these "limited editions" were the amazing Gee Bees, built by the Granville brothers in an old dance pavilion near Springfield, Massachusetts. At first glance, it seemed doubtful that the stubby little bumblebees could fly at all. The airframe was the smallest that could be devised to wrap round a massive radial engine. The cockpit appeared to have been added as an afterthought, and the tail was almost nonexistent. Jimmy Doolittle said of the ultimate Gee Bee, the R-1, "I didn't trust this little monster. It was fast, but flying it was like balancing a pencil or an ice-cream cone on the tip of your finger. You couldn't let your hand off the stick for an instant." He later added: "That airplane was the most dangerous I have ever flown."

Gee Bees won the Thompson Trophy in both 1931 and 1932, and in Doolittle's hands, the R-1 posted a world landplane speed record of 296.3 mph on September 3, 1932. (The difference made by government support is notable. Schneider Trophy floatplanes had been flying at more than 300 mph since 1927, and 400 mph had been exceeded by the S.6B in 1931.) Their achievements were costly. All seven Gee Bee racers produced eventually crashed, killing six pilots, including "Granny" Granville, the eldest of the five brothers from Springfield.

The last biplane to win a major pylon course event was the Laird Solution, which triumphed in the first Thompson Trophy in 1930 after being designed and built from scratch by Matty Laird in the month before the race. As the only biplane in the field, it was already an anomaly. From then on, only monoplanes were entered, some achieving remarkable performance from limited resources. Ben Howard built his little DGA-3 *Pete* in his spare time during eight months of 1930 and managed third place in the Thompson, pitting his 90-horsepower against power plants more than three times that size. (Howard designated his machines DGA, which stood for "Damned Good Airplane.") He went on to produce other tiny, apparently underpowered aircraft — *Ike* and *Mike* — each of which could exceed 200 mph, surprising much more heavily muscled opponents and carrying off more than their share of prize money. Howard's greatest success, however, came in 1935 with a conventional high-wing cabin monoplane called *Mister Mulligan*, powered by an 830-horsepower Pratt & Whitney Wasp. *Mister Mulligan* won the Thompson at over 220 mph, defeating such fiery hand-built specials as Steve Wittman's Curtiss D-12 engined *Bonzo* and the Keith Rider R-1.

More consistent than any in the early 1930s were the Wedell-Williams racers. Dragged along by 550-horsepower Pratt & Whitney Juniors, they claimed second place in 1931, second, third and fourth in 1932, first and second in 1933, and first and third in 1934. For a few months in 1933–34, a Wedell-Williams held the world landplane speed record at 305.24 mph. They were favorites of Roscoe Turner, who finished third in 1932 and was the winner in 1934, averaging 248 mph. He crossed the line first in 1933, too, but was disqualified for missing a pylon.

ROSCOE TURNER

In 1936, Roscoe Turner contracted with Lawrence W. Brown Aircraft Company to build a new racing aircraft. Designed by Turner and engineered by Howard Barlow of the University of Minnesota, it was a full cantilever mid-wing monoplane with fixed gear, and was powered by a 1,000-horsepower Pratt & Whitney Twin Wasp Senior. Not satisfied with the finished product, Turner had the aircraft taken apart and shipped to the Laird factory in Chicago. He then redesigned the wing, and Matty Laird rebuilt the racer. The final specifications of the Turner Racer: wingspan 25 feet; length 23 feet, 4 inches; height 10 feet; empty weight 3,300 pounds, and gross weight 4,923 pounds. It carried 215 gallons of fuel and had an oil capacity of 15 gallons.

The fuselage was covered with metal from the engine cowling to the cockpit; from this point rearward, Irish linen was used for covering. There was also a strip along the bottom of the fuselage that was metal covered to protect it from flying stones during takeoff and landings. The fin and tailplane were constructed of wood, and the elevators and rudder of steel tubing. All were fabric covered. The finish was silver gray and race number 29 was painted on the fuselage.

Turner was sponsored in 1937 by Ring Free Oil and arrived at the National Air Races wearing the name Ring Free Meteor. He finished third in the Thompson Trophy race after missing a pylon. He took the Meteor to the Thompson twice more. In 1938, the words on the fuselage said "Pesco Special," and in 1939 the sponsor was Champion Spark Plugs. In both years, Turner and the Meteor took first place.

The Meteor is now in the collection of the National Air & Space Museum, Washington, D.C., marked as it was for the 1939 Thompson Trophy race.

RIGHT *Sea Furies in close competition at the Reno air races.*

BELOW *Lyle Shelton exulting at the performance of* Rare Bear, *his highly modified Bearcat. Shelton and* Rare Bear *dominated the Unlimited class at the Reno air races from 1988 to 1991, recording a fastest average race speed of 481.618 mph, a figure not exceeded until 2003, when Skip Holm in P-51* Dago Red *averaged a phenomenal 507 mph in a qualifying race. (In 2003,* Rare Bear *was still the holder of the world's piston-engine speed record over a 3-kilometer course — 528.3 mph, set at Las Vegas in 1988.* Dago Red *has flown an unofficial 537 mph.)*

In 1936 the French intervened at the Thompson; that was the only occasion it could claim to be international. Michel Detroyat took his outstanding Caudron C.460 to Los Angeles and shocked his American hosts. Built for the revived Coupe Deutsch de la Meurthe in 1934, the blue C.460 was driven by a Renault engine of only 360 horsepower. It was sleek but strangely distorted, its long nose looking as if it belonged on a much larger aircraft. Nevertheless, with sophistications such as retractable wheels and a variable-pitch propeller, it was the fastest entrant in the Thompson, flying one early lap at more than 300 mph and then backing off to win with embarrassing ease at an average

of 273.47 mph. After this foreign interruption, the last three pre-WWII years of the Thompson were dominated by Roscoe Turner and his Laird-Turner Meteor. Designed to his specifications, it housed a 1,000-horsepower, double-row Pratt & Whitney Wasp in a slim airframe that was no larger than it had to be. In 1937, he sacrificed his chance of winning when he went back to go around a pylon he thought (wrongly) he had missed, but he made up for that error by finishing first in 1938 and 1939, averaging over 280 mph on both occasions. In the 1939 race, Turner brought the crowd to its feet after yet again going back for a missed pylon. Relegated to last place by his mistake, he fought his way through the field into the lead, lapping at well over 300 mph.

An attempt was made to reintroduce the Thompson Trophy after WWII, but it did not generate public enthusiasm. Aviation had moved on, and the glory days of reckless individualism were gone. Indeed, the glamor of the Thompson was already fading in the late 1930s. The early efforts of the largely unknown backyard builders had been exciting, with new aircraft challenging the field each year. By the mid-1930s, the novelty had worn off and the aircraft had little fresh to offer. The private builders did not have the wherewithal to conduct sophisticated research programs. If their aircraft went faster each year, it was not by much and (with the exception of the Caudron C.460) it was due more to bigger engines than to improved aerodynamics.

In 1937, *Aviation* magazine commented: "We've never been particularly impressed by the claim that air racing, national or otherwise, makes a great scientific contribution toward the advancement of flying. Talk of 'improving the breed' and 'the great laboratory of the industry'…seem to us to be the most specious form of twaddle."

In the immediate post-WWII world, the huge crowds that had supported air racing in the 1930s did not reappear. The Thompson Trophy was contested five times from 1946 to 1951. The competitors raced modified ex-military aircraft, and there were no new designs to add interest to the event. In three of the years, military jets — P-80s, FJ-1s and F-86s — flew in a separate division of the Trophy, raising lap speeds above 580 mph. The piston-powered division relied on P-38s, P-39s, P-51s, P-63s, and F2G-1s, and got close to 400 mph. Although the Thompson was awarded one last time in 1951, when Colonel Fred Ascani took an F-86 round a 100-km closed circuit at 629 mph, it died as a pylon race in 1949 when Bill Odom pulled his P-51 too tightly at a turn and snapped inverted into a house near Cleveland, killing himself, a mother and her baby son. The

influential magazine *Aviation Week* condemned "dangerous exhibitionism," adding: "The national air races no longer serve any useful purpose…. Some such tragedy as this was overdue." The National Aeronautic Association tightened regulations for air racing, and Cleveland, home of the National Air Races for so many years, abandoned the event.

Duels in the Desert

Pylon racing returned to the U.S. calendar in 1964, when Bill Stead organized a race at Sky Ranch, near Reno, Nevada. The first meeting was a success, and two years later the races moved to a former USAF base named after Bill Stead's brother. There they have flourished, drawing crowds of 150,000 or so each year. It was realized that the thrill of low-level air racing for the public is inextricably bound up with the sight and sound of propeller-driven aircraft. The program is arranged for four aircraft classes: Biplanes, Formula 1s, AT-6s, and Unlimiteds. The Biplane and Formula One categories include a variety of homebuilt designs, in contrast to the AT-6s, which all start out with basically the same airframe and engine. The races in each of those classes can be competitive and worth watching, but the Unlimited class is the biggest draw. Here there are no limitations on the machinery. It is a matter of putting the most powerful piston engine into the sleekest possible airframe and dragging them both along behind a huge propeller as fast as they can go.

ABOVE *Pit row at the Reno air races.* RIGHT *Corsair No. 57 finished third in the Thompson Trophy race of 1949 and, after several restorations, is still competing over half a century later, resplendent in red and white. (These photographs by Ron Kaplan.)*

LAIRD SUPER SOLUTION

The Laird Super Solution was from the Golden Age of air racing. It was built in Chicago for the Cleveland Speed Foundation by a team of fifteen men who lived at the Laird Airplane Factory for forty days to finish the job. Powered by a Pratt & Whitney Wasp Junior radial producing 535 horsepower, the Super Solution had a maximum speed of 265 mph. Jimmy Doolittle flew it to win the 1931 Bendix Trophy race from Burbank, California, to Cleveland, Ohio. He then flew on to set a U.S. transcontinental speed record of 11 hours, 16 minutes, from Burbank to New Jersey, including refueling stops at Albuquerque, Kansas and Cleveland.

On display at the EAA's museum, Oshkosh, is an immaculate Super Solution replica finished in the original 1931 markings of green and yellow, with a couple of flamingos on the fuselage — the logo of a sponsoring company, Skyways Inc.

The principal Unlimited competitors have been highly modified WWII fighters. Apart from the brief careers of original designs such as Burt Rutan's twin-engined *Pond Racer* and the P-51 lookalike *Tsunami* (both destroyed in fatal crashes), the field has been composed mainly of P-51 Mustangs, F8F Bearcats, Hawker Sea Furies and Yak 11s. Aircraft are assigned to heats based on their qualifying times, and those with the eight fastest times in the heats move on to the "Gold" championship race on Sunday. If numbers permit, there are two other championships in each class, the "Silver" and "Bronze" races, each with eight planes, based on their times in heats. The closed-circuit course is a little over 9 miles long, so the action is in clear view of spectators. Since speeds can approach 500 mph in the Unlimited class, a lap takes not much more than a minute, and the eight laps of the climactic Unlimited "Gold" championship race are completed in less than ten minutes. In the 1990s, the "Gold" was dominated by the P-51Ds of Bill Destefani (*Strega*) and Bruce Lockwood (*Dago Red*), and Lyle Shelton's mighty F8F (*Rare Bear*), with competitors such Dennis Sanders in the Sea Fury (*Dreadnought*) and Bob Yancey in his Yak 11 (*Perestroika*) pressing them hard. The fastest average speed for the race was recorded in 1991 when Lyle Shelton took *Rare Bear* over the course at 481.6 mph, far in excess of the performance of a standard F8F-2. *Rare Bear*'s remarkable pace has

been achieved by means of significant modifications to the original aircraft. The wingspan has been reduced by 7 feet, and the power unit is a massive Wright R-3350, which produces over 4,000 horsepower. The huge engine pumps carbon monoxide into the cockpit, which is why the pilot has to wear an oxygen mask at low altitude. Even Lyle Shelton seems mildly surprised by *Rare Bear's* performance, saying: "Short fat airplanes aren't supposed to go this fast." He showed just how fast it could go in August 1989, when he took *Rare Bear* to the piston-engined world air speed record of 528.33 mph.

Racing with Restraint

Once the Schneider Trophy was won, the British never embraced Unlimited class air racing. Two attempts to build specialized racing aircraft were made in the late 1930s, but both the de Havilland T.K.4 and the potentially very fast Heston Type 5 were destroyed in crashes and then forgotten as wartime priorities pushed all others aside. Sporting aviation in Britain flourished in the years before WWII, but it developed very differently from the way it did in the United States. A high proportion of events were arranged as handicaps, allowing flying club aircraft to be pitted against high-speed machinery and encouraging the meek to challenge the mighty. Most of the major races were cross-country affairs even when they were over a closed circuit. There was therefore

Lockheed Orion 9C Shellightning *was flown by Jimmy Doolittle while he was representing Shell Oil in the early 1930s. This aircraft (NR 12222) is the only Orion to survive. After its days with Shell, Paul Mantz acquired it and flew it in the 1938 and 1939 Bendix Trophy races. In 1976, SwissAir obtained the Orion, had it restored in the colors of one of their original "Red Dog" airliners and donated it to the Swiss Transport Museum in Lucerne.*

LEFT *G-ADLC was the prototype Miles Falcon Six, first flown by F.G. Miles on July 27, 1935. It was nicknamed* Pregnant Percy, *later shortened to* Preggers. *Only twelve Falcon Sixes were constructed, but they recorded some significant achievements. One took part in the 1934 London-to-Melbourne air race, and Tommy Rose flew* Preggers *in the 1935 King's Cup, winning at 176 mph. Early in 1936, Tommy Rose and* Preggers *broke the England-to-South Africa record with a flight of three days, 17 hours, 37 minutes.* BELOW 1938 King's Cup, *by Michael Turner. Alex Henshaw's winning Mew Gull races over Hatfield, followed by Giles Guthrie's Mew Gull and Les Cliff's Hawk Major.*

little opportunity to attract crowds to a specific place to see the racing unless an air show was planned to coincide with the finish of the handicap. If the handicappers had done their job properly, this could be an exciting thing to see, with aircraft of various types, large and small, all rushing toward the finishing line more or less together.

From its inception, one event became the most prestigious in the British air-racing calendar. In 1922, King George V, patron of the Royal Aero Club, did his best to encourage sport aviation in Britain by presenting the King's Cup. Participation was limited to British aircraft, but because it was a handicap race, there were no other limitations. Anyone could enter with any type of aircraft, but pure speed against a handicap was not enough to win, since the competition was a cross-country event. Accurate navigation and aircraft reliability were just as important as flying fast. Frank Courtney, who won in 1923 in an Armstrong-Whitworth Siskin, was of the opinion that the winner "was more likely than not to be the pilot whose equipment survived long enough for him to find his way, with luck, to the finishing point."

The 1923 race was typical in taking two days and being flown over 794 miles, outbound from Hendon to Glasgow via Birmingham and Newcastle the first day, and back through Manchester and Bristol the next. The field of twenty-two aircraft ranged from fighter types such as the Siskin and Grebe to the portly Vickers Type 61 Vulcan. Among the pilots were such distinguished names from British aviation as Henry Biard, Bert Hinkler, Hubert Broad and Alan Cobham. The route of the race varied each year, and it grew steadily in status and popularity. In 1930, there were 101 entrants, of whom 88

started the race. The competitors included several of the RAF's Schneider Trophy team, plus some names that would loom large in the development of the British aircraft industry — de Havilland, Miles, and Percival. The winner that year, however, was Miss Winifred Brown, the first woman to be awarded the King's Cup. She flew an Avro Avian and averaged 102.75 mph for the 753-mile course. Second place went to Alan Butler in a D.H.60M Moth, who was faster at 130 mph, but was defeated on handicap.

In 1931, the rules for the King's Cup were changed to permit only entrants of "amateur" status. This excluded all military and specialized commercial aircraft, confining the field to machines produced principally for the private owner. By 1938, there were only nineteen starters, but they included the impressive D.H.88 Comet that won the England-to-Australia race in 1934, and three of the remarkable Percival Mew Gulls. The winner, at 236.25 mph, was Alex Henshaw flying the Mew Gull in which he would set his record from London to Cape Town and back the following year. (See Chapter 2, Quickest to the Cape.)

The Royal Aero Club organized the first National Air Races program in 1949, and it included the King's Cup in the form of a closed-circuit race over three laps of a 20-mile course. It was open to British pilots flying British aircraft capable of at least 120 mph on a maximum of 1,000 horsepower. The next year, the rules changed again to demand a minimum top speed of 130 mph and a maximum weight of 9,920 pounds. This widened the field, allowing tiny Comper Swifts to be challenged by two Spitfires and a Hurricane, all privately registered. The race was won by a Miles Hawk Trainer, flown by Edward Day, chased home at twice his speed by Group Captain Peter Townsend in a famous Hurricane IIC (*The Last of the Many*). For a few years, a weight limitation of 3,858 pounds kept the more potent machines out, but an easing to 12,500 pounds and a relaxation of the "British only" rule set the handicappers a problem in 1967 when Charles Masefield appeared in a P-51D Mustang. Their confusion let Masefield win easily at 277.5 mph, which must have been well within the capabilities of his aircraft. They did not make the same mistake twice, however. Masefield entered the P-51D again in 1968 and was unplaced.

The subtleties of handicapping, together with frequent changes in the competition's form, have helped to ensure that the King's Cup continues to hold the interest of British aviators. It is a contest in which there is never a foregone conclusion; success does not always favor the swift or the strong. The attractions of its uncertainties have contributed to its being the longest running of all aviation competitions. First flown soon after the end of WWI, it has survived into the 21st century.

"I think it would have been cheaper to have bought a revolver."

GROUP CAPTAIN WILLY WILSON, ON SEEING ALEX HENSHAW'S MODIFIED PERCIVAL MEW GULL FOR THE FIRST TIME.

Point-to-Point

From aviation's earliest days, Americans generally were excited by the aerial challenge inherent in their continental nation. There was the Cal Rodgers epic of 1911, and Billy Mitchell's "reliability and endurance test" for the Air Service in 1919. In 1922, Jimmy Doolittle crossed from coast to coast in less than a day, and Jack Knight's persistence ensured that the air mail from San Francisco got through to New York. The Fokker T.2 of Kelly and Macready made it across nonstop in 1923. All of these attracted national headlines and intense public interest, so it was hardly surprising that Americans would be drawn to the idea of long-distance cross-country air racing.

Of all the aerial point-to-point contests in the U.S., the Bendix Trophy became the most celebrated. In 1931, Vincent Bendix, president of the Bendix Aviation Corporation, offered a trophy for an annual transcontinental race. It was to be flown in conjunction with the National Air Races, starting at some distant point and finishing at the Nationals while they were in progress. The first Bendix, from Burbank, California, to Cleveland, was won by Jimmy Doolittle flying his Laird Super Solution biplane, an improved version of the aircraft he had flown to victory in the 1930 Thompson. When he reached Cleveland in 9 hours, 10 minutes, he knew that there was a chance of breaking the coast-to-coast record, so he refueled quickly and set off for the east coast. Eleven hours and 16 minutes after leaving Burbank, he was on the ground at Newark, having taken over an hour off the previous best time and in the process adding a $2,500 prize to his Bendix winnings of $7,500. Doolittle had set a pattern, and his transcontinental record lasted only a year. In 1932, Jimmy Haizlip won the Bendix with his Wedell-Williams, making a low pass over the field at Cleveland to register his race finish and going straight on to slash almost an hour off Doolittle's coast-to-coast time. This was a period when Wedell-Williams aircraft set a number of point-to-point records. In October 1932, Jimmy Wedell himself broke Doolittle's "Three Capitals" record of 12 hours, 33 minutes, set in the Super Solution, by flying from Ottawa to Mexico City via Washington, D.C., in 11 hours, 53 minutes. Then, when the Nationals were held at Los Angeles in 1933, Roscoe Turner won the Bendix in his 800-horsepower Wedell-Williams, having made the westbound trip from New York in 11 hours, 30 minutes to claim another transcontinental record.

In contrast to Schneider Trophy developments, Unlimited air racing in the United States favored air-cooled radial engines. They were the dominant power plants in both the Bendix and the Thompson Trophy races throughout the 1930s. Sixteen of the nineteen pre-WWII Bendix and Thompson contests were won with Pratt & Whitney radials (Wasps, Wasp Juniors, Twin Wasps, and a Hornet), and they powered those that finished second in the other three. The disadvantage of the air-cooled radial's large frontal area could be largely offset by its better power-to-weight ratio, its reliability, and by the use of aerodynamic cowlings that reduced the drag penalty.

One of the most recognizable air racers in the Unlimited class is P-51 Mustang Miss America. Now owned by Dr. Brent Hisey, a neurologist of Oklahoma City, Oklahoma, this fighter embodies the color and flash of high-speed air racing.

LEFT Running up at dusk, Miss America strains the brakes.

BELOW Miss America shows off her unmistakable form. These wings have been shortened for increased turning rate. The morning sun turns the highly polished propeller into a silver disk.

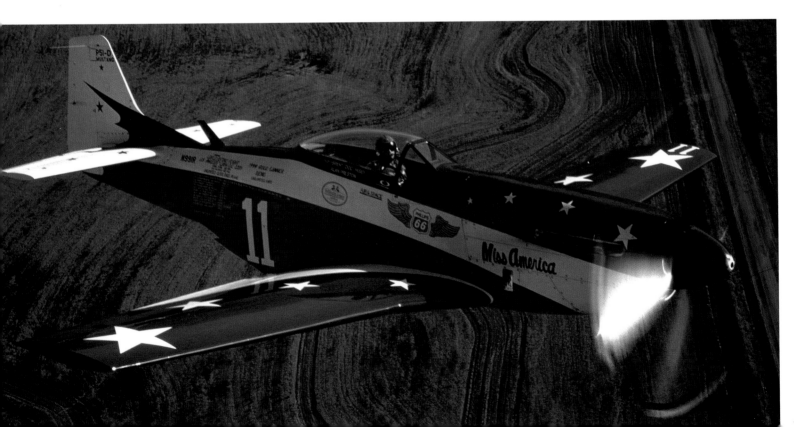

ABOVE *Over the shoulder of Brent Hisey.*
TOP *Dr. Brent Hisey and his "professional distraction."*
LEFT *The pilot's view in a pylon turn, low and fast. This photo was made from the back seat and with a relatively wide-angle lens, so the viewer will appreciate how close to the ground the racer is in these high-speed turns.*

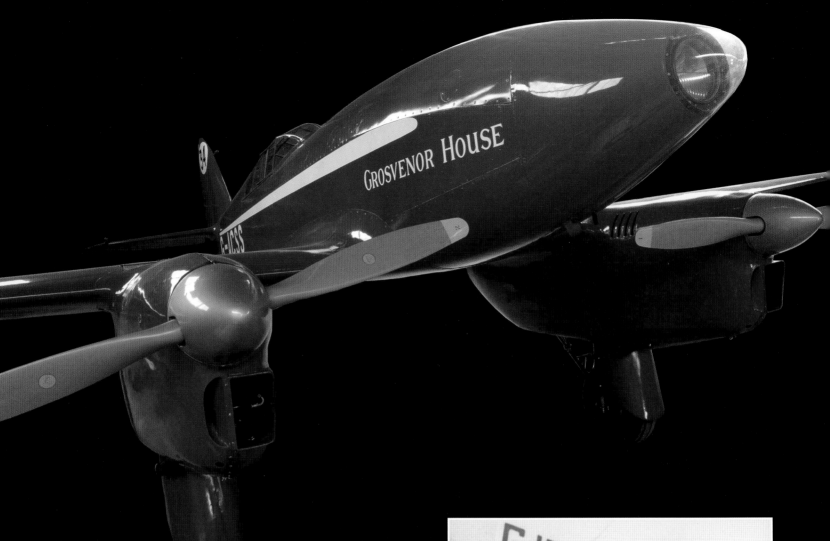

In 1934, Sir MacPherson Robertson offered a prize of £10,000 for the winner of an air race from England to Australia. Three de Havilland D.H.88 Comets were built specially for the event. The race winner was Comet G-ACSS Grosvenor House, *entered by the managing director of the London hotel of that name. It was flown by C.W.A. Scott and Tom Campbell Black, who completed the race in 70 hours, 54 minutes.*

The last historic flight by G-ACSS was one of its greatest. Flown by Arthur Clouston and Victor Ricketts (right), it took off from Gravesend, near London, on March 15, 1938, reached Sydney in 80 hours, 56 minutes, crossed the Tasman Sea to Blenheim, New Zealand, in 7½ hours, stopped overnight, and returned to Croydon on March 26. The 26,450 miles had been covered in ten days, 21 hours, 22 minutes, to set a record that still stands. The Comet then went back to Gravesend, where it remained under tarpaulins until 1951. After protracted restoration, Grosvenor House *was restored to flying condition and is now preserved and flown by the Shuttleworth Trust in England.*

A good example of an outstandingly clean airframe built round a radial engine is the Hughes H-1. In 1935, eccentric millionaire Howard Hughes decided to build an aircraft that would be fast enough to accomplish three goals — to break the world landplane speed record, win the Bendix and Thompson Trophies, and achieve the fastest coast-to-coast crossing of the United States. A 750-horsepower P&W Twin Wasp Junior was chosen, and it was enclosed in an airframe painstakingly designed to reduce drag. Its features included a close-fitting aerodynamic cowling, curved wing-root fillets, undercarriage doors blended into the wing, flush rivets and countersunk screws, and an enclosed cockpit that barely disturbed the line of the fuselage. Hughes was so satisfied with the first flight of the H-1 that he immediately made an attempt on the landplane record. Ignoring superstition, he flew on Friday, September 13, 1935, completing the required four runs at an average of 352.39 mph, nearly 40 mph above the previous mark. His success denied him the opportunity of achieving his second goal. Competitors in the Bendix and Thompson races cried foul, brushing aside the original intention of the races (to promote the development of faster landplanes) and claiming that Hughes' access to vast resources gave him an unfair advantage. To avoid acrimony, Hughes withdrew, but then showed what the H-1 was capable of by moving on to his third goal. On January 19, 1937, after fitting the H-1 with higher aspect ratio wings to improve long-range performance, Hughes flew from Los Angeles to Newark in less than seven and a half hours, averaging 333 mph over the 2,490 miles. Its job done, Hughes retired the H-1 to storage in California. It next crossed the continent in 1975, when it was transported to the National Air & Space Museum, its permanent resting place.

The list of entrants for the 1936 Bendix was disappointing, and the result seemed to be a foregone conclusion. Ben Howard in *Mister Mulligan* beat Roscoe Turner's Wedell-Williams by a mere 23 seconds in 1935 (Howard revealed that he had inadvertently penalized *Mister Mulligan* by flying most of the second half of the race, between Kansas City and Cleveland, with his flaps down), but in 1936 there did not appear to be another aircraft with *Mister Mulligan's* speed. Evidence that nothing is certain came during the race when *Mister Mulligan* threw a propeller blade and crashed, seriously injuring both Howard and his wife. With the favorite so dramatically removed, the 1936 Bendix turned into a runaway for the ladies. Louise Thaden and Blanche Noyes were first home in their Beechcraft C17-R Staggerwing, followed by Laura Ingalls in a Lockheed Orion. For the last three pre-WWII Bendix races, the character of the competition was changed by what was in effect a military aircraft. The Seversky S2 was almost identical to the P-35, which in 1937 was undergoing U.S. Army trials. Several of these formidable aircraft were lent to private individuals and used in competition. S2s gained easy victories in the 1937, 1938 and 1939 Bendix races, Frank Fuller's two wins sandwiching one by Jacqueline Cochran.

The Bendix returned in 1946, but it was never the same. Run in separate classes for pistons and jets, it was initially dominated by P-51s and P-80s. From 1951 onward, it was run as a race between USAF jets only, and from 1953, only a single type was involved each year. U.S. Navy F-4s competed between themselves for the trophy in 1961, and the USAF had the last word in 1962. In that year, a Convair B-58 Hustler flew from Los Angeles to New York in a fraction over two hours, averaging 1,215 mph. Even Howard Hughes must have been impressed. Nobody having the heart to take on such blistering opposition, the Bendix Trophy was quietly retired.

Race to the Antipodes

Of all the aerial point-to-point contests, the 1934 MacRobertson Race from England to Australia has a claim to being the most prestigious ever flown. The race was organized as part of the centenary celebrations for the city of Melbourne, and Australian millionaire Sir MacPherson Robertson provided the prizes. It was a competition in two categories — handicap and outright speed — that were run concurrently and were open to all competitors. There were four mandatory control points along the route where landings had to be made: Baghdad, Allahabad, Singapore

> *"To the pilot, [the King's Cup] gave a chance for the amateur to compete with the professional and, in some instances, the mediocre to defeat the brilliant…"*
>
> ALEX HENSHAW, COMMENTING ON AIR RACING IN BRITAIN, 1938

and Charleville, Queensland. Sixteen days was the maximum time allowed to complete the course.

By the time the competitors gathered at Mildenhall airfield on race day, October 20, 1934, the list of sixty-four entrants was down to twenty starters, but they were a varied collection. Seventeen were standard production aircraft, ranging from airliners as large as the Douglas DC-2 and the Boeing 247D to light aircraft such as the D.H.80A Puss Moth and the British Klemm Eagle. Several civil-registered military designs were there, too, including two Fairey Fox light bombers and a Fairey IIIF long-range reconnaissance aircraft. The remaining three starters were de Havilland D.H.88 Comets, which had been designed and built specifically for the MacRobertson race. Sleek low-wing monoplanes, the Comets were modestly powered by two 230-horsepower Gipsy Six engines, but they cruised at 220 mph and had a range of nearly 3,000 miles.

Until they reached India, the leaders were Jim and Amy Mollison in the first of the Comets, but there they were stopped by mechanical problems, and the second Comet (named *Grosvenor House*), flown by Charles Scott and Campbell Black, took over. Scott and Campbell Black went on to win the race, arriving at Melbourne two days, 22 hours and 54 minutes after leaving Mildenhall, averaging 159 mph for the 11,333 miles, including stops. Only nine starters got as far as Melbourne within the time limit. It was a magnificent achievement and a great reward for the de Havilland design team. However, the real significance of the race was revealed in the aircraft that finished second and third. The DC-2, operated by a KLM crew, reached Melbourne in three days, 18 hours, and the Boeing 247D, flown by Roscoe Turner and Clyde Pangborn, was not far behind. As Sir MacPherson Robertson observed: "This was just the result I wanted. To show that a transport plane could reach Australia in four days." The lesson of the DC-2's performance was not lost on the rest of the world. KLM quickly ordered more Douglas aircraft and U.S. airlines joined the rush. A British press report looked beyond the euphoria over the Comet's victory, pointing out that, although a British aircraft had won the greatest air race in history, Britain was not well placed in the race for commercial and military supremacy: "No British [air]liner, no British service machine in regular use…is fast enough to have finished the race within a thousand miles of the

American machines…" True enough, but it is worth noting that de Havilland's experience with the Comet served them well when they set out to build another twin-engined wooden machine in WWII — the ubiquitous Merlin-powered Mosquito.

By Jet and Chopper

In the jet age, there have been a number of international point-to-point races to stir the blood, but none have captured world attention nor have held practical implications for the future in the way that the MacRobertson Race did. In July 1959, a race was organized between the Arc de Triomphe in Paris and London's Marble Arch in celebration of the 50th anniversary of Blériot's flight across the English Channel. The winner, Squadron Leader Charles Maughan, began with a motorcycle ride to a waiting Sycamore helicopter, which took him to an RAF Hawker Hunter for a flight to Biggin Hill airfield in Kent. Another Sycamore rushed him from there to Chelsea Embankment on the River Thames, where a motorcycle picked him up for the dash to Marble Arch. The whole thing took just 40 minutes and 44 seconds.

A similar but more ambitious event was "The Great Trans-Atlantic Air Race of 1969," organized by the *Daily Mail* newspaper to mark the 50th anniversary of the first nonstop flight across the Atlantic by Alcock and Brown. It was run in both directions, between the top of New York's Empire State Building and the top of the Post Office Tower in London. Almost 400 entrants competed for twenty-one prizes worth a total of $150,000. The fastest eastbound time was recorded by Lieutenant Commander Peter Goddard, RN, who crossed the Atlantic in an F-4 Phantom II and reached the pinnacle of the Post Office Tower in 5 hours, 11 minutes. The westbound race was won by Squadron Leader Tom Lecky-Thompson, RAF, whose spectacular vertical takeoff in a Hawker Siddeley Harrier from a site near the Post Office Tower was a highlight of the competition. He took 6 hours, 11 minutes to the top of the Empire State Building. All of this was very exciting but did not suggest a method of intercity travel likely to be used by the everyday passenger. In later years, the transit times of Goddard and Lecky-Thompson between city centers, which looked remarkable in the 1960s, could be matched by anyone prepared to pay the premium for traveling by limousine and Concorde.

A WORLD OF AIR SHOWS

Many people in the world undoubtedly felt they had seen enough aircraft between 1939 and 1945 to last them a lifetime, particularly those who had suffered from their destructive attentions in Europe and the Far East. Nevertheless, it was not long after the end of WWII that air shows were once more offered as public entertainment and as shop windows for the aircraft industry. Before 1945 was out, the victorious Allies held air shows featuring the machines that won the air war, together with captured enemy aircraft. In the bombers hastily converted to carry passengers, and in hopeful proposals for new commercial airliners, there were hints of what might be done to return the aeronautical world to more peaceful pursuits. For the first time, the general public was exposed to the wonders of aircraft without propellers, and were able to see the fire-breathing monsters of the dawning jet age at first hand. It was all done with relief that the war was over, self-satisfaction at a job well done, and hope that the promise of aviation could at last be fulfilled.

Air shows proliferated after WWII, matching the growth of the aeronautical world as a whole. Major commercial gatherings, open days, "warbird" shows, vast association get-togethers or local club "fly-ins" — there is now hardly a day on the calendar when an air show of some sort is not being held somewhere on the planet. The month of July 1999 was typical of the international air show scene at the end of the 20th century, with air displays being given at air rallies, air fairs, air tattoos, air-racing weekends, military open days, precision flying competitions, gliding championships, club fly-ins, warbird and "old-timer" meets, aerobatic championships, balloon festivals, and state and county fairs. In North America, there were 116 air-show days of one kind or another during that month, while in the United Kingdom there were 101. Nine European countries (Austria, Belgium, Czech Republic, Eire, France, Germany, Netherlands, Poland and Switzerland) added another eighty-one. Twenty-two other countries from four continents held events during the year (Argentina, Australia, China, Croatia, Finland, Greece, Israel, Italy, Japan, Malta,

A few of the big radials to be seen at a Duxford air show. Several times each year, the Imperial War Museum's airfield at Duxford, near Cambridge, England, is the venue for spectacular air shows featuring restored warbirds. Here two French-registered Douglas AD-4 Skyraiders (foreground) line up with a British AD-4 (402, owned by the Fighter Collection) and a Boeing B-17F Flying Fortress before flying in the display.

ABOVE Photographer Ty Greenlees made this stunning image during the 2003 Dayton Air Show, at the Dayton International Airport during the Centennial Year of Powered Flight. Sean D. Tucker flew in formation with the camera aircraft over record crowds.

BELOW AND RIGHT Smaller but equally enthusiastic gatherings at small airfields around the world are drawn by the sound and appearance of such famous aircraft as this Spitfire. In 1999 at Andrews Field in Essex, England, this restored Spitfire performed a low-level display shortly after serving as a photo opportunity for a future pilot and his mom. Restorer and pilot Clive Denney looks on.

Malaysia, New Zealand, Norway, Philippines, Russia, South Africa, Spain, Sweden, Thailand, Turkey, United Arab Emirates and Vietnam).

The largest international air show for the aviation industry is held annually in Europe, with France and Britain alternating as hosts. Its scale can be judged from the program for the 1996 show organized by the Society of British Aerospace Companies at Farnborough, near London, over seven days of September. Forty-two manufacturers displayed over 100 types of aircraft, either in the air or on the ground. In the vast exhibition halls, there were 716 stands and booths of varying size where companies large and small set out their aeronautical wares, which ranged from turbofan engines of over 100,000 pounds thrust to tie pins, and from global navigation systems to aviation magazines. The flying display ran from 11 A.M. to 6 P.M. each day and included demonstrations by aircraft as modern as the Eurofighter 2000 and as old as an Avro 504. Attendance was in the hundreds of thousands, and almost $18 billion worth of sales were announced. At the 1998 show, that figure was more than $35 billion, and at Le Bourget in 1999, nearly 300,000 visitors confronted 1,860 exhibitors and 204 aircraft.

While the commercial shows at Paris and Farnborough are large by any standards, even they are surpassed in scale by the Experimental Aircraft Association's annual convention (AirVenture) at the Wittman Regional Airport outside Oshkosh, Wisconsin. In 1998, there were over 2,700 show aircraft, a staggering 12,000 "fly-in" aircraft, and nearly 900,000 visitors during the week of the convention. Among the 2,700 aircraft registered as being in the show, there were more than 700 described as antiques and classics, some 680 homebuilts, 547 warbirds, 265 ultralights, and 178 floatplanes and amphibians. There were 1,225 manufacturers and dealers from many countries on hand to display their wares. Among the hordes of visitors were a number who had chartered airliners to get to Oshkosh, including more than 400 who arrived from the far side of the world in an Air New Zealand Boeing 747-400, and 100 more from the

U.K. aboard a British Airways Concorde. Gary Burns and Alex Shenk were among those who brought their own aircraft and set a world record point-to-point in getting to the convention, flying a Lancair IV from Brisbane to San Francisco at an average speed of 290 knots.

At any air show, at least half the enjoyment for those who attend is in the act of coming together with likeminded enthusiasts to gorge at the aeronautical feast. Even at shows like Farnborough and Paris, where the emphasis is heavily on commercial promotion, it is still possible to look beyond the salesmen, taking pleasure in being with the aviation fraternity and savoring the wonders of the aircraft. At the huge Oshkosh show, there is so much to hold the attention on the ground — endless lines of parked aircraft, countless stalls and booths, lectures and classes on aeronautical subjects of all kinds — that the flying display is almost incidental. Nevertheless, it is there, and the eye is constantly caught during the day by the sight of a rare aircraft flying by or by a spectacular demonstration of aerobatics.

"First a loop with both engines…now another with one prop feathered…and finally one using only the windscreen wipers."

COMMENTATOR COVERING A DISPLAY BY A
DE HAVILLAND HORNET, FARNBOROUGH AIR
SHOW, 1948

The Aerobatic Art

After Adolphe Pégoud developed the basic aerobatic maneuvers in 1913, it became increasingly common practice for them to be included in the flying program at air shows, and, as aircraft grew more agile and powerful than Pégoud's Blériot, so pilots sought to expand their repertoire, elaborating on the basic themes and arranging the aerobatics into a sequence. By the early 1930s, aerobatics were an art form, sufficiently developed to inspire competition at both national and international level between pilots keen to show off their aerial mastery and challenge each other for the title of champion.

The first World Aerobatic Championship was held in June 1934, at Vincennes, Paris. Nine competitors from six nations took part, performing in front of a crowd of 150,000. Each pilot had to fly an eight-minute compulsory program and a ten-minute display of his own choosing. Wholly original maneuvers were accepted, but by 1934 most of those attempted were already included in a published list

of eighty-seven aerobatic figures. The Paris championships were marred by the deaths of two pilots, but were nevertheless flown to a finish, with Gerhard Fieseler of Germany narrowly defeating Michel Detroyat of France to be declared the winner. (Gerhard Fieseler is better remembered as the designer of the Storch, the Luftwaffe's STOL aircraft.) It was not entirely coincidental that high-powered aircraft took the top two places. Aircraft such as the D.H. Tiger Moth or the Avro Tutor, with engines of 150 horsepower or less, often struggled to cope with the demands of the aerobatic programs. Fieseler's F2 Tiger had the luxury of 450 horsepower, while Detroyat had 500 horsepower energizing his parasol Morane-Saulnier 225. The benefits of having a big engine were apparent, but it was not always true that the most successful pilots were those with power to spare. In the world championships held in parallel with the 1936 Olympic Games in Berlin, the winner was once more a German, Otto von Hagenburg. Flying a 150-horsepower Focke-Wulf 44 Stieglitz trainer, he was in eighth place after the compulsory program but, with a virtuoso freestyle performance, he defeated a Czech team equipped with 350-horsepower Avia Bal 22s. Hitler, glad of every opportunity to glory in German achievements, was pleased to have such positive evidence of Germany's aeronautical prowess.

After WWII, championship aerobatics developed into an intensely competitive and highly esoteric sport. It would be a mistake to equate the flying done during a competition with the aerobatics flown at an air show or just for fun. The need to come as close as possible to perfection while taking an aircraft through a sequence of maneuvers few other pilots would even attempt, the demands of continually flying at the edge of a machine's performance envelope, and the constraints imposed by the limits of the display box (a 1,000-meter cube with its base 100 meters from the ground), combine to make championship aerobatics one of the most mentally and physically challenging activities voluntarily undertaken by human beings in any field of endeavor.

The modern era of the World Aerobatic Championships dawned at Bratislava, Czechoslovakia, in 1960, when Ladislav Bezák won flying a Zlin 226. So superior was the Zlin that

At an evening air show in Piqua, Ohio, given by the Hartzell Company for its employees, Patty Wagstaff etches a circle over the cornfields and into the late September sky.

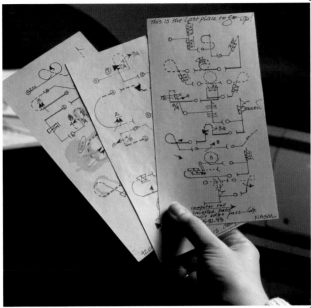

ABOVE *At the National Air & Space Museum, the Aresti Cards of Patty Wagstaff.*
RIGHT *Patty Wagstaff, the first woman to win the title of U.S. National Aerobatic Champion, sitting on the cockpit rail of her* Extra 300. *She will be enshrined in the National Aviation Hall of Fame in 2004.*

thirty-three of the sixty-one contestants in the first two World Aerobatic Championships chose to fly it. The 1960s also saw the adoption of a formal scoring method and a notation system describing aerobatic maneuvers. It was based on a system devised by a Spanish grandee, Colonel José Luis de Aresti Aguirre, who demonstrated the Polikarpov 1-16 Rata during the late 1930s. He wrote an Aerobatic Flight Manual for the Ejército del Aire (Spanish Air Force) and gave lively low-level displays in his favorite aerobatic aircraft, a Bücker Jungmeister. In 1961, he published his *Sistema Aresti*, a comprehensive dictionary of all possible aerobatic maneuvers, and the Spanish Aero Club urged its adoption internationally. With Spain as the host of the 1964 World Championships, an agreement was reached, and the Aresti Dictionary has remained in use ever since, growing from an initial 3,000 or so maneuvers to a maximum of some 15,000, all with their own symbols and difficulty coefficients. Aresti also donated a huge gold trophy surmounted by a silver Jungmeister, the Aresti Cup, awarded to each

world champion. In 1962, the U.S.S.R. donated the Nesterov Cup for the men's team event, and in the 1980s, the women's competitions were recognized with the Royal Aero Club Trophy for the individual champion and the FAI Challenge Trophy for the winning women's team.

Besides the adoption of the Aresti system, the 1964 World Aerobatic Championship in Bilbao was notable for the addition of a third element to the competition. An Unknown Compulsory program joined the Known and Freestyle components. Each of the competing teams selected one maneuver, the judges put them together into a sequence, added a few figures where necessary to make the combination work, and the pilots had to fly them straight off, without practice. It was a stroke of genius, a real test of a pilot's fundamental skill by means of maneuvers chosen by his peers.

Since internationally agreed-upon disciplines for championship aerobatics were established, the sport has gone from strength to strength, and the aircraft used now bear little resemblance to the Steiglitz and Tiger of the 1930s champions.

Aviation Gothic, 2003. Bob and Patty Wagner are longtime air-show participants. Bob is one of the most qualified air-show pilots in the world, and is happy to spread his knowledge and mentor less experienced aviators. Patty, now a retired wingrider, performed on top of the red Stearman flown by Bob at air shows across the United States. Patty is an early and steadfast member of Women in Aviation International.

In 1964, the Spanish Air Force team was successful with the latest Zlin, but in 1966 the Soviet team swept the competition with their 260-horsepower Yak-18PMs. By the early 1970s, the aircraft to beat was the diminutive Pitts S1-S, a 180-horsepower biplane with four ailerons. Its power-to-weight ratio allowed the Pitts to draw long lines in defining aerobatic figures, and its small size made minor errors hard to judge. The Pitts Special reached the apex of its fame in 1972 at Salon de Provence, France, when Charlie Hilliard performed the "Torque Roll" (a delayed tailslide where the airplane continues to roll while falling backward) and became America's first World Champion. The Pitts also took the American team of Hilliard, Gene Sourcy and Tom Poborezny to the Nesterov Cup.

In the post-Pitts era, monoplanes have dominated, with aircraft such as the Zlin 50, Extra 300, Sukhoi 31, Staudacher S300D, Yak 55M, Laser 200, and Texas Hurricane competing for the top places. Perhaps the outstanding design of the 1990s was the CAP series from Avions Mudry in France. The CAP 231, 231EX and 232 between them carried pilots to success in three out of four World Championships and won more medals than any other aircraft. Equipped with CAPs, the French aerobatic teams of the 1990s were able to dominate the competition.

Colonel Joseph C. Macky flew the only metal-skinned Waco at the 1936 International Air Games in Paris, and his performance earned him the Grand Prize Trophy as well as $10,000. Macky continued to use this special Waco to earn many other awards for his aerobatic excellence, including the coveted Freddie Lund Trophy. B.F. Goodrich, whose Wheel and Brake Division resides in the former Waco plant in Troy, Ohio, acquired the airplane and supervised its restoration to 1936 form. Here it is flown by Bob Wagner of Troy, Ohio, returning to Ohio skies in September of 1996.

Tom Poberezny is the president of the EAA and has been Chairman of the annual EAA Fly-In Convention at Oshkosh since 1977. The event attracts more than 800,000 people and 12,000 aircraft. As president of the EAA Aviation Foundation, he led the development of the EAA Aviation Center in Oshkosh that houses the EAA Air Adventure Museum. Tom is also an aerobatic champion. In 1970 and 1972 he was a member of the team that won the World Aerobatics Championship for the U.S., and in 1973 he won the individual U.S. National Unlimited Aerobatics Championship.

Excellent aerodynamic design is not the only reason for the CAP 232's lively performance. Its 300-horsepower Lycoming engine is more than adequate for its low empty weight, kept to less than 1,300 pounds by its small size (24-foot wingspan) and carbon fiber construction. Control response is superlative, with ample ailerons offering a neck-snapping roll rate of up to 420 degrees a second. At the 1998 championships in the Slovak Republic, where competitors from twenty nations took part, Patrick Paris got the best out of his CAP 232 and prevailed over the SU 31s of the Russians to become the last world champion of the 20th century.

All Together Now!

The art of flying in formation was developed of necessity by the air services of WWI. Once adopted as operational policy, it became a matter of professional pride with military aviators that they should do it well. Mastery of every aspect of formation flying was not only needed for survival in combat, it demonstrated the expertise of individual pilots and drew attention to the discipline and professionalism of their unit. It was a natural progression for formation skills honed in wartime to be put on public show between the wars. Aircraft performing maneuvers en masse were an impressive sight, and their appearance at air shows when military budgets were parsimonious helped to convince people that air forces were worth having. Britain's Royal Air Force had to struggle particularly hard to remain independent, and public air displays began at Hendon in 1920. Five Sopwith Snipes of the Central Flying School were on the program, looping, rolling and flying inverted, and giving people their first look at formation aerobatics.

The CFS Snipes having set the pattern, it was repeated at subsequent RAF displays, later teams elaborating on the original theme by outlining their maneuvers with smoke or performing with wingtips tied together. In 1926, No. 25 Squadron's nine Gloster Grebes introduced the novelty of responding to wireless instructions passed to them from the ground by King George V while the crowd listened in via loudspeakers. The following year there was a team of nine Siskins from No. 41 Squadron, but they did it to music.

A brass band played to inspire the formation leader with tunes such as "I'm an Airman," "Chick, Chick, Chick, Chick, Chicken!" "Here We Go Round the Mulberry Bush," and "Rolling Home." Before signing off with the RAF March, the band leader added a more obscure title for the benefit of the fighter pilots frolicking above — "The Frothblower's Anthem."

Formation aerobatic displays went on developing throughout the biplane era, but the coming of WWII denied monoplane squadrons the opportunity. Remarkable as it later seemed, many pilots were gloomily predicting the end of military display flying as a spectacle because they believed that it would not be possible to keep the faster, heavier monoplanes within a reasonable distance of spectators during a show. As it happened, the display baton was picked up immediately after WWII by the first jet squadrons, an eventuality that the biplane pessimists would have viewed with disbelief.

> *"No. 4 — if you don't move out just a little, we are all going to fly into the ground."*
>
> SQUADRON LEADER HARRY BENNETT, 64 SQUADRON AEROBATIC TEAM LEADER, COMPLAINING TO THE AUTHOR ABOUT HAVING THE AIR OVER THE TAIL OF HIS METEOR 8 DISTURBED DURING RECOVERY FROM A FORMATION LOOP, 1954.

Part-timers and Professionals

In the late 1940s, the U.S. Navy was the only service with a professional aerobatic team. Showing off to the public was generally left to front-line squadrons, who met their display responsibilities while retaining their primary operational duty. In Britain, No. 54 Squadron, RAF, formed an aerobatic team of five D.H. Vampires in 1947, and they crossed the Atlantic the next year to fly in U.S. shows. In the years that followed, Gloster Meteor squadrons came to the fore, notably the five-man team of No. 64 Squadron based at Duxford, which represented the RAF for the 1953–54 seasons. The Meteor was replaced by the RAF's first swept-wing fighter, the Hawker Hunter, and one Hunter unit in particular, No. 111 Squadron, led by Squadron Leader Roger Topp, set new boundaries for formation aerobatics in the late 1950s. Known as the Black Arrows because of their shape and shiny black paint scheme, they progressed through teams of five, seven, nine and sixteen aircraft, devising sequences to show off the Hunter to best effect while leaving their audience gasping at the sight of so many machines performing in harmony. No. 111 Squadron reached the peak of their ambition (and probably the limit of sensible behavior) at the 1958 Farnborough Air Show, when they opened their display with two consecutive loops in a mighty arrowhead of twenty-two Hunters. The audience of some quarter of a million people seemed to stop breathing when this colossus appeared and did not exhale until it had reduced itself to a more modest diamond sixteen.

When the English Electric Lightning replaced the Hunter as the RAF's front-line fighter, the practice of selecting a squadron to provide a display team continued. Nos. 74 "Tigers" and 56 "Firebirds" Squadrons flew diamond nines with the Lightning, but it became clear that providing a team for the increasingly crowded display season was incompatible with remaining operationally effective in such a demanding aircraft. In 1964, it was decided to use Folland Gnat jet trainers for aerobatic displays, and the responsibility was given first to No. 4 Flying Training School, and then to the RAF's Central Flying School. In 1969, the team was finally given professional status as a permanent RAF unit. It flew nine Gnats painted bright red and so was named the Red Arrows. Since then, the team has generally flown nine aircraft and has given shows all over the world, averaging some 100 public displays each season. In 1980, they reequipped with the British Aerospace Hawk, a delightful aircraft in the tradition of the Hunter as a pilot's machine. With it, they developed displays that flowed smoothly and gracefully from one maneuver to another, using colored smoke to trace intricate patterns against the sky. It is no accident that press reviews of their shows have often included words such as "aerial ballet" and "artistic design." Formation aerobatics in jet aircraft has truly become an art form.

Having been one of the first to give formation aerobatic displays in public, the RAF was much later than other services to establish a professional aerobatic team. The first was the U.S. Navy's Blue Angels, which began its demonstrations under the unvarnished title of "The U.S. Navy Demonstration Team" at an air show in Jacksonville on June 15, 1946.

LEFT *The aerobatic team of No. 64 Squadron flying Gloster Meteor 8s from Duxford represented the Royal Air Force at air shows during the 1953 and 1954 seasons. (Leader, Harry Bennett; No. 2, Johnny Izzard; No. 3, Reggie Spiers; No. 4, Ron Dick; No. 5, John Heard.)* TOP *In the 1961–63 display seasons, the English Electric Lightning was flown by the RAF aerobatic teams of 74, 56 and 92 Squadrons. Here four of No. 92 Squadron's F.2A Lightnings pull up in line astern. The U.S. Navy was the first service to establish a professional aerobatic team, in 1946. The Blue Angels have been performing at air shows ever since, always using front-line fighters. Starting with the Grumman Hellcat, they moved on to a succession of Grumman fighters — Bearcat, Panther, Cougar (seen here), and Tiger. Then came the McDonnell Douglas Phantom II, the Douglas Skyhawk and the McDonnell Douglas Hornet.*

The name Blue Angels was adopted two months later. They were the inheritors of a tradition traced to the Three Sea Hawks who flew Boeing F2B-2s from North Island, San Diego, in 1928. Other USN teams of the 1930s included the High Hatters, Three Flying Fish and Three Gallant Ls. The Blue Angels began by flying F6F-5 Hellcats, and have since progressed through F8F Bearcats, F9F-5 Panthers, F9F-8 Cougars, F11F Tigers, F-4 Phantom IIs and A-4 Skyhawks to the F/A-18 Hornet. This long-standing practice of flying displays in front-line fighter aircraft is unmatched by any other team.

The premier USAF aerobatic team is the Thunderbirds. They were established in June 1953 at Luke AFB near Phoenix, Arizona, and moved to their permanent home at Nellis AFB, near Las Vegas, Nevada, in 1956. Like the Blue Angels, the Thunderbirds have a tradition of using front-line fighters for their displays. Starting with the F-84G Thunderjet, they went on to the F-84F Thunderstreak, and then the world's first true supersonic fighter, the F-100 Super Sabre. Apart from a very brief period with the F-105 Thunderchief in 1964, the F-100 served the team for fourteen years, during which time they traveled through four continents and performed 1,111 displays. In 1969, the team converted to the F-4E Phantom, which they flew until 1974, when they broke with their fighter heritage and moved to the more fuel-efficient T-38 Talon supersonic trainer. The year 1983 saw the Thunderbirds return to using front-line

fighters when they reequipped with the F-16 Fighting Falcon, now their longest-serving aircraft and one shaped to show off the team's striking red, white and blue Thunderbird paint scheme to perfection.

The international community of military formation aerobatic display pilots is an elite. At any one time, its worldwide total numbers little more than one hundred. Among the great teams at the close of the 20th century were the Patrouille de France (Alphajet), the Italian Frecce Tricolori (Aermacchi MB-339), Brazil's Esquadrilha da Fumaca (Embraer Tucano), Canada's Snowbirds (Canadair Tutor), Singapore's Black Knights (A-4 Skyhawk), Finland's Jaska 4 (BAe Hawk), New Zealand's Kiwi Red (A-4 Skyhawk), the Australian Roulettes (Pilatus PC9), and the Silver Falcons (Atlas Impala) of South Africa. Each team pursued excellence in its own way, but all of them combined professionalism with superb showmanship. The displays they flew included loop, rolls, wing-overs and steep turns in formations that shifted smoothly from one shape to another, or suddenly broke apart only to come together again in a different form. Solo pilots pulled away to perform synchronized maneuvers in between passes by the main formation, flying as a "mirror" pair (one inverted over the other) or rolling past each other at crossing speeds of 1,000 mph. Speed, noise and colored smoke were used to

LEFT *The Snowbirds were officially named the Canadian Forces Air Demonstration Team in 1977, and became No. 431 Demonstration Squadron in the following year. They fly their displays with nine Canadair Tutors and change the shape of the formation frequently during each show.*

BELOW *The Thunderbirds have represented the USAF since 1953 Their aircraft have included the F-84 Thunderjet and Thunderstreak, F-100 Super Sabre, F-105 Thunderchief, F-4E Phantom II, T-38 Talon (here over Hoover Dam), and F-16 Fighting Falcon. The Thunderbirds fly some 100 shows each year and have displayed in over fifty countries.*

heighten dramatic effect, and the show often ended in a spectacular starburst disintegration of the formation, the tension of the display relaxing as each aircraft was finally released from the bonds that held it to its fellows. The physical and mental demands of formation aerobatic performances on the pilots are great — but so are the rewards.

AIRCRAFT AS ARTIFACTS

Away from the sound and fury of the air show circuit, aviation museums hold displays of a different kind in their quiet halls. Aircraft stand alone, hang from the roof, or form part of a scene from their previous existence. Some are uniquely famous, or are examples of a legendary type; others may not be so celebrated, but are nevertheless typical of a period in aviation history. They may be awesome or glamorous, inspir-

ing or mundane, but they all had personalities and each one has a tale to tell. Now they are silent and inanimate, gathering dust in their manmade caves, but once they "slipped the surly bonds of earth and danced the skies on laughter-silvered wings." Their engines roared and their airframes trembled, and each of them carried people into the wonders of the third dimension, vibrantly realizing the dreams of earlier centuries. Behind their now motionless framework of wood and fabric, metal and plastic, are the shadows of the designers, builders, aircrew, technicians and passengers for whom they lived. There is magic in their stories.

During the latter half of the 20th century, there was a great awakening of interest in preserving more of the artifacts of aeronautical history. Until the 1950s, it would have been possible to list the aviation museums of the world on no more than a page or two. Since then, the growth has been dramatic. Hundreds of collections, great and small, public and private, have arisen in countries on every continent. The most comprehensive, as might be expected, are in North America and Europe, a few of which have been in the business of accumulating aeronautical artifacts since the earliest days of manned flight.

Hallowed Halls

The aviation museums of the United States suitably reflect the prominent role Americans have played in the history of aviation. At the upper end of the scale are the major collections of the National Air & Space Museum (NASM) in Washington, D.C., the USAF Museum near Dayton, and the Museum of Naval Aviation at Pensacola, Florida. Between them they hold a high proportion of the world's unique

Bob Rasmussen is the Director of the National Museum of Naval Aviation at Pensacola, Florida. He spent thirty years as a naval aviator, and for three of those years he flew both the Cougar and the Tiger in formation aerobatic displays with the Blue Angels. He served during the Vietnam War as commander of Fighter Squadron 111. He retired as a captain in 1983 with 650 carrier traps and 5,000 flight hours in his logbook. In the years he has been the director of the Pensacola museum, he has tripled its size. Captain Rasmussen is a talented artist and sculptor, and his aviation paintings, some of which can be seen in the museum, earned him the R.G. Smith Award for excellence in naval aviation art.

ABOVE *Ted Inman has every reason to smile. He is the director of the Imperial War Museum airfield at Duxford, near Cambridge in England. As a center of aviation history, Duxford can justifiably claim to be the most comprehensive in Europe. The museum's aircraft collection is spread among several hangars and includes dozens of civil and military British machines.*

LEFT *Under Ted Inman's direction, Duxford's award-winning American Air Museum in Britain came into being. It was designed by Lord Foster and officially opened in August 1997 by Her Majesty, Queen Elizabeth II. The AAM, which stands as a memorial to the 30,000 Americans who died flying from the U.K. in WWII, houses an outstanding collection of American military aircraft and highlights the role of U.S. air power in the World Wars and subsequent conflicts.*

aviation jewels. In NASM's entrance hall alone can be seen the 1903 Wright Flyer, Lindbergh's *Spirit of St Louis*, the Fokker T-2 of Kelly and Macready's 1923 transcontinental flight, the Douglas World Cruiser *Chicago* of 1924, the Curtiss R3C-2 with which Jimmy Doolittle won the Schneider Trophy in 1925, Amelia Earhart's transatlantic Lockheed Vega, the Bell X-1 that Chuck Yeager flew faster than sound in 1947, and an X-15 that reached speeds above Mach 6 and altitudes of more than 50 miles. In 2003, the NASM extension at Dulles Airport opened, a vast new building capable of displaying up to 200 aircrafts.

Near Dayton, the USAF Museum's vast collection includes the Loening OA-1A flown by Ira Eaker during the 1927 goodwill tour of Central and South America, the combat veteran B-17G *Shoo Shoo Baby*, the B-29 *Bockscar* that bombed Nagasaki to end WWII, and the A-1E Skyraider in which Bernie Fisher carried out the rescue that earned him the Medal of Honor in Vietnam. At Pensacola there is the NC-4 that completed the first aerial crossing of the Atlantic, and examples of aircraft from every period of naval aviation. Frozen into a moment of their display, the "Blue

Angels" A-4 aerobatic team is suspended in time beneath the Museum of Naval Aviation's roof.

There are aviation history museums on hundreds of sites in every part of North America. Besides the big three in the United States, among the most varied collections are those at the Museum of Flight in Seattle; the Pima Air & Space Museum near Tucson; Planes of Fame in Chino, California; the San Diego Aerospace Museum; the Museum of Aviation at Warner Robins, Georgia; the Mid-America Air Museum in Liberal, Kansas; the Kalamazoo "Air Zoo" in Michigan; Old Rhinebeck Aerodrome, New York; the Lone Star Flight Museum, Galveston, Texas; and the EAA's Air Adventure Museum at Oshkosh, Wisconsin. Canada, too, has impressive aircraft collections. Two of the largest are the Canada Aviation Museum in Ottawa, and the Canadian Warplane Heritage Museum at Hamilton. There are over 100 aircraft in the museum in Ottawa, many of them rare birds indeed, such as the Sopwith Snipe and the Avro CF-105 Arrow. At Hamilton, most of the warplanes are restored to flying condition and are often flown at air displays. The standard of the aeronautical artifacts displayed at these and at most other North American aviation museums is high, and time with their collections is well spent.

Given its size, Britain is blessed with more than its share of aviation museums, and the best of them compare favorably with those anywhere in the world. At the upper end of the scale are the RAF Museum, the Imperial War Museum and its airfield at Duxford, and the Fleet Air Arm Museum. The RAF Museum at Hendon is five museums in one — RAF Historic Hangars, Bomber Hall, Milestones of Flight, Grahame-White Factory, and Battle of Britain Hall. Exhibits trace the history of the world's oldest air force from its roots in the Royal Flying Corps and the Royal Naval Air Service to its involvement in turn-of-the-century operations supporting the UN and NATO. The entrance to the Bomber Hall is guarded by the two principal instruments of destruction used in the assault on Hitler's Germany — a B-17G resplendent in the colors of the 94th Bomb Group, Eighth Air Force, and the RAF's most famous surviving Lancaster, its nose adorned with Göring's boast that "No enemy plane will fly over the Reich territory" and with symbols recording the 137 combat sorties flown in defiance of his arrogance. In the Battle of Britain Museum, the Luftwaffe's Heinkels, Junkers and Messerschmitts stand facing examples of the Hurricanes and Spitfires that fought them in 1940. The Fleet Air Arm Museum tells the story of British naval aviation, including WWI dioramas and a tour offering a noisy glimpse of life on board an aircraft carrier. In an adjacent hall are some distinctly non-naval machines, among them a Concorde and two of the research vehicles used in its development — a Handley Page 115 and a BAC 221 that started life as the Fairey Delta 2 used by Peter Twiss in setting the first world air-speed record of over 1,000 mph.

The Imperial War Museum's airfield at Duxford has a claim to being the most complete aviation history package on view anywhere. Before becoming the site of a major aeronautical collection, Duxford played a significant role in the Battle of Britain, and was later home to the 78th Fighter Group of the Eighth Air Force. Jet fighters moved in after the war, and Meteors of No. 64 Squadron formed the RAF's aerobatic display team in the early 1950s. Duxford has since relived its past more than once, hosting the makers of the movies *Battle of Britain* (1969) and *Memphis Belle* (1990). The aircraft on site cover all aspects of aviation, military and civil, and are housed in several buildings, some of them the original pre-WWII RAF hangars. Newer structures include a "superhangar" holding the British Aircraft Collection, and the superb American Air Museum in Britain, a dramatic glass-fronted single-arch shell containing aircraft as large as a B-52 and as small as a WWI SPAD XIII. Prominent among the displays are a dozen airliners of the Duxford Aviation Society. Over a hundred aircraft of all kinds are to be seen as static exhibits, and then there is the bonus of two hangars full of flyable warbirds operated by private owners.

Elsewhere in the United Kingdom, there are important collections at the Museum of Army Flying, Middle Wallop; Cosford Aerospace Museum; the Hall of Aviation in Southampton; Newark Air Museum; the Midland Air Museum, Coventry; East Fortune Aerodrome in Scotland; the Yorkshire Air Museum; the Shuttleworth Collection; and the historic airfield and motor racing track at Brooklands. Among the dozens of smaller museums are many with remarkable aircraft — for example, the de Havilland Heritage Museum at London Colney has the prototype Mosquito in its hangars, and the Lincolnshire Aviation Heritage Centre, near RAF Coningsby, has a wonderfully original Lancaster. However, perhaps the U.K.'s prize collection is held in a gallery of London's Science Museum, where there are some unique and historically significant aircraft. The Vickers Vimy of Alcock and Brown commands the floor, with Amy Johnson's D.H. Gipsy Moth overhead. The Supermarine S.6B that brought the Schneider Trophy to Britain in 1931 and was the first aircraft to exceed 400 mph is nearby, and just beyond is a Spitfire IA from the Battle of Britain. The Gloster E28/39 that first lifted Frank Whittle's jet engine into the air is at one end of the room, facing A.V. Roe's 1909 Triplane and a Fokker Eindecker, the first true fighter, at the other. In the quiet hours before the rush of visitors arrives, the gallery has a cathedral atmosphere, with such historic machines serving as aeronautical icons, commanding the admiration and respect of aviation's faithful.

Across the Channel and Beyond

Each of the world's major aviation museums promises a unique experience to the visitor. The greatest of them offer aeronautical feasts to glut the senses, stupendous collections of aircraft and related artifacts which could hardly be examined in a lifetime. One of the oldest and most impressive is the Musée de l'Air et de l'Espace near Paris. Founded in 1919, the collection suffered from a number of forced moves and a series of inadequate quarters until it became properly established at Le Bourget in the 1970s. Even without the collection, this is a wonderfully atmospheric place. Le Bourget airfield was active in WWI when it was home to Caudrons and Nieuports, and in the 1920s, it was where passengers boarded Latécoère and Farman airliners. Nungesser and Coli took off from here on their ill-fated attempt to cross the Atlantic, and French people by the thousand rushed over Le Bourget's grass to welcome Lindbergh and the *Spirit of St. Louis* to Paris. As if all this were not enough, the museum's hangars hold a collection of aircraft that, both in number and character, are hard to match. A large proportion of the machines on view are types that cannot be seen elsewhere. They are arranged in several halls, each one of which is an Aladdin's cave for the aviation enthusiast, offering treasures of every age from the pioneering days before WWI to the marvels of the jet propulsion era — from the creations of Blériot and Santos-Dumont to the Mystères and Mirages of faster times.

After seeing Le Bourget, the traveler in aviation history might begin to feel that there is little left to discover, but the rest of the world has a great deal more to offer. In Europe particularly, air museums are to be found everywhere. There are major collections to examine in Italy (Vigna di Valle and Trento), Spain (Madrid), Switzerland (Dübendorf and Luzern), Germany (Berlin, Munich, Hermeskeil and Sinsheim), Belgium (Brussels), the Netherlands (Soesterberg), Denmark (Stauning), Norway (Bodø), Sweden (Linköping), Finland (Helsinki and Tikkakoski), Poland (Kraków), the Czech Republic (Prague and Kbely), and Russia (Monino). Each museum has many exhibits unique to itself — Tikkakoski's Martinsyde F.4 Buzzard, for example, or the ambitious Swiss N20 Aiguillon jet fighter at Dübendorf. Madrid's CASA collection is matched by Linköping's homegrown SAABs, while Kraków and Prague have aircraft never seen in Western museums. The contributions of Italy and Russia to aviation have often been dramatic, a fact well illustrated in their aeronautical collections. At Monino the display features the aircraft of such great designers as Ilyushin, Tupolev, Mikoyan and Yakovlev, while Trento concentrates on the work of Italian pioneer Count Caproni. However, it may be at Vigna di Valle that the aviation enthusiast's pulse races fastest, for it is there that visitors are dazzled by the blazing scarlet of the surviving Italian Schneider Trophy aircraft, the beautiful Macchis that raced for Italy in the competition's closing years. Best of all, there is the wonderful Macchi MC.72, holder of a world speed record unlikely ever to be surpassed — encumbered with floats but still capable of 440 mph in 1934.

Visitors to the Musée de l'Air et de l'Espace at Le Bourget, near Paris, are welcomed by a formation of Fouga Magisters, frozen into the first part of a break by the Patrouille de France aerobatic team. Many of the Le Bourget buildings were there when Charles Lindbergh landed on the adjacent airfield from his Atlantic crossing in 1927.

The Old Flying Machine Company was formed in 1981 by Ray Hanna and his son Mark with the intention of preserving and maintaining rare vintage aircraft in airworthy condition. The collection has grown in reputation and size to become one of the foremost in the world, with the great WWII piston-engined fighters at its core. Along with air displays, the OFMC specializes in film work and advertising, flying in the majority of European based aviation productions since 1987. If you have seen a movie with aircraft in it, you have probably seen the OFMC. Among the company's movie credits are Empire of the Sun, Battle of Britain, Memphis Belle, A Bridge Too Far, Saving Private Ryan, *and the James Bond film* Tomorrow Never Dies. *Ray Hanna flies all the OFMC aircraft and, during his RAF career, led the Red Arrows aerobatic team for four seasons.*

Further afield still, the Royal Thai Air Force Museum in Bangkok includes such rarities as a Curtiss Hawk 75 and a Tachikawa Ki 36, and Rio de Janeiro's Aerospace Museum has a Curtiss Fledgling and a Waco CPF-5 that flew the Brazilian air mail service in the early 1930s. The Royal Australian Air Force Museum at Point Cook, Victoria, concentrates principally on types flown by the RAAF, many of them designed overseas but built in Australia. Perhaps the rarest machines at Point Cook are two Hawker Demons, rebuilt from wreckage found in Tasmania and South Australia, one of them restored to flying condition. The Royal New Zealand Air Force Museum at Christchurch also has a splendid collection, arranged in imaginative settings. In the atrium, four generations of aviation hang suspended in a descending arc, tracing progress from a Blériot XI through a D.H. Tiger Moth and a D.H. Vampire to a Douglas A-4 Skyhawk. In the main hall, visitors are taken through a succession of days from air force history, going from dawn to dusk as they walk past aircraft seen in typical surroundings, with air and ground crews portrayed going about their business.

History in the Air

Rewarding though they are, most aviation museums do not allow their visitors to experience the full effect of their principal artifacts. The aircraft generally are inanimate. The sound of engines starting or roaring at full throttle, the smell of fuel and hot oil, the sight of the machine breaking ground and maneuvering in its element — these things can be recreated artificially on film or in a computer program, but it is seldom that an aircraft from a major museum collection can relive its glory days. However, as anyone who has been to an air show knows, old aircraft in flying condition do exist and are regularly flown. They are operated by a variety of owners — museums willing and able to support flyable aircraft, private individuals with money enough to indulge their passion, professional armed services flying for public relations purposes, charter companies giving joyrides, and warbird organizations.

In the United States, private owners abound, flying classics of all kinds, as can be seen from the flight line at the annual EAA air show at Oshkosh, and there are a number of museums that fly at least some of their aircraft. Among the most prominent are the Kermit Weeks Air Museum in Florida; the Planes of Fame Museum at Chino, California; the Kalamazoo "Air Zoo" in Michigan; Old Rhinebeck Aerodrome, New York; and the Lone Star Flight Museum, Galveston, Texas. The Commemorative Air Force (originally formed as the Confederate Air Force, the CAF welcomed the new millennium by changing its name) with its headquarters in Midland, Texas, has flyable aircraft in its American Airpower Heritage Museum, and is the center of an organization that ties together CAF units in a majority of the states and in four other countries, all of which strive to maintain and fly warbirds, the majority of which are piston-engined aircraft from WWII. A number of those flown regularly are unique. For example, the CAF's B-29, *Fifi*, is the only flyable example of this type in the world.

The aviation heritage of France is splendidly represented at the grass airfield of La Ferté Alais, south of Paris. This is the home of the Jean Salis Collection, an impressive array of antique aircraft, many of them in flying condition. Originals include a Bréguet 14 bomber converted to a mailplane after WWI, a Dewoitine D.27, and assorted Moranes. The Blériot XI replica built by Jean Salis and flown across the Channel by him in 1954 and 1959 is here, as are a number of admirable replicas built and flown for the movies — WWI Nieuports, Fokkers and S.E.5s among them. A similarly nostalgic organization in the United Kingdom, the Shuttleworth Collection at Old Warden Airfield, is maintained by a trust that specifies that the aircraft are to be kept in flying condition. A visit to Old Warden on a flying day is one of the most exciting experiences possible for an aviation enthusiast.

ABOVE *One of the most experienced of warbird pilots, Squadron Leader Paul "Major" Day filled the role of Fighter Leader for twenty-four seasons with the RAF's Battle of Britain Memorial Flight, and commanded the BBMF from 1996 to 2003, flying Spitfires and Hurricanes. He joined the RAF in 1961 and flew Hunters in the Far and Middle East until 1971. He then flew Phantoms in the U.K., Germany and on exchange duty with the USAF at Luke AFB in Arizona. Conversion to the Tornado F.3 occurred in 1988, and he flew that aircraft in the U.K. and the Falklands until 1995. "Major" Day has amassed 8,500 flying hours in fighter aircraft.*
RIGHT *The flight line at a Duxford air show: P-51s fly over a line including a Wildcat, two Corsairs, a Sea Fury, and a Hawker Hind.*

Tom Allison standing in front of a restored Hawker Hurricane and the fuselage of the Curtiss Hawk 1A Gulfhawk. Head of the National Air & Space Museum's collection division, Tom Allison has overseen the restoration of many irreplaceable aviation artifacts, including the B-29 Enola Gay. He has also been responsible for the movement of the museum's stored collection from the Garber Facility at Silver Hill to the huge extension building at Dulles International Airport near Washington, D.C.

Singular machines are on every side, with aircraft such as the 1909 Blériot XI, Arrow Active and Gloster Gladiator taking to the air.

Needing more comprehensive support but of similar rarity is the RAF's splendid Avro Lancaster. Britain's Royal Air Force and Royal Navy are unusual in operating their own historic aircraft, having them flown and maintained by regular serving personnel. The RAF's Battle of Britain Memorial Flight owns the Lancaster, several marks of Spitfire, two Hurricanes, a Dakota and a Devon, all of which make regular appearances at air shows. The RN's Swordfish is also a popular performer, invariably raising a cheer from the crowd as it flies by in review, the observer standing at the salute in the back cockpit, and the Navy's ensign fluttering in the 80 mph slipstream.

Prominent as well-established warbird organizations in the U.K. are those that share Duxford Airfield with the Imperial War Museum. The one flyable B-17 based in Britain, *Sally B*, and the only Bristol Blenheim are there, as are two of the largest of the professional warbird operators — the Old Flying Machine Company and the Fighter Collection. The OFMC was founded in 1981 by Ray Hanna, the former Red Arrows leader, and his son Mark, with the aim of acquiring vintage military aircraft to fly in displays or for film work. Types flown have ranged from an F-86A Sabre to a replica Fokker D.VII, and have included most of the celebrated WWII fighters. The Fighter Collection, owned by Stephen Grey, houses equally exotic aircraft in a neighboring hangar, a B-25D, P-63C and Hurricane IIC among them. A Bristol Beaufighter, being lovingly restored to flying condition, is one of the rarest warbirds in existence. When the Fighter Collection and the OFMC join forces to fly in the Duxford air shows, it is an aviation historian's dream, with the sky over the airfield as the setting for the machines of more than half a century before, and the sounds of powerful piston engines filling the air. On other days, both companies are often kept occupied with scripts, storyboards and camera angles, adding to their film credits, which include the television series *Piece of Cake*, and such major movies as *Empire of the Sun* and *Memphis Belle*.

GREENLAND EXPEDITION

Cincinnati, Ohio, industrialist Bob Ready mounted an expedition in the summer of 1999, searching for B-17s forced down during WWII. In June 1942, a flight of three B-17s from the 97th Bomb Group, the first deployed to England, was forced down over the ocean because of bad weather and fuel exhaustion. This expedition was looking for the Sooner, *a B-17E ditched in this fjord. The other two B-17s,* Alabama Exterminator *and* My Gal Sal, *crashed on Greenland's icecap.*

RIGHT *Evening comes early to the icebergs and rocky coastline near Narsaq, Greenland.*

FAR LEFT *Gary Larkin, leader of "The Air Pirates," a uniquely talented group of aviation history experts. These men have searched the globe for the remains of historic aircraft. Climate challenges and extreme conditions do not faze these hardy men.* LEFT *Author Ron Dick (left), along with Gary Larkin (center) and Bob Ready (right) review the charts of the fjord and recreate the events of June 1942, when the* Sooner, *low on fuel, broke out of low cloud and faced the very few options remaining to the crew. This effort along with the recollections of Paul Blada, led to the discovery of a piece of an airplane. Apparently the* Sooner *had been ground up by the huge icebergs that flow from this fjord and out to sea.*

BOTTOM LEFT *Paul Blada, 97th Bomb Group, Eighth Air Force. The bombardier of* Sooner, *Paul joined the effort to recover the bomber he last saw just off the beach of one of these small rocky islands in June of 1942.* BELOW *The* Ocean Wrestler *picking its way through the ice.*

*The efforts of the 1999 expedition did not result in the recovery of a B-17.
One of the other bombers lost while flying to war, My Gal Sal, had been
recovered earlier and was acquired by Bob Ready. Now nearing a complete
but nonflying restoration, this is the only B-17E that has been completely
returned to 1942 operational condition. When completed, this B-17 will
stand as the centerpiece to "The Ultimate Sacrifice" memorial to be built
in Cincinnati, Ohio. One of the walls of the building will carry the names
of all the American airmen lost during the conflict.*

RIGHT *My Gal Sal being gently lifted into the Ohio hangar for completion of the restoration.* LEFT *After partial restoration by Gary Larkin's
craftsmen in California, sections of* My Gal Sal *were trucked to this hangar near Cincinnati, Ohio, where a dedicated group of volunteers
devoted many hours and inestimable knowledge to the restoration of this rare aircraft.* BELOW *Bob Ready and his living memorial to the
American airmen of World War II.*

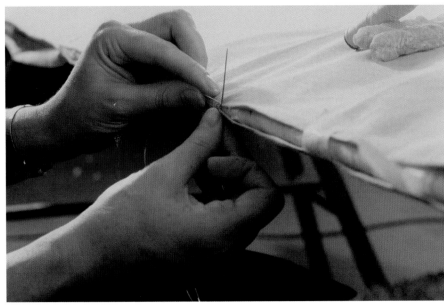

The workshop of Vintage Fabrics, owned and operated by Clive and Linda Denney. This couple has painstakingly researched the methods and building techniques used to construct aircraft in England in the early years of aviation. The Denneys are another family whose lives are consumed by aviation; sons Glenn and Andrew also participate in the business.

ABOVE LEFT *The hands of Clive Denney, along with the tools of his craft: curved needles for sewing around airplane structural pieces; red "dope" to tighten and seal the fabric; expensive cotton tapes that are hand frayed, a method of construction used in the 1920s and 1930s when this rudder to a Hawker Nimrod was originally built.*

ABOVE *Clive Denney removing the masking around the identification letters on another project. Although the methods of the past are used for construction, the paints and means of application, such as this spray booth, are up to date.*

LEFT *Linda Denney's talented fingers sew the edges along the trailing edge of an antique airplane in the shop.*

ABOVE *One of the restoration shops that Clive and Linda work closely with is Hawker Restorations in Milden, Suffolk. Under the direction of Tony Ditheridge, this shop works on aircraft from the earliest days of aviation, and WWI, as well as Hawker Hurricanes from WWII. Seen here is a complete restoration of a Hurricane. (The finished product can be seen in the third book of this series,* Aviation Century World War II.*)*

BELOW LEFT *Clive Denney applying a finishing touch to a Spitfire V. Once a fireman at Duxford, Clive, whose broad East End accent might belie his talents, told his mates many years ago when a Spitfire taxied past, "I'm gonna be flying one of them someday." They may have laughed, but Clive went on to learn the crafts of aviation engineering and restoration, and became a pilot who now flies Spitfires.*

RIGHT *Linda applying the very potent and aromatic red dope to a rudder.*

The United States Air Force Museum has one of the most complete and talented aircraft restoration facilities on earth.
ABOVE *Bob Spaulding, chief volunteer at the United States Air Force Museum. All of the great museums of the world count on the time and talents of these dedicated men and women. Bob Spaulding, who knows where everything is, seen here in front of a Douglas B-23 Dragon, one of many restoration projects undertaken by volunteers.*
TOP LEFT *The Boeing P-12 undergoing restoration in 1983. This airplane (also seen on the opening page of this chapter) had to be completely rebuilt, the restoration even including the recreation of metal forms and stampings for control surfaces.*
BOTTOM LEFT *An AFM restoration specialist buffing a high sheen onto the aluminum skin of the newly restored Northrop A-17 attack bomber from the pre-WWII Army Air Corps.*

To Fly or Not to Fly?

A large and sincere body of opinion has always held that flying venerable and historic aircraft is unnecessary, irresponsible, dangerous, and costly in terms of both our aviation heritage and human lives. The accident statistics may seem to support this view. Between 1965 and 1990, over 250 WWII combat aircraft were destroyed in crashes in the U.S. alone, and more were added every year. Disturbingly, a high percentage of the crashes were attributed to pilot error. The figures suggest that it would be better if old flying machines were never flown at all. Such a Draconian solution, however, is neither constructive nor practical. It merely borrows from the ultimate but ludicrous flight safety measure of reducing aviation's accident rate to zero by stopping all flying. It also ignores the other side of the fence. Not all losses of historic aircraft occur in flying accidents. Fire and natural disaster have taken their toll. A fire at San Diego's Aerospace Museum reduced the complete collection to ashes in 1977, and another at the Musée de l'Air near Paris in 1990 destroyed forty-three irreplaceable aircraft. Besides these and similar catastrophes, insidious deterioration is occurring daily in museums from natural corrosion, particularly where many aircraft are necessarily kept outside, exposed to all weathers.

The solution to these problems is, as it always has been, to satisfy the requirements of both operators and curators by raising flying, engineering and curatorial standards. There is plenty of evidence that this evolutionary process was underway in the later years of the 20th century. Even so, perfect museum care and complete freedom from accidents are too much to hope for. That being so, there are lines to be drawn. Some aircraft (such as Stephen Grey's Beaufighter)

A splendid example of the aircraft restorer's art is the Supermarine Walrus displayed at the Royal Australian Air Force Museum, Point Cook, Victoria. Originally allocated to the RAAF's 9 Squadron in 1943, it survived an emergency landing in 1944 and a period of storage before being allocated to the RAAF's Antarctic Flight in 1947. It was destroyed in a storm on December 21, 1947. Restoration of the pieces to a whole aircraft began in 1991, and the process was completed in 2003.

may be both valuable and rare without being individually historic. They have been and will be flown, but handled gently. Others, such as Lindbergh's *Spirit of St. Louis* or the Vimy of Alcock and Brown, are aviation's icons. Carefully preserved in aerospace temples, they can be suitably revered by generations to come.

For some people, raising standards and ensuring the preservation of the truly historic have never been enough. Their criticisms, renewed after every accident, are based on the premise that flying veteran aircraft of any kind is intrinsically wrong. The argument fails to recognize that much of the recovering and restoring of old aircraft is privately funded. The numbers of fully restored aircraft would be far smaller if there had not been people prepared to spend the money to find and recover aircraft that had been either wrecked or junked. Public institutions have not been inclined to finance such ventures, particularly when they have involved expeditions to remote swamps or icefields. That being the case, both the operators and the curators have surely earned the gratitude of the wider aviation community for their differing but complementary efforts to maintain our priceless aeronautical heritage.

Picking up the Pieces

The business of aircraft restoration is a difficult and highly esoteric art, besides being expensive. The first problem is to find and acquire the aircraft, or at least the parts from which an aircraft may be reconstructed. In the latter part of the 20th century, many valuable warbirds were rescued from military bases, where they had been standing duty as gate guardians for years, exposed to all weathers and steadily deteriorating. In many cases they were replaced by

engine frames still obtainable? If not, can T45 be used instead? Is low-grade T50 equal to high-grade T45? Can British AGS (Aircraft General Spares) rivets, nuts, bolts, screws, pins, et cetera be found and used? After that comes research on the actual aircraft — who flew it, with which units; what was its paint scheme?

accurate fibreglass replicas which served the symbolic guardian purpose admirably. Warbirds recovered in this way may have been weatherworn and corroded, but it was often possible to use 70 to 80 percent of the original aircraft. Most projects are recovered from places such as the Siberian tundra, the Greenland ice cap, the jungles of Papua New Guinea or some other remote location and are likely to be little more than a pile of wreckage. Even when an aircraft is discovered reasonably intact, it will be heavily corroded, and will usually have lost parts to local people or souvenir hunters. Finding an aircraft is, of course, merely the first stage in a long process. The next step is to acquire it, and that often takes the patience of Job and ambassadorial diplomatic skills, as well as funds to satisfy the current owners and arrange for transportation to the restoration site.

Once in a workshop, the aircraft (or its assorted parts) is laid out on the floor to establish what can be salvaged. Meticulous research is needed before the project can be taken further. The design authority must be consulted, engineering drawings and modification states examined, material specifications and alternative material usage checked. The availability of specific materials has to be investigated. In the case of one Spitfire restoration done in the U.K., the questions asked included: Are the proper T50 steel tubes for

All aircraft parts have to be jigged — a framework must be prepared within which the fuselage, tail unit, wings, flying controls and so on will be accurately arranged in relation to one another. The jigs must be built, a difficult and exacting task that has to be accurate, or a distorted aircraft will emerge at the end of the project. Once the components are jigged, the process of restoration can begin. All components are taken apart, derivated and sent for cleaning, corrosion removal, crack testing and treating. Treating could involve cadmium plating on steel or anodizing on aluminum. Once deemed reusable, the components are etch primed, epoxy primed and then painted in the finish topcoat. Ideally, the topcoat should be as close as possible to the original color. A good restoration can be ruined by the application of incorrect colors. Old but serviceable components are then fitted into the jig and new items added as required. Major components — the fuselage, wings, and tail — usually have to be derivated regardless of condition. (For example, over the years, British rivets set up an electrolysis against the skin and the heads pop off.) When all this work is done, the fuselage is taken out of the jig and is ready to accept the wings and tailplane.

At this point, most people expect the aircraft to be almost ready, but there is still much work to be done on

ABOVE *This gorgeous yellow Fokker Super Universal, from the Western Canada Aviation Museum near Calgary, Alberta, was taken off the museum floor and returned to flight status to participate in the National Air Tour.* TOP RIGHT *A New Standard, designed for air-show rides with an enormous front cockpit, and powered by the legendary Wright Whirlwind, also followed the tour.* BELOW *The ramp of the Lewis A. Jackson airport in Greene County, Ohio, filling up with rare airplanes during the 2003 National Air Tour.*

the aircraft systems (hydraulics, pneumatics, electrics, pitot head and lines), plus the engine and propeller. If they are all there, the restorers praise their good fortune, otherwise they have to find them or have them made. For a restoration team to produce a top-quality Spitfire might take two to three years. Even then, with the Spitfire outside the hangar — wings on, engine in, propeller on, fuel in the tanks — there is still a long way to go. The first engine run can be daunting, but very exciting. The aircraft comes to life, changing from a mere collection of parts into a piece of living history. Engine runs and adjustments completed, the time is approaching when the machine might fly. The regulatory authority (FAA/CAA) will have kept an eye on the project as it progressed, but now aviation is about to be committed, so they will need to check the paperwork and conduct their final inspection. The aircraft is weighed and the center of gravity

calculated, the compass is swung and at last the aircraft is almost ready for the big day.

Next comes the vexed question of who will fly the warbird for the first time. Plenty of people would love to, but ideally it should be a pilot with test experience, and preferably one who has flown the type. If the test program is completed and satisfactory, a permit to fly can be applied for. Once it is received, the question of who will fly the aircraft returns. Most owners are naturally eager to experience the joys of their creation themselves, but they need to be honest about their capabilities. To be qualified to fly a Spitfire (or any other warbird with a tailwheel), experience in a tail-dragging type is essential. In any event, whoever the pilot(s) might be, competence and professionalism are prime requirements if the expenditure of time, patience and money are to be regularly rewarded with the sights and sounds of a great aircraft operating in its natural element.

Aircraft of the 2003 National Air Tour.
LEFT *A flying advertisement: the New Standard sells its services.* BELOW *The only flying Ryan mail plane in the world landing at Lewis A. Jackson airport near Dayton, Ohio. The bloodlines of Ryan designs can be seen here and in a more famous airplane, the* Spirit of St. Louis, *on pages 120–127 of this book.* OPPOSITE *Into the clear blue skies of late September, three trimotors bank into the crosswind section of the pattern. The left and center airplanes are Ford Trimotors; upper right is a Stinson.*

BIBLIOGRAPHY

Abate, Rosario, Gregory Alegi, and Giorgio Apostolo. *Aeroplani Caproni.* Trento, Italy: Museo Caproni, 1992

Allen, Peter. *The 91 Before Lindbergh.* Eagan, MN: Flying Books, 1984

Anderton, David A. *History of the U.S. Air Force.* New York: Military Press, 1981

Angelucci, Enzo. *World Encyclopedia of Civil Aircraft.* New York: Crown Publishers, 1982

Angelucci, Enzo. *Rand McNally Encyclopedia of Military Aircraft.* New York: Military Press, 1983

Apple, Nick, and Gene Gurney. *The Air Force Museum.* Dayton, Ohio: Central Printing, 1991

Armitage, Michael. *The Royal Air Force.* London: Arms & Armour Press, 1993

Arthur, Max. *There Shall Be Wings.* London: Hodder & Stoughton, 1993

Baker, David. *Flight and Flying: A Chronology.* New York: Facts on File, 1994

Baldry, Dennis, ed. *The Hamlyn History of Aviation.* London: Hamlyn, 1996

Barker, Ralph. *The Schneider Trophy Races.* Shrewsbury, U.K.: Airlife, 1981

Bauer, E.E. *Boeing in Peace & War.* Enumclaw, WA: TABA Publishing, 1991

Bernhard, Toni. *Fliegermuseum Dubendorf.* Dubendorf, Switzerland: VFMF, 1989

Bickers, Richard Townshend. *A Century of Manned Flight.* Broadstone, U.K.: CLB, 1998

Bonds, Ray, ed. *The Story of Aviation.* New York, Barnes & Noble, 1997

Bowers, Peter M. *50th Anniversary Boeing B-17.* Seattle, WA: Museum of Flight, 1985

Bowyer, Chaz. *History of the RAF.* London, Hamlyn, 1982

Bowyer, Chaz. *The Age of the Biplane.* London: Hamlyn, 1981

Bowyer, Chaz, and Michael Turner. *Royal Air Force.* Feltham, U.K.: Temple Press, 1983

Boyd, Alexander. *The Soviet Air Force since 1918.* New York: Stein & Day, 1977

Boyne, Walter J. *The Leading Edge.* New York: Stewart, Tabori & Chang, 1986

Boyne, Walter J. *The Smithsonian Book of Flight.* Washington, D.C.: Smithsonian Books, 1987

Boyne, Walter J. *Silver Wings.* New York: Simon & Schuster, 1993

Brett, Bernard. *History of World Sea Power.* London: Hamlyn, 1985

Brown, David, Christopher Shores, and Kenneth Macksey. *Air Warfare.* Enfield, U.K.: Guinness Superlatives, 1976

Bryan, C.D.B. *The National Air & Space Museum.* New York: Harry N. Abrams, Inc., 1980

Burge, C.G., ed. *Encyclopaedia of Aviation.* London: Pitman, 1935

Cacutt, Len, ed. *Classics of the Air.* New York: Exeter Books, 1988

Cameron, Rebecca Hancock. *Training to Fly.* Washington, D.C.: Office of Air Force History, 1999

Catalanotto, B., and B. Pratt. *Once Upon a Sky. 70 Years of Italian Air Force.* Roma: Lizard Edizioni, 1994

Chant, Christopher. *20th Century War Machines (Air).* London: Chancellor Press, 1999

Chant, Christopher. *The History of Aviation.* London: Tiger Books International, 1998

Chant, Christopher. *Pioneers of Aviation.* Rochester, U.K.: Grange Books, 2001

Chesnau, Roger. *Aircraft Carriers of the World.* Annapolis, MD: Naval Institute Press, 1984

Chichester, Sir Francis. *Solo to Sydney.* New York: Stein & Day, 1982

Christienne, Charles, and Pierre Lissarrague. *Histoire de L'Aviation Militaire Francaise.* Paris: Charles-Lavauzelle, 1980

Coffey, Thomas M. *Hap.* New York: Viking Press, 1982

Cooksley, Peter G. *Air Warfare.* London: Arms & Armour Press, 1997

Cooling, Benjamin Franklin, ed. *Close Air Support.* Washington, D.C.: Office of Air Force History, 1990

Copp, DeWitt S. *A Few Great Captains.* New York: Doubleday, 1980

Corn, Joseph J. *The Winged Gospel.* New York: Oxford University Press, 1983

Coster, Graham, ed. *The Wild Blue Yonder.* London: Picador, 1997

Cross, Robin. *The Bombers.* New York: Bantam Press, 1987

Cunningham, Robert E. *Aces High.* General Dynamics Corporation, 1977

Dick, Ron, and Dan Patterson. *American Eagles.* Charlottesville, VA: Howell Press, 1997

Divone, Louis and Judene. *Wings of History.* Oakton, VA: Oakton Hills Publications, 1989

Donald, David, ed. *The Classic Civil Aircraft Guide.* Edison, NJ: Chartwell Books, 1999

Doolittle, James H., with Carroll Glines. *I Could Never Be So Lucky Again.* New York: Bantam, 1991

Dudgeon, A.G. *The Luck of the Devil.* Shrewsbury, U.K.: Airlife, 1985

Ellis, Ken. *Wrecks & Relics.* Leicester, U.K.: Midland Publishing, 1998

Emde, Heiner. *Conquerors of the Air.* New York: Bonanza Books, 1968

Evangelisti, Giorgio. *Un'aquila nel Cielo.* Firenze, Italy: Editoriale Olimpia, 1999

Foxworth, Thomas G. *The Speed Seekers.* Newbury Park, CA: Haynes Publications, 1989

Franks, Norman. *Aircraft versus Aircraft.* New York: Macmillan, 1986

Friedman, Norman. *U.S. Aircraft Carriers.* Annapolis, MD: Naval Institute Press, 1983

Friedman, Norman. *British Carrier Aviation.* Annapolis, MD: Naval Institute Press, 1988

Fritzsche, Peter. *A Nation of Fliers.* Cambridge, MA: Harvard University Press, 1992

Garvey, Jude. *A Guide to the Transport Museums of Great Britain.* London: Pelham Books, 1982

Gibbs-Smith, Charles H. *Aviation: An Historical Survey.* London: Science Museum, 1985

Gildemeister, Jerry. *Avian Dreamers.* Union, OR: Bear Wallow, 1991

Glines, Carroll V. *Round-the-World Flights.* New York: Van Nostrand Reinhold, 1982

Glines, Carroll V., Harry M. Zubkoff, and F. Clifton Berry. *Flights.* Montgomery, AL: Community Communications, 1994

Green, Geoff. *British Aerospace.* Wotton under Edge, U.K.: Geoff Green, 1988

Green, William. *Warplanes of the Third Reich.* New York: Galahad Books, 1986

Green, William, and Gordon Swanborough. *The Complete Book of Fighters.* New York: Smithmark, 1994

Greenwood, John T., ed. *Milestones of Aviation.* New York: Hugh Lauter Levin Associates, 1989

Gunston, Bill. *The Development of Piston Aero Engines.* Yeovil, U.K.: Patrick Stephens Ltd., 1993

Gunston, Bill, ed. *Chronicle of Aviation.* London: Chronicle Communications, 1992

Gwynne-Jones, Terry. *Wings Across the Pacific.* Atglen, PA: Schiffer Military/Aviation History, 1995

Hallion, Richard P. *Legacy of Flight.* Seattle, WA: University of Washington Press, 1977

Hallion, Richard P. *Strike from the Sky.* Washington, D.C.: Smithsonian Institute Press, 1989

Harris, Stephen K. *The B-17 Remembered.* Seattle, WA: Museum of Flight, 1998

Harrison, James P. *Mastering the Sky.* New York: Sarpedon, 1996

Henshaw, Alex. *The Flight of the Mew Gull.* Shrewsbury, U.K.: Airlife, 1998

Henshaw, Alex. *Sigh for a Merlin.* Wilmslow, U.K.: Air Data Publications, 1996

Heppenheimer, T.A. *A Brief History of Flight.* New York: John Wiley & Sons, 2001

Hildebrandt, Erik. *Front Row Center.* Minneapolis, MN: Cleared Hot Media, 2000

Holmes, Donald B. *Air Mail.* New York: Clarkson N. Potter, 1981

Howson, Gerald. *Aircraft of the Spanish Civil War.* Washington, D.C.: Smithsonian Institution Press, 1990

Hunt, Leslie. *Veteran & Vintage Aircraft.* New York: Charles Scribner's Sons, 1974

Huttig, Jack. *1927 Summer of Eagles.* Chicago: Nelson-Hall, 1980

Jablonski, Edward. *Flying Fortress.* New York: Doubleday, 1965

Jackson, Donald Dale. *Flying the Mail.* Alexandria, VA: Time-Life Books, 1982

Jackson, Donald Dale. *The Explorers.* Alexandria, VA: Time-Life Books, 1983

Jackson, Robert. *The Sky Their Frontier.* Shrewsbury, U.K.: Airlife, 1983

Jacobs, Peter. *Hawker Hurricane.* Malmesbury, U.K.: Crowood Press, 1998

James, Derek N. *Schneider Trophy Aircraft.* London: Putnam, 1981

Jarrett, Philip, ed. *Biplane to Monoplane.* London: Putnam, 1997

Johnson, J.E. "Johnnie." *The Story of Air Fighting.* London: Hutchinson, 1985

Jones, David. *The Time Shrinkers: Africa.* London: Beaumont Aviation Literature, 1977

Josephy, Alvin M. *The American Heritage History of Flight.* New York: American Heritage Publishing, 1962

Kasmann, Ferdinand C.W. *World Speed Record Aircraft.* London: Putnam, 1990

Knott, Richard C. *The American Flying Boat.* Annapolis, MD: Naval Institute Press, 1979

Koc, L.W., and E. Quirini. *The Polish Army and the Polish Navy.* Central Warsaw: Military Booksellers Magazine, 1939

Larkins, William T. *Battleship and Cruiser Aircraft of the United States Navy.* Atglen, PA: Schiffer Military/Aviation History, 1996

Lee, David. *Never Stop the Engine When It's Hot.* London: Thomas Harmsworth, 1983

Lewis, Peter. *British Racing and Record-Breaking Aircraft.* London: Putnam, 1970

McKay, Ernest A. *A World to Conquer.* New York: Arco Publishing, 1981

March, Daniel J., and John Heathcott, eds. *The Aerospace Encyclopedia of Air Warfare (Vol. 1).* London: Aerospace Publishing, 1997

Markham, Beryl. *West With the Night.* San Francisco: North Point Press, 1983

Mason, Francis K. *Aces of the Air.* New York: Mayflower Books, 1981

Mason, Francis K. *The British Bomber since 1914.* London: Putnam, 1994

Mason, Francis K. *The British Fighter since 1912.* London: Putnam, 1992

Maurer Maurer. *Aviation in the U.S. Army 1919-1939.* Washington, D.C.: Office of Air Force History, 1987

Millbrooke, Anne. *Aviation History.* Englewood, CO: Jeppesen Sanderson, 1999

Moll, Nigel. *Confederate Air Force: Past Perfect.* Osceola, WI: Motor Books, 1987

Mondey, David, ed. *Aviation.* London: Octopus Books, 1980

Moolman, Valerie. *Women Aloft.* Alexandria, VA: Time-Life Books, 1981

Morley-Mower, Geoffrey. *Flying Blind.* Las Cruces, NM: Yucca Tree Press, 2000

Murray, Williamson. *Strategy for Defeat.* Secaucus, NJ: Chartwell Books, 1986

Musciano, Walter A. *Warbirds of the Sea.* Atglen, PA: Schiffer Publishing, 1994

Nevin, David. *Architects of Air Power.* Alexandria, VA: Time-Life Books, 1981

Nowarra, Heinz J. *Die 109.* Stuttgart: Motorbuc-Verlag, 1979

Nowara, H.J., and G.R. Duval. *Russian Civil and Military Aircraft.* London: Fountain Press, 1971

Oakes, Claudia, ed. *Aircraft of the National Air & Space Museum.* Washington, D.C.: Smithsonian Institution Press, 1981

Ogden, Bob. *Great Aircraft Collections of the World.* New York: Gallery Books, 1986

Oliver, David. *Wings over Water.* Edison, NJ: Chartwell Books, 1999

O'Neil, Paul. *Barnstormers & Speed Kings.* Alexandria, VA: Time-Life Books, 1981

Pisano, Dominick, and F. Robert van der Linden. *Charles Lindbergh and the Spirit of St. Louis.* New York: Harry N. Abrams, 2002

Prentice, Colin W. *Monino.* Shrewsbury, U.K.: Airlife, 1997

Price, Alfred. *The Spitfire Story.* Poole, U.K.: Arms & Armour Press, 1987

Prior, Rupert. *Flying: The Golden Years.* London: Tiger Books, 1994

Rabinowitz, Harold. *Conquer the Sky.* New York: Metro Books, 1996

Rawlings, John D.R. *The History of the Royal Air Force.* Feltham, UK: Temple Press, 1984

Redding, Robert, and Bill Yenne. *Boeing, Planemaker to the World.* Greenwich, CT: Bison Books, 1983

Rickenbacker, Edward V. *Rickenbacker: An Autobiography.* Englewood Cliffs, NJ: Prentice-Hall, 1967

Ross, Tony, ed. *75 Eventful Years.* Canterbury, U.K.: Wingham Aviation Books, 1993

Sherry, Michael S. *The Rise of American Air Power.* New Haven, CT: Yale University, 1987

Shores, Christopher. *Air Aces.* Greenwich, CT: Bison Books, 1983

Smith, Herschel. *A History of Aircraft Piston Engines.* Manhattan, KS: Sunflower University Press, 1986

Smith, Peter C. *The History of Dive Bombing.* Annapolis, MD: Nautical & Aviation Pub. Co., 1981

Stone, Ronald B. *Aircraft & Aerospace Museum Guide.* Olathe, KS: Bruce/Beeson Publishers, 1998

Sturtivant, Ray. *British Naval Aviation.* Annapolis, MD: Naval Institute Press, 1990

Taylor, John W.R. *Combat Aircraft of the World.* New York: Putnam, 1969

Taylor, John W.R. *C.F.S. Birthplace of Air Power.* London: Putnam, 1958

Taylor, John W.R., Michael Taylor and David Mondey. *Air Facts & Feats.* Enfield, U.K.: Guinness Superlatives, 1977

Taylor, John W.R., and Kenneth Munson. *History of Aviation.* New York: Crown Publishers, 1972

Taylor, Michael J.H. *Great Moments in Aviation.* London: Prion, 1989

Terraine, John. *A Time for Courage.* New York: Macmillan, 1985

Thetford, Owen. *Aircraft of the Royal Air Force.* London: Putnam, 1988

Thomas, Lowell. *Famous First Flights that Changed History.* New York: Doubleday, 1968

Thruelsen, Richard. *The Grumman Story.* New York: Praeger, 1976

van der Kooij, Otger. *European Wrecks & Relics.* Leicester, U.K.: Midland Publishing, 1998

van der Linden, F. Robert. *Aircraft of the National Air and Space Museum.* Washington, D.C.: Smithsonian Institution Press, 1998

Vorderman, Don. *The Great Air Races.* New York: Doubleday, 1969

Willmott, H.P. *B-17 Flying Fortress.* London: Arms & Armour Press, 1980

Wohl, Robert. *Aviation and the Western Imagination.* New Haven, CT: Yale University Press, 1994

Wood, Tony, and Bill Gunston. *Hitler's Luftwaffe.* New York: Crescent Books, 1979

Wragg, David. *Wings Over the Sea.* New York: Arco Publishing, 1979

Yenne, Bill. *The Aerobats.* New York: Mallard Press, 1991

BOOKS BY CORPORATIONS AND MUSEUMS

Dateline Lockheed. Burbank, CA: Lockheed Corporate Communications, 1982

Forty Years On ... London: Handley Page Ltd., 1949

National Museum of Naval Aviation. Pensacola, FL: Naval Aviation Foundation, 1996

Pedigree of Champions: Boeing Since 1916. Seattle, WA: The Boeing Company, 1977

The Pratt & Whitney Aircraft Story. Hartford, CT: Pratt & Whitney Aircraft, 1950

United States Air Force Museum. Wright-Patterson AFB, OH: Air Force Museum Foundation, 1997

ANNUAL PUBLICATIONS

Aviation Year Book. New York: Aeronautical Chamber of Commerce of America

Jane's All the World's Aircraft. London: Jane's Yearbooks

Jane's Fighting Ships. London: Jane's Yearbooks

MAGAZINES

Aeroplane Monthly. London: IPC Media Ltd.

Air & Space Smithsonian. Washington, DC: Smithsonian Business Ventures

Flight Journal. Ridgefield, CT: Air Age Inc.

INDEX BY SUBJECT

Note: Page numbers in bold indicate an illustration.

GENERAL INDEX